LIBERAL BY PRINCIPLE

The Politics of John Wodehouse
1st Earl of Kimberley, 1843–1902

SOURCES FOR MODERN BRITISH HISTORY

General Editors: Kathleen Burk, John Ramsden, John Turner

THE CRISIS OF BRITISH UNIONISM: The Domestic Political Papers of the Second Earl of Selborne, 1885–1922
Edited by George Boyce. 1987

LABOUR AND THE WARTIME COALITION: From the Diary of James Chuter Ede, 1941–1945
Edited by Kevin Jefferys. 1987

THE MODERNISATION OF CONSERVATIVE POLITICS: The Diaries and Letters of William Bridgeman, 1904–1935
Edited by Philip Williamson. 1988

THE CRISIS OF BRITISH POWER: The Imperial and Naval Papers of the Second Earl of Selborne, 1895–1910
Edited by George Boyce. 1990

MY DEAR MAX: The Letters of Brendan Bracken to Lord Beaverbrook, 1925–1958
Edited by Richard Cockett. 1990

PATRICK GORDON WALKER: Political Diaries, 1932-1971
Edited by Robert Pearce. 1991

PARLIAMENT AND POLITICS IN THE AGE OF BALDWIN AND MACDONALD: The Diaries of Sir Cuthbert Headlam, 1924–1935
Edited by Stuart Ball. 1993

DUTY AND CITIZENSHIP: The Correspondence and Papers of Violet Markham, 1896–1953
Edited by Helen Jones. 1994

A LIBERAL CHRONICLE: Journals and Papers of J.A. Pease, 1st Lord Gainford, 1908–1910
Edited by Cameron Hazlehurst and Christine Woodland. 1994

LIBERAL BY PRINCIPLE

The Politics of John Wodehouse
1st Earl of Kimberley, 1843–1902

Edited with an introduction by

John Powell

British Library Cataloguing in Publication Data

A copy of the catalogue entry for this publication can be obtained from the British Library

ISBN 1-872273-02-5

PUBLISHED BY THE HISTORIANS' PRESS
9 DAISY ROAD, LONDON E18 1EA

Printed in England by Antony Rowe Ltd

For Janice

Contents

Preface

Lord Kimberley was active in Liberal politics from 1848 and a cabinet-level politician from 1868 until his death in 1902. Garrulous in conversation, he was surprisingly lucid and succinct in writing. During a long career, he produced thousands of letters, despatches, memoranda, annotations and minutes, most of which have been preserved among official records, in the archives of his colleagues, and in his own large and well organized collection of papers. Given this mass of materials from Kimberley's hand, as well as hundreds of speeches and contemporary reports, readers of this work will want to know the principles upon which this study has been based.

Liberal by Principle is neither a biography nor a political history, but rather a study in the political personality of an individual and a party. It incorporates a fifty-page introductory essay and a fully-annotated collection of 274 contemporary documents drawn from more than fifty archival sources. It has been designed as a whole in order to do two things. First, it attempts to illustrate the nature of Kimberley's liberalism, both in theory and practice. What circumstances shaped his thinking; what did he read and how did he make use of it; what was the relationship between his theory of liberalism and the way he practiced it within the party structure? That is, what was Kimberley's personal liberal creed? Second, this study then seeks to situate his personal philosophy and practice in the context of contemporary Liberal politics. How did the political community perceive him, what role did he assume within the political process and how did he interact with colleagues, operating from the personal ground which he occupied?

I have necessarily avoided dealing with other issues which will in future require further attention. Although this work contains the most complete biographical record of Kimberley's life to date, it is no substitute for proper biography. There are large gaps in this sketch of his life, which provides principally the context in which his political ideas were developed. I say little about matters such as family, religion, estate management and Norfolk society, all of which were important to him, and therefore necessarily significant to the biographer. To the degree that these matters touch politics, as in the relationship between the established church and Irish policy, they become visible in this study, but are not treated systematically. Too, I have paid relatively little attention to the details of what Kimberley actually did politically. The outline of his cabinet career is relatively well known and much of his departmental work has been expertly analyzed. Where these conditions do not apply, as in the case of his early political career and his later role in Irish policy development, I have provided summary accounts and, later, suggestive documents, but have not attempted more. Instead, I have focused on the political perception of what Kimberley did and the manner in which he did it.

In adopting this approach, I am less concerned with introducing new material (though most of the documents are printed here for the first time) than with creating a fuller context for understanding Kimberley's role in the familiar events traditionally associated with the rise and fall of Gladstonian liberalism. This is particularly relevant to Kimberley's career, as he has consistently been portrayed as the very representative of Victorian stolidity — honest, thoughtful, dutiful, cooperative and competent, ready to be directed by the prime minister. He was associated with no transcendent event, as were Lowe, Forster, or Goschen; he displayed no eminent gifts, as did Bright, Harcourt and Granville; he never changed parties or created political scenes, as did Chamberlain and Hartington; and he had no reputation apart from politics, as did Morley, Bryce and Trevelyan. The history of Victorian politics has been studied very much as if Kimberley were a cypher. However, the leadership of the Liberal party did for a variety of reasons care about Kimberley's allegiance, though their expressions of concern were usually unknown to both the public and the rank-and-file within the party. The record of Kimberley's political role is suggestive of forces shaping the Liberal Party, forces which reflected not just ideology or vision, but also perception and interpersonal relations.

This study will reinforce the immediacy of practical concerns, which were comparable in importance within the political process to the ideological viewpoints they were meant to serve. It should further reinforce the point that no one at cabinet level maintained a position for long on sufferance. It is widely known why Churchill thought it necessary to shove Northcote into the Lords, and why Gladstone ditched Bruce and spent considerable energy in devising a plan to rotate Dodson and Fortescue out of the cabinet. However, no one has yet quite delineated the positive reasons that a quiet politician like Kimberley, facing plenty of competition year in and year out from whigs, Peelites, university and municipal liberals, and a variety of radicals, was perceived as integral to virtually every actual and proposed Liberal government between 1868 and 1902. To understand what this required beyond departmental competence is to perceptibly enhance one's understanding of Liberal politics a whole.

In keeping with the general purposes of this study, 278 items were selected for inclusion, with the following types of documents given precedence:

1) *Out-letters*, which on the whole are the most reliable guides to Kimberley's political thought and relations.

2) *Correspondence with political confidants*, which was usually private, and grounded in specific political situations.

3) *Documents representing principles of governance*, suggestive of Kimberley's political motivations.

4) *Items related to national and Cabinet politics*, rather than local and departmental politics.

5) *Items related to the nature of personal relationships and centres of authority within governments*, including letters suggestive of the role of personality in the course of policy development.

It is hoped that this selection of 251 letters, 14 political memoranda, 9 private memoranda, one minute, and three addresses will representatively reflect the nuances of Kimberley's personal political creed and method, and the way in which these fitted into the larger framework of Liberal politics. In terms of content, his early career and his role in Irish policy have received more attention than the departmental work of the 1870s and 1880s, because they have been less studied. However, in this emphasis I have been careful to provide representative documents in which the essential principles upon which he dealt with hundreds of issues in thousands of letters and despatches written as Irish Viceroy and Colonial, Indian and Foreign secretary should stand clear. So should the nature and significance of his most important political relationships, which are fairly represented by the distribution of correspondents.

In most cases, letters and memoranda are printed in full. It seemed to me preferable to provide fewer complete letters, giving context to the broader political process, than a greater number of fragments in which the seemingly important detail is separated from valuable information which may at first seem trivial. There are, therefore, a number of references to 'fair harvests', 'first rate roots' and 'receipts for former bills', though such asides made to political colleagues tended to be brief. Original spellings and, in most cases, punctuations, have been maintained, though in some instances the intended mark of punctuation is far from clear. Those relatively few illegible words — for Kimberley normally wrote in a clear hand — are indicated thus: [ill.].

Annotation has required line-by-line selectivity. However, I have generally followed these principles:

1) *References to Cabinet politics are more thoroughly annotated than those of general interest*, and generally include historiographical references.

2) *British subjects receive fuller biographical treatment than non-British subjects*. In keeping with point number one, the more closely one is related to Cabinet politics, the fuller the reference.

3) *Family members and political figures with whom Kimberley worked closely over long periods of time are treated in an alphabetised Portrait Gallery, rather than in notes*. It is recommended, therefore, that the twenty-eight brief

portraits be read first to provide a sense of relative immediacy to Kimberley.

Acknowledgements

In the course of this work I have incurred many debts which I am pleased here to acknowledge. I must first thank the following for permission to reproduce letters and documents: the Earl of Kimberley; Earl St. Aldwyn and the Gloucestershire Record Office; Lord Derby and the Liverpool Record Office; the Honourable Mrs. Crispin Gascoigne; Lord Monk Bretton, Lord Clarendon, Lord Bonham-Carter, and the Bodleian Library; Mrs. Sheila Sokolov Grant; the Borthwick Institute of Historical Research; the Board of Trinity College Dublin; the Trustees of the Broadlands Archives Trust; the Somerset Record Office; the Suffolk Record Office, Ipswich Branch; the National Register of Archives and Her Majesty's Stationery Office; the Norfolk Record Office; the Leicestershire Record Office; the University of Birmingham; the Public Record Office; and the British Library.

Librarians and archivists at some ninety locations have been invariably kind and helpful. I would like specially to notice those whom I have troubled most: Ms. Jean Kennedy of the Norfolk County Record Office and Mrs. Christine North of the Cornwall County Record Office. Dr. Brian Blakeley introduced me to Kimberley and guided me through the initial stages of my acquaintance with him. I must thank him for this, and for not insisting on 'Labuan and the Colonial Office'. I am grateful to Barry Tharaud, Karen Sauer, Otto Nelson, Barry Morgan and Dan Frankforter for assisting me with a variety of linguistic matters associated with Kimberley's extensive use of non-English languages. I must thank many scholars who at various stages have provided useful information or made helpful suggestions: Tony Cartwright, Monica Cartwright, Ronald Fiske, Patrick Jackson, Idris Traylor, Angus Hawkins, Colin Matthew, Mark Curthoys, Padraic Kennedy, David Bebbington, Derek Blakeley, Susan Farnsworth and James Patrick Smith. Mr and Mrs Ronald Buxton were gracious hosts at Kimberley Hall on more than one occasion, going out of their way to reveal unusual features of the estate. For much personal help and a defining approach to high politics, I thank Professor John Vincent. I am thankful for research assistance from Hannibal-LaGrange College and Pennsylvania State University, the Behrend College. As to my family – Janice, Grady, Tessa and Ellen – I can hardly thank them sufficiently for their good-natured toleration of my wandering mind and body. I am grateful to all of these, but most indebted on both personal and intellectual grounds to one who has made 'almost an art of remaining in the shadows.' A medal to Dr. Andrew Croker for a life well lived.

All errors and infelicitous statements are of course my own.

Portrait Gallery

The following entries are meant to be suggestive rather than exhaustive, focusing upon information relevant to the subject's Cabinet career and relationship to Kimberley. Choice of surname or title has been dictated by common usage during the period of most active asscociation. Thus, *Ripon* rather than *de Grey*, *Goderich* or *Robinson*.

Campbell-Bannerman Sir Henry (1836–1908) Educ. Glasgow University and Trinity College, Cambridge. M.P., Stirling, 1868–1908); Financial Secretary to the War Office, 1871–74, 1880–82; First Secretary to the Admiralty, 1882–84; Chief Secretary for Ireland, 1884–85; Secretary of State for War, 1886, 1892–95; Prime Minister, 1905–08. Worked closely with Kimberley on Indian and foreign policy matters from 1892, and on party questions from 1899 when he became leader of the Liberal opposition. They were not personal friends, but always worked together cordially; both committed to the principle of strength through diversity within the Liberal Party.

Clarendon George William Frederick Villiers, 4th Earl of (1800–70). Educ. St. John's College, Cambridge. Minister to Spain, 1833–39; Lord Privy Seal, 1840– 41; Chancellor of the Duchy of Lancaster, 1840–41, 1864–65; President of the Board of Trade, 1846–47; Lord Lieutenant of Ireland, 1847–52; Secretary of State for Foreign Affairs, 1853–58, 1865–66, 1868–70. Early mentor, who from the mid-1850s spoke regularly in favour of Kimberley's advancement. More nearly reflected Kimberley's liberal credo than Russell, Palmerston or Gladstone. Close political friends.

Currie Bertram Wodehouse (1827–96). Educ. Eton. City banker, partner and active manager of Glyn, Mills, Currie and Company; Member of the Council of India, 1880–95; played an important role in the Baring financial crisis, 1890; represented England at the International Monetary Conference in Brussels, 1892; served on Indian Finance Committee, 1893; founded the Gold Standard Defence Association, 1895. Widely considered by the 1890s the foremost City authority on banking matters. A firm Liberal, but relatively uninterested in politics. Second son of Raikes Currie and friend of Gladstone; Kimberley's cousin and close personal friend.

Currie Philip Henry Wodehouse (1834–1906), joined the Foreign Office as a clerk in 1854; served under Kimberley at St. Petersburg, 1856–57; served as secretary to Salisbury on diplomatic missions to Constantinople and Berlin, 1876, 1878; Permanent Under-Secretary for Foreign Affairs, 1889–93; Ambassador to Turkey, 1893–98; Ambassador to Italy, 1898–1903. Fourth son of Raikes Currie; Kimberley's cousin. Essentially non-political, but a valuable source of diplomatic information. Kimberley served as his professional mentor, and the two remained close.

Currie Raikes (1801–81), City banker, partner in Glyn, Mills, Currie and Co.; Liberal M.P. for Northampton, 1837–57; unsuccessfully contested Lord John Russell's London seat in 1857; an early advocate of national education, church reform and vote by ballot. From 1847 served as Kimberley's financial advisor in repairing the fortunes of Kimberley estate, and as his earliest political mentor. The two remained personally close, though Currie was less active politically after 1865. At his death, Kimberley wrote: 'Indeed, he was almost a father to me.'

Derby Edward Henry Stanley, 15th Earl of (1826–93). Educ. Rugby and Trinity College, Cambridge. Conservative M.P. for Lynn Regis, 1848–69; Under-Secretary for Foreign Affairs, 1852; Colonial Secretary, 1858, 1882–85; President of the Board of Control, 1858; Secretary of State for India, 1858–59; Foreign Secretary, 1866–68, 1874–78; leader of the Liberal Unionists in the Lords, 1886–91. An undoctrinaire centrist, like Kimberley. The two worked closely and cordially after Derby succeeded Kimberley at the Colonial Office. Maintained their London friendship after 1886.

Dodson John George, First Baron Monk Bretton (1825–97), Liberal M.P. for East Sussex, 1857–74, for Chester, 1874–80, for Scarborough, 1880–84; Deputy Speaker of the House of Commons, 1865–72; Financial Secretary to the Treasury, 1873–74; President of the Local Government Board, 1880–82; Chancellor of the Duchy of Lancaster, 1882–84. Liberal Unionist from 1886. He and Kimberley were contemporaries at Eton and at Christ Church, Oxford, where they each took a first in Classics in 1847. Lifelong personal friends.

Duff Sir Mountstuart Elphinstone Grant (1829–1906). Educ. Balliol College, Oxford. Liberal M.P. for Elgin Boroughs, 1857–81; Under-Secretary of State for India, 1868–74; Under-Secretary of State for the Colonies, 1880; Governor of Madras, 1881–86. Gained a reputation as a foreign policy expert during the 1860s; published *Studies of European Politics*, 1866. Devoted the last years of his life to literature. Took a second in Classics, Balliol, Oxford, 1850. Worked for Kimberley at the Colonial Office and as Governor of Madras. Close personal friends, with common tastes in literature and politics.

Forster William Edward (1818–86). Educ. at Quaker schools. M.P. for Bradford, 1851–86; Under-Secretary of State for the Colonies, 1865–66; Vice-President of the Committee of the Privy Council for Education, 1868–74; Chief Secretary for Ireland, 1880–82. Kimberley thought highly of his abilities, though they disagreed over Forster's Irish policy; they were political associates who seldom had occasion to work together.

Fortescue Chichester Samuel, Baron Carlingford (1823–98), Liberal M.P. for Louth, 1847–74; Lord of the Treasury, 1854–55; Under-Secretary of State for the Colonies, 1857–58, 1859–65; Chief Secretary of Ireland, 1865–66, 1868–71; President of the Board of Trade, 1871–74; Lord Privy Seal, 1881–85; Lord President of the Council, 1883–85. An elder contemporary of Kimberley at Christ Church, Oxford, where he took a first in Classics, 1844. Kimberley and Fortescue were personal friends whose claims to office became inextricably tangled, particularly in 1861, 1865, 1870 and 1880. Kimberley feared that Fortescue's wife, Lady Waldegrave, was not good for his character.

Gladstone William Ewart (1809–98). Educ. Eton and Christ Church. Conservative M.P. for Newark, 1832–45; Liberal-Conservative, Liberal M.P. for Oxford, 1847–65; Liberal M.P. for South Lancashire, 1865–68, for Greenwich, 1868–80, for Midlothian, 1880–95; Under-Secretary of State for War and the Colonies, 1835; Vice-President of the Board of Trade, 1841–43; President of the Board of Trade, 1843–45; Secretary of State for War and the Colonies, 1845–46; Chancellor of the Exchequer, 1852–55, 1859–66; Prime Minister, 1868–74, 1880–85, 1886, 1892–94. Kimberley mistrusted Gladstone's diplomatic instincts, but admired his liberal principles, parliamentary skill, and popular genius. The two were close politically, but seldom saw or wrote to one another out of session.

Granville Granville George Leveson-Gower, Second Earl (1815–91), educ. Eton and Christ Church; Whig M.P. for Morpeth, 1836–40, for Lichfield, 1841–46; Under-Secretary of State for Foreign Affairs, 1840–41; Vice President of the Board of Trade and Paymaster-General, 1848–51; Secretary of State for Foreign Affairs, 1851–52, 1870–74, 1880–85; Lord President of the Council, 1852–54, 1855–58, 1859–66; Chancellor of the Duchy of Lancaster, 1854–55; Ambassador Extraordinary to Russia, 1856; Secretary of State for the Colonies, 1868–70, 1886. Formed a good opinion of Kimberley from their first close political contact in 1856; Kimberley admired his diplomatic skill, with the usual reservations regarding nonchalance. Always a cordial working relationship, especially close from 1880. When Granville was ill, Kimberley frequently filled his place as leader in the Lords.

Harcourt Sir William George Granville Venables Vernon (1827–1904), educ. Trinity College, Cambridge. Liberal M.P. for Oxford, 1868–80; for Derby,

1880–95; for Monmouthshire, 1895–1904. Solicitor-General, 1873–74; Secretary of State for Home Affairs, 1880–85; Chancellor of the Exchequer, 1886, 1892–95; Liberal leader in the House of Commons, 1894–98. Called to the bar, 1854; wrote for the *Morning Chronicle*, *The Times* and the *Saturday Review*, 1849–67; Professor of International Law, Cambridge, 1869–87. Kimberley admired his Liberal principles and his ability to make a 'slashing' speech, but ever questioned his political manners. They were in almost constant conflict during the Rosebery administration over policy issues, but worked cordially together in leading their respective houses, 1896–98.

Hartington Spencer Compton Cavendish, Marquess of (1833– 1908) and 8th Duke of Devonshire, educ. Trinity College, Cambridge; Liberal M.P. for North Lancashire, 1857–68; for Radnor Boroughs, 1869–80; for Lancashire N.E., 1880–85; for Lancashire N.E., Rossendale, 1885; Liberal-Unionist M.P. for Lancashire N.E., Rossendale, 1886–91, whereupon he succeeded his father as 8th Duke of Devonshire. Under-Secretary of State for War, 1863–66; Secretary of State for War, 1866, 1882–85; Postmaster General, 1868–71; Chief Secretary for Ireland, 1871–74; Secretary of State for India, 1880–82; Lord President of the Council, 1895–1903; President of the Board of Education, 1900–02. Got on well with Kimberley in the course of business, but they moved in different social circles.

Morley John (1838–1923), educ. Cheltenham and Lincoln College, Oxford. Liberal M.P. for Newcastle-on-Tyne, 1883–95; for Blackburn, Montrose, 1896–1908. Chief Secretary for Ireland, 1886, 1892–95; Secretary of State for India, 1905–10, 1911; Lord President of the Council, 1910–14. Biographer and man-of-letters, edited *Fortnightly Review* (1867–82), *Pall Mall Gazette* (1880–83) and *Macmillan's Magazine* (1883–85); wrote biographies of Cobden (1881) and Gladstone (1903). Worked cordially with Kimberley, though in largely different areas. Kimberley admired his scholarship, and in 1886 copied the following selection from *On Compromise* into his commonplace book: 'A man does not become celebrated in proportion to his general capacity, but because he does or says something which happened to need doing or saying at the moment.'

Northbrook Thomas George Baring, 1st Earl of (1826–1904), Kimberley's contemporary at Christ Church; Liberal M.P. for Penryn and Falmouth, 1857–66, when he succeeded as Second Baron Northbrook. Under-Secretary of State for India, 1859–64; Under-Secretary of State for Home Affairs, 1864–66; First Secretary to the Admiralty, 1866; Under-Secretary of State for War, 1868–72; Viceroy of India, 1872–76; First Lord of the Admiralty, 1880–85. Kimberley, being the chief landowner in Falmouth, took special interest in Northbrook's role in Liberal politics there. They thought highly of one another's abilities, and often consulted one another on foreign affairs; personal friends.

Overstone Samuel Jones Loyd, 1st Baron (1796–1883), educ. Eton and Trinity College, Cambridge; partner in London and Westminster Bank; M.P. for Hythe, 1819–26; influential writer on currency matters from 1837, especially *Thoughts on the Separation of the Departments of the Bank of England* (1844); frequently consulted by Sir Charles Wood, Lord John Russell and Lord Granville. Intimate friend of Raikes Currie (q.v.) and frequent promoter Kimberley's talents within the financial community into the mid 1860s.

Palmerston Henry John Temple, 3rd Viscount (1784–1865). Educ. Harrow, Edinburgh, and St. John's College, Cambridge. Tory M.P. for Newport, 1807–11; for Cambridge University, 1811–31; for Bletchingly, 1831; Liberal M.P. for South Hampshire, 1832; for Tiverton, 1835–65. Secretary at War, 1809–28; Secretary of State for Foreign Affairs, 1830–34, 1835–41, 1846–51; Secretary of State for Home Affairs, 1852–55; Prime Minister, 1855–58, 1859–65. Invited Kimberley to dine and shoot; thought highly of his diplomatic ability and wide knowledge of European affairs.

Ripon George Frederick Samuel Robinson, Lord (1827–1909), styled Viscount Goderich, 1833–59; 3rd Earl De Grey and 2nd Earl of Ripon, 1859; 1st Marquess of Ripon, 1871. Privately educated. Under-Secretary of State for War, 1859–61, 1861–63; Under-Secretary of State for India, Jan.-July 1861; Secretary of State for War, 1863–66; Secretary of State for India, 1866; Lord President of the Council, 1868–73; Viceroy of India, 1880–84; First Lord of the Admiralty, 1886; Secretary of State for the Colonies, 1892–95; Lord Privy Seal, 1905–08. More radical than Kimberley, though they shared fundamental Liberal principles. Kimberley's closest political friend from the 1860s, despite Ripon's conversion to Catholicism in 1874.

Rosebery Archibald Philip Primrose, Lord (1847–1929), styled Lord Dalmeny, 1851–68; 5th Earl of Rosebery, 1868. Educ. Eton and Christ Church, Oxford. Under-Secretary of State for Home Affairs, 1881–83; Lord Privy Seal and First Commissioner of Works, 1885; Secretary of State for Foreign Affairs, 1886, 1892– 94; Prime Minister and Lord President of the Council, 1894–95. Worked closely with Kimberley from 1886, with broadly similar views regarding colonial and foreign affairs. Became more intimate personally during the tumultuous Rosebery ministry, though they later drifted apart.

Russell Lord John (1792–1878), 1st Earl Russell, 1861. Educ. Westminster and Edinburgh University. Whig M.P. for Tavistock, 1813–17, 1818–19; for Huntingdonshire, 1820–26; for Bandon Bridge, 1826–30; for Devon, 1831; for Devon South, 1832–35; for Stroud, 1835–41; for London, 1841–61. Paymaster-General of the Forces, 1830–34; Secretary of State for Home Affairs, 1835–39; Secretary of State for War and the Colonies, 1839–41; Prime Minister,

1846–52, 1865–66; Secretary of State for Foreign Affairs, 1852–53, 1859–65; Cabinet Minister without office, 1853–54; Lord President of the Council, 1854–55; Secretary of State for the Colonies, 1855; First Commissioner to the Vienna Congress, 1855. Requested Kimberley's assistance at the Foreign Office in 1852 and generally promoted his career during the fifties and sixties, though they differed on Italian policy.

Spencer John Poyntz, 5th Earl (1835–1910), styled Viscount Althorp, 1847–57. Educ. Harrow and Trinity College, Cambridge. Liberal M.P. for South Northamptonshire, 1857. Lord- Lieutenant of Ireland, 1868–74, 1882–85; Lord President of the Council, 1880–83, 1886; First Lord of the Admiralty, 1892–95; Liberal leader in the Lords, 1902–05. Friends from around 1860, Norfolk estates, fox hunting and the Volunteer movement brought them together. Worked closely together from 1868, principally on Ireland. Next to Ripon, Kimberley's closest friend in the Cabinet.

Wodehouse Anne (1802–1880), Kimberley's mother. Born Anne Gurdon, daughter of Theophilus Thornagh Gurdon of Letton, Norfolk. Married Henry Wodehouse, 7 April 1825; four children: John, 1826–1902; and twin Annette, 1826–33; Laura, 1827–35; Henry, 1834–73. Widowed, 29 April 1834. Devout Anglican. Close relations with extended family including Gurdons, Wodehouses and Curries. Doted on her younger son, some said to the exclusion of Kimberley.

Wodehouse Armine (1860–1901), Kimberley's younger son. Married in 1889 Eleanor, daughter of Matthew Arnold. Private Secretary to Kimberley, 1886, 1892–95; Executive Committee of the Eighty Club, 1899. Liberal M.P. for Saffron Walden, Essex, 1900–01. Recurrent illnesses from 1871 demanded frequent attention; educated at home under his father's tutelage. Kimberley was particularly fond of Armine, in part because he had lost another son in infancy (Alfred, 1856–58).

Wodehouse Henry (1834–73), Kimberley's brother, born after their father's death. Educ. Balliol College, Oxford. Entered the foreign service 1855, serving successively in St. Petersburg, Stockholm, Constantinople, London, the Hague, Madrid, Vienna, Paris (1868–72) and Athens (1872–73). Died in Athens of typhoid fever. Served with Kimberley in St. Petersburg, 1856–58; and on the Schleswig-Holstein mission to Berlin and Copenhagen, 1863–64. Universally liked in the diplomatic corps. Kimberley, eight years his senior, was more serious and treated him almost as a son. Nevertheless, the brothers got on well together.

Wodehouse Florence Fitzgibbon (1825–95), married Kimberley on 16 Aug. 1847. First daughter of the 3rd and last Earl of Clare. Never enthusiastic about her husband's political and diplomatic responsibilities; devoted to Armine, much as Anne Wodehouse had been devoted to her younger son; well liked throughout the extended family. Kimberley loved her deeply throughout their marriage; she seems to have been less satisfied. Lord Dufferin recalled their first meeting at a ball, where Kimberley 'fell a victim to the pair of large soft eyes he married, but behind the eyes there was nothing.' The proposal of marriage came after only ten days' acquaintance.

Wodehouse John (1848–1932), Kimberley's elder son. Educ. Eton and Trinity College, Cambridge. Spent extravagantly, failed to graduate and finally filed bankruptcy, 1872. Active in Norfolk politics, serving from the 1880s as a Liberal agent in Mid and East Norfolk; heavily funded party activities after the death of his father. County Councilman for North Walsham from 1889. County magistrate until being removed for personal assault during the campaign of 1895. In later years referred to in the London press as the 'Labour Earl'. Despite disappointments, father and son remained very close both personally and politically.

Wood Charles (1800–85), 1st Viscount Halifax, 1866. Educ. Eton and Oriel College, Oxford, where he took a double first in 1821. Private secretary to Earl Grey; Liberal M.P. for Great Grimsby, 1826–31; for Wareham, 1831–32; for Halifax, 1832–65; for Ripon, 1865–66. Joint Secretary to the Treasury, 1832–34; First Secretary to the Admiralty, 1835–39; Chancellor of the Exchequer, 1846–52; President of the Board of Control, 1852–55; First Lord of the Admiralty, 1855–58; Secretary of State for India, 1859–65; Lord Privy Seal, 1870–74. Aided Kimberley early in his career; considered by his younger colleague to be an uncommonly shrewd and quick witted politician, who suffered from poor speaking and 'his incurable habit of telling a fool he was a fool.' The two were politically close and personally friendly.

Introduction

He was supremely excellent as an average British statesman with more than the average amount of capacity.

Eastern Daily Press on Lord Kimberley at his death.

How neatly Winston Churchill reduced the era of his youth to 'an age of great men and small events', an age in which personal potential was often thwarted by the circumstances attending a sustained period of national success.[1] It is true that the Victorians were not threatened with civil war, foreign invasion, or national bankruptcy; but then, each age requires its own kind of heroism. In an era of peace it was perhaps necessary for high-minded politicians to believe with John Morley that a man did not 'become celebrated in proportion to his general capacity' but because he did or said 'something which happened to need doing or saying at the moment.'[2] The century between Waterloo and the Great War required maintenance in foreign affairs, no small task but one unsuited to the heroic temperament of men like Wellington and Churchill. Instead of military and diplomatic campaigns to defend the homeland, the Victorian circumstance presented the less urgent but more complex task of governing an expectant nation at peace. The generals in this campaign of control and management have received substantial attention; the lieutenants have fared less well. A good example of this neglect may be found in the case of John Wodehouse, first Earl of Kimberley.

There is no question here of finding a lost Liberal leader. Lord Kimberley's temperament was too conciliatory, his need for approbation too slight, for him to play the political game with all his might. Ambition and an array of solid talents earned early opportunities for distinguishing himself both diplomatically and in government, but two factors worked against a more overt political role. First, he never sat in the House of Commons. He was bitterly disappointed at being thrust at the age of twenty-one into the 'icy atmosphere' of the Lords, with its host of indolent members. In the 1850s serving in the august upper house did not seem to matter so much; in fact, he shone in comparison to his peers.

---

[1] *Great Contemporaries* (London: Reprint Society, 1941), p. 13.
[2] *On Compromise* (London: Macmillan, 1886), p. 213; cited in Kimberley's commonplace book, KP1 15/K2/12.

But in doing business there he gradually adopted their tone, and lost forever the habit of public politics which would have strengthened his hand immeasurably after 1867.

Just as the democracy made itself an irresistible rather than manageable force, Gladstone emerged after 1865 to dominate the Liberal landscape, further limiting the possibilities and combinations which might have made more room for an ambitious and clear-thinking young nobleman just entering his prime. Gladstone's genius for combining brazen political warfare with high legislative purpose was an irresistible shield – at least subconsciously – for an earnest liberal who suspected the democracy and wished to have as little as possible to do with the compromises it required. Gladstone seemed to manage this unruly tandem in a way that Kimberley was ready enough to admit he could not. An occasional disagreement over method was not worth the price of rebellion, for he had no intention of giving up the pleasures and responsibilities of Norfolk life in pursuit of an impossible dream. The great point was to govern, and he believed that Gladstone did it supremely well. The natural qualities of leadership which many saw in Kimberley in the 1850s were under Gladstone funnelled into administrative rather than political channels.

Had their policy objectives diverged substantially, Kimberley might well have developed a different political identity. But they did not. Even before leaving school, Kimberley was committed to policies which Gladstone would later embrace and gradually come to symbolize – Peelite finance, free trade, liberty of conscience, extension of education, imperial decentralization, and, perhaps most importantly, the process of collective government. Where Kimberley changed, especially in promoting more aggressive imperial policies and Home Rule for Ireland, he was responding to the same circumstances which led Gladstone to judge moments ripe for his own initiatives. Because they began with common assumptions and attitudes, it is not surprising that they should have evolved politically along similar lines, an evolution reinforced by the strength of Gladstone's personality without being initially motivated by it.

If Kimberley was thus the most unlikely of Liberal leaders, his role in Victorian Liberal politics nevertheless has been imperfectly understood.[3] In the quintessential chronicle of Victorian high politics, A. B. Cooke and John Vincent warned that the 'highly experienced Whig ministers' could not 'easily be understood', then characterized Kimberley as one who 'could be relied upon to leave party politics to the party leaders.'[4] Access to the Derby diaries in 1974, however, led Vincent to add Kimberley to 'the list of Gladstone's ministerial

---

[3] At Kimberley's death, George Shaw-Lefevre represented the view of most Liberal ministers in saying that 'in proportion to his real weight in the inner circle' of the Liberal Party, there was no one 'so little known to the rank and file of it.' 'Lord Kimberley: A Reminiscence', *The Speaker*, 12 April 1902, p. 37.

[4] *Governing Passion*, p. 119.

confidants in autumn 1885.'[5] Colin Matthew, after two decades of research in the Gladstone diaries, suggested that Gladstone's 'inner group of the Cabinet' included 'Granville, Hartington, Harcourt, and perhaps Kimberley.'[6] Such intimations alone are nevertheless unlikely to dispel the caricature of Kimberley as Gladstone's 'loyal lieutenant', competent, hard-working, high-minded, and self-sacrificing; the only soldier to persist from first to last in each of Gladstone's ministerial campaigns, for there is undeniably a large element of truth in the epithet.[7] Over a long career, he displayed each of these qualities in abundance. However, one should recall that he enjoyed a distinguished Liberal career while Gladstone was still searching for a party, that he twice threatened resignation in order to win his way, and that he ultimately refused to support his 'chief' over naval estimates in 1894.

Like any caricature, the traditional view of Kimberley conveys an essence which falls short of precision and misleads as to detail. In point of policy-making, Kimberley was no Gladstone, but neither was he a Fortescue, as he is sometimes portrayed, unimportant but occasionally 'useful'.[8] During more than thirty years of cabinet-level manoeuvring, Kimberley's title to high office was never seriously questioned, in fact was scarcely mentioned apart from problems elsewhere, as in the Queen's refusal of Derby for the India Office in 1882.[9] He served continuously in Liberal cabinets between 1868 and 1895 as Lord Privy Seal (1868–70), Colonial Secretary (1870–74; 1880–82), Indian Secretary (1882–85; 1886; 1892–94), and Foreign Secretary (1894–95), and ambitious cabinet-makers as diverse as Chamberlain, Herbert Gladstone, and Edward Russell pegged him for high office in imaginary governments either anticipating or following Gladstone's retirement.[10] But if Kimberley were not simply a minion of Gladstone, what then was his role, and why has it been shrouded?

The reasons for Kimberley's obscurity are understandable. The bulk of his extensive archive was closed to research from 1959 until 1994, inhibiting general studies and assessments which might at any moment have proven incomplete or erroneous. As collections of his out-letters gradually have become available elsewhere, Kimberley has been cited more frequently, suggesting a breadth

---

[5] *DD3*, pp. 25a, 34.

[6] *Gladstone Diaries*, 10:lviii.

[7] Typical is the casual reference to Kimberley as one of Gladstone's 'minions'. Richard Jay, *Joseph Chamberlain, A Political Study* (Oxford: Clarendon Press, 1981), p. 47. See too *Norwich Mercury*, 9 April 1902, p. 4; *Governing Passion*, p. 119.

[8] See, for instance, Owen Chadwick's intimation that Kimberley might have been a 'superfluous veteran' in 1892. *Acton and Gladstone* (London: Athlone Press, 1976), p. 44; on Fortescue, *Gladstone Diaries*, 10:lvii.

[9] See letter 116, herein.

[10] Chamberlain to Dilke, 7 January 1885, DkP 43887; 9 April 1902, *Norwich Mercury*, p. 2; Herbert Gladstone to Campbell-Bannerman, 4 January 1900, CBP 41215, f. 193; *Liverpool Daily Post*, 9 February 1901.

of political activity previously unknown.[11] Renewed access to the Kimberley papers following their purchase by the Bodleian Library in December 1991 now make it possible to better understand his party role. In the meantime, the effects of this long period of historiographical caution need to be addressed, for they are not self-evident. Because his name figures prominently in a number of well executed departmental studies published since the late 1950s, one might imagine that Kimberley has been well served.[12] Safe studies rooted firmly in the records of the Colonial, Indian, and Foreign Offices give the illusion that Kimberley has fared singularly well at the hands of historians. Yet safe studies, like notions of safe sex, can be dangerously misleading. While *what* Kimberley did administratively from the time he moved to the Colonial Office in 1870 until the fall of the Rosebery ministry in 1895 has been well studied, *who* he was and how his personality influenced Liberal politics has remained a mystery. Virtually nothing has been done on his early life, education, county career, rise in politics, or early administrative performance.[13] What little has been written about his role in Cabinet, where the most important political decisions of the era were made, is frequently misleading. For all practical purposes, he is still the politician who, in Rosebery's phrase, 'went loyally where he was told to go', leaving party politics to others.[14] But Rosebery's own self-regard kept him surprisingly naive of political circles of which he was not the centre.[15] In

---

[11] Ubiquitous citations from his 'Journal of Events during the Gladstone Ministry, 1868–74' have established Kimberley as a reliable source and an integral factor in the high politics of the first ministry. However, although his party role grew steadily during the following twenty years, he is seldom mentioned in the absence of convenient journal references. On references to Kimberley from the recently accessible Northbrook and Cartwright papers, see J. P. Parry, *Democracy and Religion, Gladstone and the Liberal Party, 1867–1875* (New York: Cambridge University Press, 1986); T. A. Jenkins, *Gladstone, Whiggery and the Liberal Party, 1874–1886* (Oxford: Clarendon Press, 1988).

[12] The most notable being Rose Louise Greaves, *Persia and the Defence of India, 1884–1892: a Study in the Foreign Policy of the Third Marquis of Salisbury* (London: Athlone Press, 1959); W.D. McIntyre, *The Imperial Frontier in the Tropics, 1867–75* (London: Macmillan, 1967; D.M. Schreuder, *Gladstone and Kruger: Liberal Government and Colonial 'Home Rule', 1880–1885* (London: Routledge and Kegan Paul, 1969); Arnold Kaminsky, *The India Office, 1880–1910* (Westport, Conn.: Greenwood Press, 1986); Gordon Martel, *Imperial Diplomacy: Rosebery and the Failure of Foreign Policy* (Kingston: McGill-Queen's University Press, 1986).

[13] For examples of the value of such prosaic studies, see H.C.G. Matthew, *Gladstone, 1809-1874* (Oxford: Clarendon Press, 1986), chaps. 1 and 2; Michael Bentley, 'Gladstone's Heir', *English Historical Review*, 107 (Oct. 1992), pp. 901–24; Andrew Adonis, 'Aristocracy, Agriculture and Liberalism: The Politics, Finances and Estates of the Third Lord Carrington', *Historical Journal*, 31 (1988), pp. 871–97; Roy Foster, *Charles Stewart Parnell: The Man and His Family* (Atlantic Highlands, N.J.: Humanities Press, 1976).

[14] Extracts, Kimberley memoir, RsP 10186, p. 253.

[15] Kimberley's ignorance of much political intrigue is well known, but it tended to be wilful and was never as profound as Rosebery and others imagined it to be. While

working closely with Kimberley, Rosebery grew fond of his elder colleague, but had little understanding of his inner life. To understand Kimberley's political role, one first needs to sense his political presence. This is no easy task, for subsequent events often have obscured the reasons for contemporary perceptions. Yet some combination of factors caused Clarendon in 1858 to peg Kimberley as a future foreign secretary, and Knatchbull-Hugesson as late as 1874 to give him a good chance of one day becoming prime minister. The key to Kimberley's role in Liberal politics lies buried in the two decades prior to Gladstone's first ministry. Of course he had to manage departmental work with some success thereafter, but his colleague's perceptions of his performance were inevitably tinged by their predisposition to believe that Kimberley was exercising the kind of ability and judgement proven across time. Thus he could, for example, authorize with Cardwell a military expedition against the Ashanti without serious dispute from the left, or support Ripon's progressive Ilbert Bill without arousing a fatal reaction from the Liberal right.[16]

Wordsworth's observation that 'moderation naturally keeps out of sight' suggests the most fundamental reason for Kimberley's obscurity.[17] In Kimberley's case, it was a moderation which operated in two ways. First, he consciously avoided attention and was careful about what he said and what others were allowed to publish regarding his career.[18] Second, because he was committed to Cabinet consultation, he never became associated in the public mind with a single, transcendent event or crusade. This combination of personal reticence and public accident meant that most of his political activity went unnoticed by the public, and much by the Liberal rank-and-file. When his papers became available for research in the late 1940s, when there were still living memories to supplement incomplete written records, it was no longer fashionable to study

recuperating in January 1901, Kimberley responded to Campbell-Bannerman's account of party machinations: 'Altho' Spencer has kept me (generally) informed of what has been going on, I did not before thoroughly understand the situation which is indeed as you say 'hideous'.... the 'subterranean' personal intrigues are detestable.' Gladstone's characterization of politics as both a game and as high art is suggestive here, for Kimberley's own concept of politics leaned strongly toward the latter, and tended to define the levels at which he chose to participate. See Extracts, Kimberley memoir, RsP 10186, pp. 278–79; Robert Rhodes James, *Rosebery* (London: Weidenfeld and Nicolson, 1963), pp. 330–32, 511; Kimberley to Campbell-Bannerman, 1 January 1901, CBP 41221, ff. 204–05; Matthew, *Gladstone, 1809–1874*, p. 177.

[16] *Gladstone Diaries*, 8: 372–73; Wilfrid Blunt, *India under Ripon, a Private Diary* (London: T. Fisher Unwin, 1909), p. 18.

[17] Wordsworth to Walter Savage Landor, 21 January 1824, in Alan G. Hill, ed. *Letters of William Wordsworth, A New Selection* (Oxford: Oxford University Press, 1984), pp. 221-222.

[18] See, for instance, Wemyss Reid to Kimberley, 16 November 1894, KP1 15/K2/21, and note; Kimberley to Spencer Childers, 20 July 1900, KP1 15/K2/21; Kimberley to A.G. Symonds, 12 August 1901, Symonds Papers, 18-E, Perkins Library, Duke University; 2nd earl of Kimberley to Spencer, 20 October 1902, SP K372.

rational, self-contained individuals who adhered to fixed standards of personal and public morality.[19] This was especially true for members of the Lords, for it was clear that the important work of government during the Gladstone era had been done in the Commons. As a result, the tendency has been to focus upon departmental work, with little reference to its broader political implications. In Kimberley's case, having never been memorialized with a biography, his political role has been extrapolated from information drawn from a few standard sources, primarily the *The Times* obituary, the *Dictionary of National Biography*, the *The Complete Peerage*, and, since 1958, Ethel Drus's introduction to Kimberley's 'Journal of Events during the Gladstone Ministry, 1868–1874'. All are useful, but each is flawed. Collectively they have portrayed the administrative stalwart without suggesting his party presence, which must be an important characteristic in understanding the role of any cabinet minister.[20]

Publication of the Gladstone diaries, along with greater access to archives generally, has now provided a framework for interpreting both the conclusions of departmental studies and the many laconic references from contemporaries. It is not surprising that the shifting perception of Kimberley's political role emanates from such sources. But in tracing the development of a political career, it is perhaps more necessary in his case than in most to return to the beginning, for in private and public life, in character and approach to politics, he consistently bore witness to the 1887 observation of Lord Dufferin, who had known him since Eton in the 1830s, that Kimberley was 'less changed from what he was as a boy than any person I ever knew.'[21] Even that repository of condensed truth, the commonplace book, testifies to the constancy of his fundamental assumptions, entries from the 1840s and 1850s often resurfacing forty years later.[22] Through more than fifty years of public life he supported the extension of education, promoted free trade and the removal of civil disabilities, encouraged colonial and international self-determination, and preached fiscal responsibility. He sometimes changed opinions; as in relaxing his hostility toward Roman Catholicism, and in reversing his opposition to Irish Home Rule. In both cases, he freely admitted his *volte face* in parliament, arguing that it

---

[19] Cf. praise such as Walter Bagehot's in the 1850s and 1860s for stolidity and dullness in parliamentary government as a 'test of its excellence, an indication of its success.' 'Dull Government', in *The Collected Works of Walter Bagehot*, ed. Norman St. John-Stevas (London: The Economist, 1974), 6:81.

[20] For a full discussion of the treatment of Kimberley in standard sources, see Appendix 2.

[21] Dufferin to Grant Duff, 30 June 1887, GDP MSS Eur F 234, no. 12. Lady Wantage's 1907 categorization of Kimberley with the 'men of Lord Overstone's generation' suggests a similar perception. 'The type of mind of one generation', she observed, differs from another 'as does the style of dress.' Yet Kimberley is grouped with Overstone and eight friends, who, on average, were more than thirty years older. *Lord Wantage: A Memoir* (London: Smith, Elder, 1907), p. 286.

[22] Cf. Kimberley's two commonplace books, KP1, 15/K2/7; 15/K2/12.

was 'very unwise to persevere in a course of action which is proved to have failed'.[23] But these were not so much conversions of principle as reconciliations with reality, thought about and weighed in light of the experience of many years. If anything, such changes tended to reinforce broader liberal principles, such as religious toleration and self-determination, which he had held from the beginning of his career. On the whole, Kimberley's political mind was made early.

Kimberley was fortunate in having been born healthy, intelligent, and first. His self-regard was developed through the support of a large, extended family with an ancient pedigree and a substantial if somewhat impoverished Norfolk estate. As a boy, he could see and smell and touch his past. The richly embroidered, red velvet hangings of a throne prepared for the great Queen Elizabeth in 1578 imbued the house with a distinct importance, and also recalled the Wodehouse connection with the Boleyns.[24] He could unroll great parchment maps and carefully spread red-sealed royal warrants in the muniment room at Kimberley Hall, or peer into the awesome 'Japanned chest' which contained the material relics of the family's glory: a gold-spangled bodice worn by the great Elizabeth, a rosary presented by Henry V's queen after Agincourt, and Archbishop Laud's personal copy of the *Book of Common Prayer* — enough glorious association to fire the imagination of any young nobleman.[25] His parents provided him with love, a comfortable home, discipline, travel and the surety of places at Eton and Christ Church, where Wodehouses had attended for more than a century. Still, he was forced to deal with the many personal sufferings common to that age. Because he was healthy and his family was not, he learned the lessons of a survivor. Within the four months between December 1833 to April 1834, his twin sister and father died, ages seven and thirty-four. Less than a year later and within a few days of his arrival at school, his younger sister died, upon which he dutifully wrote to that he was sure he had 'great reason to thank God' that his mother had been spared.[26] Anne, a devout Anglican who had been devastated by the string of deaths, at first tried to hide the news, and then compensated for her losses by an absolute devotion to the care of her boys. Instead of an emotional intimacy, however, young Johnny Wodehouse

---

[23] 3 *Hansard*, 346 (11 July 1890): 1446; 3 *Hansard*, 186 (28 March 1867): 711–12.

[24] See Bulletin Note, 'An Elizabethan Throne', which notes that the throne 'was carefully preserved and handed down in the family', most of the material being 'the original ruby red velvet with its enrichment of gold and silver tissue tinted with colours and edged with gold bullion thread.' The Burrell Collection, Glasgow. Also, Kimberley, *The Wodehouses of Kimberley* (London: Privately Printed, 1887), pp. 38–39.

[25] Throughout his life, Kimberley took great interest in his family history, at various times organizing and annotating documents, researching family legends, and finally producing his only publication, *The Wodehouses of Kimberley*. On the 'Japanned chest' and its contents, see 'Inventory and Valuation at Kimberley Hall and Witton Park, Norfolk', KP7, p. 5; *The Wodehouses of Kimberley*, pp. 19–39; Annotated biographical register of portraits at Kimberley Hall, in author's possession.

[26] 17 February 1835, KP1 15/K2/18.

turned inward, stoically accepting the vagaries of life and death and gradually developing an emotional independence which Anne could not fully appreciate in a boy so young. She increasingly doted on the frail baby Henry, who had been born after his father's death in 1834. Though she may have done this to the 'exclusion of Kimberley', who was less dependent, the brothers got on well together. Henry was not ambitious and usually deferred with good grace to his brother's fatherly admonitions.[27]

While Henry stayed home, John was sent away to school at the age of nine. Though clearly clever, even at Rev. Thomas Kerchever Arnold's rectory in Lyndon, Rutlandshire, he was thought to be 'slightly more reserved and self-contained than some.'[28] This may also have had something to do with floggings at the good reverend's hand, though he was later thankful for Arnold's having 'extirpated' a 'vile habit of falsehood', and for having compelled him to be 'accurate' in his lessons. 'Whatever may be said in favour of "moral suasion" as contrasted with corporal punishment,' Wodehouse later wrote, I disliked being flogged, and took care afterwards at Eton to avoid it by attention to lessons and discipline.'[29] After a summer tour of Belgium, Switzerland and the Rhineland, at twelve years of age Wodehouse entered the hallowed– and dirty– halls of Eton. Rather big for his age, he was not much bullied, but 'hated' school– the food was bad, the discipline severe, and the surroundings sordid, altogether depressing for a young man of refined sensibilities.[30] And the lack of privacy impinged upon his reflective personality. He had a few close friends – most notably John George Dodson, Anthony Henley, and his younger cousins, Bertram and Maynard Currie – but was already developing an independent political viewpoint which placed him distinctly in the minority. Once he shocked 'the august assembly of "Pop", defending in a set speech the execution of Charles I',[31] drawing only one vote from the assembled boys. Kimberley nevertheless proved to be an exemplary student. He was known throughout the college as 'one of the cleverest boys', and was 'sent up for good' more than twenty times.[32].

---

[27] Edmund Monson to William Monson, 1 September 1873, Monson Papers, Perkins Library, 18-G. See too, Extract from Miss Throckmorton to Miss Mellish, September 1873, KP1 15/K2/20. On fraternal relations, see Kimberley, Travel diary, 22 August 1838, KP1 15/K2/5; Kimberley to Edward Buxton, 21 November 1857, K1 3/2; Henry Wodehouse to Kimberley, 8 April 1859, KP1 3/2; John Wodehouse to Henry Wodehouse, 18 December 1860, in *KJ*, p. xi.

[28] May Kerchever Arnold, Letter to the Editor, 14 April 1902, *Morning Leader*, KP6 MS.eng.c.4483, f. 38.

[29] Kimberley journal, KP6 MS.eng.e.2790, p. 2.

[30] On conditions at Eton, see C. Kegan Paul, *Memories* (London: Kegan Paul, Trench, Trubner and Co., 1899), pp. 91–94; H. C. Maxwell Lyte, *A History of Eton College (1440–1910)*, 4th ed. rev. (London: Macmillan, 1911), pp. 450–55.

[31] Kimberley journal, KP6 MS.eng.e.2790, p. 5.

[32] Kimberley journal, KP6 MS.eng.e.2790, p. 3; E. H. Pickering to Anne Wodehouse, 14 May 1843, KP6 MS eng.c.4476, f. 1; Alfred Lyall, *Life of the Marquess of Dufferin*

The spring and early summer of 1843 were spent in Europe under the direction of Rev. Constantine Frere. While in Hamburg, Kimberley met the precocious, radical historian, Henry Buckle,[33] who was already full of plans for his massive *History of Civilisation in England* (1857, 1861). Both young men being full of ambition, great talkers, alive to current events, and interested in languages, they fell in together, spending two months in Dresden before parting company.[34] Upon his return, Wodehouse matriculated into Christ Church in June. Tradition and taste dictated association with the 'fast set', which in his case primarily meant riding with the Bicester pack.[35] Ambition, however, proved stronger than country pleasures. While many gambled, rioted and generally neglected their studies, Kimberley read *sub rôsa* with the young philosopher Henry Mansel,[36] and took a first in Classics in May 1847, reputed to be one of the best in years.

Upon the death of his grandfather, second Baron Wodehouse, John left Christ Church after the Trinity term of 1846, returning in October as a nobleman. Matriculating at the same time was John Charles Henry Fitzgibbon, eldest son and heir of the third Earl of Clare,[37] and brother of Florence, a pretty Dublin socialite. Within a short time, John and Florence were introduced; ten days later he put the question at a breakfast given by the Duchess of Bedford. After their marriage on 16 August 1847, Lord and Lady Wodehouse spent four months in Italy before settling on the Kimberley estate.

Anne Wodehouse regretted that she had 'made an idol' of her son, but determined to concentrate her attention on the one 'still dependent' upon her.[38] Henry, who did not marry until 1872 and who even then continued to write fulsome missives full of the routine affairs of life, was clearly his mother's favourite by temperament, but there is little evidence to suggest that either Kimberley or Anne considered their relationship anything other than an extension of natural dispositions, and much to suggest that they remained close, if not emotionally

---

and Ava, 2 vols. (London: John Murray, 1905), 1:23.

[33] Henry Thomas Buckle (1821–62), scholar; son of a wealthy London shipowner; no formal training, but widely travelled and well read. Reputed to have known 19 languages by the age of thirty.

[34] Alfred Henry Huth, *The Life and Writings of Henry Thomas Buckle*, 2 vols. (London: Sampson, Low, Marston, Searle and Rivington, 1880), 1:30–31.

[35] Kimberley journal, MS.eng.e.2790, p. 4 ; *Norwich Mercury*, 9 April 1902, p. 2. Though associations with the 'fast set' appear to have declined from the 1850s, it is interesting to note his long friendship with Francis Lawley, Gladstone's private secretary, who was dismissed in 1854 for gambling, and later became a sporting journalist. See Lawley to Kimberley, 19 May 1895, KP1 15/K2/22.

[36] Henry Longueville Mansel (1820–1871), scholar and tutor at St. John's College, Oxford from 1844; strong Tory and high churchman.

[37] Subsequently killed in the charge of the Light Brigade at Sevastapol, where he was serving with the 8th Hussars.

[38] Anne Wodehouse, Anniversary book, September 1847, KP1 15/K2/27.

intimate, until her death in 1880.[39] If Kimberley had not the time in the course of his career to write of Russian princesses and balls and silver knives,[40] it was, she conceded, because he was busy fulfilling the larger duties which she herself had taught him must accompany his station in life.[41]

Kimberley's mother need not have worried that the gentleman's 'temptation to idleness' would entice him. Realising how poorly Christ Church had prepared him for a life in politics, Kimberley immediately laid out a plan for educating himself in political and moral philosophy, political economy, jurisprudence, and European history, gradually bringing shape to the 'Liberal principles' which he had adopted at Eton.[42] The honeymoon trip to Italy led to the study of Italian, a useful addition to his already fluent French. For five years, Kimberley read the classic accounts in each field of study, carefully recording critiques in an indexed notebook. Frequently he would refer to the author's sources in judging the validity of conclusions which had been drawn, seldom adopting any argument whole. Typical of his approach to the word of authorities is his assessment of Coleridge's *The Friend*, with which he had 'been much entertained' though not 'converted to [his] extreme idealism':

> I must acknowledge, that there is something far more attractive to me in their Theories, than in those of the materialists or rather Sensationalists. I sincerely wish that the Existence of Ideas originally implanted in the mind could be demonstrated to my satisfaction, but my Reason demurs.[43]

The gulf between philosophy and practice was one of Kimberley's earliest concerns, and led to the development of a political philosophy at once both doctrinally progressive and practically conservative. He admired the sheer intellectual power of philosophers such as Mill and Kant, and worked systematically through their arguments.[44] He tended, however, to minimize the importance of all theoretical applications, appealing rather to circumstance and the lessons of history. Education was a process of training the mind, rather than filling it with ready-made doctrines.[45] At first enthusiastic in his commitments, even 'radical'

---

[39] For instance, various family letters in KP1 15/K2/18, 20; and PkP DE 1749.

[40] For Henry Wodehouse's long letters to his mother, see KP1 15/K2/20. Cf. Kimberley's, which frequently began in the manner: 'I have been a very bad correspondent lately but I have been really so harassed with every kind of business private and public....' 29 September 1856, KP1 15/K2/18.

[41] Anne Wodehouse, Anniversary book, KP1 15/K2/27, Sept. 1846 and throughout.

[42] Although he remained an avid reader of the classics, Kimberley held that they did little to aid a politician. See Blakeley, *Colonial Office*, p. 45. For his plan of reading, see KP1 15/K2/6, [pp. i–iii].

[43] Notes on Books, KP1 15/K2/6, p. 13.

[44] KP1 15/K2/6, pp. 56–57; Grant Duff, *Notes from a Diary, 1896–1901*, 1:311

[45] See, for instance, his July 1850 address to the Royal Agricultural Society in Exeter, KP6 MS.eng.d.2492, p. 5.

in his ideas, by the time he was brought into Aberdeen's government in 1852 he had moved far toward the growing 'Liberal' centre, ever more careful to temper his enthusiasms. In many ways Kimberley represented the new wave of mid-century politicians who, according to Cornewall Lewis, approached politics with a 'well-placed confidence' which avoided 'the Scylla of misplaced confidence and the Charybdis of "practical resistance to the Principle of Authority in every form."'[46]

Kimberley had ability and initiative, but he was not bound to succeed in politics. Born into an ancient family with a modestly distinguished record of service to the Crown, but with few high connections, his progress may be seen as particularly personal in nature, a thorough mixture of personality, ambition, hard work and skilful cultivation of the few insiders with whom he was acquainted.[47] Well built, above the average height, and accustomed to a sporting life, Kimberley was seldom ill, which enabled him to maximize his energy in simultaneously fulfilling heavy family, estate and county responsibilities, while at the same time pursuing a national career.[48] Bitterly disappointed at being deprived of an opportunity in the House of Commons, he made the best of the situation by becoming unusually active in the Lords, going up for important votes even when ministers felt 'sure of a majority', serving on committees, and making himself available for debate.[49] Though far from 'admiring' Lord John Russell's policy, particularly in Italy, he worked closely with Lord Albermarle[50] in promoting Liberal interests in Norfolk. Though they failed in the election of 1852, Kimberley continued to canvass the local gentry in support of Liberal candidates,

---

[46] Cited in R.K. Webb, 'A Crisis of Authority: Early Nineteenth-Century British Thought', *Albion*, 24 (Spring 1992), p. 16.

[47] Contrast Fortescue, with similar credentials and better connections. In 1858 Goldwin Smith observed that 'a little more ambition or effort' would have placed him in the company of 'Ld. Wodehouse, Ld. Carnarvon, Lord Stanley, Mr. Fredk. Peel, & Mr. Cairns' as 'the most rising young men in official life...', cited in O.W. Hewett, ed. '...and Mr. Fortescue', *A Selection from the Diaries from 1851 to 1862 of Chichester Fortescue, Lord Carlingford* (London: John Murray, 1958), p. 131. After several political disappointments, in 1880 Fortescue was 'well aware that my inertness in the House of Lords throughout these years of opposition tells agst. me .... I grew lamentably, culpably inert.' Carlingford diary, 26 April 1880, CfP 63688.

[48] In a telling account from the Schleswig-Holstein mission of 1863–64, his brother observed that while 'the subalterns were more or less knocked up' *en route* to Berlin, 'Wodehouse seems in the rudest health .... He sleeps profoundly in the railway, and has the most astonishing appetite and spirits — in fact envy of him is the only grievance we have to complain of. Henry Wodehouse to Florence Wodehouse, [13 December 1863], KP1 15/K2/20.

[49] Kimberley journal, KP6, p. 4; Caroline Currie, *Bertram Wodehouse Currie, 1827–1896: Recollections, Letters, and Journals*, 2 vols. (Roehampton: Manresa Press, 1901), 1:440.

[50] George Thomas Keppel (1799–1891), Russell's private secretary; M.P. for East Norfolk, 1832–35, for Lymington, 1847–50.

and in 1857 he played a major role in electing the first Liberal in East Norfolk since 1832.[51] By all accounts, at a time when oratory was aimed mainly at fellow parliamentarians and judged by erudition and logic rather than enthusiasm, he was a good debater, who carried a strong instinct for the political fray.[52] He was intelligent, well read and got on well in society. He spoke French fluently, as well as several other languages, which made him all the more valuable for diplomatic positions. His grasp of financial principles, fostered by his uncle and fortified by a careful study of political economy, was turned to good advantage in London. Raikes Currie introduced him to City bankers and politicians, talked up his abilities, and helped secure his election to the Political Economy Club on 6 March 1851, at a moment when financial matters were especially prominent in national politics.[53] Fundamental to the employment of all these advantages was Kimberley's moral conviction that social privilege carried with it responsibility, and that duty came before all else.[54] His mother prayed for this attitude, Eton and Christ Church fostered it, philosophers justified it, and Kimberley adopted it, not as a public façade, but as the natural expression of a world view in which the individual could choose, for good or ill, the course of his conduct.

[51] 'Has not Norfolk done its duty well?', he asked Raikes Currie, adding that he took some credit for the good showing, 'as I may say without egotism that the party was stirred up and kept together mainly by my exertions in the face of the most tiresome lukewarmness and apathy....', 11 April 1857, KP1 3/1; Currie, *Recollections*, 1:501. For papers related to Kimberley's role in organizing Norfolk liberals, see KP1 3/2.

[52] See letter 14, herein. For a good example, see Kimberley's sharp attack on both Derby's equivocation on free trade and his manner of debate, in which he 'was very fond' of accusing the opposition of 'factiousness', and taking 'all the advantage of the discussion to himself.' 3 *Hansard*, 123 (22 November 1852): 290–93. Kimberley found Derby, 'with rare exceptions...unscrupulous in debate'. Extracts, Kimberley memoir, RsP 10186, p. 261; also Malmesbury, *Memoirs of an Ex-Minister, An Autobiography*, 2 vols., 3rd ed. (London: Longmans, Green and Company, 1884), 2:159. Generally on Kimberley's speaking, see Charles Knight, *Passages of a Working Life during Half a Century*, 3 vols., reissue (London: Knight and Company, 1873), 3:154; Currie, *Recollections*, 1:300, 355; *Correspondence of Lord Overstone*, 3 vols., ed. E.P. O'Brien (Cambridge: Cambridge University Press, 1971), 1:756.

[53] Kimberley's course of study in political economy from August 1850 until June 1852 included Morier Evans, 'The Commercial Crisis of 1847 and 1848'; John Stuart Mill, *Principles of Political Economy* and *Essays on some Unsettled Questions of Political Economy*; James Mill, *Elements of Political Economy*; J.R. McCulloch, *Principles of Political Economy* and *On Taxation*; Adam Smith, *Wealth of Nations*; and a wide variety of related pamphlets, including a number written by fellow members of the Political Economy Club. KP1 15/K2/6, pp. 30–49; Catalogue of the Kimberley library, KP7. See Overstone's recommendation to G.W. Norman, director of the Bank of England, of Kimberley's 'remarkable document' surveying Russia's financial crisis of 1857. *Correspondence of Overstone*, 1:750–58.

[54] Kimberley wrote that 'the approach to Kings and principal persons' was valuable only as a 'vantage ground' for doing good. If this today seems tendentious, his personal habits and political career give it plausibility as a substantial aspect of his motivation. KP1 15/K2/7, pp. 4–5. See too, Extracts, Kimberley memoir, RsP 10186, p. 281.

By the early 1850s, Kimberley's combination of intellect, education, indefatigability, and political instinct had attracted the attention of Whigs such as Grey, Russell, Clarendon and Overstone who, like many at the time, were sensing a creeping 'crisis in Whig talent'.[55] In December 1852, Aberdeen, at Russell's request, offered Kimberley the post of Under-Secretary at the Foreign Office, though he had no special interest or training in foreign affairs, and would have preferred a position at the Board of Trade.[56] In fact, he could hardly have done better at twenty-six, for the foreign office in the 1850s afforded many opportunities for displaying ability, both in the office and in the Lords. Kimberley's earnest manner was well suited to a situation in which Russo-Turkish conflict, Indian mutiny and Italian unification were continually investing foreign affairs with a certain sense of urgency. He was asked to research precedents and write memoranda for the cabinet on delicate and complex issues. He was routinely privy to confidential information about the gravest matters from all parts of the world. And though he was exceedingly cautious and was implicitly trusted by Clarendon, still he *knew* things — and everyone knew it. In the ordinary course of work he met many foreign dignitaries, and often had occasion to assist important people. Whether it was 'writing a few lines' to let Molesworth know what the newspapers did not 'seem to know' about the Eastern Question, or cutting red tape for Cobden in a consular appointment for his brother-in-law, Kimberley was brought into regular contact with people who, if they were pleased with his work and manner, might later help him.[57] With the formation of Palmerston's government in February 1855, Herbert offered him charge of Colonial affairs in the Lords, but he declined, preferring to remain at the Foreign Office.[58] Clarendon was so pleased with Kimberley's performance that he appointed him to the difficult position of minister plenipotentiary to Russia in the wake of the Crimean War.[59] Though some found his diplomacy heavy-handed, it exactly suited Clarendon, who preferred to convey a bluff superiority.[60] Kimberley resigned in March 1858 in the wake of the conservative victory, 'having no confidence in Lord Derby and his government'. However, when Palmerston's government was formed in June 1859, he was reappointed to the Foreign Office

[55] Michael Bentley, *Politics without Democracy, Great Britain, 1815–1914* (Totowa, N.J.: Barnes and Noble, 1984), p. 130.

[56] Frances Balfour, *Life of George, Fourth Earl of Aberdeen*, 2 vols. (London: Hodder and Stoughton, 1923), 2:175; Kimberley journal, KP6 MS.eng.e.2790, , p. 12. Only in 1856, according to Granville's account, did he declare that his goal was the foreign office. Cf. assertions since that it had been a lifelong ambition. Fitzmaurice, *Life of Granville*, 1:180; McIntyre, *Imperial Frontier*, p. 53; Bentley, *Politics without Democracy*, p. 381.

[57] Molesworth to Wodehouse, 21 September 1853, KP6 MS.eng.c.3998, f. 132; Cobden to Wodehouse, 16 December 1859, KP6 MS.eng.c.4002, f. 133.

[58] Wodehouse to Herbert, 10 February 1855, KP6 MS.eng.c.4475, ff. 4-5.

[59] Letter 21, herein; Clarendon to Wodehouse, 15 July 1856, KP3 46692, ff. 29–30.

[60] For instance, Clarendon to Wodehouse, 16 June 1857, KP3 46693, f. 118; 6 January, 14 February 1858, KP3 46694, ff. 51, 127.

where he served with considerable distinction until Russell was elevated to the peerage in July 1861.[61] After 'maturely considering' Russell's request that he remain as Under-Secretary, Kimberley chose to resign, citing five-and-a-half years of successful service at the Foreign Office and two years as the head of 'an important mission' abroad as factors making his continuance under a chief in the same house impossible.[62]

Palmerston and Sir Charles Wood immediately tried to arrange for his transfer to the India office, though the vacancy could not be arranged.[63] During the following seventeen months, Kimberley refused the embassy at Constantinople, governorships of Madras and Bombay, and the governor-generalship of Canada. Though no permanent position could be found until his appointment as Under-Secretary to the India Office in April 1864, Liberal leaders were anxious to find a suitable place for him in the government. He was clearly frustrated, principally because ambition, coupled with his rapid political progress during the fifties, had made important posts abroad and lesser positions at home equally unattractive. Finally, in October 1864 he reluctantly accepted the Lord Lieutenancy of Ireland, though he and Palmerston agreed that the post eventually should be abolished. The ceremony was odious and the work abroad. On the other hand, it was one of the few positions outside the Cabinet offering real opportunities for political distinction, while allowing Kimberley to keep in touch with the pulse of party politics. As Henry comforted their fretting mother, he suggested that Kimberley was not likely to be away long, and reminded her that the newspapers were treating him extraordinarily well. 'The article in *The Times* itself at once brings him into *universal* notice, which is such an enormous thing'.[64] To be noticed is, after all, the first requisite of politics.

This brief survey of Kimberley's early career suggests a man of talent on the rise, but scarcely reflects the political rapids which he was required to navigate during the first decade of political life, when all his most important political connections were being formed. Yet his later political role must be misunderstood if the 'whig' and 'radical' labels so often applied by journalists and scholars are glibly repeated. Recent studies by T. A. Jenkins, J. P. Parry, Peter Mandler and Boyd Hilton have done much to unravel the complexities of political nomenclature during the mid-Victorian era. Such studies have, however, tended to be fundamentally about political process rather than the politicians themselves.[65]

---

[61] Wodehouse to Hammond, 27 February 1858, HmP FO 391/3; Palmerston to Russell, 8 December 1859, RIP 30/22/20, ff. 291–92; Russell to Cowley, 10 December 1859, RIP 30/22/103, f. 160; Cowley to Russell, 12 December 1859, RIP 30/22/53, f. 536; Palmerston to Russell, 5 September 1860, RIP 30/22/21, f. 219.

[62] Letter 31, herein; cf. letters 28, 30, herein.

[63] On efforts to provide Kimberley with a position, see Appendix 2.

[64] Henry Wodehouse to Anne Wodehouse, 13 October 1864, KP1 15/K2/20.

[65] Hilton's article provides an exception: 'Whiggery, Religion and Social Reform: the Case of Lord Morpeth', *Historical Journal*, 37 (December 1994): 829–59. T. A. Jenk-

If one wishes to understand Kimberley as an individual within the process, one must look to the unique circumstances which shaped his political role and which led to the particular form of its later representation.

In its obituary notice, the *Manchester Guardian* described Kimberley as a 'utilitarian radical of the Benthamite type'. This might be dismissed as journalistic rhetoric were the radical label not applied fairly broadly throughout his life.[66] His association with radicalism was rooted in the principle of *laissez faire* broadly applied to society and the economy, and reified in his participation in a variety of political ventures based in part upon the assumptions of philosophic radicalism. His first commitment to a political organization, predating association with the Whig Party, was to the Colonial Reform Society, founded in 1849 upon the premise that English colonies, 'if emancipated from the Downing Street incubus' would 'encircle England with a brotherhood of first-rate cognate nations faithful to the same crown'.[67] This search for organic reorganization recommended itself to a variety of reformers, including John Arthur Roebuck, Joseph Hume, Sir William Molesworth, Richard Cobden and Thomas Milner Gibson – 'men of all parties' as Kimberley proudly noted.[68] Kimberley's spirited defence of the Australian Colonies Government Bill during May and June of 1850, in which he argued for a complete re-examination of the 'principles' governing colonial relationships, can be linked to the speeches and pamphlets of Molesworth, Gibbon Wakefield's *Art of Colonization* and Roebuck's *The Colonies of England*, all of which Kimberley had read with interest.[69] During 1850, 1851 and early 1852, election to the Political Economy Club, advocacy of

ins, *Gladstone, Whiggery and the Liberal Party, 1874–1886* (Oxford: Clarendon Press, 1988), intro.; Parry, *Democracy and Religion*; Peter Mandler, *Aristocratic Government in the Age of Reform: Whigs and Liberals, 1830–1852* (Oxford: Clarendon Press, 1990). See too Angus Hawkins, *Parliament, Party and the Art of Politics in Britain, 1855–59* (London: Macmillan Press, 1987), intro.; J. W. Burrow, *Whigs and Liberals: Continuity and Change in English Political Thought* (Oxford: Clarendon Press, 1988).

[66] *Manchester Guardian*, 9 April 1902, p. 6. Lady Kimberley, according to Carlingford, 'abused Kimberley for his Radicalism...' A.B. Cooke and J.R. Vincent, eds., *Lord Carlingford's Journal: Reflections of a Cabinet Minister, 1885* (Oxford: Clarendon Press, 1971), p. 75. Gladstone himself suspected Kimberley of republicanism and noted that he had 'more than once strenuously voiced the Radical view.' *KJ*, p. 33; 'Two Colleagues on Lord Kimberley', *Leeds Mercury*, 10 April 1902, KP6 MS.eng.c.4481, f. 95. See also, H.H. Asquith, *Fifty Years of British Parliament* (Boston: Little, Brown and Company, 1926, p. 8; *Eastern Daily Press*, 9 April 1902, p. 3.

[67] Childe-Pemberton, *Life of Lord Norton, 1814–1905*, pp. 78–82; 18 November 1850 Circular, 'The Society for the Reform of Colonial Government', 29 January 1850, KP6 MS.eng.c.3995, ff.110–11. For the organization's relationship to philosophic radicalism, see A.M. Thornton, *The Philosophic Radicals: Their Influence on Emigration and the Evolution of Responsible Government for the Colonies* (Claremont: Pomona College, 1975).

[68] Kimberley journal, MS.eng.e.2790, p. 8.

[69] Kimberley, Notes on Books, KP1, 15/K2/6; 'Catalogue of the Kimberley Library', p. 7, KP7; 3 *Hansard*, 110 (31 May 1850): 519.

extension of education before mechanics' institutes and agricultural meetings, and favourable allusions in parliament to the application of the theories of political economy and the necessity of granting full civil rights further reinforced the public perception that Kimberley was in league with the utilitarian radicals.[70] Given that he still had not committed himself politically, and publicly had spoken only upon subjects associated with radical causes, it is understandable that frequent social company among more outspoken men like John Bright, John Bowring, George Grote, George Warde Norman, Adderley, Molesworth and Hume would lead many to suspect Kimberley of radical inclinations.[71]

Radicalism, however, was only one aspect of his evolving political perspective, and not very deeply ingrained. Though Kimberley was satisfied that the Colonial Reform Society had 'put the finishing stroke to the "liberation" of the Colonies from the incessant muddling of the Colonial Office', it was short-lived and its focus narrow, and he recognized that he still needed a party, as well as a political, persona. It is suggestive that his 'most valuable acquaintance' among the Radicals was Sir William Molesworth, the single Radical member of the Aberdeen Cabinet, whom Gladstone considered 'practically rather nearer in colour to the Peelites than to the Whigs.'[72] He hunted with Palmerston and dined at Lansdowne House. He met foreign dignitaries. Foremost, he educated himself in the wider world of European politics, making himself useful, and building bridges in all directions. Clarendon was a model in both style and viewpoint– capable, moderate and cosmopolitan; ambitious but not aiming for the top; and leaning toward the Peelites.[73] Frequently Kimberley agreed with radical theory, while arguing against its practice. In 1850, for instance, much of Richard Whately's argument against transportation in *Secondary Punishment* struck him as 'unanswerable', but he could not agree that the practice ought to be discontinued. Kimberley confessed that he disagreed with Whately, not 'from any fault in the argument', but rather from 'the seeming impossibility' of finding an alternative at the moment.[74] This tendency to balance doctrine and practice is fairly represented in his 1856 assessment of Harriet Martineau's *History of England during the Thirty Years' Peace, 1815–46*:

> It is a very useful account of current events.... Strong radical opinions, hatred of the Whigs, and deification of Peel for his Free Trade Measures. There are however

---

[70] *Correspondence of Overstone*, 1:509–10; Item 13, herein; Currie, *Recollections*, 1:300, 309; 3 *Hansard*, 119 (15 March 1852): 1032.

[71] See, for instance, R.A.J. Walling, ed. *The Diaries of John Bright* (New York: William Morrow, 1931), p. 137; Childe-Pemberton, *Life of Norton*, pp. 79–80; J.K. Laughton, *Memoirs of Henry Reeve*, 2 vols. (London: Longmans, Green and Company, 1898), 1:260; Harriet Sarah Loyd-Lindsay, *Lord Wantage, A Memoir*, p. 286.

[72] Kimberley journal, KP6 MS.eng.e.2790, pp. 6–7, 9; *PMP: Gladstone*, 1:78.

[73] Mandler, *Aristocratic Government in the Age of Reform*, p. 101; letters 17, 21, herein.

[74] Notes on Books, KP1 15/K2/6, p. 28.

many just remarks in the book. The antipathy to Palmerston and praise of Aberdeen is exaggerated and unsound.[75]

This is vintage Kimberley who seldom found any well constructed argument without merit, or any doctrine without fault.

By the mid-1850s, adherents of the Manchester school would not have considered him a radical. He was sometimes progressive, but the difficulty in distinguishing shades of progressivism is suggested in Cobden's letter of July 1852 supporting William Gardiner's decision not to cooperate with the 'old Whigs' in opposing new liberal members in Leicestershire: 'After all, how can they justify themselves in joining their old enemies in a contest with men whose only fault is (politically speaking) that they go a little faster on the same road that the pure Whigs have professed to be travelling on. Because they cannot go the pace of the radicals is no reason why they should turn round and run back.'[76] Kimberley, who cut his political teeth on free trade, had worked with Cobden in the Colonial Reform Society, and had remained on friendly terms with him, might be ascribed a 'form of radicalism' without going at Cobden's pace, based upon an intellectual freedom from what Asquith called an inert 'Whig laissez faire'.[77] All attributions of radicalism essentially suggest that he simply was not a 'pure Whig', confirming John Vincent's often unheeded observation that 'the great bulk of the Liberal M.P.s were neither Whigs nor Radicals but simply commonplace wealthy Englishmen whose political actions were bound neither by affiliation to great houses nor by theoretical intransigence.'[78] Still, calling Kimberley 'radical' sits ill beside frequent references to him as a 'whig', particularly after 1870. And the difficulty is heightened by the almost universal adoption of the latter designation since his death.[79] Who were these Whigs to

[75] Ibid., pp. 72–73.
[76] Cobden to Gardiner, 30 July 1852, CbP 43668, f. 174. Cf. Lord Stanley's observation of December 1852, that 'the Whigs and Radicals blend so closely that distinction is impossible'. *DD1*, p. 90.
[77] Asquith, *Fifty Years of British Parliament*, p. 8; Escott, *Pillars of the Empire*, p. 173.
[78] Though speaking principally of the House of Commons, Vincent's observation well applies to Kimberley. *Formation of the Liberal Party*, p. xxxiv.
[79] George Shaw-Lefevre, who sat with Kimberley in two cabinets, suggested that he was 'one of the last survivors of the pure Whigs, who governed the country for so many years after the Reform Act of 1832. *The Speaker*, 12 April 1902, p. 37. Consider Donald Southgate's suggestion that Kimberley had been pulled from the 'Whig top drawer' in the mid-1850s; E.D. Steele's that Kimberley was 'a moderate and sensible Whig' in the 1860s; and Colin Matthew's identification of him as 'leader of the younger Whigs' of the 1870s. Southgate, *The Passing of the Whigs, 1832–1886* (London: Macmillan, 1962), p. 285; Steele, *Irish Land and British Politics: Tenant-Right and Nationality, 1865–1870* (Cambridge: Cambridge University Press, 1974), p. 56; Matthew, *Gladstone, 1809–1874*, pp. 174, 178. See too Schreuder, *Gladstone and Kruger*, p. 31; McIntyre, *Imperial Frontier*, pp. 51–52; and J.P. Parry, *The Rise and Fall of Liberal Government*

whom Kimberley supposedly belonged?

There was of course the 'Whig Party', but this was all but defunct as an entity by the time Kimberley entered government.[80] In terms of an individual designation, G.W.E. Russell later identified two kinds of whigs: those who came from whig families, but 'by their public acts . . . have associated themselves with the general body of modern Liberalism'; and 'the Whigs as a separate section' – men like Lord Cowper, who was a 'warm adherent of the Liberal Party' but who refused to 'pledge' himself for the future.[81] Under these terms, Kimberley was no sort of whig at all, for he had no whig lineage and was by the 1860s clearly a party man. In the 1850s, it was the Whig party to which he 'refused to "pledge" himself'; by the mid-1860s, no one doubted that he was a strong Liberal partisan. He was courted by the Whigs in the 1850s, not as a landowning nobleman, but as an energetic and able young peer who could help supply the want of young talent in the party. Kimberley's support for Russell reflected a commitment to the 'vague rectitude over notions of "progress", "improvement" and "liberty"' which held diverse individuals together, rather than any kind of social identification or commitment to whiggism *per se*.[82] Perhaps this is the reason that 'a generous Derby' complimented him on his maiden speech of 1852, while he was little encouraged by his 'supercilious exclusive friends the Whigs.'[83]

Indeed, if Russell were right, it was as impossible to 'become a Whig as to become a Jew'.[84] And how much more difficult when one was not trying. Kimberley was simply a landed liberal rising through a chaotic political order in which it was still assumed that one might exercise private judgement in making political decisions. Yet a *pro forma* adherence to the Whig party and an eleven-thousand-acre estate predisposed many later observers to ascribe his political actions to a social and political philosophy which contemporary observers could not have imagined. When H.C.G. Matthew cites Kimberley in support of his assertion that 'Gladstone remained the Whigs' last, best hope', the reader may misinterpret the basis of Kimberley's support. In suggesting that only Glad-stone could 'steer the party in an even course' between 'right and left wings', Kimberley was speaking, not for the Whigs, but for the diminishing centre which was bound neither by historical association nor ideological commitment. Without this centre, he recognized that 'whiggish' members might well become conservatives, leaving only the radicals in opposition on the left, a possibility

---

in Victorian Britain (New Haven: Yale University Press, 1993), p. 259.

[80] Mandler, *Aristocratic Government in the Age of Reform*, pp. 1–3, 275.

[81] Russell, 'A Protest against Whiggery', *Nineteenth Century*, 13 (June 1883): 922–23; Francis Cowper, 'Desultory Reflections of a Whig', *Nineteenth Century*, 13 (May 1883): 738.

[82] See Hawkins, *Art of Politics*, pp. 5-6.

[83] Kimberley journal, KP6 MS.eng.e.2790, p. 5.

[84] Russell, 'A Protest against Whiggery', p. 923.

which Labouchere and others had long cherished.[85] By the turn of the century, then, the growing vacuity of both 'radical' and 'whig' allowed Kimberley to be characterized as both. It is hardly surprising that Dilke thought the use of party names had become 'defective'. 'I naturally think "Radical" the best of a bad lot' he argued for himself. 'But then the Tories have stolen it for application to politicians who to me appear to be the ordinary Whigs of my youth.'[86] When he wrote this, Dilke might well have been thinking of Kimberley, who had joined Aberdeen's government under Russell's sponsorship when Dilke was nine years old, and who was then being touted for his radicalism.

From the beginning, however, Kimberley thought of himself as a Liberal, an ardent free-trader who would nevertheless cooperate with men of all parties. The first event which he recorded as having marked his political philosophy was a dinner at Raikes Currie's in 1842, where the sixteen-year-old Kimberley listened as Currie, George Grote, Charles Buller, and others debated the importance of Peel's introduction of a sliding scale on corn tariffs. By some expressions which Peel had 'let fall', they were convinced that 'he intended eventually to repeal the Corn Laws.'[87] As the parties began to break up over repeal, new opportunities for independent liberal action presented themselves. Until 1852 Kimberley was not in any sense a party man, but rather a member of the Lords who usually supported Russell's government but carefully maintained his independence.[88] In fact, until he entered Gladstone's cabinet in 1868, Kimberley was seldom identified as either a Whig or a Radical.[89] How, then, did he come to acquire such titles from a later generation?

In the first instance, Kimberley's manner was responsible for failing to create a precise political persona. Rising through the liberal ranks in the 1850s, he mastered the intricate art of masking doctrine with performance. That he was simultaneously acceptable to both Gladstone and Chamberlain in 1885, and at his death proclaimed both a 'radical' and a 'pure Whig', is not indicative

---

[85] *Gladstone Diaries*, 10:xlvii; cf. Kimberley's account of a conversation with Derby at Knowsley: 'He fears (not perhaps without reason) Gladstone's plans about Ireland. When he saw him lately he found him inclined to make large concessions in the Home Rule direction. Ireland, we both agreed, was the pivot on which the political future turned.' Kimberley later added, 'He evidently expects some measure in the direction of Home Rule. He made this prophecy (since come true). If such a policy is adopted by Mr. G. you will be for it, I against.' Kimberley and Derby were still interested in the details of any proposed plan, and relatively unconcerned about 'class' interests. Kimberley journal, KP6 MS.eng.e. 2793, pp. 170–72; on Labouchere, see his letter to Dilke, 10 October 1882, DkP 43892, f. 139.

[86] Charles Dilke, 'Some Lessons of the War', *New Liberal Review* 1 (1901), p. 63.

[87] Kimberley journal, KP6 MS.eng.e.2790, pp. 9–10.

[88] Kimberley journal, KP6 MS.eng.e.2790, p. 5; Currie, *Recollections*, 1:394, 488.

[89] The first reference that I find to Kimberley personally as a Whig — distinct from his association with 'the Whig ranks' of the early 1850s — is from the *Vanity Fair* caption, 16 July 1869, p. 36. Prior to that time, he was usually identified by title or some similar reference — 'such a young nobleman' or 'one whose political views are Liberal'.

of an absence of political principle, but rather a reflection of his belief that results would ultimately justify the reasoning upon which they were based. Too, Kimberley's socialization with a variety of political figures, including radicals, whigs, liberals and Peelites, could variously be used as a basis for political characterization . English society, however, is a notoriously unreliable guide to political proclivities.[90] Problems of nomenclature associated with the obliquity of Kimberley's manner and society were exacerbated by turn-of-the-century attempts to interpret what was by then an ancient past from the perspective of a later, more disciplined party structure. This created in Kimberley's case the false dilemma of 1886, with the notion that he and the other 'whigs' had been forced to make a fundamental choice between whiggery and Gladstone over Home Rule.[91] This formulation misunderstands the nature of Kimberley's politics specifically, and Liberal party politics more generally, for it presupposes a Liberal orthodoxy which scarcely could have been resisted without harming one's position in the party. However true that may have been for politicians who came of age during the last quarter of the nineteenth century, promising politicians at mid-century gained considerable tactical advantage and personal distinction by wisely exercising their independence. Indeed, to have identified oneself too closely with a specific party or person in the 1850s might well have put a politician on the fast track to the lower reaches of government.

The origins of Kimberley's politics are undoubtedly unusual. His ancestors had been Tory since the seventeenth century. However, his grandfather, with whom he often sat 'on the platform', supported Peel and gave his proxy vote for repeal of the Corn Laws shortly before his death in 1846.[92] His uncle and chief political mentor, Raikes Currie, was a reform-minded City banker who married into the gentry and served as Liberal M.P. for Northampton from 1837 to 1857. Currie is perhaps best known as the Liberal Representation Society nominee to fill Lord John Russell's seat for the City of London in the general election of 1857, the LRS opposing Russell's 'aristocracy, his poor attendance,

---

[90] Though clubs were often important centres of political activity, John Hogan goes too far in saying that they 'were at the social heart of the parties.' 'Party Management in the House of Lords, 1846–1865', *Parliamentary History*, 10 (Summer 1992), p. 137. Stefan Collini has provocatively nominated the Atheneum as a 'suggestive symbol' of the 'relative homogeneity of the intellectual elite' in Victorian Britain. One might do the same for whig political culture with Brooks's's; for shrilly apolitical political culture with Grillion's; for distinguished peripatetic and diplomatic culture with the Traveller's; and for a friendly elitism with the Cosmopolitan. Kimberley was a member of all five clubs. Collini, *Public Moralists* (Oxford: Clarendon Press, 1991), chap. 1.

[91] W.C. Lubenow cogently argues that 'the home-rule defection was a crisis in the regime, not a crisis in society.' 'Irish Home Rule and the Social Basis of the Great Separation in the Liberal Party in 1886', *Historical Journal*, 28 (March 1985), p. 141.

[92] Kimberley, *The Wodehouses of Kimberley*, p. 58; *Leicester Post*, 17 April 1902, KP6 MS.eng.c.4484, f. 92.

and alleging insincerity in support of the admission of Jews to Parliament.[93] Kimberley, long skeptical of Russell's foreign policy and deeply committed to the removal of Jewish disabilities, wrote from St. Petersburg to wish Currie well.[94] It is both ironic and indicative of the contemporary political dynamic that the two most important figures in promoting his early career thus should have come into conflict. Kimberley played it carefully, privately identifying with Currie's position, but remaining on good terms with Russell and continuing to make himself useful to the party. To further confound his political associations, Kimberley had married the great-granddaughter of the notorious arch-Tory, John Fitzgibbon, first Earl of Clare and prime mover of the Irish Act of Union (1800). So in terms of family association, Kimberley was influenced by Tory, Peelite, and Liberal sentiments, lacking only the Whig and Radical pedigrees most frequently assigned to him.

Having examined Kimberley's early political associations, it will now be useful to identify some of the practical and intellectual factors which shaped, reinforced and modified family traditions. The 'Swing' riots[95] of November and December 1830 may well have been his introduction to public affairs. The Norfolk phase of the movement began on 19 November 1830. Labourers demanding elimination of threshing machines addressed the bench of North Walsham, chaired by John Wodehouse, Kimberley's grandfather and Colonel of the East Norfolk militia. As barns and crops were torched and machinery destroyed throughout East Anglia during the following fortnight, officials and property holders spread throughout their districts seeking to prevent disturbances. Kimberley's father was forced 'to harangue' the Kimberley tenants, and to help in raising special constabulary forces in the troubled districts. However, although he acknowledged that the region was in 'a most critical state', he tended to view the disturbances as isolated expressions of discontent, rather than manifestations of a general upheaval.[96] John Wodehouse arrested some thirty rioters, but he and the other North Walsham magistrates issued a public notice indicating both a determination to enforce the law and a recommendation that owners 'discontinue the use of Threshing Machines, and increase the wages of Labour' in order to meet legitimate demands.

The disturbance was serious and potentially threatening to the ancestral estate which young Kimberley often visited. If it would be foolish to say that the 'Swing' riots imbued him, as a five-year-old, with a liberal social theory, it

---

[93] Although he warned that 'Johnny...has still power enough to knock over any Liberal Government which excludes him.' See Spencer Walpole, *Life of Lord John Russell*, 2 vols. (London: Longmans, Green, and Company, 1889), 2: 284–89; Southgate, *Passing of the Whigs*, pp. 286–91.

[94] Wodehouse to Currie, 7,14 & 21 March 1857, KP1 3/1.

[95] For a detailed account of the 'Swing' riots in Norfolk, see E.J. Hobsbawm and George Rudé, *Captain Swing* (New York: Pantheon, 1968), chap. 8.

[96] For Henry Wodehouse's reports to his family, see KP1 15/K2/15.

would be an equal folly to suppose that he was altogether indifferent to the dangers and excitement of his father's mission, that he never in later years discussed the crisis with his father and grandfather (the latter who lived until Kimberley was twenty), or that he never reflected upon the means by which a potentially revolutionary situation had been successfully resolved.[97] These are matters of conjecture, but it is clear that as a young man he trusted circumstances rather than doctrine as the surer political guide, that he took more than a passing interest in the causes and courses of revolutions, and that he eventually adopted the moderation of his father and grandfather, rather than the more virulent Toryism of his great-grandfather and most of his ancestors. Toward Ireland, for instance, Kimberley was as consistent as any official of his time in supporting simultaneous measures for stringent law enforcement and redress of grievances, just the method which had been adopted by his grandfather on the North Walsham bench when confronting local rioters.[98]

According to his own account, written in 1862, Kimberley had adopted liberal principles 'purely from conviction' while still at Eton, further suggesting that early experiences were central in his evolving political philosophy.[99] Shortly after graduating from Christ Church, he had opportunity to consider these amorphous convictions in the field. While on their honeymoon tour of Italy, he and Florence unexpectedly found themselves caught up in the revolutionary wave which rolled through Lombardy and Venetia in March 1848.[100] The feeling of the moment was electrifying. For six days between March 20 and 25, while progressing from Florence to Venice, Kimberley found himself weighing wars and rumours of wars, speaking in broken Italian to throngs of cheering revolutionaries who warmly responded to his support for their 'liberal' revolution. It is not surprising that after such an experience he lamented over 'the icy cold atmosphere of the House of Lords' upon his return.[101] However, upon reach-

---

[97] It is difficult to know precisely what Kimberley knew of the riots at time. However, given the warm relationship between father and son, the fact that Henry Wodehouse regularly wrote home during his policing tour, and that he sent messages in these letters directly to his son, it is far more likely that Kimberley was impressed in some way by the event than otherwise. Whatever the impressions at the time, Kimberley certainly reread the letters as an adult.

[98] A response to Lord Derby in the Established Church Bill debate is typical: 'Are we to be told that disaffection is not enough, and that we must wait for tumults and rebellion? ... Parliament has shown ... that they can repress disaffection and maintain law in Ireland; but I say that, having done this, Parliament and Government are bound to see whether there are not grievances of which the Irish justly complain, and, if there are, to show an eagerness to consider them — and especially at a time when the civil liberties of the country have been suspended.' 3 *Hansard*, 192 (15 June 1868): 2117.

[99] Kimberley journal, KP6, MS.eng.e.2790, p. 5.

[100] See letters 3 and 4, herein.

[101] Nevertheless, he quickly made political peace with his nobility and came to accept the necessity as a virtue. Ibid., p. 4. Cf. his later comments on speaking in the House of Lords. Grant Duff, *Notes from a Diary, 1886–1888*, 1:131–32.

ing Venice, Kimberley turned in his reading from the literary and philosophical reflections of Bacon, Tasso, Manzoni and Dante to the political pamphlets of Azeglio on Jewish emancipation and Italian unification. In calm reflection he believed that Italian liberals had since 1847 'far overstepped the bounds of the prudence which the moderate party would have wished'. 'It is to be hoped,' he continued, 'that there still remains a sufficient number of generous minds impressed with the ideas of Azeglio to restrain the extreme ardour of some who may be hurried on by their unexpected success to measures, which might endanger the usefulness of the whole movement.'[102] After returning to England in April with both the progressive and destructive possibilities of revolution clearly on his mind, Kimberley spent six months studying Smyth's *Lectures on the French Revolution*, Mackintosh's *Vindiciae Gallicæ*, Burke's *Reflections on the Revolution in France*, Alison's *History of the French Revolution*, and the memoirs of Madame Roland, Bertrand de Noleville, and Jean-Sylvain Bailly; and then another four months in relating the lessons of the French revolution to England and Europe during the preceding two hundred years.[103] As personal reflection and Austrian reaction reified the heady experience of unrestrained liberalism in practice, Kimberley's support for Italian unification markedly displayed the tempering of his family's early conservatism.[104] Considering reform, whether legislative or revolutionary, he clearly adhered to Burke's veneration for 'usage and precedent', and took seriously the dictum that one who 'despises little things shall perish little by little'.[105] To this attitude may be owed both his lack of grand political ideas, and his mastery of policy detail, for he constantly sought to make small, careful adjustments, preferring them to large, systemic shocks.[106]

And so it was in every kind of government business. Burke was his philosopher; his commitment to 'usage and precedent' was fundamental, and in retrospect has reinforced the general sense of his whiggery.[107] Still, his regard

---

[102] Notes on Books, KP1 15/K2/6, p. 5.

[103] Ibid., pp. 5–19.

[104] When selecting Kimberley as a representative to the abortive Congress of Villafranca in 1859, Russell noted that he was 'eager for Italy but has no bad name on account of his opinions...'. Russell to Cowley, copy, 10 December 1859, RIP 30/22/103, f. 160. For a suggestive comment regarding the unusual combination of radicalism and conservatism in Lady Kimberley's great grandfather, about which Kimberley was certainly aware, see R.B. McDowell, *Ireland in the Age of Imperialism and Revolution, 1760–1801* (Oxford: Clarendon Press, 1979), pp. 307–08.

[105] Extract from *Jesus, Son of Sirach*, KP1 15/K2/7, p. 15. Cf. his memorandum regarding reform of the Book of Common Prayer, item 71, herein.

[106] In moving the second reading of the Irremovable Poor Bill in 1861, for instance, he 'ventured to think it was better for their Lordships to make small and well-considered changes than to wait till matters grew to such a head that they might be driven to adopt some sweeping legislation.' 3 *Hansard*, 164 (23 July 1861): 1350.

[107] See, for instance, George Leveson Gower's complaint that Kimberley might in 1894

for the past never quite overwhelmed his commitment to reform. As Kimberley himself argued in the debate over re-establishing diplomatic relations with Rome in 1860, 'the question was entirely one of time and opportunity'. In this case, as in many others, 'he thought he could show their Lordships that the present was not a convenient time or opportunity for taking any step to produce the change.'[108]

Such caution today seems perilously close to the 'inert Whig laissez faire' which was sometimes complained of by a new generation of politicians in the late nineteenth-century, but it was seen by many as positively bracing at mid-century. And throughout a long career, it never hardened Kimberley against reform. His belief in the potential for progress through administration was so prominent a part of his political philosophy that no one prior to the 1870s ever mistook Kimberley for a conservative. Cautious support for the compromise Factories Bill in 1850, for instance, was support nonetheless, and may be measured against the fact that Shaftesbury abstained from voting. Though 'interference in matters of this kind' was viewed as 'a dangerous policy', Kimberley was ready to admit that the case of factory operatives was 'exceptional'.[109] He never argued that reform need come quickly or in the context of a particular set of circumstances, but that its consideration should not be excluded merely because of tradition.[110] In all questions of reform, whether involving the remediation of obvious evils or the implementation of more efficient measures of governing, Kimberley was likely to ask Bentham's question, 'is it useful', and then to add, 'will it work?' In considering flogging as a punishment, for instance, he first noted his moral reprobation, then quickly added, 'but that is quite apart from the questions before us.... The Question here is whether corporal punishment... is likely to effect the object which we have in view.' Long experience had shown, he argued, that it would not.[111] Likewise, he refused to rely solely upon 'his own interpretation of the obscure passages in Scripture', upon which the opponents to the Marriage Law Amendment Bill originally had based their 'principal opposition', but he confidently asserted that the law as it stood 'affected injuriously very many persons who had already contracted marriages of the kind, or who, as amongst the lower classes, did what was worse, by living without

---

have prevented the unwarranted creation of new benefices by withholding his sanction as Lord President of the Council. 'He did not increase my estimation of either his energy or his ability by declining to exercise his authority, mumbling a few platitudes about "there being no precedents," "an unusual exercise of power," etc. etc.' *Years of Endeavour*, pp. 133–34. On adherence to usage, see too Kimberley to Francis Cavendish, 2 March 1882, Perkins Library, Great Britain Papers (Political) 18-G; Kimberley to Henry Wodehouse, 1 August 1861, KP1 15/K2/19.

[108] 3 *Hansard*, 159 (8 June 1860): 155.

[109] 3 *Hansard*, 112 (15 July 1850):1360–61.

[110] See his argument for dismissing 'old feelings and prejudices' in ending religious inequality in Ireland. 3 *Hansard*, 192 (25 June 1868): 2122.

[111] 3 *Hansard*, 334 (2 April 1889): 1367–68.

marriage with their deceased wife's sister.[112]

Whether reform was rooted in 'natural rights' was problematic. But he believed strongly enough in 'civil liberty' as 'one of the highest attributes of the human character' that it served as the foundation of his commitment to the repeal of all civil disabilities.[113] He was not, however, a democrat, believing 'absolute equality a chimera'.[114] Rather, the polity should be governed by those of intellect and means, who were not burdened by enslaving circumstances.[115] Pure democracy could not then work, simply because the majority of the populace lived in circumstances which prohibited development of the intellect. Agreeing with Coleridge, he found that the state of dependence applied in varying degrees to women generally, to the 'poor and infirm, to men in embarrassed circumstances, to all in short whose maintenance be it scanty or be it ample, depends on the will of others.'[116] Kimberley was not an elitist *per se*, but rather a pragmatist, reflecting on the world as he found it, both hopeful for the improvement of society and painfully aware of the dangers and inadequacies of revolution. He was not a racist in the modern sense of the term; he did not believe that Africans, Indians, or Irishmen were biologically inferior. However, he did believe that individual character was in large measure a natural outgrowth of cultural circumstances, and that these cultural tendencies could only be changed across long periods of time. In developing Colonial policy, for instance, he took account of the Bengalis' long association with the British, which had made them clever and likely to surpass other Indian ethnic groups in examinations; and the Hausa martial tradition, which made them better troops than their Fanti counterparts. Kimberley's attitude toward race may in some measure be gauged by a dispute with John Pope-Hennessy, Administrator of Sierra Leone, who in 1872 proposed the foundation of a West African University, 'where not only the sons of rich Africans could be educated, but where, like in the early Irish Universities, and some of the Continental Universities of our own times, even the poorest youths who had talents and a real taste for knowledge might . . . have an opportunity of cultivating learning.' Kimberley found the proposal 'extremely interesting', and suggested that the Indian example be studied, for 'mere missionary education will never effect much.' However, later when Pope-Hennessy began to quote Sir Richard Burton on the intellectual superiority of the black race, Kimberley

---

[112] 3 *Hansard*, 151 (23 July 1858): 1983–84. See too his arguments against the Convict Prisons Bill and, later, for maintenance of the opium trade. 3 *Hansard*, 110 (12 April 1850): 192; Kimberley to Gladstone, 20 March 1886, GP 44228, f. 232.

[113] Kimberley very early adopted the cause of Jewish civil rights. See notes on Azeglio's pamphlets, 18 March 1848, KP1 15/K2/6, pp. 4–5; extract from Smyth's *Lectures on the French Revolution*, KP1 15/K2/7, p. 17; 3 *Hansard*, 118 (17 July 1851): 875–77.

[114] KP1 15/K2/7, p. 29.

[115] Ibid., pp. 17, 23.

[116] Extract from *The Friend*, Ibid., p. 33.

wrote that it was 'impossible not to distrust the judgement of a man who can write in this strain.'[117] He frequently spoke of the racial characteristics of the Irish for instance, but his policies suggest that he agreed with Goldwin Smith's observation that there was no 'inherent depravity or even inherent weakness' in Irishmen, but rather an arrested training in civilization.[118] Such ethnic and racial attitudes were to have important consequences in India and the colonies, where the pace of self-government was for many years largely determined without reference to the cabinet, according to Kimberley's perceptions of a people's ability to govern themselves.[119] To a lesser extent they influenced Irish policy through Kimberley's role as Lord Lieutenant and as a prominent member of the cabinet.

Domestically, Kimberley demonstrated considerable faith in the rugged common sense of the English and Scotch, particularly before the advent of mass campaigning. This may have contributed to his early belief in the civilising effect of education, which he promoted by participating in agricultural and mechanics' organizations and by supporting Liberal measures for the extension of public education.[120] The masses who were without the means of governing he regarded with a benevolent detachment, his sense of social justice owing more to a 'generous indignation at the selfishness of the oppressor' than to sentimentality or an 'enthusiasm of humanity' so frequently associated with Victorian radicalism.[121] He found that workers were 'in fact neither much better nor much worse than other men'.[122] But whatever may be seen as whiggish in these attitudes emerged primarily from study and experience rather than social position or historic association. Before Gladstone's budget battle of 1853, Kimberley already had grounded himself in a conservative progressivism which resembled Gladstone's in fundamental ways, and which would contribute to his entry into the cabinet almost twenty years later.

Regardless of the specific issues, however, or the fundamental questions involved, Kimberley adhered foremost to principles of method. Whether his personal views on a matter might be considered radical, Peelite, conservative, or

---

[117] James Pope-Hennessy, *Verandah, Some Episodes in the Crown Colonies, 1867–1889* (London: George Allen and Unwin, 1964), pp. 118–19.

[118] Goldwin Smith, *Irish History and Irish Character* (Oxford: Parker, 1861), p. 194. Kimberley called it 'an admirable sketch'. KP1 15/K2/6, p. 143.

[119] See John Powell, 'A Whig Facade: Indian Policy Development under the Liberals during 1883', *Quarterly Review of Historical Studies*, 30 (Oct.-March 1990–91): 70–86.

[120] Many of his early speeches outside parliament dealt at length with the benefits of education. KP6 MS.eng.d.2492, throughout. See too extracts from Coleridge's *The Friend* and Hallam's *Europe during the Middle Ages*, KP1 15/K2/7, pp. 31, 61; item 13, herein; Kimberley to Ripon, 27 October 1867, RP 43522, f. 116.

[121] Grant Duff, *Out of the Past*, 2:184.

[122] Similarly, during the 1884 debates over the Representation of the People Bill, he argued that agricultural labourers were no more likely to abuse the vote than their urban counterparts. KP1 15/K2/6, facing p. 23; 3 *Hansard*, 290 (7 July 1884): 98.

whiggish, his method was consistently liberal. The most important aspect of Kimberley's liberalism was adherence to the great *via media*, cautiously steering between 'the rocks of Distinctions, and the Gulfs of Universalities',[123] between 'the despotism of the few and the despotism of the many',[124] between the demands of reason and appeals to the imagination. Few problems were easily resolved, for each could be variously contextualized. As Kimberley observed, for instance, in the Lords in 1850 on the Australian Colonies Government Bill, the problem was 'how to reconcile colonial freedom with the Imperial supremacy', two fundamentally irreconcilable principles.[125] When governments were routinely required to tread such dangerous ground, it simply was not prudent to take a dogmatic line.

His second rule of method was that, while pursuing progress, one should not childishly 'cry for the moon'. His sense of the pragmatic was rooted in the experience of a family of politicians and owed much to his study of European history. But regardless of its exact provenance, all traces of utopianism had been eradicated from Kimberley's political thinking by the time he entered parliament.[126] He was firmly committed to Burke's prescription that everything 'really beneficial' lay 'within the reach of an informed understanding and a well-directed pursuit.'[127]

Third, Kimberley's method was inherently cautious. Although not so careful as Sir George Cornewall Lewis, whose reasoning he characterized as that of a 'pure whig', he too was sceptical of 'all opinions which are diffused rapidly by impressions on the nervous susceptibilities of a numerous audience.' Having himself been carried somewhat beyond his convictions by the emotional fervour of revolutionary Italian crowds, he well knew how faulty judgements might be 'when formed under such circumstances.'[128] Over the course of a long career, Kimberley accepted the need for a steady course of Liberal reforms. Gladstone

---

[123] From Bacon, in KP1 15/K2/7, p. 9.

[124] From Coleridge, in KP1 15/K2/7, p. 33.

[125] 3 *Hansard*, 111 (31 May 1850): 519; cf. his arguments to Gladstone in the Australasian differential tariff controversy of 1871–73, Kimberley to Gladstone, 15, 22 May 1871, GP 44224, ff. 132–35, 137–38.

[126] See, for instance, his assertion regarding the 'rights of men': 'of one thing I am sure that a reign of Neros would not be worse than a reign of metaphysicians, and that whatever may be our abstract opinions as to the right of all men to "liberty and equality", until all men are made *really equal* in every thing, to make them equal in political power is about as absurd as it would be in a vessel to issue an equal stock of provisions to every soul on board, man woman or child, because as human beings they had an equal right to be supplied ...'. Item 5, herein; also, 3 *Hansard*, 151 (23 July 1858): 1984.

[127] KP1 15/K2/7, p. 49. Cf. his answer to Argyll's criticism of the Home Rule Bill almost forty years later, admitting difficulties, but thinking that 'these questions can be solved.' 3 *Hansard*, 306 (10 June 1886):1273; also Wodehouse to Grey, 8 December 1864, letter 44, herein; Kimberley to Gladstone, 5 April 1892, GP 44229, ff. 23–27.

[128] KP1 15/K2/12, p. 23.

as the man of measures was his natural leader, though Kimberley was never altogether comfortable with the means by which the prime minister wrought his magic. If Gladstone could not automatically depend upon his support, he knew that Kimberley fundamentally leaned in his direction, and that his caution could always be removed by a careful argument and a workable piece of legislation.

Administratively, Kimberley would have been an asset to any government.[129] Despite the fact that he was well educated and bright, he still thought it worth his time to study issues in considerable detail, especially in preparing for debate. This was, for him, a part of Burke's 'well-directed pursuit'. Normally he grounded himself in both the philosophical and practical aspects of a matter, identified the principle at issue, admitted various points of view, then made a judgement on balance of reason, rather than according to self-evident truths.[130] Paying attention to the peculiar circumstances of each problem, he developed a reputation for delving more deeply into matters than most politicians, and therefore as one who could not be easily disregarded or overthrown in argument. Seldom was he indiscreet or caught off-guard, because he knew his ground. In preparation lay the secret of many minor and apparently effortless successes.[131] He may be faulted for reading a 238-page report on a minor case at the Colonial Office, but it was only an extreme example of the thoroughness upon which he based his intellectual independence. In Kimberley's mind, the details of any measure ultimately outweighed the principle, for they alone determined legislative success. He always preferred to let others propose legislation, but he was a keen critic in Cabinet and a good defender in debate.[132]

---

[129] Cf. Mandler's description of how individualists such as Clarendon made their way, performing 'well in difficult and technical jobs that high whigs would not or could not fill.' *Aristocratic Government in the Age of Reform*, p. 101.

[130] In preparing his maiden speech on the Convict Prisons Bill, for instance, Kimberley read Gibbon Wakefield's *A View of the Art of Colonization*; Roebuck's *Colonies*; Terry's *New Zealand*; Mitchell's *Australian Exploration*; Sturt's *Two Expeditions into the Interior of Southern Australia, 1828–1831*; Mackay's 'Australian Bill' and *Western World* (probably volume one of *The World as it is*); Whately's *Secondary Punishment*; and pamphlets by Wakefield, Adderley, Molesworth, and Lord Lyttleton. KP1 15/K2/6, pp. 23–28; 'Catalogue of the Kimberley Library', KP7, p. 7. Cf. 3 *Hansard*, 110 (12 April 1850):191–94.

[131] Toward the end of his career, Kimberley was faulted by some younger politicians for lack of preparation – it was wrongly said that 'he never used notes' in his speaking. His lack of polish in presentation however seldom represented a lack of preparation. Kimberley's large fund of experience and habitual study of affairs made extensive preparation in every case unnecessary. See *A Victorian Diarist: Later Extracts from the Journals of Mary, Lady Monkswell, 1895–1909*, ed. E.C.F. Collier (London: John Murray, 1946), p. 15; Herbert Gladstone, *After Thirty Years* (London: Macmillan, 1928), pp. 209–10; Henry Lucy, *The Balfourian Parliament* (London: Hodder and Stoughton, 1906), pp. 24, 150.

[132] On the long report, see Blakeley, *The Colonial Office*, p. 44. Cf. Hartington's challenge, in a cabinet discussion on the threat of war with Russia, to a 'vociferous and

Although Kimberley had established his credentials throughout Westminster and Whitehall by the early 1860s, his role in late Victorian Liberal Party politics cannot be understood apart from his relationship with Gladstone, which was by no means simple. Kimberley's political advent coincided with the prolonged party disarray occasioned by Corn Law repeal and the residual effects of Gladstone as a Peelite spokesman on colonial affairs. Between 1849 and 1852, both Kimberley and Gladstone were significantly involved in the 'export nationalism' of the Colonial Reform Society and the Canterbury Settlement.[133] Though Gladstone had maintained an official independence from these organizations in which Kimberley cut his political teeth, the fact that Kimberley solicited votes in the midst of Gladstone's hotly contested Oxford election of January 1853 suggests that their contact had been more than incidental prior to the formation of Aberdeen's ministry. The pained response from Kimberley's old tutor, Henry Mansel, suggests the mixed nature of the Cabinet which makes it difficult to draw broad conclusions regarding purely political affinities:

> There is much in the constitution of the present ministry to alarm the Conservatives of Oxford, which can only be met by a distinct explanation of Mr Gladstone's present views on matters both of public and of University interest.... That you should be in it is only natural and consistent with the political views which you have always held.... But you must allow that some of the Liberal members of the ministry, particularly Lord John Russell, must be objects of distrust among the Conservatives of Oxford, and the connection with the Irish Brigade is alarming enough with the Protestants; for notwithstanding some painful theological quarrels, I believe that the main body of the University is still at heart, in the best and most liberal sense, Protestant. There are unpleasant rumours about, on what appears to be good authority, that Mr. Gladstone, though originally an opponent of the Oxford Commission, has finally signified his approval of most of the suggestions of the Blue Book. These rumours derive some confirmation from his present popularity with Dr. Jeune and the radical reformers of Oxford.... With these views I cannot help feeling that for me to support Mr. Gladstone now, would be more than an error – it would be a sin.[134]

Though Mansel admitted that others of more 'enlightened views' might regard Gladstone's apostasy differently, he spoke for many Conservatives who admired

unreasonable' Harcourt: "'Now I bet a 100 to 1 you haven't read any of the papers", which he could not deny.' *CJ*, p. 80. Also, Meade to Ripon, 26 December 1894, RP 43558, ff. 53–54.

[133] *Gladstone Diaries*, 3:xxxv–xxxvi; 4:485. KP6 MS.eng.c.3995, ff. 116– 70. See generally Patricia Burns, *Fatal Success: A History of the New Zealand Company* (London: Heinemann Reed, 1989), chap. 28; W. David McIntyre, 'Salvaging the Canterbury Plan: Henry Sewell and the Founding of Canterbury', in *Provincial Perspectives: Essays in Honour of W. J. Gardner* eds. Len Richardson and W. David McIntyre (Christchurch: University of Canterbury, 1980), pp. 41–49.

[134] Mansel to Wodehouse, 7 January 1853, MS.eng.c.3998, ff. 61–64; *Gladstone Diaries*, 4:485–86. On Gladstone's role in producing the controversial Oxford University Bill, see Matthew, *Gladstone*, pp. 83–85.

Gladstone's abilities but were not sure of his political philosophy. He seemed so willing to move with the political chaos, and to contribute to it, that it was difficult for many to know what were his fundamental principles, if indeed he had any. Nevertheless, Gladstone's financial acumen, allied with enormous physical strength and discipline, made him an asset to any ministry, and a danger in opposition.

Kimberley's politics were simpler, if only because he had done and said fewer things which circumstance had called into question. Before 1852, however, he like Gladstone had been searching for a political haven. He had from the first disliked Russell's Italian policy, and though he favoured colonial reform, disagreed with what he considered Lord Grey's timorous paternalism. On the other hand, he made a special point to travel to London for the vote to repeal the Navigation Acts, spoke eloquently in favour of the admission of Jews to parliament and eagerly embraced Russell's anti-Papal campaign. Since no perfect correspondence of party and principle was to be found, Kimberley necessarily had to be vigilant in reading the political landscape in order to secure the footing which must be every politicians first order of business. Upon seeing Kimberley's name appearing often on the Government's side in division lists, Bertram Currie hoped that his cousin had not attached himself too firmly to 'Lord Grey and his colleagues'.[135] Indeed he had not, having maintained a studied independence, refusing to vote against Brougham's hostile motion on Canadian policy in 1849 and once declining to move the address so as to 'not associate too closely with the Government'.[136] Nevertheless he was a liberal by principle, and there could be little doubt which direction he would go once the fallout over protection settled and party structure re-emerged.

Formation of the Aberdeen coalition hardly settled the party question, though it did represent an important step toward the creation of a party of 'Liberals', as Kimberley had styled himself.[137] His commitment to free trade had preceded Gladstone's, and his interest in the removal of Jewish disabilities and colonial reform were less suspect.[138] More important to their relationship at this stage was a common political ethic. They both believed in the principle of change by degrees, which allowed for co-operation while leaving plenty of room for disagreement as to method and timing.[139] From the beginning of his official

---

[135] Bertram Currie to Raikes Currie, 11 August 1850, in Currie, *Recollections*, 1:394.

[136] Kimberley journal, KP6 MS.eng.e.2790, pp. 5–6.

[137] See Roebuck's reference to the coming of 'a combination so-called Liberal ministry'. Robert Eadon Leader, *Life and Letters of John Arthur Roebuck, with Chapters of Autobiography* (London: Edward Arnold, 1897), p. 241.

[138] For instance, see Shannon, *Gladstone*, p. 266; Ged Martin, 'The Canadian Rebellion Losses Bill of 1849 in British Politics', *Journal of Imperial and Commonwealth History* 6 (October 1977): 3–22.

[139] Both Kimberley and Gladstone owed much to Burke. On Kimberley, see pp. 23–4, 27–8, herein. On Gladstone and Burke, see *Gladstone Diaries*, 10:92; Richard

career in 1852, Kimberley had proven to be a distinctly 'safe' politician, much
as Gladstone had been considered in the same year a departmentally 'safe pair of
hands', who 'did not make mistakes', and 'did not have to take things back.'[140]
Both were intelligent, ambitious, hardworking, and high-minded. Both were
Christians of faith who refused to allow religious orthodoxy to stand in the
way of political prudence, which entailed its own subsidiary morality.[141] On
the whole, belief in the efficacy of administration and diligence in its practice
made them highly compatible. Of course this was of little moment at this stage.
Kimberley was a junior minister seventeen years younger than Gladstone, who
had little reason to wonder what a young lord's views might have been on these
or other matters– unless, perhaps, he could sway an Oxford vote or two.

There were differences. Where Gladstone had been dismayed by Russell's
anti-Papal agitation of 1851, Kimberley actively had opposed both 'foreign interference' and 'Romish practices' in the Anglican Church, which had 'encouraged,
if not caused, that interference.'[142] Kimberley supported Palmerston in the 'Don
Pacifico' debate, and generally throughout the 1850s found Gladstone's 'message of mercy and peace' regarding foreign relations naive and pusillanimous.[143]
That foreign affairs proved to be their foremost battleground throughout four
ministries should not be surprising, for they had from the first been at odds
here. Too, they inhabited different societies, sat in different Houses and on the
whole devoted themselves to different concerns. Kimberley's absence in Russia
(1856–58) and Gladstone's from the government (1855–59) made it unlikely
that any practical correspondence of interests would develop. Still their under-
lying approach to the political process, and commitment to reduced expenditure
and free trade as the best guarantees of good governance, were enough to sur-
mount less important differences. Less tangible though perhaps more important,
neither of them had the least difficulty in doubting Disraeli's sincerity, a question which would increasingly reflect upon Conservatives generally, and thus
heighten the moral pretensions of Liberal politicians. Their early association
had been cordial, and Kimberley had found ways of making himself useful to a
rising force of nature in British politics.[144]

Helmstadter, 'Conscience and Politics: Gladstone's First Book', in *The Gladstonian
Turn of Mind: Essays Presented to J. B. Conacher*, ed. Bruce Kinzer (Toronto: Toronto
University Press, 1985), pp. 17–34.

[140] Matthew, *Gladstone*, p. 83.

[141] One is reminded of Gladstone's fear that religion might spoil his morality. Morley,
Life of Gladstone, 2:185; David W. Bebbington, *William Ewart Gladstone: Faith and
Politics in Victorian Britain* (Grand Rapids, MI: William B. Eerdmans, 1993), pp. 234–
35. On Kimberley's sense of political morality, see letters 187–89, herein.

[142] Though he later recanted. See above. Shannon, *Gladstone*, p. 229; letters 10–12,
herein.

[143] Kimberley journal, KP6 MS.eng.e.2790, p. 6; letter 23, herein.

[144] Though it should be remembered that Gladstone's mass appeal was not yet apparent. See Eugenio F. Biagini, *Liberty, Retrenchment and Reform: Popular Liberalism in*

With a decade of political turmoil and a variety of diverse experiences behind them, Kimberley and Gladstone both joined Palmerston's government in July 1859 with clearer goals, firmer principles, and new opportunities for co-operation. Kimberley, at the age of thirty-three, became chief foreign affairs spokesman in the House of Lords; Gladstone, almost fifty, became Chancellor of the Exchequer for the second time. Though as a rule their official positions would have afforded few opportunities for co-operation, three interrelated issues— Italian policy, the French commercial treaty, and the budget— brought them into greater contact than would ordinarily have been the case. Gladstone's acceptance of office under Palmerston was suffused with a mixture of political and psychological designs, but clearly owed something to his interest in bringing a 'happy settlement' to the Italian question.[145] Fired by his experiences in northern Italy while returning from the Ionian Islands, in April he had published a fervent article on 'War in Italy' in the *Quarterly Review*, publicizing his mission of 'Peace founded upon Justice', and four months later had made an 'impassioned speech on Italian affairs' which, some believed, 'overstepped the bounds of discretion'.[146] Kimberley, the Lords spokesman on foreign affairs, was also opposed to Austrian dominance, but had, with the instincts of a rising Under-Secretary, been more moderate in his pronouncements. In December 1859 he was appointed co-commissioner with Lord Cowley to the abortive Congress of Villafranca, Palmerston recognising that though only an Under-Secretary, he was an Italian expert, 'a peer, has been Minister P.[leni] P.[otentiary] and might be so commissioned for the Congress.'[147] Clarendon was pleased with the appointment. Greville reflected the general estimate of the political world, then absorbed in the Italian question, when he wrote that Kimberley was 'clever, well informed, a prodigious talker and a great bore, speaks French fluently, and has plenty of courage and aplomb; his opinions are liberal but not extravagant'.[148] Cobden wrote to congratulate him, though he doubted whether any politician in England would 'break the 10th Commandment' by envying his appointment.[149] Gladstone was no diplomat, but he knew that war was bad for budgets, so had every reason to closely follow Italian affairs.[150]

---

the Age of Gladstone, 1860–1880 (Cambridge: Cambridge University Press, 1992), pp. 379–81.

[145] Shannon, *Gladstone*, pp. 388–89; Ramm, *William Ewart Gladstone*, pp. 42–43. Also on Gladstone's relations with Palmerston, see John Powell, 'Small Marks and Instinctual Responses: a Study in the uses of Gladstone's Marginalia', *Nineteenth-Century Prose*, 19 (Special Issue 1992): 8–10.

[146] *Quarterly Review*, April 1859, p. 564; T. A. Jenkins, ed. *The Parliamentary Diaries of Sir John Trelawny, 1858–1865*, Camden Fourth Series, v. 40 (London: Royal Historical Society, 1990), p. 91.

[147] Palmerston to Russell, 8 December 1859, RIP 30/22/20, f. 292.

[148] *Greville Diaries*, 7:446–447.

[149] Cobden to Wodehouse, 16, 23 December 1859, KP6 MS.eng.c.4002, ff. 133–36.

[150] For a succinct account of Gladstone's interest, see Ramm, *William Ewart Glad-*

As a result of Gladstone's Italian enthusiasm, Kimberley found himself in the middle of a peculiarly personal feud, defending the Chancellor of the Exchequer in the House of Lords from a sustained attack on a foreign policy issue. In calling for despatches relating to the Duchy of Modena, the Marquis of Normanby,[151] accused Gladstone of circulating 'throughout Europe' false accusations against the Duke of Modena.[152] Normanby read eleven letters exchanged between himself and Gladstone, in which he failed to find satisfactory explanations. Gladstone himself wished to pursue the matter, but realized the impossibility of speaking to the criticism from the Commons, and the possible detriment to his own work which might follow if the argument were prolonged. He therefore asked Kimberley to quash the 'loose statements' and remarked that he was 'quite at ease', knowing that his case was, with Kimberley, 'in very safe hands'.[153] Following Gladstone's line, On July 22 Kimberley vigorously responded to Normanby, alluding to the difficulties involved in a Peer attacking a member of the House of Commons, smartly suggesting how 'very disagreeable' it would be to Gladstone's accusers 'to meet him face to face'. Kimberley conceded what Gladstone had admitted already — that an error had been made regarding one particular case in Modena — then defended the validity of Gladstone's principal accusation of arbitrary government on the part of the Duke.[154] It was perhaps a tempest in a teapot, but one which nevertheless tested Kimberley's partisanship, his manner of handling such personal matters, and the degree to which he would involve himself on Gladstone's behalf.[155] And while it must always be difficult to document the impact of the performance of expected duties, the cumulative effect of *the way* in which they are performed must necessarily have had its effect as Gladstone later cast about among the host of prospective Cabinet ministers.[156]

Gladstone's budget campaign of 1860–61, including hard battles over every aspect of the French Commercial Treaty and repeal of the paper duties, constituted one of the great political triumphs of the Victorian era. Yet he considered it 'the most trying part' of his entire political life, and the 'nadir' in his 'pub-

stone, pp. 42–44; also, Shannon, *Gladstone*, pp. 395, 403–05.

[151] Constantine Henry Phipps (1797–1863), first Marquis of Normanby, Ambassador to Paris, 1846–52; Minister to Florence, 1854–58.

[152] Including the assertion that the Duke had issued an edict calling for the execution of a seventeen-year old found guilty of murder, despite a law which prohibited capital punishment of anyone under twenty-one.

[153] Gladstone to Kimberley, 5 July 1861, KP6 MS.eng.c.4002, ff. 75–76.

[154] 3 *Hansard*, 169 (22 July 1861): 1247–63.

[155] Though one would expect a hearty defence by colleagues, even at the risk of some personal compromise, there were no clear guidelines. Gladstone had refused to defend Aberdeen in July of 1854. He was not universally popular personally, and this was essentially a personal matter. Shannon, *Gladstone*, pp. 292–93.

[156] On Gladstone's inclination to judge men by their character, see Vincent, *Formation of the Liberal Party*, pp. 211–15.

lic estimation.'[157] When it is remembered that he was opposed by virtually the whole of the cabinet on one or both of these issues, that he saw little prospect for attaining Liberal leadership, that he was hated by the whigs and 'old tories',[158] and that it was still wondered aloud whether he could harness his great gifts,[159] one is reminded of Gladstone's precarious personal position. '*Ill*; vexed and *indignant* at the possible and probable conduct of the peers' in the spring of 1860, Gladstone could hardly fail to be pleased with hearty support from any quarter. Preparing for his speech in the Lords, Kimberley requested ammunition. 'I send in this box some papers', Gladstone wrote on March 15, 'which bear upon various points of the Treaty and which I think you may find useful. . . . I cannot afford the time to sit through in the House of Lords but I expect during most of the evening to be here [11 Downing Street] and will come at a moment's notice if sent for'.[160] Kimberley warmly supported the Commercial Treaty with France and pressed for repeal of the paper duties as the 'true policy'.[161] Of course the devil is in the details, and Kimberley was in no position to have much impact there. Nevertheless, as Under-Secretary at the Foreign Office he could provide relevant foreign information, as a member of the Lords he could support the budget and French Treaty at a time when perhaps it mattered for a change, and as an individual he could demonstrate his partisan credentials. While Gladstone still had to win his major battles in the country, Commons and Cabinet, the events of 1860–61 provided him with tangible reasons for keeping Kimberley in mind for future consideration.[162]

Kimberley had been careful through an assiduous but pragmatic attention to his responsibilities not to create rifts with Liberal leaders. As Sidney Herbert, Sir James Graham, Cornewall Lewis, the Duke of Newcastle, and Palmerston passed from the scene between 1861 and 1865, Gladstone emerged as heir apparent to Russell as Liberal leader, with the less ambitious Granville and Clarendon near the top. Kimberley was not intimate with any of the four, but through his work in St. Petersburg, Dublin, and at Foreign Office, he had at some point worked closely with each of them and had gained a reputation

---

[157] *PMP: Gladstone*, 1:83.

[158] Morley, *Life of Gladstone*, 2:29–31.

[159] *DD1*, p. xv; Walter Bagehot, 'Mr. Gladstone' (1860), in *Biographical Studies*, 2nd ed. (London: Longmans, Green, and Co., 1889), pp. 104–15.

[160] 15 March 1860, KP6 MS.eng.c.4003, ff. 50–51; also Kimberley to Gladstone, 11 May 1860, letter 27, herein; Gladstone to Kimberley, 5 June 1860, MS.eng.c.4003, f. 61.

[161] 3 *Hansard*, 157 (15 March 1860): 579–84; Gladstone to Kimberley, 17 March 1860, GP 44224, f. 9; letters 26, 27, herein.

[162] In 1894, Gladstone recalled in a letter to Courtney 'pleasing recollections of repeated indications of friendliness and fairness' on Kimberley's part from 1863. The precise date is less important—for written spontaneously in a letter thirty years later it may be wrong— than the perception of friendliness from the early years of that decade. Gooch, *Life of Courtney*, p. 335.

for toughness, pragmatism and energy. Nevertheless, positions near the top were few. Kimberley was painfully aware that his ministry in Russia might make him 'look higher than would be reasonable' at the moment; what he wished to avoid was either a step down or a foreign post.[163] Upon the Duke of Newcastle's resignation in April 1864 and Cardwell's vacating the Duchy of Lancaster, Clarendon 'advised Palmerston most strongly to put Wodehouse in Cardwell's place, but he would not...'. Reluctantly accepting the Irish Viceroyalty in October 1864, Kimberley was congratulated by Clarendon, who again would have preferred to see him 'in an office more worthy of you *at home*'.[164] Though ascent toward the charmed circle of leadership was crowded and full of uncertainty, it was widely understood that he then stood very near the Cabinet.[165] Toward the end of a surprisingly active and successful Viceroyalty, he felt bold enough to write to Russell asking that no other peer be put in the Cabinet ahead of him.[166] Even some 'old and implacable repealers' would admit that he had used his powers with both firmness and fairness, testifying to Kimberley's claim to be a reformer who would nevertheless enforce the law.[167] Kimberley corresponded with Gladstone on Irish questions, seeking metropolitan financing for arterial drainage and declaring himself in favour of a land bill, concurrent endowment and an inquiry into the question of national education. It is impossible to say exactly at which points the two influenced one another. Kimberley entered the Viceroyalty with liberal convictions, hoping to modernize Irish administration and upgrade her agriculture. Yet he was convinced that Ireland would 'improve very slowly', and that it could not 'for a long time be governed according to English principles'.[168] His official position gave a

[163] Wodehouse to Granville, 13 June [1859], KP6 MS.eng.c.4475, ff. 9–10. On the difficulty in obtaining suitable employment, see Appendix 2 and letter 39, herein.

[164] Herbert Maxwell, *Life and Letters of George William Frederick Fourth Earl of Clarendon*, 2 vols. (London: Edward Arnold, 1913), 2:287; Clarendon to Wodehouse, 9 October 1864, KP6 MS.eng.c.4475, f. 49.

[165] According to Ripon, his next post '*must* be in the Cabinet'. DeGrey to Wodehouse, 30 September 1864, KP6 MS.eng.c.4475, f. 41. Also Henry Wodehouse to Anne Wodehouse, 13 October 1864, KP1 15/K2/20; Constance Strachey, ed. *Letters of Edward Lear to Chichester Fortescue, Lord Carlingford, and Frances Countess Waldegrave* [1907] (Freeport, N.Y.: Books for Libraries Press, 1970), pp. 299–300; letter 40, herein.

[166] Wodehouse to Russell, 8 February 1866, copy, KP6 MS.eng.c.4475, ff. 62–63. John Wodehouse was created Earl of Kimberley on 1 June 1866 in recognition of services related to the Fenian uprising of 1865–66. Rosebery judged the Lord Lieutenancy to be Kimberley's 'best piece of work.' Rosebery memorandum, Kimberley memoir, RsP 10186, p. 252.

[167] O'Neill Daunt, *History of Eighty-five Years, 1800–1885*, 2 vols. (London: Ward and Downey, 1886), 2:170.

[168] Kimberley to Raikes Currie, 2 December 1864, KP1 3/1. See, too, J. L. Hammond, *Gladstone and the Irish Nation*, 1938), p. 22. On his perception of the difficulty in transplanting institutions, see Kimberley's citation from Alison's *History of the French Revolution*: 'Many examples are to be found of institutions being suddenly imposed

vantage point for acting, while Gladstone's *obiter dictum* of 17 December 1864 to an evaluation of Irish financial arrangements, in which he argued that there were certainly matters 'not of finance, in which as I think present justice to Ireland is both desirable and obtainable', left a window of approach, utilized by Kimberley, on the subject of Irish measures generally before Gladstone had a title to a 'special voice' on such questions.[169] In any event, Kimberley was considered a strong Lord Lieutenant with a thorough knowledge of Ireland and good judgement in handling delicate political matters. After leaving Dublin in the summer of 1866, he agreed in Gladstone's policy of 'consistent moderation' toward reform, until the Liberal defections of 8 April 1867 led him to conclude that 'the only sound settlement' was 'household suffrage pure and simple.'[170] 'What an impudent liar...Disraeli is', Kimberley wrote to Raikes Currie seven months later, disgusted with the Conservatives' *volte face* on electoral reform. 'It is a disgrace to the country to governed by such men.'[171] Instead, he was looking for honest, 'cool and courageous men at the helm' to guide the country in a 'new and unquiet era of politics'.[172] Though Gladstone himself was 'anything but cool', Kimberley was thrilled at the crushing Liberal victory at the polls in 1868. When offered the Privy Seal in December 1868, he was satisfied that the new Prime Minister had done well to balance his popular genius with the talents of solid men like his old Foreign Office mentor, Lord Clarendon, and his personal friend, Lord Ripon.[173]. He was also extremely pleased to be sitting at last in Cabinet.

For thirty years after 1868, Kimberley's inclusion in the Cabinet was a foregone conclusion. His name was seldom mentioned in the flurry of correspondence related to the cabinet-making of 1880, 1886, 1892 and 1894, for it was understood that he would hold one of the great 'Whig' preserves related to foreign policy. If he were not quite necessary to the government[174]—for he was

---

upon a people; none of those so formed having any duration.' KP1 15/K2/7, p. 27. On his desire to abolish the Viceroyalty, see Kimberley to Palmerston, 27 September 1864, PP GC/WO/2/1; letter 43, herein.

[169] Gladstone to Kimberley, 17 December 1864, copy, GP 44224, ff. 27–30; Kimberley to Gladstone, 12 February, 30 July 1866, GP 44224, ff. 31–42, 52. Cf. Morley, *Life of Gladstone*, 2:237–41; Matthew, *Gladstone*, pp. 144– 45.

[170] Matthew, *Gladstone*, p. 142; Kimberley to deGrey, 9 April 1867, letter 54, herein.

[171] 4 November 1867, KP1 3/1.

[172] Kimberley to Currie, 7 June 1866, KP1 3/1; Kimberley to deGrey, 25 November 1867, letter 56, herein.

[173] *KJ*, p. 7.

[174] The qualification is necessary to account for the offer of the Indian Viceroyalty in 1880. Although Gladstone judged its importance second only to cabinet positions at the Foreign and India Offices, it was nevertheless an offer which would have removed Kimberley from English politics for five years. *Gladstone Diaries*, 7:505–08. When the Viceroyalty had fallen vacant in 1872, Granville thought 'Kimberley would be excellent, but could not be spared.' *Gladstone-Granville Corresp. 1*, 2:307–08.

unlikely to intrigue against it—his range of skills and breadth of experience could not be matched. Gladstone's legislative agenda required a cabinet with both ability and stamina. If Kimberley sometimes talked too much, he wrote clearly, worked hard, exercised sound judgement, and enjoyed wide experience, especially in Irish and foreign affairs. Too, he had a flexible attitude, which recommended itself to Gladstone. Kimberley thought the highest positions in government should go to those with 'force of character', who could listen intelligently to a wide range of opinions, then take an independent line.[175] Thus, he was pleased to sit as a conservative Liberal in a Cabinet with Bright, who 'always gave us exactly what we wanted, namely, the view which would be taken of the matter under discussion by the Radical Party'.[176] Although Kimberley's capacities have been judged almost wholly from studies of his Colonial and Indian secretariats, his work there merely confirmed what Gladstone already knew when first inviting him to join the Cabinet. He was not required to prove himself in the departments—he really had to fail to be noticed—, and was accordingly little interfered with by either Gladstone or the Cabinet. His career as a departmental minister has been widely explored, and there can be little doubt that his judgement, capacity for work, and commitment to collective governance were instrumental in maintaining his position. However, the question of his political role remains. Did he have a political presence apart from his departments?

It is easy to cite specific cases in which Kimberley influenced Gladstone and the Cabinet. He argued against the Imperial antipathy of Gladstone, Lowe, and Cardwell, and generally dampened Gladstone's instinctive moralism.[177] By patient and studied determination, he convinced Gladstone that any attempt to prohibit Australian colonies from passing differential tariff measures in 1872 would be detrimental to the empire, and that the annexation of Fiji, which Gladstone had gone to great lengths to prevent, was sound policy.[178] He and Cardwell sanctioned the Ashanti expedition in 1873 without consulting either Gladstone or the Cabinet.[179] He refused the annexation of Samoa, Namaqualand and Damaraland, and the Cameroons in 1882, the latter over the objections of Dilke and Granville;[180] Had it not been for Kimberley's firm resistance to his

---

[175] Grant Duff, *Notes from a Diary, 1896–1901*, 1: 311; cf. Vincent, *Formation of the Liberal Party*, p. 215.

[176] Grant Duff, *Notes from a Diary, 1889–1891*, 2:13–14.

[177] On the moral motive, see Herbert Paul, ed. *Letters of Lord Acton to Mary Gladstone* (London: George Allen, 1904), p. 96; also, letters 187, 189 herein; Kimberley to deGrey, 20 October 1871, RP 43522, ff. 180– 83; *KJ*, pp. 18, 29–30.

[178] McIntyre, *Imperial Frontier*, pp. 211, 246– 59; Kimberley to Gladstone, 15, 22 May 1871, GP 44224, ff. 132–35, 137–38; *KJ*, p. 29; Kimberley to Gladstone, 9 February 1872, GP 44224, f. 253.

[179] See letter 81, herein.

[180] Granville in cautioning the frequently thwarted Dilke in 1882 suggested Kimberley's weight in reminding him that 'on a colonial matter, we cannot fly in the face of the Col. Secy.' 2 March 1882, DkP 43880, ff. 138–39.

old friend's expectant demands, Ripon would have moved India more rapidly toward self-government, or crippled the government under the strain of Viceregal and Council bickering.[181] In 1884, he convinced a reluctant Gladstone that Dufferin ought to be Indian Viceroy and resisted the Prime Minister's wish that Dufferin's departure be delayed in order to accommodate party need on a vote in the Lords.[182] And he refused the annexation of Formosa on his own authority in 1895.[183] To the extent that these were departmental matters, they seem to fall outside the scope of this study. However, by the 1870s departmental affairs and popular politics had substantially merged.[184] Cumulatively, Kimberley's policy decisions helped give the lie to polemic characterizations of Gladstone as a 'Little Englander', whose governments would doctrinairely divest Britain of imperial authority at every opportunity.[185] With Kimberley at the India Office, for instance, a tea planter worried over Ripon's pace of reform was consoled with the assurance that 'the people now in office, Lord Kimberley, Lord Northbrook, and Lord Granville, were as little likely to do anything really in the direction of freeing the Indians as any three Tories in the kingdom.'[186] If an exaggeration of Kimberley's conservatism, the observation nonetheless points to Kimberley's influence as an exponent of that wing of the party.

Gradually, Liberal colonial policy was transformed during the Gladstone era, first by reversing Peelite retrenchment during the 1870s, then by selective expansion which concentrated British imperial resources on the protection of India and southern Africa during the 1880s and 90s. As Gladstone set about his domestic work in 1868 with Liberal principles but no clear agenda, Kimberley similarly entered the departments.[187] Notwithstanding public pronouncements and personal preferences, Gladstone's imperial policy as a whole was moderately expansionist and not infrequently vigorous, a trend established in considerable part by Kimberley's management of colonial affairs, and carried forward at the India Office, where he was frequently consulted by Granville, Hartington, Rosebery, Derby, and Ripon. In a time when departments still often determined

---

[181] Powell, 'A Whig Facade', pp. 70-88.

[182] *Gladstone Diaries*, 11: 185, 218; Kimberley to Gladstone, 5 October 1884, GP 44228, ff. 158–60.

[183] Letter 253, herein.

[184] See, for instance, Kimberley's arguments for action against the Ashanti in 1873: 'We cannot leave them quietly in occupation of the Protectorate. Public opinion would not allow us to do so, if we ourselves desired it...' Kimberley to Cardwell, 26 July 1873, CdP 30/48/5/33, ff. 48–51.

[185] An impartial observer could not, for instance, credit Louis Jennings with more than partisan exaggeration in arguing that 'in the end' Gladstone's international policies revealed 'the same spectacle of national humiliation and misfortune....' *Mr. Gladstone: A Study*, p. 71; see 'Lord Kimberley on Current Politics', *The Times*, 26 January 1899, p. 5.

[186] Blunt, *India under Ripon*, p. 18.

[187] See Matthew, *Gladstone, 1809–74*, p. 171.

policy, no individual contributed more than Kimberley to the shape of British imperial policy between 1870 and 1895.

Sometimes the relationship between the departments and domestic politics was more specific. D.M. Schreuder has carefully traced the parallel development of crises in the Transvaal and Ireland in October of 1881, when Gladstone simply wanted African matters out of the way in order to concentrate upon Ireland. Had Kimberley pressured the Boers on a mere point of honour after Majuba, as many urged, war in South Africa might well have been renewed, making a simultaneous stand against Parnell more difficult. As it was, Kimberley's patience and reputation, bolstered by Gladstone's authority and tactical skill, paid rich political dividends. Together they deflected a growing sentiment within the Cabinet for coercion, allowing time for a peaceful Boer acceptance of the terms of the Transvaal Convention.[188] The point is not that Kimberley's policy was always right, especially in this instance, but that the routine soundness of his judgements allowed colleagues to leave matters in his hands with confidence, and thus to attend more carefully to their own business. In Gladstone's case, this meant more time for procedural matters and 'big bills', which by 1870 were already hindering the conduct of business.[189]

Kimberley's quietly tenacious defence of imperial interests provided a middle ground between those generally inclined to pacifism and economy on the one hand, and Tory and Radical jingos on the other. He had a large hand in what many considered to be disgraceful Liberal handling of circumstances in South Africa, Merv, Penjdeh, the Sudan and the Belgian Congo. Still, he drew clear lines at Zulficar and the Zambezi River, from which India and South Africa were adequately protected at a reasonable cost, and which enabled Britons still to regard their empire in reasonably grand terms. No one mistook Kimberley for 'a Little Englander', as they might have done with Gladstone.[190] However, the Prime Minister could accept this, and may even have wished for it as a foil for his Irish and domestic policies. By the 1890s, Kimberley could stand before large crowds on the hustings, without fear of reasonable contradiction in the papers, and say both that 'Mr. Gladstone' could not be suspected of wishing to 'saddle this nation with heavier responsibilities than were unavoidable', and that in the course of his career he had added 'not a few territories to the dominions of the empire.'[191] The line between imperial camps was drawn

---

[188] Schreuder, *Gladstone and Kruger*, pp. 238–49.

[189] Agatha Ramm, 'The Parliamentary Context of Cabinet Government, 1868–1874', *English Historical Review*, 99 (October 1984), pp. 739–41; Matthew, *Gladstone*, pp. 205–06. See too, for instance, Gladstone's response upon being consulted by Kimberley on the Indian currency question: 'Harcourt is I believe going abroad but I hope the rule will not be made general that on that account his work is to come to me . . . .', *Gladstone Diaries*, 13:70.

[190] *Pall Mall Gazette*, special ed., 9 April 1902, p. 1.

[191] Item 267, below.

more sharply after Gladstone's departure in 1894, when the blustering Harcourt
became the peaceful left's best advocate. With little study and much reflex,
his demands for concession, arbitration, and forbearance in an increasingly taut
international environment fell upon deaf ears at the Foreign Office, Kimberley
in the main agreeing with Rosebery in a firmer foreign policy in order to counter
the escalating aggressiveness of Germany, France, and Russia. Still, he tempered Rosebery's instinctive secrecy, gently pushing the prime minister toward
greater co-operation with the Cabinet.[192]

By the 1870s, Kimberley's political longevity already had invested his opinion with a certain weight. At the end of the decade, T. H. S. Escott wrote that
his competence in foreign affairs was 'indisputable', citing Kimberley's association with the 'mazes of European complications' at Magenta and Solferino,
St. Petersburg, and Syria.[193] By the turn of the century, it was difficult to resist
the historical attraction of an elder statesman who had emerged relatively un-
scathed and hopeful, not only from the vagaries of four Gladstone ministries and
a Rosebery addendum, but also from skirmishes with the Fenian brotherhood
and Bismarck in the 'seemingly distant sixties'; from the continental wiles of
Gorchakov and Morny in the remote fifties; and even from the fires of the 1848
Italian revolution itself. It made great copy for journalists to contrast Kimberley with illustrious colleagues who had also served at the Foreign Office: Lord
Salisbury 'still engaged in writing articles for the Press when Lord Kimberley
was holding important office. He was sent on a special mission to Russia before
Lord Rosebery had gone to school.'[194] By the 1890s, it is little wonder that
Morley, Bryce and a host of younger, civic-minded Liberals often sought Kim-
berley's advice on foreign matters. Principally concerned with other matters,
they still needed something to say on the platform about Chitral and the Eastern
Question.[195]

Kimberley's political longevity was more a function of method than opinions,
either liberal or conservative. Gladstone himself could be erratic as an exemplar
of Liberal doctrine.[196] In approaching complex issues, however, he valued an
open-minded diligence, in part no doubt because it left greater latitude for his
powers of persuasion.[197] This approach to the Cabinet method, so successful
during the first ministry, broke down in the second when Chamberlain's ambi-

---

[192] See, for instance, letters 200, 202, 221, herein.

[193] *Pillars of the Empire*, p. 174.

[194] *Illustrated London News*, 12 April 1902, p. 518; *Daily Chronicle*, 9 April 1902,
KP6 MS.eng.e.4478, f. 110.

[195] See letters 167, 252, 258, 264, herein; Bryce to Kimberley, 21 November 1900,
KP2 10249, ff. 97–98; George Shaw-Lefevre, 'Lord Kimberley: A Reminiscence', *The
Speaker*, p. 37.

[196] See, for instance, his 'pleading, so to speak, on behalf of human sacrifices.' Gladstone to Kimberley, 4 September 1873, in *Gladstone Diaries*, 8:383.

[197] James Bryce had early noted Gladstone's political flexibility, a theme further developed in various contexts by J.A. Spender, D.A. Hamer, and H.C.G. Matthew. Bryce,

tion, Parnell's dogmatic persistence, and the growing cacophony of Press voices began to destroy the fragile framework of mutual respect which had seen the Liberal Party through a good deal of internal tension. After Gladstone's retirement and Campbell-Bannerman's ascension, Kimberley continued to function as the conservative conscience of the Liberal Party, valued for his perspective and commitment to the value of divergent views. He would speak both knowledgeably and pointedly in opposition, within the party or without, yet in the end could be counted on to defer with good grace to the collective wisdom.[198] No man, he believed, was immune to the temptation of pride, and only a fool would insist upon a particular course when every avenue was fraught with danger.

Both Gladstone and Rosebery took advantage of Kimberley's political simplicity, but, for two reasons, less frequently than one might expect. First, the Cabinet process admitted adjustment in virtually every kind of business and at every level. Gladstone's, or anyone else's, views could be overturned, or, more frequently, modified through private argument, committee proceedings, and the process of drafting and revising legislation and despatches.[199] This allowed proponents of a policy to gain their principal end, while less interested Cabinet colleagues, usually in groups, were satisfied in having had the opportunity of refining. Second, despite the pragmatic gloss on Kimberley's political behaviour, he clung tenaciously to a few irreducible minimums, and was willing to resign when issues which he considered of supreme importance went against him.[200] Used sparingly, the threat of resignation was a measure of both influence and integrity, and one which Gladstone probably valued, as it allowed him to give way on honourable ground.

Throughout forty years of political association, there were relatively few conflicts between Kimberley and Gladstone. In part, this reflected their different spheres of interest. Apart from the Irish Viceroyalty, Kimberley held no executive positions related to domestic affairs. In these, he was content to follow the lead of others, actively playing his part in the Lords and Cabinet but recognizing

---

William Ewart Gladstone: His Characteristics as Man and Statesman (New York: The Century Co., 1898), pp. 23– 26; Spender, *The Public Life*, 2 vols. (London: Cassell and Co., 1925), 1:72; Hamer, *Liberal Politics in the Age of Gladstone and Rosebery*, pp. 73–76; Matthew, *Gladstone Diaries*, 10: xxxvii–xliv.

[198] When Lowe was forced to revise his budget in April 1871, Kimberley remarked that probably it would not have been necessary had he given the Cabinet an opportunity to discuss it, especially since it included 'experienced financiers such as Cardwell, Halifax & Goschen'. 29 April 1871, *KJ*, p. 22.

[199] In general terms of revision in council, see *KJ*, pp. 12, 18–19, 32; for a single example of the potential significance of drafting revisions, see Kimberley to Gladstone, 5 June 1893, GP 44229, ff. 90–91.

[200] He threatened resignation twice: in 1873 over resistance to the Ashanti invasion, and in 1893 over Pease's Opium motion. See Wolseley, *The Story of a Soldier's Life*, 2 vols. (London: Archibald, Constable and Company, 1903), 1:268; letters 188, 189, and accompanying notes, herein.

the necessarily dominant role of the Commons. His attitude emanated in part from a commitment to wide-ranging but gradual reform, which, by the 1870s, required principally restraint of the multifarious initiatives of others; and in part from his deference to the legislative energy and genius of Gladstone. More importantly, their relative harmony reflected a mutual admiration for hard work and a grudging willingness to be convinced in argument. Believing that each circumstance required its own answers, Kimberley was impervious to ideological argument, yet susceptible to plausible reasoning. In this, both Gladstone and Rosebery could be masterful in their spheres. On the broad borderlands of Kimberley's convictions, where no clear answers presented themselves, he was content, having voiced his opinion, to follow. However, in all departmental matters he led, and almost always got his way.

It has proven impossible to trace the evolution of Gladstone's thinking on Irish reform, but is clear that Kimberley's initiatives of the mid-1860s[201] contributed to his growing perception that Irish questions were becoming ripe for settlement. Kimberley is best known for his administrative work at the Colonial and India Offices, yet he had been brought into the 'charmed circle' of the cabinet on the strength of his Irish experience, and his first nineteen months there were filled principally with Irish work.[202] Serving on committees to study the Irish Land, Church, and Peace Preservation Bills, Kimberley was involved in the evolution of every phase of Irish policy during Gladstone's first ministry. The increased work load as a Secretary of State during the second, third, and fourth ministries precluded the same level of direct involvement, but he continued to be consulted by Gladstone and was courted as an ally in increasingly divided cabinets.[203] As late as 1892, Spencer was still apologizing for Kimberley's exclusion from regular discussions of the Home Rule bill.[204]

As Kimberley's departmental work steadily increased in both amount and importance after his appointment as Colonial Secretary in 1870, so did opportunities for failure or success. His inveterate caution seldom won public acclaim,

---

[201] See letters 44–45, 47, 52.

[202] Henry Wodehouse to Anne Wodehouse, 13 October 1864, KP1 15/K2/20; *The Times*, 9 December 1868, p. 8. See Palmerston to Kimberley, 25 September 1865, PP GC/WO/11 on the dearth of candidates for the Lord Lieutenancy. Cardwell was in the cabinet, but Sir Robert Peel had been ineffective as Chief Secretary and Chichester Fortescue proved less formidable than expected. On Kimberley's committee work, see *KJ*, especially pp. 2, 11–13.

[203] See, for instance, Morley, *Life of Gladstone*, 3:50; Kimberley to Monk Bretton, 30 September 1879, MBP; Kimberley to Ripon, 4 October 1880, RP 43522, f. 259; Kimberley to Gladstone, 19 October 1880, GP 44225, ff. 227–28; Gladstone to Kimberley, 13, 20, 21 January & 10 June 1881, GP 44544, pp. 256, 259, 260, 358; Kimberley to Gladstone, 21 January 1881, GP 44226, f. 11; *Gladstone Diaries*, 10:lvii–lviii, 11: 520–22, 672; *DD3*, p. 34.; *EHJ3*, pp. 31, 202.

[204] Spencer to Kimberley, 30 July 1892, MS.eng.c.4474, ff. 46–47.

and not infrequently roused the ire of younger Liberals,[205] but it ideally suited a Prime Minister wishing to legislate, who desired nothing more than calm and competence from the departments.[206] Nor did Kimberley 'create events'. If strong measures were urged, as in sending Wolseley to the Gold Coast in 1873 or in instructing Dufferin in 1885 that 'an attack on Herat will mean war between us and Russia everywhere', even the most pacific ministers were inclined to concede its necessity.[207] Gladstone so frequently adopted this line of defence that observers wondered if he were not taking leaves from the Tory book.[208] On the political level, competent departmental management minimized Liberal fracturing and made campaigning at the next elections easier, limiting occasions for Press importunity.[209] Although Gladstone found no shortage of Liberals with high claims to office in 1868, the administrative failures of Lowe and Bruce, the illness of Bright, the inactivity of Dodson, the scandal surrounding Monsell and the Post Office, and the relative ineffectiveness of Carlingford made safe hands more necessary than ever.[210] Kimberley continued in successive ministries to administer his departments with energy and acumen as Liberal ministers for various reasons either left or were abandoned—Argyll, Forster, Dodson, Northbrook, Carlingford, Dilke, and the Unionist host which departed in 1886. If his opinion carried weight with seasoned diplomats like Clarendon and Henry Bulwer in the 1850s, and his breadth of experience was valued by Gladstone and noted by the Press in the 1870s, it is little wonder that his political stock rose during the turbulent 1880s.[211] If only for the chance of stability, Gladstone could ill afford to lose Kimberley, who was perhaps the Liberal's best administrative official next to himself.[212]

---

[205] See, for instance, Herbert Gladstone, *After Thirty Years*, pp. 209–10; Gwynn & Tuckwell, *Life of Dilke*, 1:400–01, 547; *EHJ2*, p. 239.

[206] See, for instance, Gladstone's secret advice to Rosebery in 1886, urging that disturbing issues be avoided 'while we have this big Irish business in hand.' *Gladstone Diaries*, 11:541–42.

[207] After Bright's remonstrance at news of a British expedition to repel the Ashanti invasion of the Gold Coast, Granville mollified him with Kimberley's explanation, arguing that he could understand Bright's 'doubts and regrets', but sure that he would have 'a different feeling when looking back some years hence.' 3 September 1873, BP 43387, ff. 81–82. On Gold Coast, see *Gladstone Diaries*, 7:372; on Herat, Greaves, *Persia and the Defence of India*, pp. 227–37.

[208] See, for instance, *EHJ1*, 1: 324–25. Also, Kimberley's account of Gladstone as imperialist, item 267, herein.

[209] See, for instance, Morley, *Life of Gladstone*, 2:389–90; Stephen Koss, *The Rise and Fall of the Political Press in Britain, the Nineteenth Century* (Chapel Hill, N.C.: University of North Carolina Press, 1984), pp. 198–99.

[210] One colleague thought Kimberley to Carlingford was like comparing a 'whale to a sprat'. Cited in McIntyre, *Imperial Frontier*, p. 54.

[211] Bulwer to Wodehouse, [?] 1855, KP6 MS.eng.c.3995, f. 79; Escott, *Pillars of the Empire*, pp. 173–74.

[212] Although Kilbracken was speaking only of officials with whom he had worked,

Similar in point of daily usefulness to Gladstone was Kimberley's ability to refine complex issues. Though a legend of garrulousness in conversation, he had consistently surprised colleagues with 'admirably concise and lucid' letters and memoranda, shorn of 'irrelevant matters'.[213] These written observations helped facilitate the time-consuming process of business by committee. In Cabinet he irritated some by speaking frequently, but he was one of the few ministers prepared to discuss the range of topics which regularly came before them.[214] If Kimberley never found the heaven-born answer of the moralist, he was adept at clarifying the points upon which profitable discussion might turn, facilitating the process of Cabinet debate. Recognizing Kimberley's experience, and knowing that he would consult with Granville, Hartington and Rosebery when appropriate, his colleagues were generally content to leave Colonial and Indian affairs to the experts in order to move on to more pressing domestic business.

An elevated conception of the Cabinet's central function in government almost necessarily inhibited Kimberley's development as a party leader.[215] Though he

and is one of the few authors specifically to rank politicians as departmental ministers – Gladstone in a class by himself, Kimberley 'a good second', then 'a perceptible interval'– the evidence suggests that many would have agreed with him. Godley to 2nd Earl of Kimberley, 9 April 1902, KP1 15/K2/21; *Reminiscences*, p. 157. Cf. Chamberlain, *Politics from Inside*, p. 68; Stuart Rendel, *The Personal Papers of Lord Rendel* (London: Ernest Benn, 1931), p. 228; *Free Lance*, 19 April 1902, KP6 MS.enc.c.4484, f. 143; George Shaw- Lefevre, 'Lord Kimberley: A Reminiscence', *Speaker*, 12 April 1902, p. 37.

[213] Gladstone to Wodehouse, 28 April 1860, KP6 MS.eng.c.4003, f. 52; *Gladstone Diaries*, 7:464; 10:345. See too *EHJ1*, 2:736; Ramm, *Gladstone- Granville Corresp. 1*, 1:92–93, 2:384; Ramm, *Gladstone-Granville Corresp. 2*, 2:421, 458; Greaves, *Defence of Persia*, p. 234; letters 152, 155–58, herein. Kimberley's loquacity was recalled by virtually every memorialist. Among dozens of references, see Durand, *Life of Lyall*, pp. 350–51; Grey, *Twenty Five Years*, 1:17; *Letters of Lord Blatchford*, p. 347. Most who worked with him, however, considered this a superficial fault. Dilke, Rosebery, and Morley, all of whom first sat with him in Cabinet during the mid 1880s, found him wiser than first impressions had led them to believe. *EHJ1*, 2:830; Dilke, undated annotation on his diary entry for 30 August 1881, DkP 43924, f. 59; *St. James's Budget*, 11 April 1902, KP6 MS.eng.c.4481, f. 325; Morley to Minto, 19 February 1908, copy, MtP MSS Eur. D573/3.

[214] On Kimberley's manner in Cabinet, cf. Lord Rendel's recollection of Gladstone's having called Kimberley 'the most long-winded man he had ever known in a cabinet', with Shaw-Lefevre's reference to 'frequent' but 'short and pithy' interpositions, and Childers' complaint of Kimberley having spoken 'nineteen times'. Rendel, *Personal Papers*, p. 57; Shaw-Lefevre, 'Lord Kimberley', *Speaker*, 12 April 1902, p. 37; *EHJ1*, 2:830.

[215] Had Kimberley's goals been otherwise, he might have been more politically successful. No amount of ambition could have won him the premiership with Gladstone on the scene, (though from the 1870s, he was on several occasions considered a potential though unlikely Prime Minister), but he might well have secured the Foreign Office earlier. Clarendon had thought him, at the age of thirty-two, destined for the Foreign Office. See, for instance, McIntyre, *Imperial Frontier*, p. 54; Crewe, *Life of Rosebery*,

had been extremely ambitious as a young man, a secretariat in 1870 had quite satisfied his desire for influence.[216] This was due in part to a recognition of his own limitations, particularly as a popular orator.[217] But it also reflected a growing awareness of concomitant problems—residence abroad,[218] intrigue added to business, the constant demand for compromise and mental gymnastics[219]—and a growing desire to be with his family and to play the part of a Norfolk squire. Commitment to the Cabinet process is indicative of his epistemological doubts and his political philosophy. It provided a suitable mechanism by which ministers might be simultaneously straightforward, courageous, receptive, and wrong, without fear of immediate personal consequence or much danger to the public good. When Kimberley learned that he might have the Indian Viceroyalty in 1872, he characteristically observed that 'the office of Cabinet Minister' was really higher than such 'a dazzling prize.... It sounds grandly to be Viceroy over 180 millions of men, but it is in truth a much greater thing to be a member of the governing Committee of the whole Empire, India included.'[220] Perhaps this was a species of political vanity equal to any other, but it nevertheless helped to create the unique political moment which made 1869–72 a period of such legislative success, and it helped keep the dissentient Liberal cabinets of the eighties together long beyond their natural life. Kimberley was more than willing to defend the cabinet principle publicly, retorting, for example, to Argyll's attacks on Spencer over the Home Rule Bill, that he considered himself 'as much responsible for that part of the policy of the Government as Spencer.'[221] After the debilitating divisions of Gladstone's second ministry, in which personal and parliamentary claims so frequently were put ahead of the government's,

2:440.

[216] Cf. Kimberley's provocation at being 'shelved in the prime of life when I am boiling over with energy' with Gladstone's seeking 'great things to do' and 'losing the best years of my life out of my natural service'. Rosebery extracts, Kimberley memoir, RsP 10186, p. 256; Matthew, *Gladstone*, p. 106.

[217] Kimberley to Currie, 9 April 1864; 7 June 1866, KP1 3/1; *KJ*, pp. 5, 24; see pp. 47–50, herein.

[218] Kimberley believed that his infant son, Alfred, who had died in St. Petersburg in 1858, might have been saved had they been living in England; Anne Wodehouse and Lady Kimberley were distressed at having to live in Dublin; Kimberley hated being away from the ever-changing face of home politics.

[219] Kimberley, while heartily conceding Gladstone's genius, always suspected his reasoning. 'His ingenuity in shifting his ground, and in probing every weak point in his adversary's armour render him almost invincible. Unfortunately he is often led astray by his own subtility, and thus gives exaggerated weight in council to arguments useful perhaps in debate but more plausible than sound.' 2 March 1870 in *KJ*, p. 12. Cf. Salisbury's taunt that Kimberley had 'not at his command that wealth of ambiguous language which would have enabled him to appear to answer them without leaving any distinct impression on his hearers' minds.' 3 *Hansard*, 306 (10 June 1886): 1274.

[220] *KJ*, p. 28.

[221] 3 *Hansard*, 306 (10 June 1886): 1273.

Gladstone reflected upon a letter from Kimberley: 'how different is the Cabinet Minister of the older type from him of the newer, as to relations, obligations, attitude.'[222] Gladstone's observation had little to do with political viewpoint, but rather with the manner in which business was conducted. The quiet self-effacement and commitment to public business, so characteristic of Kimberley and associated in Gladstone's mind with the French Commercial Treaty and the peaceful first ministry, became more distinctive and a cause for reflection when practised during the second.[223] Gladstone managed the parts, but could not have maintained the whole without a core of ministers who, in addition to departmental competence, displayed a principled loyalty to the Government and refrained from constantly demanding personal satisfaction — Clarendon, Granville, Kimberley, Spencer, and Ripon each fulfilled this role in varying degrees; Kimberley was the only one to serve continuously through all four ministries.

If Kimberley's political philosophy precluded a drive for greater personal visibility, it fitted him to perform a wide variety of unofficial duties which were important to the party. He served as messenger in delicate situations;[224]; as a mediator of inter- and intra-party disputes, especially after 1886;[225]; and as an unselfish facilitator in cabinet-making.[226] Such services individually were

---

[222] Ramm, *Gladstone-Granville Corresp. 2*, 2:421–22. Edward Hamilton, in a position to hear, noted in 1894 what 'exalted ideas' politicians had of their own claims. *EHJ2*, p. 118. On Gladstone's response to personal claims during the calmer first ministry, see Ramm, *Gladstone-Granville Corresp. 1*, 1:103–04; 2:395–97.

[223] *PMP: Gladstone* 1:96. On commitment to public business, see Kimberley's reply to Raikes Currie's congratulations on a speech in the Lords, written six days after the onset of ten- year-old Armine's convulsions and paralysis due to a disease of the brain and spinal cord: 'It was indeed with a heavy heart that [I] sat thro' seven hours debate on the Test Bill. . . . I was very ill reported, but I think the reply really was successful. A kind of desperation stirred me up more than usual.' 10 May 1871, letter 73, herein; see too Kimberley to Anne Wodehouse, 28 August 1873, KP1 15/K2/20.

[224] Ramm, *Gladstone-Granville Corresp. 1*, 1:92–93; letter 65, herein. Kimberley's preference in the latter case to have told Gladstone what passed 'by word of mouth' suggests the plausibility of a number of unrecorded personal missions of this sort. It is perhaps significant that the committee to investigate 'leakage from the Cabinet' in 1882 included Granville, Carlingford, Spencer, and Kimberley. *Gladstone Diaries*, 10:190.

[225] Michael Hurst, *Joseph Chamberlain and Liberal Reunion* (London: Routledge and Kegan Paul, 1967), p. 75; Rendel, *Personal Papers*, pp. 136, 143; West, *Diaries*, p. 278; letters 220–235, herein; *KJ*, p. 16

[226] His offer to resign the Irish Viceroyalty in 1866 in order to make way for Fortescue in the Cabinet, and his willingness to transfer from the Colonial Office to the India Office in 1882 in order to make room for Derby are the two most notable examples. Upon Gladstone's retirement in 1894 he was willing 'to serve anybody in any capacity.' *EHJ2*, p. 117. See too Ramm, *Gladstone-Granville Corresp. 2* , 1:403. The great exception, which left Gladstone 'rather stunned', was Kimberley's refusal of the Indian Viceroyalty in 1880. Gladstone must have been aware of Kimberley's reticence to go in 1872, but may not have known of his eldest son's bankruptcy in the same year and the

small and went unnoticed by the public, but collectively were fundamental to the higher legislative process. Kimberley's affability in such matters, allied with wide experience, proven judgement and official capacity, quietly left the impression with most observers that there was no politician quite like him.[227]

His abilities as a parliamentarian, usually obscured by the façade of administrative work, were a decided asset to Gladstone. As the legislative logjam increased during the 1870s, limiting the number of measures which might be passed in order to satisfy factions, Kimberley's skill as a draftsman became increasingly important.[228] He was a good manager of indolent Lords, speaking their deliberate language and determined to get the utmost from the small Liberal band in the upper house.[229] He proved to be a popular leader in the Lords, both in the absence of Granville, occasionally ill from 1884, and as leader in his own right from 1891–94 and again from 1897 until his death in 1902. A lifelong study of human nature, and a humanistic perception that imperfect men were the only means of governing, imbued him with a sympathetic understanding of politicians as people, which men like Gladstone and Rosebery were prone to overlook in the context of larger international, moral, or redemptive designs.[230] If Gladstone's insensitivity toward men like Ripon, Harcourt and Rosebery was not immediately destructive, its effects tended to multiply, greatly contributing to factiousness in Rosebery's administration and enhancing the need for a Cabinet peacemaker.[231]

In speaking during the Cabinet years, Kimberley began with the advantage of a thorough knowledge of his field and an integrated sense of the interplay

---

continuing poor health of his youngest son. Gladstone to Kimberley, 25 April 1880, GP 44225, ff. 161–62.

[227] As Kimberley lay dying, Northbrook wrote to Curzon that it would be difficult to fill his place in the Lords: 'He was excellent in debate, courteous and popular on both sides. Rosebery, though of course far more eloquent, would never have made so good a leader.' 28 February 1901, CzP, Pr. #243. See too Appendix One, letter 1, herein.

[228] *KJ*, pp. 29–30, 34; Ramm, *Gladstone-Granville Corresp. 2*, 2:358; *Gladstone Diaries*, 11:672; Ramm, 'The Parliamentary Context of Cabinet Government, 1868–1874', 739–69.

[229] See, for instance, letter 256, herein; Thomas Lister, *Impressions and Memories* (London: Cassell, 1927), pp. 184–86; Crewe, *Life of Rosebery*, 2:374; KP2 10248, throughout.

[230] A classic example is Gladstone's taking up 'the cudgels' for the Greek government in a conversation with Ripon, shortly after Ripon's brother-in-law had been murdered by Greek brigands. According to Kimberley, this was 'to be Philhellene with a vengeance.' *KJ*, p. 13. Events surrounding the assassination marked the beginning of Ripon's conversion to Roman Catholicism. More generally, see Bebbington, *William Ewart Gladstone: Faith and Politics*, pp. 242–43.

[231] Rosebery's independent spirit during the fourth ministry stemmed in part from his resentment toward Gladstone. James, *Rosebery*, pp. 273–74, 281–85; Magnus, *Gladstone*, pp. 400–401. On Harcourt, see *PMP: Gladstone*, 4:107. Rosebery's thin skin was legendary, and might be seen in direct contrast to Kimberley's nature in Esmé Howard, *Theatre of Life*, 2 vols. (London: Hodder and Stoughton, 1935), 1:163–68.

between departmental and political factors. On the other hand, he had had little opportunity for developing a popular style. Imagine the demoralizing effect on a young man of ambition who had prepared a major speech in the Lords, finding only a handful of peers in the House at the appointed hour. 'Then one reads in the newspapers,' he wrote in disgust, 'that "the debate in the Lords was a far better one than in the Commons." The debate!! 6 or 7 peers versus the red benches.'[232] Inured to the indifference of the Lords, he adapted himself to their style. He could say what he wanted logically, cogently, and without committing blunders.[233] As in his letters and memoranda, he bypassed superfluous arguments thrown up in debate to deal with the central issues at hand.[234] Even unpopular imperial policies seemed more plausible under Kimberley's sedate and minutely-informed defence. In the debate over the motion of censure after the death of Gordon, for instance, he pointed out that, despite the public mood, those familiar with Gordon's past conduct, the intricacies of Egyptian affairs, and the deteriorating situation in Central Asia could not glibly support honorific measures. In carefully reasoned terms, Kimberley admitted that the rescue had failed, dismissed the possibility of political motivation, boldly criticized Gordon for miscalculation and misleading the government, then pushed beyond the failure to conclude with an appeal to the goal of Liberal policy: disentangling Britain from the Sudan in order to strengthen their position in Egypt and enable the country 'to secure objects of other kinds which are, if possible, even more closely connected with, and of more importance to, the interests of this country.'[235] If an imperfect defence, it was nevertheless as good as the Liberal policy was likely to get without cries of special pleading. Kimberley accepted responsibility, spread the blame widely, and made it clear to those who were listening that there were some matters over which no party had control.

A frequent auditor in the Commons,[236] Kimberley was capable of responding in his own speeches to the mood as well as the content of topics under discussion in the lower house. He reluctantly accommodated himself to speaking outside Parliament, doing so when necessary and more often than most Peers, but never feeling at home when popular enthusiasms were involved. Although publicly he

---

[232] Kimberley journal, KP6 MS.eng.e.2790, f. 95.

[233] For a concise general assessment, see the *Spectator*, 17 March 1894, p. 363.

[234] See, for instance, Kimberley's unwillingness to enter into a secondary debate over party motivations following Gordon's death. 3 *Hansard*, 294 (27 February 1885): 1536–37. Also, Justin McCarthy, *A History of our Own Times: from the Diamond Jubilee 1897, to the Accession of Edward VII* (London: Chatto and Windus, 1914), p. 210.

[235] 3 *Hansard*, 294 (27 February 1885):1536–43. For months prior to the debate, the papers were full of portents of war with Russia. Four days before the debate, *The Times* reported that in India, the almost 'universal opinion' was that Russia was taking advantage of 'difficulties in Egypt to press claims which she knows to be preposterous.' 23 February 1885, *The Times*, p. 5.

[236] *KJ*, pp. 3, 11; *Birmingham Post*, 9 April 1902, KP6 MS.eng.c.4478, f. 85; Edward Russell, *That Reminds Me* (London: T. Fisher Unwin, 1899), pp. 253–54.

argued in the 1880s that he was not impressed by a 'man's being able to work up an audience which is prepared to agree with him', he was clearly more terrified of falling flat with the Liberal public than of facing the hostile Lords, 'the most terrifying audience', according to Salisbury, which 'a man can address.'[237] Nevertheless, by the 1890s he was speaking to large crowds throughout the country.[238] Recognizing the need for change but not altogether comfortable in this role after decades in the cool atmosphere of the Lords, the degree of his achievement as a Liberal popularizer is suggested by the terms of Herbert Gladstone's recommendation of Kimberley as dinner speaker to a gathering of colonial representatives during the Boer War: ' . . . the gathered clans will expect to hear the voice of some chief. Uncle Kim if he will go would be safer, in a sense, than A[squith], but not nearly so effective.'[239] But however reticent, Kimberley took considerable pleasure in the plaudits of more popular audiences, fulfilling in some degree the missed opportunity for a Commons career, which he had always regretted.[240]

Although the nature of Kimberley's speeches varied little over fifty years, it is instructive to notice the change in their reception. Until about 1880, he was almost uniformly praised as an effective, even 'first rate' speaker.[241] From the early eighties, about the time Kimberley himself began to regularly note the almost universal drift toward 'platform oratory', assessments become mixed. Kimberley is frequently praised for 'an admirable answer' or a 'high standard of excellence',[242] and just as frequently derided for being 'comparatively in-effective' or lacking the gift of 'oratory'[243] This may in part be explained by party bias or the variable quality of individual speeches, but praise and criticism

---

[237] On Kimberley's attitude, see Grant Duff, *Notes from a Diary, 1886–1888*, 1:132; Kimberley to Granville, 13 October 1885, GrP 30/29/22A/5, ff. 223-25. For the Lords as audience, see Andrew Adonis, *Making the Aristocracy Work: The Peerage and the Political System in Britain, 1884–1914* (Oxford: Clarendon Press, 1993), pp. 57–58.

[238] Which may have contributed to his election as president of the Eighty Club in 1900.

[239] H. Gladstone to Campbell-Bannerman, 26 March 1900, CBP 41215, f. 245.

[240] Kimberley journal, KP6, MS.eng.e.2790, p. 4.

[241] Knight, *Passages of a Working Life*, 3:154; Currie, *Recollections*, 1:300; *Letters of Lord Blatchford*, p. 340; Henry Austin Bruce, *Letters of Lord Aberdare* (London: Oxford University Press, 1902), 1:340; 'Ripon Diary', pp. 29, 125, 132, 140; on Kimberley as a 'first-rate speaker', Hamilton, *Parliamentary Reminiscences and Reflections*, p. 97.

[242] By Granville in Ramm, *Gladstone-Granville Corresp. 2*, 2:177; and, remarkably, by Herbert Gladstone, *After Thirty Years*, p. 209; also, Kay-Shuttleworth to Campbell-Bannerman, 18 November 1900, CBP 41221, f. 214; Gathorne Hardy, *A Memoir*, 2:363, 372; *EHJ1*, p. 589; Crewe, *Life of Rosebery*, 2:374; Northbrook to Curzon, 28 February 1901, CzP Pr. #243.

[243] Kilbracken, *Reminiscences*, p. 158; *Spectator*, 10 March 1894, p. 326. Also Herbert Paul, ed. *Letters of Lord Acton to Mary, Daughter of W. E. Gladstone* (London: George Allen, 1904), p. 108.

crossed party lines, and single speeches elicited varied responses,[244] suggesting a period of transition in political taste. Nevertheless, he spoke well for his department, was unusually well-suited by temperament, experience, and willingness to speaking at short notice, and could easily manage every kind of party business before the Lords.[245] By the time Gladstone retired, it certainly made little legislative difference whether or not one could move the 'cold critical' House of Lords, but all these speaking jobs, small in themselves and unnoticed in success, had to be done credibly if the Liberal Party were to avoid Conservative censure and fractious Liberal aggression over the divisive issue of reform of the Lords.

Kimberley had no illusions about the power of the Lords, but his efficient conduct of business made it difficult for critics to argue as stridently or as confidently against a second house. It was commonly observed that he belonged to a small group of men who, by diligent attention to business, had 'really been the saviours' of the House of Lords. 'Paradoxical as it may seem,' wrote one journalist, 'while Lord Kimberley thus unconsciously prevented the realisation of the democratic ideal of popular representation, he was one of the best friends the common people ever possessed.'[246] He was criticized, along with most members of his House, for being unresponsive to the populace,[247] but no one denied that he did his parliamentary and departmental work well, a powerful point in eventually bringing Harcourt and Morley in line with Rosebery's cabinet arrangements in 1894, and thus in maintaining a modicum of Liberal solidarity. He was almost always willing to manage the tedious business of the Lords, as in the electoral reforms of 1884–85, and almost always prepared for handling the most intricate measures, as in the Parish Councils Bill a decade later.[248] Accomplishing anything in a House where the Liberals were so greatly

---

[244] See, for instance, letter 276 and note, herein.

[245] See, for instance, Ramm, *Gladstone-Granville Corresp. 1*, 2:403. On almost any foreign matter, Kimberley was prepared to 'save' a colleague in debate. Schreuder, *Gladstone and Kruger*, p. 312. Also, see Morley seeking information for his own speech on Salisbury's Eastern policy, probably a more typical occurrence than written documentation would suggest: 'Of course one may say broadly that it has turned out as ill as possible.... I find it less easy to *put my finger* accurately on this and that error'. Letter 258, herein.

[246] 12 April 1902, *Wigan Observer*, KP6 MS.eng.c.4482, f. 182. As early as 1871 Kimberley had noted 'the impotence of the House'. *KJ*, p. 25. On the political potential of the Lords as a body, see Adonis, *Making Aristocracy Work*, part I.

[247] This of course is a relative judgement. In a curious example of radical perceptions, while Dilke complained that Kimberley, Hartington, and Northbrook knew nothing 'about popular feeling', Labouchere abused Dilke as 'one of the great ones of the earth', living in Government offices but 'never really understanding the bent of public opinion.' 27 October 1882, in Gwynn & Tuckwell, *Life of Dilke*, 1:547; Labouchere to Dilke, 10 October 1882, DkP 43892, f. 139.

[248] See Rosebery's encomium of 1906, Extracts, Kimberley memoir, RsP 10186, p. 277; *EHJ3*, pp. 232, 237; Ramm, *Gladstone-Granville Corresp. 2*, 2:286; *Eighty*

outnumbered required both the respect of the House generally and a cogent argumentativeness made relevant by its apparent transcendence of party polemic, both of which Kimberley possessed in marked degree. This led to criticism, especially from younger Liberals, for abandoning the cause, but he would merely have argued that Liberals must accomplish what they could.

Kimberley came late and reluctantly to his role as party leader. In the oppositions of 1874–80 and 1886–92, he largely retired to country life and politics, leaving party direction to Gladstone, Granville, and Hartington. However, Rosebery's observation that he remained out of touch politically and in seclusion is wrong, reflecting more accurately Rosebery's own isolation from the Gladstonian wing of the party after 1895 than the state of Kimberley's political activity. After 1895 he continued to mediate between party factions until both Rosebery and Harcourt resigned house leaderships making way for more harmonious intra-party relations. Until Campbell-Bannerman clearly emerged as party leader around the turn of the century, Kimberley served as an important link with the past, guarding the individualist assumptions and Peelite ethic in the eroding Gladstonian tradition. His patience, tact, and moderation helped to ensure that the Liberals did not altogether destroy themselves, particularly over prosecution of the Boer War, and that Campbell-Bannerman would enter the election of 1905 at the head of a relatively unified party. While Kimberley's influence in opposition during the last years of his life is difficult to isolate, it is significant that as late as 1900 Herbert Gladstone was arguing that the party might stand the defection of Grey and Fowler, but that it was 'very desirable' to retain Asquith and Kimberley, who represented the solid centre of Gladstonian liberalism.[249] It was Kimberley's commitment to the principle of party diversity, honed during the Gladstone ministries, which Campbell-Bannerman most valued after becoming leader. When Ripon despaired of Liberal prospects after hearing Kimberley's answer to the King's Speech in 1901, in which he had argued that it would be impossible 'to establish any safe condition of affairs in South Africa' until Boer resistance had been overcome, Campbell-Bannerman reassured him. 'After all, Kimberley and I were only describing opposite sides of the shield, he dwelling more on energy and I on conciliation.'[250]

By the 1870s, Kimberley's capacity for the highest offices of state was universally granted by both Liberals and Conservatives. Knatchbull-Hugesson, who served under him at the Colonial Office, thought that he stood 'a good chance of being one day Prime Minister.'[251] Morley later put him at the 'top of the Whigs' he had known, based upon his 'capacity, industry, probity, independence, en-

Club Yearbook, 'The Crisis in Foreign Affairs', p. 6; *Norwich Mercury*, 1 December 1894, p. 3.

[249] Herbert Gladstone to Campbell-Bannerman, 4 January 1900, CBP 41215, f. 193.

[250] 4 *Hansard*, 88 (14 February 1901): 40; Spender, *Life of Campbell-Bannerman*, 1:321.

[251] Cited in McIntyre, *Imperial Frontier*, p. 54.

tire single-mindedness.'[252] Virtually everyone who sat with him in Cabinet or worked with him in the departments thought him a first-rate man of business. But Kimberley's political role remains difficult to isolate because it was never defined by a single issue or character trait. Rather, his position within the political structure emerged through the exercise of a unique conjunction of abilities across decades of time and experience. No Liberal political figure of the last quarter of the nineteenth century, excepting Gladstone and perhaps Granville, had wider experience, and none could treat a variety of topics as competently as Kimberley. After 1880 he was routinely consulted on large matters of foreign and colonial policy,[253] and continued to advise on Irish policy. He was not Gladstone's confidant, (Granville alone might be said to have filled that role), but to a large extent the Cabinet collectively satisfied the Prime Minister's *amour propre* regarding consultation, and in its deliberations Kimberley always played a prominent role. An excellent lieutenant, he nevertheless criticised, and wielded enough influence to sometimes alter the course of events. From a broader perspective, he was the kind of politician who made classical Cabinet government work, a clever, talented peer with no taste for Bagehot's 'dignified' service and no scope for 'efficient' work except within Cabinet.[254] In following Gladstone, Kimberley bowed to the hand of management, rather than authority. Well after most cabinet-level politicians either had been made redundant or had adopted the stump, the political faction, the party organization, or the polemic point-of-view, Kimberley maintained an almost obsessive individualism which yielded only to the collective wisdom of the Cabinet. Having successfully carved his political footing in the turbulent 1850s, he maintained it largely by hard work and ability rather than adaptation, no small feat at the highest levels of government where a single misstep might have spelled the end of a career. However, he was not impervious to change and avoided all ideological commitments, staying just close enough to contemporary trends to maintain political influence.[255] If Gladstone eventually abandoned consultative government as an impediment to legislation, he never failed to appreciate the qualities which had made it work so well between 1868 and 1872. Kimberley's consistency, self-reliance, discipline, and amiable detachment were personal triumphs with political implications. As a sound though undoctrinaire utilitarian, he never indulged in the temptation to

---

[252] Morley to Minto, 19 February 1908, Minto Papers, MSS Eur. D573/3. Cf. Morley, *Recollections*, 2:247, in which his diary entry of the same day includes both Kimberley and Spencer in an almost identical evaluation.

[253] Indeed, the lines between the two became increasingly blurred after 1880. On consultation, see for example, Gladstone to Hartington, 5 March 1885: 'I rather think and a conversation with Kimberley confirms me....' *Gladstone Diaries*, 11:304.

[254] See Morley to Minto, 19 February 1908, Minto Papers, MSS Eur. D573/3.

[255] After the 1850s, he never imagined, for instance, that his own individualistic values might be applied to society at large. In contrast, see Herbert Spencer's 'purer', ideological liberalism in *The Man versus the State* (London, 1884).

isolate himself and his increasingly old-fashioned views— at least not during the session. So long as influential people believed that the most important end of politics was the selection of 'honest, trustworthy, and competent' men to direct British affairs, as a significant number did well into the twentieth century, there was a place for Lord Kimberley.[256]

Kimberley's ability to fashion a long career between 1847 and 1902 reflects both the strengths and weaknesses of classical Liberalism as a political movement. However, it also reflects the achievement of one man traversing an uncertain political landscape. If the nature of his influence has been suggested in this study, its extent remains speculative. It is enough to say here, with Edward Hamilton, that he was in the 'first class' of Liberal Cabinet ministers, and with Morley, that he represented the best of old landed liberalism.[257]

[256] W.E.H. Lecky, *Democracy and Liberty*, 2 vols. (London: Longmans, 1896), 1:120.
[257] *EHJ2*, p. 262; Morley to Minto, 19 February 1908, MIP, Eur. MSS D573/3.

1

Early Career

John Wodehouse was born into a land-poor Tory family on 7 January 1826. His father, Henry, stood heir to the Wodehouse barony (cr. 1797), but expressed little interest in politics. Young John Wodehouse was raised in a happy but politically undistinguished home, surrounded by books and guns, destined for Christ Church, but with little expectation of a national career. However, the deaths of his father, great-grandfather, and two sisters during the 'most sorrowful' fourteen months between December 1833 and February 1835 both impressed upon him the seriousness of life and opened the way for a career in politics, the Wodehouse peerage then resting upon his sixty- three-year-old grandfather.

Having just turned nine, Wodehouse was sent to school at Lyndon, Rutlandshire, and from there to Eton, where assistant master William Cookesley spoke of him as 'one of the cleverest boys.' Wodehouse recalled being 'tolerably successful', being 'sent up for good' more than twenty times. He nevertheless hated school. In the summer of 1843 he matriculated into Christ Church, Oxford, where he 'read hard' until his studies were interrupted by his accession to the barony in May 1846 upon the death of his grandfather. Among those enrolling when Wodehouse returned in October was his future brother-in-law, John Charles Henry Fitzgibbon, eldest son and heir to the third Earl of Clare. In May 1847 Wodehouse took a first in classics, and in August married Florence Fitzgibbon. After a five-month tour of the continent and some first-hand experience of the 'romantic revolutions' of 1848, the Wodehouses returned to live at Kimberley Hall, a modest Georgian house situated on a 10,000-acre estate near Wymondham, Norfolk.

Wodehouse like his father enjoyed sport and books, and for several years filled his days out of the parliamentary season with study, hunting and estate management. He avoided the 'temptation to idleness' which his mother had so greatly feared, regularly attending parliament, taking an active role in the development of the Colonial Reform Association, and reading systematically in order to educate himself in law, history, and political economy, areas for which his Oxford training had little prepared him. The result was a maiden speech, 12 April 1850, of 'great promise'. Through committee work, speaking on behalf of colonial reform, and membership in the Political Economy Club, he gained the favour of a number of prominent men, including Sir William Molesworth,

Joseph Hume, Lord Overstone, Lord Grey and Lord John Russell. By December 1852 he managed with the help of Raikes Currie, his great-uncle and political mentor, to secure appointment as Aberdeen's Under-Secretary at the Foreign Office.

1. John Wodehouse to Anne Wodehouse[1]   Christ Church, Oxford
February 1843
KP1 15/K2/18

.... I have a great deal of news to tell you; indeed for the last few days or rather week we have all been in such a state of excitement that I scarcely know whether I am on my head or my legs, and today is the first day that I have thought about anything. The cause of all this is that last Wednesday night the censors came up into *Stanley's*[2] rooms and there found gambling going on — at hazard with dice — (I ought to have premised that there has been a good deal of gambling this term). There were five men playing at hazard, 8 at whist (*with low stakes*) 12 I think at Vingt un [sic] and *myself* who never gamble or play at cards, as I may say sincerely, reading one of Walter Scott's novels in a corner.[3] This was in the evening after tea. All or most of the men were friends or acquaintances of mine. We were sent for the day but one after to the Dean — and then Curzon,[4] who was playing at hazard was sent away which was no more than we expected — and then greatly to everyone's astonishment and disgust Dodson[5] and Campbell.[6] — Ogilvie,[7] Seymour,[8] Parker,[9] and Stanley, all friends of mine, were rusticated till after the long Vacation and will very probably at least 3 of them not come back again. Some more who were playing at whist are confined to hall and Chapel for the rest of the term; and I and some others were warned of our misdeeds — reading Scott's novels, I suppose! — and so dismissed. Now as to Curzon's being sent away, and the 4 men (all of

---

[1] Misdated sometime after June 1866 as Wodehouse sorted his papers. The correct date is almost certainly February 1845. Wodehouse did not officially matriculate until 8 June 1843. I am grateful to Dr. Mark Curthoys for his assistance in identifying persons and dates relative to this letter.

[2] Edward James Stanley.

[3] Subsequently identified as *Anne of Geierstein*. T. H. S. Escott wrote that Wodehouse 'never gambled... he earned the reputation of combining hard riding with hard reading better than any other member of the fast set with which his hunting naturally brought him into contact.' *Norwich Mercury*, 9 April 1902, p. 2.

[4] Henry Dugdale Curzon.

[5] John George Dodson.

[6] Archibald Campbell.

[7] David Graham Drummond, Baron Ogilvy, later 7th Earl of Airlie; remained one of Wodehouse's closest friends.

[8] Alfred Seymour.

[9] John Skipwith Parker.

whom were playing at hazard) being rusticated, it was all fair enough: but that Dodson and Campbell should be sent away: the former of whom *never* gambled himself and had a good character, but had had gambling in his rooms, which *many others* had had who were only confined, and the latter *never* gambled, *never* had hazard in his rooms, and had always passed good examinations and collections till last time, and as you know used to be a reading man — that these two should be *sent away* whilst others who were equally — some much more culpable were only rusticated or actually confined, appears positively *monstrous*. All this is ascribed to Jelf[10] who represented them in an unfair light to the Dean — and the whole college has been in a ferment about it. That evening we had a bonfire in the quad which made all Oxford think Christ Church was on fire — and yesterday morning when we went to Chapel *all the doors* from Canterbury gate to Chapel nine or ten the number including the Dean's, Subdean's, Canon's, Jelf's, doors and were painted *bright red*. On some of them were painted death's heads and Crossbones in white with a red ground — on one, a very large door, was a monument with an undergraduate's cap and gown painted (*wonderfully well*), and Dodson, Curzon and Campbell in large letters.

On Jelf's door which was painted bright red was written in immense letters, 'Dirty work done here' — and on the Dean's 'Ursa major' — which means the *great bear* — Under the archway was painted in letters about 2 yards long — on one side — No Spies — and on the other walls have ears — All this was done so well, and neatly that they would have done for village signs — Conceive the horror of the 'Dons' .... All the scouts and porters are paid spies on everything one says and Jelf has been seen listening under windows at night. If caught, he will probably be half killed. The painters have not been found out....

I had been reading but have been quite put out by all this 'row' — I am *very sorry indeed* for Dodson and Campbell both of whom I had hoped would have stayed to take a degree and gone up for a class — in fact now I have no one of my year whom I know, and going to stay.... [11]

2. Wodehouse to Anne Wodehouse   Rome
    7 December 1847
    KP1 15/K2/18

A grand ceremony took place at St. Peter's on Advent Sunday when the Pope officiated in person; we did not go to it because we could not have gone to our own church, and that we thought was to be preferred. We went in the afternoon when there was some fine singing and we saw the Pauline Chapel lighted up for

[10] William Edward Jelf, Student and Censor of Christ Church.
[11] On Oxford friends, see Algernon West, *Recollections, 1832 to 1886*, 2 vols. (London: Smith, Elder, and Co., 1899), 1:53, 194–95; Dufferin to Grant Duff, 30 June 1887, GDP MSS Eur. F234/12; Northbrook to Kimberley, 23 December 1901, KP6 MS.eng.c.4472, f. 35.

the adoration of the Sacrament which is carried there by the Pope himself and then worshipped for 40 hours. Without incharitable bigotry I think one may say that more complete idolatry it would be impossible to see except the kissing the toe of the image of St. Peter. What a miserable sight it is to see all the people high and low go reverently up to it and kiss the toe! It is a fact that a new toe has been put lately because the old one was worn out with kissing. I saw a ladylike person with two very little children and a tall footman in attendance who had after praying for a long time before the altar walk up to St. Peter's image, and then up stalked the tall footman and lifted each of the children up in his arms for them to kiss the toe. What could the children possibly think, except that they were to worship the image. I am more convinced of the extreme errors and superstitions of the Roman Catholic Church every day that I live here and no one who does not come to the headquarters of Roman Catholicism can form a true idea of what it is when thoroughly carried out. I wish some of those Englishmen who from a leaning to Puseyism have such a bad practice of glossing over the errors of Roman Catholicism could come here and judge for themselves. We should not then hear such stuff talked as the unhappy Reformation and all the rest of the Pharisaical way of destroying every thing sound in our Church. As I am very much inclined to think that the Puseyites have done a great deal of good in rousing up the Church of England from her long slumber and also in recalling a great many forms and ceremonies to us which have been most unwarrantably neglected, so I am persuaded that the thing required to raise our Church to the position she ought to hold is that there should be a strong party if party it must be called, which should be essentially Protestant and anti-Roman Catholic but at the same time avoid the cant and bigotry of Exeter Hall and all that school:[12] in fact you will say attain that impossible thing more particularly in religion *viz* the *juste milieu*. You perhaps may wonder why I treat you to this religious dissertation, but when one comes to Rome, naturally one is expected to have first impressions of some kind on seeing so famous and interesting a place. Mine are such as I have tried hurriedly to put on paper above, probably very much suggested by the discussions occasioned in the English newspapers by the appointments to archbishopric of York and bishopric of Hereford and . . . [13] I think of the old Romans and their temples and philosophers . . . that if they could see this city as it now is they would be . . . to ask whether much change has in reality taken place . . . . would say that the priests only professed their religion as an . . . of power, just as their priests and upper classes did, without believing a shred of it themselves and that just as in their time the multitude sunk in

---

[12] On the aggressive evangelicalism of Exeter Hall, see George W. E. Russell, *A Pocketful of Sixpences* (London: Thomas Nelson, n.d.), pp. 241–47. On Wodehouse's anti-Catholicism, see letters 10, 12, 155, herein; Ramm, *Gladstone-Granville Corresp. 1*, 2:102–03; Kimberley Journal, KP6 MS.eng.e. 2792, pp. 340–41.

[13] To the end of this paragraph damage from the letter seal has left certain portions illegible.

superstition, were mere tools in their hands. The conclusion would not be true because the Christian religion is the Christian religion after all, and much is now being done to emancipate the Italians, and give them again a political existence, but still it would be very naturally suggested to a spectator....

This whole country is in a turmoil, though there is nothing to disturb us as visitors. When we were at Florence, as I wrote you word, the Florentines were continually about to do something very tremendous and they actually did about a week before we arrived incite an insurrection and seize upon all the police; since we have been here there has been a great procession to the Capitol on the occasion of the municipal deputies, who form a kind of senate, holding their first meeting. They went in the Pope's state carriages and others belonging to the cardinals and princes, and were escorted by the *Garde Nationale* which the Pope has lately granted them, in their new uniforms and helmets with red horse hair plumes exactly copied from the old Roman helmets. It is a very handsome uniform and they are very proud of it. They are really a fine body of men, only one gets tired of the eternal press and noise which they are always making in the streets with processions and last night they escorted the body of the deputy from Bologna to a church where he was to be buried or lie in state, I could not make out which; he died very suddenly a rumour says was poisoned by the anti popular party but I don't believe it for there are always rumours of all sorts every day, which generally turn out false or immensely exaggerated. I believe however that two reports which have been *the* reports of the last two days are true *viz* that Civita Vecchia and Leghorn have imposed 14 days quarantine upon all vessels from Marseilles because a case of Cholera is *supposed* to have occurred there! and that Sicily is in a complete state of revolt from the Neapolitan Government....

3. Wodehouse to Anne Wodehouse   Venice
   26 March 1848
   KP1 15/K2/18

The extraordinary events which have taken place since I wrote to you from Florence may have prevented that letter from reaching you[14] and I have no idea when or how this may get to you, as no post has left this for England for many days or arrived, thence, though it is hoped that one may arrive tonight. With this preface about our correspondence I may tell you that we arrived here yesterday quite safe and well, but our journey here was the most extraordinary I ever want. We were at luncheon at Mrs. Harcourt Vernon's last Sunday[15] where we met

---

[14] Popular demonstrations in Vienna on March 12 forced Prince Metternich's resignation the following day. News of the Vienna uprising led to widespread revolution throughout Lombardy and Venetia, culminating in the proclamation of the Venetian Republic on March 22. There are no letters in the Kimberley archives written by Wodehouse from Florence.

[15] March 19.

Mr. Hamilton, Sir G. Hamilton's brother. I asked him if he had heard a rumour just arrived about an insurrection in Lombardy and revolution at Vienna and he said he had but hardly believed it. He promised to let me know the next morning if he heard anything authentic likely to make it prudent not to start. I heard nothing more, and we started on Monday for Bologna which we reached after a very cold journey over the Apennines on Tuesday evening seeing nothing of the banditti who were said to infest the road, and robbed the diligence some months ago. In Bologna the intelligence about Vienna was all confirmed and we heard of the outbreak at Modena. 3000 Bolognese, composed of the Guardia Civica and as many volunteers as they could find arms for had marched to Modena on the first news of the rising of the people after a night march of about 25 miles, they arrived just in time to decide the affair. The Duke at first had been inclined to resist but the Modenese troops having force and the people he abdicated and proclaimed a regency, which was to prepare a constitution. This however would not satisfy them, and with the arrival of the Bolognese the Austrian troops in the town capitulated being allowed to depart. The Duke fled, unmolested, to Mantua and I believe then to Verona and the people set up a Provisional Government. This all passed while we were at Bologna. I saw the English Vice Consul who advised us to go on, as he did not think there was any danger of being stopped so on Thursday we went from Bologna to Ferrara (of course we left Bologna frantic with joy, illuminations, mass in a temporary Church, &c., &c.) Ferrara we found in a state of great excitement. The Austrian garrison had all retired into the citadel (a rather strong position just outside the town, though inside its walls, which encircle a great deal of ground enveloped by the dwindled away modern town). The colonel commanding had been summoned to surrender by one of the common people but had refused. The English consul told me that fears were entertained that he might bombard the town but the cardinal legate had been accompanied by the consuls to beg him to forbear which he had promised to do if not attacked. The whole town was illuminated that night; the people pouring to the churches and crowding the streets reading the last news from Lombardy; every one wearing the tricolor; it had a wonderful effect as contrasted with the dead old world appearance of the town. News arrived that night of the defeat of the Austrians at Milan, a report of the capture of the commander in chief, Radetsky,[16] and a confirmation of the news that Venice had declared itself a republic. As you may suppose we were in great doubt what to do; if we stayed we might witness a fight between the Austrians and the inhabitants; to go on appeared equally dangerous; however by the advice of the consul we decided to go on, hearing that all was quiet at Padua and on the road. I saw the consul immediately before we started (on Friday morng.). He said that the inhabitants were very violent and anxious to attack the fortress; it

---

[16] Josef Radetzky, Austrian field marshal. The report was false, but Radetzky had been forced to retreat.

is to be hoped that they did not as they had no cannon and there would have been dreadful carnage probably the Bolognese as was expected marched to their assistance and the Austrians capitulated as the commander had already promised to do so if the people would oppose to him a respectable force. However we started, armed with a proclamation just published of the news from Milan, and a proclamation of the Venetian Republic; these in fact were our passports. We crossed the Po without interruption by the *pont volant* a few miles from Ferrara; on the other bank we found an Austrian custom house officer still in authority and an Austrian sentinel the only one we have seen! As you may suppose we were not searched. At the first post station a small village, Polesella, we fell into the thick of it; we were stopped at the entrance in doing which very suddenly our postillions ran us against a wall luckily without damage, but the patriots were exceedingly civil. They had just disarmed a few Austrian soldiers, and Hungarians; picture to yourself a respectable and at other times probably very tranquil old gentleman in a long snuff coloured frock coat, with a huge sword buckled on under it, very hot in the face, gesticulating very violently and you have before you the *capo di luogo*[17] the head of the revolution in the village, exactly my idea of Oldbuck in *The Antiquary*[18] when he turned out at the fear of invasion. Our news electrified them; and I was sworn friends with a crowd of patriots immediately; and in return I received an account of the disarming their little garrison; the long and short of which was that they had treated them very mildly much to their credit, plundering them of nothing and letting them to depart where and when they liked. Of course we had hoisted the tricolor in hats, button holes, &c. We surmounted with the Italian white and yellow, and away we drove amidst cries of Viva l'Inghilterra. The next place Rovigo, which is a considerable town we found in a state of frantic enthusiasm; the regiment of Italian cacciatori stationed there had fraternised with the people, and the rest of the troops Hungarian hussars left the town. We soon heard an immense crowd assembled and I was in the midst of patriots detailing the state of the country, the news from Modena, from Bologna, Ferrara, and of all of which we were the first bearers. I shook hands with a countless number; and they offered us an escort of armed peasants upon which an Italian soldier who stood by, drew his bayonet and planted himself before the carriage exclaiming 'Ci sono io'[19] — no doubt he would have been as he intended a host in himself. However I politely declined the escort and only requested post horses — the answer was 'Siete padroni; potete andare, o rimanere; quando ritornate, troverete amici, fratelli, patria!'[20] There is a speech for you, away we went amidst deafening cries of

---

[17] Probably meant for *capo del luogo*, 'head of the place'. Wodehouse's self-taught Italian was still imperfect, having just begun in January with the study of Tasso's *Gerusalemme Liberata* and Dante's *Inferno*. KP1 15/K2/6, pp. 2–3.

[18] Novel of 1815 by Sir Walter Scott.

[19] 'I am at your service', literally 'I am here'.

[20] 'Be seated, gentlemen; you are free to go or stay; when you return you will find

Viva l'Inghilterra! Viva *Lord Palmerston*! whose name had been discovered on the passport — of course we responded Viva l'Italia, Viva la Lombardia! — one of our postillions had buckled on a sword, a trophy of an Austrian officer, so that we presented a terribly insurgent appearance. At the Adige brigands guarding the *pont volant*; they were however exceedingly civil and it was very amusing to see the simulation of military regularity with a few rusty old single barrelled guns and pistols evidently not loaded. Then I should mention we were deprived of our only defence as our postillion disposed of his sword to another patriot for 3 Zwanzigers,[21] reserving however the sash and tassel which he buckled on as a trophy. At the next station Monselice we heard the news that the Austrians had capitulated at Padua, and all quiet; and we arrived there without any further interruption and exactly one hour and a half after the troops had capitulated without fighting to the people and the main body left the town. The remainder did not go away till late that night and some Austrian officers were in our hotel till early next morning. The town was in a state of miraculous quiet; no one could have dreamt that a successful revolution had just been accomplished; that night at 11 o'clock the provisional Government of Padua declared their adhesion to the Venetian Republic and sent off a courier to announce it. I have only told you the main incidents of these adventurous journeys.

I cannot give you an idea of the extraordinary scene, how often I shook hands, how many harangues I held in my imperfect Italian (which however was of wonderful use to me),[22] how all the people shouted, and to us appeared to start from their eyes, as they recounted each their share of the revolution, how the very air appeared to be full of Evviva la patria, Evviva la Italia[23], which appeared to proceed spontaneously from every field, and at the same time the groups of peasantry, and the sulky looking soldiers without arms, altogether a scene I shall never forget. We left Padua yesterday and arrived here by the old plan of the gondola, communication by the Railway having been stopped but I believe opened again to day. Some American and English gentlemen who left Ferrara at the same time as we did were stopped for many hours at Rovigo, as the diligence would not go on, and had much difficulty in reaching Padua next morning. We found Mr. Bagot and his sister here whom we had slight acquaintance with at Rome; they had attempted to go to the Tyrol a few days ago,

friends, brothers, homeland!'

[21] A twenty-kreuzer coin; most frequently referring to those struck in 1753 in Austria, Hungary and southern Germany.

[22] Wodehouse was a good linguist, fluent in French, conversant in German, Italian, and Spanish, and thoroughly grounded in Greek and Latin. He studied Russian and Polish while envoy to St. Petersburg (1856– 58) and Icelandic from the 1870s at the suggestion of Robert Lowe. According to the G. W. E. Russell, writing in the *Manchester Guardian*, Wodehouse spoke modern languages 'with a fluency which rivalled that of his English speaking — and that was not saying a little.... [He was] stenographically tested, the most rapid speaker of his time.' 9 April 1902, p. 6. See letter 154, herein.

[23] 'Long live the nation, long live Italy'.

but had been stopped at Vicenza and returned here to find the communication stopped to Trieste which they had hoped to reach. Venice is at this moment perfectly tranquil.

4. Wodehouse to Anne Wodehouse   Innsbruck
   31 March 1848
   KP1 15/K2/18

.... Of course on our arrival here we found the usual quantity of perplexing reports; revolutions, republics, abdications, in the midst of which I am delighted to see that England remains tranquil. I shall not make any political allusions here, all is quiet in the German Tyrol at present: the rest you know. We start tomorrow for Munich by way of Tegernsee. I hope we shall be able to travel through Bavaria without interruption, and thence to the Rhine, but in these times of commotion, one cannot count on anything beforehand. Florence is much as usual; she sends you her love. I have no time to write you any more — we shall go straight home from hence by Augsburg, Stuttgard, Rhine, &c. if revolutions permit.

5. Wodehouse, Notes on Reading   London
   14 July 1848
   KP1 15/K2/6

Finished Mackintosh, *VindiciæGallicæ*[24] [June 23]
Finished Burke's *Reflections on the French Revolution*.[25] [July 14]
Instead of attempting any criticism on Burke's *Reflections on the French Rev.* and Mackintosh's *Answer*, I shall try to give some of my impressions on reading them of the validity of their arguments. On the whole question viz. the success of the Revn., Time, the surest of all arbitrators, has decided completely in favour of Burke, yet it does not follow but that there may be truth in much of Mackintosh's defence, it is unfortunately quite certain that the experience of that Revolution has not taught men to avoid revolutions or to appreciate at their real value the abstract theories which are the constant pretexts for a defence of radical changes. On the question of the abolition of the French Established Church, I can neither agree with Burke, that the resumption of the Church property by the State was violation *of private property*, nor with Mackintosh, that it was no injustice to deprive the actual possessors of their vested life interest without complete compensation. The *abolition of titles* was I think as needless as the abolition of *nobility* was unwise.... All that Burke says about the wisdom of

[24] Sir James Mackintosh (1765–1832), English philosopher, published *VindiciæGallicæ* in 1791 in answer to Burke, but was later converted.
[25] Edmund Burke (1729–97), English statesman, published *Reflections on the Revolution in France* in 1790.

amending the existing edifice of the constitution instead of rashly pulling down good and bad together with the view of replacing it by some Utopian perfection I most cordially agree with. Perhaps the present anarchy of Europe is a bitter lesson to men to keep steadily to the 'narrow and dastardly coasting which never ventures to lose sight of usage and precedent', and avoid that hazardous enterprise, which is to bring them by the 'polarity of reason' to unexplored regions of felicity.

The *rights of men* are a more difficult question, but of one thing I am sure that a reign of Neros would not be worse than a reign of metaphysicians, and that whatever may be our abstract opinions as to the right of all men to liberty and *equality*, until all men are made *really equal* in every thing, to make them equal in political power is about as absurd as it would be in a vessel to issue an equal stock of provisions to every soul on board, man, woman, or child, because as human beings they had an equal right to be supplied with food. I hold it to be an axiom in politics, that, what is true in theory is frequently false in practice, that circumstance, to use Burke's words give to every political principle their distinguishing colour and discriminating effect. Lastly I consider that it is an infringement on the abstract rights of men that a minority should be obliged to cede to a majority, and an infringement which no form of government, whatever be its professions as to perfect liberty, can possibly avoid.

On the other hand I agree entirely with Mackintosh in his condemnation of monachism; the splendour of Burke's apology[26] for that institution cannot change may opinion, that a more useless, and hurtful institution cannot exist in a State.

Many of the abuses enumerated by Mackintosh in the English Constitution have been remedied, a practical vindication has been shown of that excellent maxim of Burke, that a '*disposition to preserve* and an *ability to improve*' are the true standard of successful statesmen.

In conclusion, to Mackintosh's panegyrics of Reason as the new polar star, by which every thing is to be guided, I oppose an observation of Aristotle, which tho' applied by him to Ethics is equally connected with Politics (of which Ethics are in the wide sense of [ill.] but a part) and shortly points out the insufficiency of bare reason to direct us in matters, where feelings and dispositions, virtues and vices play as prominent a part as in the scene of the social and political world — the observation is this —

εὐπραξία [γὰρ] καὶ τὸ ἐναντίον ἐν πράξει ἄνευ διανοίας καὶ ἤθους οὐκ ἔστι[ν]· διάνοια δ᾽ αὐτὴ οὐθὲν κινεῖ[,] ἀλλ᾽ ἡ ἕνεκά του καὶ πρακτική . . . . διὸ ἢ ὀρεκτικὸς νοῦς ἡ προαίρεσις, ἢ ὄρεξις διανοητικὴ καὶ ἡ τοιαύτη ἀρχὴ ἄνθρωπος [27]

[26] *Reflections on the Revolution in France*, ed. Conor Cruise O'Brien (London: Penguin,1968), pp. 267–71.
[27] 'Good action and its opposite cannot exist without a combination of intellect and

6. Wodehouse, [Historical Notes]
  ca. March 1849
  KP1 15/K2/9

Points to be considered in *James II*, the *reign of James II* and *the Revolution of 1688*.[28]

The *state of the nation at his accession* . *Political*. the Depression of the Whig party at James' accession, and after the Defeat *of Monmouth and Argyll* — the great power of the King supported by the Tory party and the *Church*.

James' character — his excessive *bigotry*, how far his mistakes are to be ascribed to *stupidity* —

His manifest determination to destroy *the Church* and the *Liberties* of England — his *disgraceful dependence on Louis XIV*.

His *want of faith* as shown in his utter disregard of the professions made at the beginning of his reign.

His *cruelty* — needs some further proof than I have seen, for although I think he has not the *smallest claims* to the character of a merciful Prince, since the few persons whom he did pardon, were, as is well shown by Macaulay, exactly those he ought to have punished, yet his conduct is hardly to be ascribed to direct cruelty, but more to culpable indifference, and to an *extremely vicious judgement*/.

As to his pretensions to be considered the advocate of religious freedom I doubt not, if he had lived in an age when it was possible, he would have lit the fires of Smithfield,[29] but I must allow that he probably succeeded in deceiving himself somewhat on this point, and by constantly boasting of his liberal opinions as to religion at last really believed he was liberal from conviction, when he was liberal simply from necessity —

His Queen seems to have been even from the account of her professed apologist, Miss Strickland,[30] a *mere harmless cypher*.

James' characters and political views are no where more clearly shown than in his 'Advice to his Son' — indeed to me nothing more is required to prove the *absolute necessity of the Revolution*, than the knowledge there given of his principles of Govt.

(1) to adhere to the R.C. religion.
(2) to settle Liberty of Conscience by a *Law*. (he had learnt by experience to distrust the *Dispensing power*.
 3. he calls the '*Habeas Corpus Act*' a *misfortune*! to the people and the Crown.

---

character. Intellect itself, however, moves nothing, but only the intellect which aims at an end and is practical'. Aristotle, *Politics*, Tr. W.D. Ross. Kimberley omitted the bracketted characters.

[28] Based mainly upon his reading of Clarke's *Life of James II* and Macaulay's *History of England*. KP1 15/K2/6, pp. 14–17.

[29] Where Mary Tudor martyred some 300 Protestant heretics at the stake (1555–56).

[30] Elizabeth Strickland, wrote *Lives of the Queens of England*, 1840–48.

4. Be never *without a considerable body of Catholick troops —*
5. Avoid mistresses (good advice)
6. Never embark in *an offensive war —* as contrary to Humanity, Xtianity &c. *— and* because if King of Engld. must have the help of parliament to carry it on, and if once he ran in debt, runs hazard of his Crown by having things imposed upon him &c. &c.
7. *Avoid a Parliament as much as possible on every account.*
8. Encourage Navy and Trade.
9. Keep *Scotland* as much as possible as it is, avoiding in every case union with Engd.
10. Civilise the native *Irish*, and encourage English colonists. For in spite of the Cromwellian politics of the English settlers, James had the good sense to see that nothing could be done by supporting the native Irish, which coming from him must be considered a remarkable admission, to have *no troops* in Ireland, *native Irish*.
11. Officers, Ministers &c. 3 Church of Engld.
    Commiss. of Treasury 5 1 Catholick 1 Dissenter.
    Secretaries of State — 1 Catholick, 1 Protestant
    Secry. of War — C — of Navy. P.
    Army, Household, Bed Chamber *most Catholick*
    Embassadors — C. and P — As *many Catholicks*
    as can be in 1/4 Army some Ch: of Eng: and Dissenters.

7. Wodehouse to the Editor
   November 1849
   Morning Chronicle, in KP6 MS.eng.d.2492, p. 2

Sir,

    I am much gratified to see that you have taken up the subject of University abuses, and you may therefore perhaps think it worthwhile to occupy a corner of your paper with a few hints as to the shortcomings of Christchurch, from one who, during a recent residence of three years and a half, had practical experience of them.

    The manner in which studentships are disposed of — by favour not by merit — you have already made known; and I will therefore first mention the *scholarship founded by Dr. Fell*: they are worth 40l. per annum, and may be held for six years, if the scholar continues to reside at Christchurch. You would think that such prizes as these would be made the subjects of stringent examination, calculated to stimulate men of ability to assert themselves. No such thing: they are given after a lazy and slovenly examination before the Dean, so easy that any boy in the higher forms of a public school, with moderate abilities and acquirements, would laugh at such a trial. Compare it with the Newcastle scholarship at Eton, the value of which is only 50l. per annum for three years;

there is almost as much difference in stringency between them and between the Oxford examinations for an ordinary degree and for honours.

Let me now say a few words about the system of teaching in the college — the mode, in fact, in which it professes to fulfil its duty to its *alumni* and the public. The public lectures of the college are notoriously insufficient as a preparation even for the ordinary degree examination; and strange to say, by a sort of Procrustean rule, every freshman is made to attend a certain routine of lectures, with scarcely any reference to his abilities or acquirements, so that many who, when boys at school, were reading Thucydides, Æschylus and Sophocles, on their arrival at college recede to Euripedes and the elements of the Greek grammar. But, it will be said, the deficiency is supplied by the Tutors' lectures to their pupils in private classes. How far this may be the case I leave you to judge by the fact that every candidate for honours who can afford the expense, and many for an ordinary degree, have recourse to a private tutor. Well, at any rate, you would suppose that the college, having failed itself to provide instruction, would not throw any obstacles in the way of procuring it elsewhere. But no; our dean required that every undergraduate who wished to read with a private tutor should apply to him, and accept unconditionally his selection; and as he always nominates some graduate residing in the college — usually, if not always, a student — it frequently happened that there was no graduate of high abilities resident, or if there was, his number was full, and the unfortunate candidate had to put up with a second or even third class man. But of course, as no clever man would risk his reputation in the class schools without the best preparation that could be secured, most of the candidates read *sub rôsa* with private tutors belonging to other colleges, selected by themselves — I did so for one myself. But *sub rôsa*! Do not these words speak volumes? The first college in the University of Oxford, permitting its *alumni* to qualify themselves *clandestinely*, contrary to rule, for the public examinations! I could mention a variety of details of the same kind; but as I have already trespassed far too much upon your columns, I will conclude at once, merely observing that, if some should imagine that what I have mentioned are but trifles peculiar to the accidental management of one college, I answer, that these and similar trifles, collected together, constitute a system of such gross negligence, that I am of deliberate opinion that a candidate for honours can qualify himself far better with a private tutor away from the University than in that establishment which boasts herself to be the first college in Oxford, but where, to her shame be it spoken, there are almost as many impediments as aids to the acquirement of academical distinction.

A Christchurch Man

8. John Wodehouse, Commonplace Book
   ca. January 1850
   KP1 15/K2/7

'How to reconcile the prescience of God with the freedom and responsibility of
man; how to explain the permission of evil under the reign of infinite power and
infinite goodness' —

                                                                  ([Gibbon] 5.205)

The two *impossible* problems fairly stated —

9. Wodehouse to the Editor   Traveller's Club
   18 March 1850
   Morning Chronicle, in KP6 MS.eng.d.2492, p. 3

Sir,
   When a question of such vital importance to the British empire is about to
be debated in Parliament as the form of government for some of her most
important colonies, I grieve to observe signs that it is likely to be decided rather
with reference to the petty jealousies of party than on the broad grounds of
national policy.[31] My fears have, I confess, been awakened by recent articles
in a morning journal which is usually understood to express the views of the
ultra-reforming party. I perceive, if I am not much mistaken, a desire to shrink
from a searching and honest criticism of the Government bill: a putting forward
beforehand of excuses for a sham opposition.
   The bill is represented as a concession to colonial reform, not indeed going so
far as might be wished, but yet, on the whole, calculated to give the colonies a
fair initiation into self-government, and to satisfy all reasonable men, who wish
for a liberal but a practical measure.
   Is then, opposition to the bill, after all, to be a mere pretence? I cannot
believe that honest men who are not mere partizans of the Government (and
many such we know are to be found in Parliament) will suffer themselves to
be so deluded by this Colonial Office phantom as to take their eyes off the real
object— the giving to large masses of our fellow subjects the freedom which is
their right, and the laying a sound foundation for our colonial empire....
   Opposition to the Government becomes indelibly associated in the colonial
mind with opposition to the suppressing of the empire; every oppressive act,
even the blunders of the local minister, are charged against the British connection. Can it be wondered at, that at length a feeling grows up that connection
with the mother country is synonymous with vexatious meddling and every

---

[31] Australian Colonies Government Bill. Wodehouse supported the principle of constitutional government in the Australian colonies, but opposed the single-chamber legislature
and federation of the colonies. 3 *Hansard*, 111 (31 May 1850): 520–21.

species of misgovernment? Surely this is a state of things which every patriotic Englishman would lament to see in Australia.... Lord John Russell appeals to Canada. Is not Canada at this moment a striking and melancholy example of the consequences of a statesmanship in which forethought has no part— of a liberality which gives only when refusal is impossible?

Why, again, should we send out a stereotyped form of church establishment to the colonies? Have we such reason to boast of our success in reconciling conflicting sects in our own country, or in Ireland, that we must try our hand elsewhere?... Far better to leave it to the colonists to decide for themselves what is best suited to their particular state of society.

X March 16

10. Wodehouse to Brampton Gurdon   26 Lower Brook Street
  27 November 1850
  CwP HA54 1/147 970/2000

If you have not received you have doubtless heard of the requisition from County Meeting to protest against Pope and Cardinal.[32] I have signed it, but unfortunately I was the cause of much delay, as it was sent to Kimberley and not forwarded to me for several days after it arrived there.

I am glad there is to be a meeting, and I hope there will be *a resolution, or clause in any address which may be agreed upon*, expressing in the strongest manner our *reprobation of the Tractarian practices*.[33] I look upon this as far more important than my protest against the Pope, altho' that is very proper, and necessary.[34] I shall not be able to attend the meeting but if I did I should certainly propose some such resolution, if it were not done as a matter of course or by some one else. I hope you are of the same opinion, and that you will take an opportunity of suggesting it to those who are to take the lead.

I dare not write to any one, for one never knows what the religious opinion of men, or their *wives* in these times may be. I suppose Lord Leicester[35] is not high Church. I dare say an effort may be made to omit any allusion to Tractarians on the ground of unanimity, but I hope it will not succeed. I would not give a fig for a false unanimity or compromise in such a matter.

---

[32] On the political aspects of the papal aggression controversy, see G. I. T. Machin, *Politics and the Churches in Great Britain, 1832 to 1868* (Oxford: Clarendon Press, 1977), pp. 210–28; D. G. Paz, *Popular Anti-Catholicism in Mid-Victorian England* (Stanford: Stanford University Press, 1992), chap. 7.

[33] For accounts of the meeting and the text of the resolution, see *Norfolk Chronicle*, 14 and 21 December 1850, p. 4; p. 4.

[34] Wodehouse later regretted his 'protest against the Pope' as having provided 'no security whatever for the Protestant religion'. 3 *Hansard*, 186 (28 March 1867): 711–12.

[35] Thomas William Coke, second Earl of Leicester (1822–1909), Whig and Lord Lieutenant of Norfolk from 1846 in succession to Wodehouse's grandfather.

11. Wodehouse to E. R. Pratt[36]   26 Lower Brook St.
  12 December 1850
  Norfolk Chronicle, 21 December 1850, p. 4

I regret that, being unavoidably detained in London, I am unable to attend
the County Meeting to be held on the 14th, for the purpose of protesting against
the late aggression of the Pope. In the objects of that meeting, I need scarcely
say I heartily concur.

No one can be more anxious than myself that the principles of toleration
should be maintained in their full integrity, but at the same time I think it is the
duty of every Englishman to resist foreign interference, and I may add, no less
of every true Protestant, to raise his voice against these Romish practices in our
own Church, which have encouraged, if not caused, that interference.

12. Wodehouse to Brampton Gurdon   26 Lower Brook St.
  17 December 1850
  CwP HA54/1/150 970/2003

Many thanks for your letter. Altogether your account is I think very favourable to the eloquence and good sense of our county compatriots ....

I think the Tories were used very ill, worse indeed than any one but the
Tractarians, whose 'candle' you certainly extinguished. But the poor Tories —
how they appear to have longed to grumble at the whole proceeding, really
to have entrapped them into agreement in, and participation even in passing
your liberal resolutions must have been very galling. The concurrence of Lds.
Leicester, Walsingham,[37] Sondes,[38] Mr. Peto[39] and E. Wodehouse[40] was the
lion and the lamb indeed lying down together.

Seriously however, not to weary you with any more of my nonsense, it
appears to have gone off very satisfactorily. The resolutions, if not well worded,
expressed abundance of good liberal but at the same time Protestant sentiments
in a moderate tone, and the universal expression of attachment to religious
liberty speaks volumes as to the progress which has been made in mens' minds
since the Emancipation Act.

I saw Ld. Overstone last week at Raikes Currie's. He did not at all like
having *had to reduce his rents 10 per ct.* He and C. Villiers, the Corn Law

---

[36] High Sheriff of Norfolk.
[37] Thomas deGrey, fifth Baron Walsingham (1804–70).
[38] G. W. Milles, fifth Baron Sondes (1824–94).
[39] Sir Samuel Morton Peto (1809–89), Liberal M.P. for Norwich, 1847–54.
[40] Edmond Wodehouse (1784–1855), Conservative M.P. for Norfolk, 1817–30; 1835–
55, and nephew of the first Baron Wodehouse; voted for protection in 1846. When John
Wodehouse declared for the Whigs in 1852, it was suspected that they would 'throw over
old Edmond' if they could 'get up an opposition', which they couldn't. For development
of the Liberal Party in mid-Norfolk, see letters 18, 19, 20, 24 and notes, herein.

Villiers, had a long argument,[41] Overstone asserting, and Villiers denying the existence of agricultural distress.

13. Address to the Northampton and   Corn Exchange Hall,
Northamptonshire Mechanics' Institute   Northampton
16 December 1851

Lord *Wodehouse* then came forward amidst hearty cheering.[42] He had been very unexpectedly called upon to propose the next resolution, in the absence of the very learned gentleman who had undertaken it. He very much regretted his absence, because he knew both the importance of the resolution and the justice he would have done it. It was as follows: — 'That as intelligence and education exert powerful means in giving a healthy impulse to public opinion, an advancement in knowledge should keep pace with the unceasing agencies and influence of our social progress.' Need he ask whether public opinion and its great power were appreciated in a meeting like that? There were countries, indeed, where public opinion was sometimes overborne by physical force. But here, and on the other side of the Atlantic, it reigned paramount. It was through the established institutions of the country that it reigned, and should that not therefore be an enlightened public opinion, and should they not take every means in their power to make it so? What guarantee could they have for the stability of their political institutions and for their improvement, what assurance that the people would rightly exercise that power which they were certain to possess, equal to that afforded by education? When a man came to a calm perusal of history, he saw the difference between the condition of his forefathers and the liberties he himself enjoyed, he would appreciate those liberties, and seek, by the orderly and earnest performance of his duties as a citizen, to secure the stability of the institutions under which he enjoyed them, and to promote it by all wise reforms. (Cheers.) He sincerely believed that a study of history was eminently calculated to see what really was safe in political changes. He had heard it said that religion would be endangered by the extension of education. Could anybody really believe that the cultivation of the noblest gift of the Almighty was calculated to diminish reverence for his word? He should despair for religion if it were so. But he did not believe it. It was not by an unreasoning superstition, but by calm reasoning, that religion was secured from danger. Its only sure basis was sound reason, illumed and confirmed by Divine revelation. They had listened to an earnest appeal on behalf of mechanical science. He would as earnestly plead the cause of moral improvement. He would say that

[41] Charles Pelham Villiers (1802–98), M.P. for Wolverhampton, 1835–98; moved an annual resolution against the Corn Law from 1838 until its repeal in 1846.
[42] Reported in the *Report of the Soiree of the Northampton and Northamptonshire Mechanics' Institute, Held at the Corn Exchange Hall, Northampton, December the 16th, 1851* (Northampton: Thomas Phillips, 1852), pp. 13–14.

in a very remarkable age of mechanical improvement let them not lose sight of moral improvement. No one could more appreciate the triumphs of mechanism than he did; yet he would place all moral triumphs above them. When, as at the present day, they saw in neighbouring countries anarchy and despotism; and, on the other hand, in our own country the people looking calmly forward to changes in her institutions, he saw in that spectacle a very remarkable proof that moral energy was the safeguard of a nation. Let the man who doubted whether he ought to promote the extension of education reflect whether he did not appreciate the knowledge which he himself had gained; and if he did, could he justify his refusal to extend it to others — would he not desire that those who were engaged in unceasing toil should share in that enjoyment? Whoever had helped towards communicating that enjoyment had done something, and he would, in conclusion, say, if any man should be tempted to over-value the force of human reasoning, let him look round him and that what was the great cause and origin of all. Let his thoughts revert to that Divine wisdom whence all knowledge springs, and whither it will all ultimately return. (Cheers.)

14. Grey to Wodehouse   Carlton Terrace
   12 March 1852
   KP6 MS.eng.c.3996, ff. 161–62

I hear from Bessborough[43] that he has written to ask you to come to town for the discussion we expect in the House of Lords on Monday, and I hope very much that you will not only do so, but will speak, if Lord Derby shld. take the line which is generally expected. You will see by the newspaper that Ld. Beaumont[44] has given notice of his intent in presenting a petition to call the attention of the house to the injurious effect of the uncertainty which exists as to the intentions of the new administration on the subject of protection, and that he will ask Ld. Derby whether he proposes in a new Parlt. to recommend the imposition of a duty on the importation of corn.

We have every reason to believe from what we hear that Ld Derby will try to evade giving any distinct answer to this question, and will say as he did on the first night of his appearing as a minister that his opinion is in favour of a duty on corn but that whether such a duty can be proposed must depend upon the sense of the country as tested by a dissolution. It appears to me that it is contrary to all precedent and calculated to produce the worst possible effects that such a line shld. be taken by the Government.

It has always hitherto been supposed to be the duty of the administration to take the lead upon important questions of this sort and to make itself responsible

---

[43] John George Brabazon Ponsonby, fifth Earl of Bessborough (1809–80), Chief Liberal Whip, 1850–80.

[44] Miles Thomas Stapleton, eighth Baron Beaumont (1805–54).

for proposing to Parlt. the policy it thinks best for the country, standing or falling by the decision which is pronounced.

To say that the Govt. have an opinion but is not prepared to act upon it, and must wait to know the judgement of the country, is to give a direct encouragement to agitation upon this most agitating question. I do not think that such a line wd. be justifiable on any important subject, but when one remembers that this question has for the last 10 years been the chief difference between political parties and that the great protectionist party has been kept together for 5 years and the opposition to the late administration rendered formidable entirely by the promise held out to the farmer by the leaders of the present govt. that they would obtain for them a restoration of protection, it is a little too much that they should now refuse to say whether they do or do not intend to attempt fulfilling their promises.

I have no wish to bind the new ministers to protection—on the contrary I think their frankly abandoning it wd. be such a gain to the country that if they wd. do so I shd. be quite ready to abstain from reproaching them with their conduct during the last 5 years factious as it wd. then be shown to have been. On the other hand if they explicitly decline that they do mean to adhere to protection and to propose it in a new Parlt., I think that every facility shld. be afforded to them for finishing the business of the session and appealing to the country by a dissolution, but I do not think that they are entitled to shroud their intentions in mystery and get a majority in the new Parlt. by allowing their adherents to canvass the counties as Protectionists and the Boroughs with a declaration that they are opposed to the reimposition of a duty on corn. I am convinced that such a concealment of their intentions must be most injurious to every interest in the country but more particularly so to the landed interest.

If you concur with me in these views, I am sure you wd. render much useful service by expressing your opinions in the House of Lords on Monday.[45] Ld. Albermarle will I believe immediately follow Ld. Derby and I wd. urge you to speak as soon afterwards as possible. It is highly desirable that the debate shld. be as much a possible in the hands of those who were not members of the late govt., though it is not likely that we shld. be able to avoid speaking altogether. You will find it useful to read over Ld. Derby's speech of the 28th of Feby. of last year in explaining his reasons for abandoning his attempt to form an administration.

As I am not sure whether you are at your own place in the country, I send this to your house to be forwarded.

---

[45] For Wodehouse's speech along the lines suggested, see 3 *Hansard*, 119 (15 March 1852): 1032–33; J.B. Conacher, *The Peelites and the Party System, 1846– 52* (Hamden, CT: Archon Books, 1972), pp. 103–04.

15. Wodehouse to Raikes Currie   London
[27 December 1852]
KP1 3/1

I write to you in the capacity of HM's Under Secretary for Foreign Affairs having received the offer of the appointment from Lord Aberdeen himself in the House of Lords this evening. It seems it has been decided some three days, but by some mistake between Lord A. and Lord John R. I was the only person who knew nothing about it.[46] I expect to see Lord John or Lord Granville this evening and shall ask him to let me if possible go out of town for a day or two.

I know you would not like me formally to thank you for your many kindnesses to me, but I cannot let this occasion pass without telling you how grateful I am to you for the invariable encouragement you have given me from my childhood to this day. If ever (which however I am not vain enough to expect) I should achieve any success, I shall not forget your early and constant support of my often failing courage.[47]

16. Wodehouse to Overstone   Kimberley Park
30 December 1852
OP MS.804/1063, ff. 1-2

It gives me, I assure you, the greatest pleasure to receive your kind letter this morning.[48] The ordinary congratulations of friends and acquaintances may be passed over, as mere marks of their good-will, but I venture to imagine that you would not congratulate me unless you thought me in some degree not unfit for the duties I have undertaken. It would be great affectation in me to say that I enter upon an official career with reluctance; on the contrary it has been the object of my life to obtain the opportunity, and I consider myself most fortunate in being placed under men, who, whatever may be the destiny of the Government they have formed, are undoubtedly men of the highest integrity and

[46] In order to gain Lord John Russell's support for a coalition ministry of Whigs and Peelites, Aberdeen 'willingly agreed' to Russell's request for the Foreign Office with Wodehouse as Under-Secretary. Ironically, Russell resigned the Foreign Office in February 1853 to become Minister without Portfolio. Wodehouse, who had wished for the vice- presidency of the Board of Trade, was convinced that he was selected for the Foreign Office because he 'had never expressed an opinion in public on Foreign Affairs.' Frances Balfour, *Life of George, Fourth Earl of Aberdeen*, 2 vols. (London: Hodder and Stoughton, 1923), 2:175; Kimberley Journal, KP6 MS.eng.e.2790, p. 12.

[47] Currie wrote to his son that 'if the Government last, as Johnny [Lord John Russell] can never lead the House of Commons and really do the work of the Foreign Office, this most interesting and important department will almost fall into the hands of our industrious and noble friend. Such is the reward of steady exertion! I have had something to do with it.' Currie, *Recollections*, 1:518.

[48] Congratulating Wodehouse and looking to the new government as 'a bulwark against' the further denigration of the 'character of British statesmanship.' KP6 MS.eng.c. 3999, ff. 11–12.

capacity. But I can say with perfect truth, that, though I enter now only upon subordinate duties, I feel very deeply a sense of the responsibility which I incur. I feel that having once stepped out of the ranks, I am bound to devote whatever ability and energy I may possess to the public service — I can promise nothing as to my ability (for that I have yet to prove I possess), but I think I feel that my motives are upright, and that if I fail it will be at least without dishonour.

I hope you will continue to me the advantage not only of your friendship but also your advice; both I value highly. I only came down here today to settle my affairs, and return to London on Tuesday. I have kept your Christmas gift for New Years' day, when I can give it myself to my children.

2
Years of Endeavour

Office under Aberdeen was both the goal of Wodehouse's public ambition and the end of his leisurely self-pursuits. Hard work at the Foreign Office, a quick mind, fluency in French, and an imperturbable assurance recommended him to the Foreign Secretary, Lord Clarendon, who in the aftermath of the Crimean War appointed his young protegé Minister Plenipotentiary to St. Petersburg with the full approval of Palmerston. Though some considered Wodehouse heavy-handed, his management of affairs generally was considered successful, especially in Clarendon's office, where the rule of the moment was 'meeting coldness with coldness'. Resigning his post at the outset of Derby's ministry in 1858, he was reappointed under Palmerston to the foreign office, where he mastered the complex historical and legal circumstances surrounding affairs in Italian and German states, Rumania and Syria. Russell's elevation to the peerage in July 1861 nevertheless exposed the weakness of Wodehouse's political position. Having no influence with 'the reigning cliques' and unwilling to serve subordinately in the Lords, he resigned, waiting three years to be brought back into national government. Wodehouse firmly resisted posts abroad — including Governorships of Madras and Bombay, the Governor-Generalship of Canada, and perhaps the Turkish embassy — preferring to take his chances in 'the sea of home politics.' Although no permanent position could be found, in December 1863 Russell assigned to Wodehouse the delicate task of mediating the intractable Dano-Prussian dispute over Schleswig-Holstein. Negotiations with Bismarck and the kings of Prussia and Denmark were unsuccessful, but provided further diplomatic experience and international visibility.

Though disappointed at being out of office, Wodehouse continued to study foreign affairs, served on a number of House committees, and generally kept in touch with political society at Brooks's, the Cosmopolitan, Grillion's and the Political Economy Club. In April 1864, he reluctantly accepted Palmerston's offer to serve as Under-Secretary to the India Office. His patience was rewarded, however, for in November of that year he was appointed Lord-Lieutenant of Ireland, an offer widely perceived as bringing him into the front rank of Liberal politicians. Though he disapproved of the office, as did Palmerston, he determined to administer it energetically, promoting grants-in-aid for land drainage and disestablishment of the Anglican church in Ireland. Timely suppression of the Fenian uprising of 1865 led to his elevation in the peerage, Wodehouse becoming the Earl of Kimberley on 1 June 1866. Throughout the political manoeuvring of the reform bill debates of 1866–67, he became convinced that 'household suffrage pure and simple' had become a political necessity, declaring his 'strongly liberal' sympathies in the campaign. Kimberley briefly served as governor of the Hudson's Bay Company (1868) before being brought into Gladstone's first ministry as Lord Privy Seal, an office which in itself, he observed, 'is nothing [but] puts me well on the road to promotion when the occasion offers.'

Wodehouse took an active part in Norfolk civic affairs. Beginning in 1855, he served as unofficial Liberal agent in East Norfolk, helping to secure in 1857 the first Liberal victory there 1835. He spoke frequently at local meetings such as the Turnstead and Happing Association, Norfolk Agricultural Association and North Walsham Volunteers, and for friends and colleagues at working men's institutes, industrial exhibitions and agricultural meetings. He served as a county magistrate, Poor Law Guardian, member of the Wymondham Petty Sessions, and on a number of local school boards and committees. From the first interested in the social potential of education, in 1850 he built a school in Kimberley which he continued to support, served on a number of local school boards and in 1859 began his 43-year tenure on the senate of the University of London. Until 1864 he was much involved in the financial rehabilitation of the Kimberley estate, principally through the sale of Falmouth properties as Cornwall belatedly entered the railway age.

17. Wodehouse to Raikes Currie   48 Bryanston Sq.
   20 December 1853
   KP1 3/1

Confidential

There are so many conflicting reports about Palmerston's retirement and the present state of affairs[1], that you may perhaps like to hear my notions on our past, present and future. P. has I know gone out ostensibly on the Reform Bill; I have been told that the particular part of it on which he disagreed, was the question whether the members of the borough, which are to be disfranchised, should be given to towns or counties; but I will not disguise my own opinion that his resignation has been accelerated, if not caused, by dissatisfaction at our policy in the East. I am of course precluded by my position from entering into any particulars of that policy, but I own I am greatly dissatisfied with it myself. We have placed far too much confidence in the professions of Russia, in the

[1] For a full account, see J. B. Conacher, *The Aberdeen Coalition, 1852–1855, A Study in Mid-Nineteenth Century Party Politics* (Cambridge: Cambridge University Press, 1968), pp. 215–46.

face of the worst barefaced lying and perfidy on her part; and we have been pursuing for months the vain shadow of a Quadruple Alliance against Russia the only points of which are the note and protocol, published yesterday in the newspapers.[2] The protocol is worth something as a declaration of policy, but it is more than useless if it is not to be accompanied by prompt and decided action. Whilst we are talking and writing the Russians are acting; massacring Turks, and destroying their ships under the noses of the Admiral and Ambassadors, and vigorously preparing for war in the spring. Meantime our valuable ally at Vienna is rejoicing that a wholesome reverse will dispose the Turks to peace. I don't believe it. The answer of the Turks to the note of the Ambassadors will propose terms of peace which the Emperor of Russia will instantly reject. What then is the alternative? I am, even I would venture to hope, in the opinion of our Prime Minister. I have tried hard to persuade myself that we have all along been making honourable efforts for peace and that our vacillation and timidity have been only in appearance or inseparable from conciliatory counsels. I cannot say that I have convinced myself. It is painful to feel an utter want of confidence in what we are doing or are about to do, and yet such is undeniably my real feeling. Not that I am a follower of Palmerston; far from it. On the contrary I have no confidence in *his* foreign policy. That policy has been too often to talk very big, and then to leave in the lurch those whom his big talk had encouraged to rebellion or resistance; witness his policy in Italy in 1848 which inflicted a grievous wound on our influence in Europe. I need not say that on the question of Reform, if his opinions are at all what they are represented to be, I entirely differ from him. Neither am I dissatisfied with Clarendon, whose policy I firmly believe, if he had his own way, would be such as I should entirely approve.

If you say peace is worth many sacrifices, I answer there is a limit to those sacrifices; and that limit we have reached. We are pledged in the eyes of the world to support Turkey, and I regret to say that since the Sinope affair,[3] I see no way of giving that support in an honest, straightforward manner, but by war, or measures tantamount to war. The newspapers report that Dundas[4] wanted to sail at once and endeavour to intercept the Russians on their return to Sevastopol; that would have retrieved our position, but it is said he was overruled by B. d'Hillier;[5] probably the story is an invention, but it points to what might and ought to have been done. Upon any ordinary question of home or foreign policy, a compromise of opinion in a government seems to me allowable, and even laudable, but a question of this extreme importance seems to me to admit of no

---

[2] Supporting Turkish integrity while seeking concessions from the Porte for Ottoman Christians. *The Times*, 19 December 1853, p. 6.

[3] Destruction of a Turkish flotilla by a Russian naval squadron at Sinope, on the Black Sea, 30 November 1853.

[4] Sir Richard Saunders Dundas, Vice-Admiral, 1853–1861; Commander-in-Chief of the Baltic fleet, 1855–1861.

[5] Achille, Comte Bargueys d'Hilliers, French Amassador to Turkey.

compromise, and I am grieved that those members of the Govt. (for some there certainly are) who are for more definite and vigorous measures, do not enforce their opinion, or retire from further responsibility. Amongst them I believe is Lord John and I think he owes it to his reputation and to his friends not to give way on such a point to Lord Aberdeen. Pray pardon this rather tedious expose of my malcontentment, and consider all I have written as *entirely confidential*. I think that events may yet falsify my fears, and that if we do not adapt, we may be *forced* into a different policy. Events have forced us very far already, and before the meeting of Parliament they may have forced us so much farther, as to enable the Government to present a tolerably satisfactory account to the Country.

18. John P. Boileau[6] to Wodehouse   Ketteringham
  1 October 1855
  KP1 3/2

I am sorry to say that I do not think I can get back here before the meeting fixed for the 9th inst. but should I do so I will immediately let you know and shall be very glad (as suits your convenience) either to go to you at Kimberley or receive you here, for I am much interested in the arrangements which it is desirable to make to secure a proper share in the representation of the County for the Whigs, tho' I am obliged to confess I have not the stamina left to undertake an active part in carrying the arrangements forward.

  If you can spare time from your official duties and will undertake the trouble (prepared for some disappointment) I feel sure much can be done and John[7] will I think be a zealous coadjutor — and if you will not consider me intrusive I would venture to say that in doing so you would I am persuaded confirm your personal influence and that of your family permanently.

19. Wodehouse to Birkbeck[8]   48 Bryanston Sq.
  5 November 1855
  KP1 3/2

Private/copy

  I saw Boileau on Sunday and we talked over E. Norfolk election matters. We agreed that Sir E. Buxton[9] and Custance[10] having refused, the next step must be

---

  [6] Norfolk county magistrate.
  [7] John Oddin Taylor, Norwich solicitor, Liberal agent in East Norfolk during the 1850s and 1860s. For Wodehouse's appreciation, see his letter to Taylor, 11 December 1858, KP1 3/2.
  [8] Henry Birkbeck, Norfolk county magistrate.
  [9] Sir Edward North Buxton (1812–58), Liberal M.P. for South Essex, 1847–52; East Norfolk, 1857–58.
  [10] Hambledon Francis Custance, Norfolk county magistrate.

to ask Mr. Townshend,[11] whose name was brought before the meeting, and who it was agreed would be a fitting candidate, if Buxton and Custance declined. I would at once have written to Mr. Townshend myself, if there [was] not as you know a certain impropriety in my being the organ of such a formal invitation. As Boileau wrote to Custance, perhaps you would acting on the principle of division of labour, write the letter to Townshend. It would be well to say that at the meeting his name was discussed and it was agreed that 'he would be a fitting candidate,' this I have in the minutes of the meeting. The sooner it is done the better. If Mr. Townshend refuses, it will then be time enough for you to consider as to my brother[12] ....

20. Wodehouse to Windham[13]   Foreign Office
    28 March 1856
    KP1 3/2

Private/copy

As there appears every probability of peace being shortly concluded, I am very anxious to ask you whether you would consent to become a candidate for East Norfolk on a dissolution or vacancy, which latter event is however improbable. There was a very general wish that you should come forward and at a meeting of influential persons held privately in October at Mr. Birkbeck's to consider as to candidates your name was prominently mentioned, but it was decided that at that time it was of no use to ask you as you wd. not be likely to accept as long as the war continued. Now however the case is different.

We are, I regret to say, entirely without candidates and the field is therefore open. The registration has, I am assured, been very favourable to us, and I cannot but think that you would have a very good prospect of success.[14] With regard to the expenses of an election, we could not of course expect you to bear them, but I believe there would be no great difficulty in getting a subscription of £1500 or £2000. You will say that this is an inadequate sum with wh. to defray the expense of a contest, but I am convinced a gr. deal may be done as far as legitimate expenses go with such a sum, and you would do no greater benefit to the Liberal party and to the County in general than to break the neck of the ruinous system hitherto pursued and wh. prevents many excellent candidates from coming forward.[15] If you should assent, I will with pleasure

---

[11] Probably John Townshend.

[12] Henry Wodehouse. On further attempts to enlist Henry Wodehouse as a parliamentary candidate, see letters 23 and 24, herein.

[13] Charles Ash Windham (1810–70), Major-General, Chief-of-Staff to Sir William John Codrington in the Crimea.

[14] Windham was returned unopposed on 6 April 1857, but volunteered for service in India during the summer upon the outbreak of the mutiny.

[15] On the striking electoral changes of the mid- fifties in East Norfolk, see *The Poll for*

subscribe £500 and will do my best to get others to contribute. I must beg you however distinctly to understand that I have no authority whatever to invite you to become a candidate. I write entirely as a private individual, and I should not be justified in using the name of any one in the matter. All I can promise is that if, as I hope, you will entertain the proposal, I will communicate with the Party with a view to their accepting you as their candidate.[16]

With regards to a dissolution, my own impression is that it is not so imminent as people suppose, but no one can foresee what may take place in Parliament after the Peace, and it wd. be well to lose no time in making preparation for a contest.

21. Clarendon to Wodehouse
    4 May 1856
    KP3 46692, ff. 1-2

Private

Would you like to go to Petersburg? I would not offer you the mission if I did not believe that it wd suit you and *you it*. You know as I can tell you how important and delicate a matter it will be to re-establish friendly relations with Russia as there is a bitter feeling agnt. us in that Country just now and France is meditating the closest alliance with Russia. No mission will be more closely watched by the people of Engd. and none in my opinion offers the same opportunity to a minister for distinguishing himself, wh. is the principal reason why I place it at your disposal and hope you may accept it. I myself feel the immense advantage of having had a mission abroad in difficult times[17] and I think you would find the same when you get the seal of the F.O. which I am sure you are destined to hold.

I can give no better proof of my conviction that your going to St. P. wd. be advantageous to the service and yourself than the offer I am now making because in the event of your acceptance I shd. be put to the greatest inconvenience and I really don't know how I cd. supply your place. You will like at all events to know that the Queen and Palmerston *most cordially* approve my proposal of you.

The drawback wd. be the enormous expense.[18]

a Knight of the Shire for the Eastern Division of the County of Norfolk... and an Account of the Position of Parties between the Contests of 1837 and 1858 (Norwich: R. N. Bacon, 1858), pp. iii–xxxiv.

[16] See Wodehouse to Francis Astley, 2 May 1856, KP1 3/1.

[17] As attaché to St. Petersburg in 1820.

[18] Wodehouse accepted despite the expense and feeling 'so entirely English in my habits and tastes that a residence abroad for any length of time could never be very agreeable to me.' He nevertheless was thrilled at being so highly regarded and felt duty-bound to accept, meeting the costs with a £3,000 loan from Lord Overstone. Wodehouse

22. Wodehouse to Raikes Currie   St. Petersburg
   3 January 1857
   KP1 3/1

Private

...I promised to write a few lines to you about the Persian war[19] which I consider by far the most important question at the present moment of foreign policy. The articles in the 'Times' do infinite mischief and if the opinions embodied in them are carried into practice by the people of England, I am convinced they will find themselves engaged in a far more serious undertaking than an expedition to the Persian Gulf.[20] The misfortune is that because we committed a blunder in invading Afghanistan, and by the inscrutable folly or incapacity of our agents and Generals incurred a frightful disaster, people are determined to shut their eyes to all that passes in the N.W. frontier of our Indian Empire and to correct one error by another far worse.

To talk of Herat as a far distant place in which we have no more interest than in Timbuctoo is sheer nonsense. Herat and Kandahar are the two most important points on *our frontier*. Peshawar and Shibarpin are *our* two frontier positions. Kandahar and Herat are the two important positions beyond our frontier, lying between us and Persia. There is but one road to India, that thro' these two towns — the mountains [ill.] all other routes practically impossible. Now I am no alarmist about Russia — Russia you may depend upon it does not wish at present for another war, but so *much the better* is the opportunity for securing our position in Afghanistan. What we have to fear is not a Russian invasion but the gradual absorption of the intervening territories between our Empire and the Russian Empire. Or what is nearly equivalent, that the intervening territory should fall under a paramount Russian influence. As long as we keep up a series *of buffers* between India and Russia the peace will be kept between us once we have close neighbours peace will not long continue — in Asia especially there cannot be two paramount powers side by side. This is the opinion of Russian statesmen and ought to be of English. There is no concealment of the matter here. If Persia holds Herat she may and probably will next seize Candahar and she then holds in her hand the keys of India. In her hands those keys are not safe — in the hands of independent Afghan rulers who hate the Persians from religious differences and hereditary feuds, I believe they are. Our policy is therefore to maintain things as they are or rather were. The next best thing probably would be to seize and fortify Candahar which John Bull could acquiesce in when frightened some years hence perhaps. Is it not better to

to Clarendon, 4 May 1856, KP3 46692, ff. 3- 4; O'Brien, ed., *Correspondence of Overstone*, 1:650–51, 695–97.

[19] Persian–Afghan War (1855–57), in which Persia attempted to capture Herat. Responding to Afghan appeals, Britain declared war on 1 November 1856.

[20] Sent to capture the port of Bushehr.

pursue a bold *preventative* policy than to let matters *drift* into a really dangerous situation — I can imagine nothing more senseless than to expend millions to maintain the Ottoman Empire, to go into paroxysms of fury, at the loss of Kars, and coolly to look on whilst our next door neighbours are subjugated by a faithless and imbecile Govt., ready at any moment to do Russian bidding, and in defiance of written engagements. Add to this that we have been grossly insulted and our forebearance abused and if you have not a case for strong measures, I don't know what would be — talk of prestige! where would be our prestige in Asia if we allow our beards to be pulled in the face of all India?

As to the Russians, no doubt during the war they instigated, as was natural, the Persians to do us all the harm they could, the Persians thought the opportunity a good one for seizing Herat which they have always coveted. They made a gross blunder, and we have the game in our hands if we have courage to play it. *Most confidentially* I may tell you I don't believe the Russians *now* wish the quarrel between us and Persia to proceed. It obviously is not the moment for them to play the great game in Asia. We have them at too great a disadvantage.

The long and short of it is that if we wish to maintain our splendid Empire in India, we must act as a great Asiatic Power boldly, vigorously, decisively. I believe the maintenance of that Empire to be the mainstay of our greatness as a nation. The Americans overwhelmed all the West, the Russians are great in the North, the French are the most influential Power in Europe, but in Southern Asia and the South Pacific we are lords paramount — and then we must act as becomes an Imperial nation.

I need not ask you to regard this opinion as *strictly confidential*, as I have no right to talk about current affairs in which I am myself an agent of the government. An interesting book has recently been published, 'Ferrier's Caravan Journeys',[21] which probably you have seen throwing much light upon these questions....

23. Wodehouse to Raikes Currie   St. Petersburg
   7 March 1857
   KP1 3/1

Private

We were electrified as you may suppose by the news of the defeat of the Government, and the approaching dissolution; especially after Pam's double victory on the Budget and in the Lords on China.[22] As we are yet without details

---

[21] Joseph Pierre Ferrier, *Caravan Journeys and Wanderings in Persia, Afghanistan, Turkistan, and Beloochistan: with Historical Notices of the Countries lying between Russia and India*, ed. H. D. Seymour (London, 1856), in which Wodehouse found 'some good speculations on the relative positions and prospects of the Russians and English in Asia.' Notes on books, 14 January 1857, KP1 15/K2/6, p. 79.

[22] On 8 October 1856 Chinese authorities in Canton arrested the Chinese crew mem-

it is impossible even to guess at the future but I am glad Palmerston means to fight it out. There will be great rejoicing *here* if he falls; and the measure of hatred largely tempered by respect and fear, with which he is regarded abroad, is no bad measure, such to say, of the services he has rendered to England.

Contrast his foreign policy with that which Gladstone or Lord John would have followed during the war! If the Persian difficulty is settled he will have gained an excellent position in Persia at small cost and the country ought to trust to him to extricate her from the Chinese affair.

Entre nous I think Bowring might have acted more wisely[23] — but I don't see how the Govt. at home could have acted otherwise.

My objection to Bowring's course is that he proceeded to such extreme measures in a case which had nothing urgent in it, and that he should not have mooted the question of entrance into Canton without instructions from home. If instead of resorting to force, he had declared to Yeh that the matter of the Lorcha was too grave a matter for him to decide upon without referring it home, intimating at the same time that it would probably have to be discussed with *higher authorities* than a provincial Governor, it would have been open for the Government to have made this affair the ground of a formal application to Pekin, where we might have presented our whole catalogue, a long one, of grievances. If our complaint had not been listened to a case would have been made out for war, and the English people who have to pay the piper, would have had time to understand what the ground of quarrel was and would have backed up the Government. As it is, we are involved in hostilities on a point of comparatively trivial importance — and we are accused of precipitation. *Pray don't even hint* at my sentiments on the Chinese Question, as I have nothing whatever to do with it and have no desire to mix myself up with the matter.

We shall be in a state of great uncertainty here until the new Parliament meets, and it is decided whether the Govt. remains in, as I should resign immediately if Derby[24] came in. I think it not unlikely that Henry will be invited to stand

---

bers of a lorcha flying British colours and registered in Hong Kong as the *Arrow*. Although such ships were frequently used for smuggling and piracy, Palmerston backed Sir John Bowring (1792–1872), Governor of Hong Kong, in demanding release of the prisoners and a written apology. Palmerston's support of the bombardment of Canton forts led to a March 3 vote of censure in the Commons, and a subsequent dissolution. The March elections vindicated Palmerston, however, who increased his majority some 50 seats. On the repercussions of the *Arrow* affair see Angus Hawkins, *Parliament, Party and the Art of Politics in Britain, 1855–1859* (Stanford: Stanford University Press, 1987), pp. 56–64; Shannon, *Gladstone*, 1: 333–38.

[23] This based upon Bowring's own account of his actions. See Bowring to Wodehouse, 30 December 1856, KP3 44694, f. 245. Lord Selborne later wondered of Bowring 'what fitness there may be in a fourth- or fifth-rate English politician... for the government of important colonies and the management of difficult foreign relations.' *Memorials, Family and Personal*, 2 vols. (London: Macmillan and Co., 1898) 2:319.

[24] Edward George Stanley, 14th Earl of Derby (1799–1869), briefly Prime Minister,

for E. Norfolk, and I have written in anticipation to advise him to decline, in case he is asked.[25] I cannot possibly afford any expense beyond £500 which I have promised Windham, and even if there was no difficulty as to money, it would, I believe, be a positive misfortune to him to be elected now. It is far better that he should remain where he is for the present and should acquire habits of business and above all of independence.[26] I hope you mean to fight Northampton — You would regret I am sure to leave the H. of Commons and the House can ill afford to lose your experience.[27]

Pray write and tell me how things go — I feel very much bored at being out of England at such a crisis of politics.

I should be very much obliged to you [ill.] the bills as per annexed list to be paid — and would desire the receipts to be sent to me with the receipts for former bills.

24. Henry Wodehouse to John Wodehouse   Vienna
20 March 1857
KP1 3/2

I had so much to do on Wednesday that I could not find time to answer your letter in time for the messenger. However as you had already settled the affair, there was no particular hurry about delivering my important opinion upon the subject. I quite agree with you that it would be absurd for me to give up the diplomatic line so soon, for the honor [sic] of representing my native county, and with the prospect of a continued series of expensive contests. As far as I am *personally* concerned though not particularly fond of my daily occupation of copying, I must say that at present I would much prefer to remain as I am.[28] And besides the expense would make it quite impossible at the present time when you have been 'shelling' out so profusely in the service of an ungrateful Country — and I am sure we should never screw anything out of those stingy liberals in

1852; opposed Palmerston's foreign policy.
[25] Wodehouse immediately telegraphed to Liberal chief whip W.G. Hayter that he could not support his brother's candidacy. 7 March 1857, KP1 3/2. On other attempts to enlist Henry Wodehouse as a parliamentary candidate, letter 14, herein; Edward Buxton to John Wodehouse, 3 November 1857, KP1 3/2; John Wodehouse to Buxton, 21 November 1857, KP1 3/2; Henry Wodehouse to John Wodehouse, 8 April 1859, KP1 3/2.
[26] Henry Wodehouse had entered the Foreign Service in November 1855, following graduation from Balliol College.
[27] Currie, who chose not to stand for Northampton Borough which he had represented since 1837, lost his bid for a London seat.
[28] Henry wrote to their mother of the 'very good set of attachés' and of the impressive social life of Vienna: 'I am getting on famously and am pretty well amused. The dancing is *terrific*. The floors, rooms, and music splendid. I do not think I shall ever be able to *dance* in England again. It is certainly carried to a wonderful state of excellence tho' it is more like work, than play'. 16 January 1857, KP1 15/K2/20.

Norfolk, Sir J.B., Ld. A. &c.[29] Moreover I suppose my coming in would have been very problematical, in which case the waste of money would have been very disgusting. Though I suppose that my having stood as 2d fiddle would have given me a good claim another time, it would have been rather dearly bought. I heard from England that they were going to put up Sir E. Buxton, but I should hardly think it likely that he would stand 2d to the General. Also that my Uncle B.G. was going to stand for the West or Norwich, I forget which, but both I doubt.[30] Rather a sell for the other Uncle at Colchester[31] but he can afford it very well, so I don't pity him.

My mother appears to have returned from Paris very much pleased with her trip. I should think the change will have done her good. Love to Florence.

25. Wodehouse to Hammond[32]   St. Petersburg
   12 June 1857
   HmP FO391/3

Private

I am very glad you agree that Currie[33] should go and look about in Russia in the Caspian and still more so that Lord C. authorizes an allowance to be made towards his expenses.[34] I am a little puzzled how much to allow him but I will not let him have anything extravagant. I think your suggestion that I should give him some heads under which to classify the information he may procure a very good one and I shall take care to act upon it.

I entirely agree in all that you said in your letter of the 18th on the subject of the Clayton-Bulwer Treaty — you know I have always thought that treaty a complete mistake and that it would be infinitely to our advantage if it could be got rid of.[35] As to keeping the Yankees out of Central America you may as

---

[29] Sir John Boileau and Lord Albermarle. See Currie, *Recollections*, 1:501.

[30] Brampton Gurdon was elected Liberal M.P. for West Norfolk on 30 March 1857.

[31] John Gurdon Rebow (?–1870), Liberal M.P. for Colchester, 1857–70; younger brother of J. Brampton Gurdon; upon his marriage in 1835 added Rebow to the patronymic Gurdon.

[32] Edmund Hammond (1802–90), Permanent Under-Secretary for Foreign Affairs, 1854–73.

[33] Philip Henry Wodehouse Currie, Foreign Office clerk, temporarily attached to the British legation in St. Petersburg, 1856–57.

[34] Wodehouse previously wrote to Hammond that Currie had 'made so much progress in Russian...that I think he wd. profit much by what he sees in Russia'. 23 May 1857, HmP FO391/3. For a report of his journey through Kazan, Astrakhan, Baku, and Tbilisi, see P. Currie to Wodehouse, 23 December 1857, KP6 MS.eng.c.4009, ff. 75–83. Currie was eventually paid £150 and made précis writer to Lord Clarendon, 1857–58.

[35] Anglo-American treaty of 19 April 1850 mutually guaranteeing neutrality of a future canal, and agreeing not to occupy or exercise control over any part of Central America. Hammond's letter in KP3, 46694, ff. 170–72. On Wodehouse's early opposition, see Bulwer to Wodehouse, 1855, KP6 MS.eng.c.3995, ff. 79-80.

well try to keep the water of the Mississippi from running into the Sea. From the moment they got California the fate of the Central American Republics was virtually sealed and it is now merely a question of time. The best plan as far as treaties go of securing free oceanic communication would be to make Treaties to that effect with the local Governments but even that would be of little use as if the Yankees got possession of those countries they would repudiate the treaties. The whole question to my mind practically turns on this — are the English people prepared to keep out the United States people *by force* from Central America. If as I believe every one would answer they are not, where is the use of making treaties *out of which you will have to back* if the United States won't observe them.

I also very much agree with your views as to the Principalities.[36] The great difficulty will be to get the various Powers of Europe to let anything rational be done. I see no use in making ourselves unhappy about the question. Let us only keep quiet and then interpose in a firm dignified manner when the matter is ripe for decision which it is not at present. Above all I entirely agree with you don't let us lean on Austria. She may be a card to play but can never be a prop to lean against with safety. I don't think there is so much in the Austrian rapprochement with Russia as Seymour[37] imagines, but he is quite right in supposing that there is such a rapprochement and well applied flattery and a suitable donation to Gff.[38] would do wonders. Still I don't think the former intimacy could early be renewed and you will observe from my Despatch to day on the Principalities that Gff. still speaks bitterly of Austria but certainly with *modified* bitterness, considerably modified.

[*Postscript*] I suppose I shall start Currie soon — don't forget an unpaid attache for us when he goes.

26.　Wodehouse to Gladstone
　　17 March 1860
　　GP 44224, f. 9

I return with many thanks your papers. We had not much opportunity of using them, as our opponents made violent speeches against the Budget and said very little of details of the Treaty. If you should read the report in the 'Times' of the Debate, pray don't suppose I made the absurd mistakes attributed to me in that report e.g. that 15 pr. ct. was charged on silk manufactures after 1826.[39]

[*Postscript*] I am made to commit an absurd error about the China vote instead

---

[36] Hammond arguing that matters would have to be left to 'take their own course', though he thought a federal union would be the best solution.

[37] Sir George Hamilton Seymour, Envoy Extraordinary and Minister Plenipotentiary to Vienna, 1855–58.

[38] Prince Aleksandr Mikhailovich Gorchakov, Russian Foreign Minister, 1856–82.

[39] See 3 *Hansard*, 157 (15 March 1860): 580, which reported the same.

of correcting Grey, who was quite wrong about it.

27. Wodehouse to Gladstone   Foreign Office
     11 May 1860
     GP 44224, ff. 21–22

Can you give me any materials for a speech on the paper duties. I know I am
very incapable of taking part in financial discussions, but we shall no doubt have
a long debate, and I should be glad to be prepared to do my duty. I fancy the
attack will be directed against the general finance of the year rather than against
the paper duty repeal. If you would have ten minutes to spare any day and
would let me come to your office, I should very much like to be indoctrinated
with some good arguments.

28. Wodehouse to Russell   Foreign Office
     12 September 1860
     RlP 30/22/28, ff. 253–54

Private

I returned to town yesterday and you will find me here when you come
through. I dare say Sir C. Wood[40] mentioned to you that he had offered me the
Governorship of Madras. I was pleased at his having so good an opinion of me
as to offer me so responsible a post, but I had no hesitation in declining it, as I
prefer to take my chance in the sea of home politics.[41]

[*Postscript*] I find Hammond I am happy to say in good health and spirits.

29. Wodehouse to Raikes Currie   48 Bryanston Sq.
     1 May 1861
     KP1 3/1

I am happy to say that the Falmouth Dock and Ry. Companies have arranged
their differences and in the manner, I think, most favourable to our interests.[42]
There are or were some difficulties of a technical nature which impede the
progress of the Ry. Bill[43] thro' Parlt. but I believe they will be got over.

[40] Sir Charles Wood (1800–85), Secretary of State for India, 1859–66.

[41] When George Curzon was appointed Indian Viceroy in 1898, Wodehouse observed
the 'mistake, for a man of ambition, of taking *any* post, however high, abroad'. See
letter 263, herein.

[42] Allowing for continued development and eventual purchase of approximately 20
acres of land from Wodehouse's Arwenack estate for £13,935. For a summary of railway
and dock developments see *Falmouth Packet*, 27 July and 7 September 1861; Wodehouse
to Raikes Currie, 27 April 1863, KP1 3/1.

[43] Cornwall Railway Bill, passed in August 1861.

The prospects of the Govt. as regards the Budget look brighter. By letting the Ic. Tax resolution pass, and moving a reduction on Tea duties, the opposition abandon the accusation against Gladstone's figures and the battle becomes a contest between tea and paper.[44] I will back paper — Even financially I believe a total repeal of an obnoxious excise duty is a sounder measure than a diminution of tea duty — politically and financially. I can't conceive any reasonable doubt that the paper duty repeal is the true policy.

Much might be said as to the fallacy of Gladstone's surplus, (whether justly or not,) but if you take his figures, as you must if you reduce tea, you go more than half way with him. Such at least is the opinion of Yours affectly.

30. Wodehouse to Raikes Currie   Foreign Office
    13 July 1861
    KP1 3/1

Private

I am exceedingly obliged to you for the message you sent me thro' Philip.[45] The news is corroborated from other quarters, and I have no doubt it is true, tho' I cannot make out whether the change is to take place immediately. Lord John has said nothing to me yet on the subject, and I don't think it has been mentioned to the Cabinet unless it was today.

It seems to me that a peerage will give him a *coup de grace*, as his position in the country is nothing apart from the House of Commons. My extinction of course must follow on his becoming a peer, as I could not remain with my chief in the Lords. Herbert[46] who is very ill, and gone to Spa, has it seems certainly resigned, and *Lewis*[47] succeeds him! It is evident that deGrey[48] will go back to the War Office as Under Secretary, and I fear they will then offer me the Under Secretaryship of the India Office. Ought I to accept? I have great doubts, on the one hand it is very disadvantageous to go out of office by oneself, and in my position without any connexion with the reigning cliques, and with no means of keeping myself before the public out of office, it will be very difficult ever to get back into office.[49] On the other I have been five years and a half Under

---

[44] See Shannon, *Gladstone*, 1: 436–37.

[45] Philip Currie, fourth son of Raikes Currie and Wodehouse's cousin.

[46] Sidney Herbert (1810–61), Secretary of State for War, 1859–61.

[47] Sir George Cornewall Lewis, (1806–63), Home Secretary, 1859–61; Secretary of State for War, 1861–63.

[48] George Frederick Robinson, Earl deGrey & Ripon (1827–1909), then serving as Under-Secretary at the India Office.

[49] Palmerston attempted to place Wodehouse as Ambassador to Constantinople and as Governor-General of Canada. Cavendish, *Society, Politics and Diplomacy, 1820–1864*, p. 359; Martineau, *Life of Newcastle*, p. 303; Malmesbury, *Memoirs of an Ex-Minister*, 2 vols. (London: Longmans, Green and Co., 1884), 2:257–58.

Secty. and have besides been Minister abroad at an important Court, two years, and I don't fancy going down in the world (for the Ind. Off. is very inferior to the F.O.) and beginning an apprenticeship again. It is a choice of evils, and I wish you would give me your advice. You are now outside the political world, and can judge calmly what the probable effect of either course would be on my future prospects. Any way it will not be a very encouraging termination to 7 years and 1/2 hard and conscientious work. Sir G. Grey[50] or Cardwell[51] are spoken of for the Home Office, and Cardwell some say will be C. of the Duchy instead of Grey, as he can't manage the Irish.[52] C. Fortescue will be Secy. for Ireland it is said; if so, it will show that philandering after Lady W. is more profitable than attention to business.[53]

31. Wodehouse to Russell   48 Bryanston Sq.
   16 July 1861
   RIP 30/22/28, ff. 260–61

After maturely considering your proposal that I should remain as your Under Secretary after your elevation to the Peerage I can come to no other conclusion than that I must, with however much regret, place in your hands my resignation of the office which I hold. When Lord Palmerston offered me that office on the formation of the present Government, he asked me to 'undertake to be the House of Lords organ of the Foreign Department by accepting the office of Under Secretary of State for Foreign Affairs';[54] and it is but natural that I should not continue to hold the office after being deprived of that which alone induced me to accept it....

I cannot conclude this letter without adding that I shall terminate my service under you with real and very sincere regret. I have thoroughly agreed in and admire the foreign policy which you have conducted with so much success during the last two years, and you have always treated me with such unvarying

[50] Sir George Grey(1799–1882), second baronet; Home Secretary, 1846–52, 1855–58, 1861–66.
[51] Edward Cardwell (1813–86), M.P. for Oxford city, 1853–57, 1859–74; Secretary for Ireland, 1859–61.
[52] Sir George Grey finally went to the Home Office, Cardwell to the Duchy of Lancaster, and Sir Robert Peel to the Irish Office, but without a cabinet seat. See *DD1*, pp. 175, 367 n. 44.
[53] Chichester Samuel Fortescue (1823–98), Under- Secretary for the Colonies, 1857–58, 1859–65; Chief Secretary for Ireland, 1865–66, 1868–70; fourth husband of the politically ambitious Frances, Countess Waldegrave (m. 1863). On the strangely recurring competition between Wodehouse and Fortescue, see Wodehouse to Fortescue, 1 June 1866, KP6 MS.eng.d.4048, ff. 8-9; Arthur Irwin Dasent, *Life of John Thadeus Delane*, 2 vols. (London: John Murray, 1908), 2:161; Extracts, Kimberley memoir, RsP 10186, p. 259; *CJ*, pp. 153–58; Carlingford Journal, 24–26 April 1880, CfJ 63688.
[54] 14 June 1859, KP6 MS.eng.c.4475, f. 12.

kindness that I have every personal reason to be satisfied with my service under you. Moreover I like active employment, and I should be very glad to continue in the public service if the arrangements of the Govt. permit it.

I need not say that I shall be ready to remain at the Foreign Office till Hammond comes back.

32. Wodehouse, Notes on Books   Kimberley House
   28 October 1861
   KP1 15/K2/6

Finished Gladstone's *Homer and the Homeric Age*. 3 vols. This book is a thorough reflex of Gladstone's mind. It is as full of paradox as of ability and research. The mythological discussion in vol. 2 strikes me as the weakest part of the book; the account of the Homeric characters in vol. 3 the strongest. It is very amusing to see the question of divorce in England dragged in by the ears, and the Homeric Greeks quoted as *models of conjugal morality*! I thoroughly agree in his condemnation of Virgil.[55]

33. Wodehouse to Raikes Currie   House of Lords
   17 April 1863
   KP1 3/1

Lewis is a real loss both to the Liberal party and to the whole country.[56] Every one on both sides seems to regret him.

Nothing as far as I can hear is decided as to his successor. On the whole deGrey is the favourite, and if he were not a peer would I think be sure to get the office. I have no doubt he is the best man for it.

As for myself I don't see the least chance of an opening. DeGrey's appointment would be so far good for me that it would be a precedent for admitting a man under 40 to the Cabinet, but I have ceased almost to think of the unattainable. One might as well cry for the moon.[57]

---

[55] *Studies on Homer and the Homeric Age*, 3 vols. (Oxford: Oxford University Press, 1858), 2:480–503, 3:503 ff. Sidney Colvin, who reviewed Gladstone's later condensation, *Juventus Mundi* (1869), argued that 'no Homeric critic had ever shown, along with so minute and systematically tabulated a knowledge of the text, such ingenious perversity as he in comment and interpretation.' *Memories and Notes of Persons and Places, 1852–1912* (London: Edward Arnold, 1921), pp. 193–94. On Virgil, see Frank M. Turner, 'Virgil in Victorian Classical Contexts', in *Contesting Cultural Authority: Essays in Victorian Intellectual Life* (Cambridge: Cambridge University Press, 1993), pp. 294–96.

[56] George Cornewall Lewis (1806–63), Secretary of State for War. Wodehouse observed that Lord Grey 'purloined without acknowledgement from Lewis's *Irish Disturbances and the Irish Church Question*, his scheme for paying the several Xtian sects in Ireland'. KP1 15/K2/6, facing pp. 17–18.

[57] On Wodehouse's ambition, see Extracts, Kimberley memoir, RsP 10186, p. 256; Wodehouse to Granville, 13 June 1859, copy, MS.eng.c.4475, ff. 9–10; Dasent, *Life of Delane*, 2:161.

34. Wodehouse memorandum
   4 December 1863
   KP6 MS.eng.c.4014, ff. 7–10

Private

Lord Russell at my interview with him this day at Pembroke Lodge gave me a Mem: to be shown by me to Lord P.[58] ....

I saw Hammond and Layard afterwards, Layard rather anti-Danish. I met D. of Somerset and Granville at the Traveller's in the evening; also Lord Clarendon. The Duke did not seem much up in the subject of my mission, and G. was not communicative.

I had a long and interesting conversation with Lord C. He said the Queen had had a sharp correspondence with Lord R., she complaining of his anti German despatches, he retorting that the Liberal Party, (quoting me as an instance) found fault with him as too German. The Crown Prince of Prussia Lord C. described as rabid for Schleswig-Holstein.

Lord C. found General Grey rather German, and describes his influence as growing daily more formidable.

On the 5th I saw Lord Palmerston. He rejected at once the notion of reviving his old proposal to divide Schleswig. Otherwise I do not think his conversation was very different from Lord Russell's except that it was more to the point, and less German.

35. Wodehouse to Raikes Currie   Kimberley House
   7 December 1863
   KP1 3/1

You will have seen in the newspaper that I am going on a special mission to Copenhagen. The Dano-German quarrel is a very thorny matter and I am not very sanguine that I can do any good but if I can by any means help to stave off a war, I shall be well repaid my trouble. The very short notice and the cold time of the year are unpleasant incidents and I am so rooted at home that it is not without reluctance that I undertake the duty. I am sorry I shall be away just when the Falmouth affair is approaching a settlement;[59] but I am sure you will [be] kind enough to have an eye to it in my absence. I shall tell Messrs. Coverdale to communicate with you if necessary, and when the money is paid, I dare say at the present high rate of money you can employ it advantageously for

---

[58] Related to his mission as special envoy, nominally to congratulate Christian IX on his accession to the throne, but in fact to mediate the Dano-Prussian quarrel over Schleswig-Holstein. See Russell to Wodehouse, 2 December 1863, KP6 MS.eng.c.4013, f. 20; Russell to Paget, 2 December 1863, RlP 30/22/102, f. 52; letter 35, herein. For a full account, see Keith A.P. Sandiford, *Great Britain and the Schleswig-Holstein Question, 1848–64* (Toronto: University of Toronto Press, 1975).

[59] The sale of properties to railway and hotel developers. See letter 29, herein.

me, if there is any difficulty as to paying off the incumbrances — and you will see that proper discharges are taken of those paid off. Messrs. Coverdale will have to send the mortgage deeds by messenger to Copenhagen. I am delighted that Philip[60] is going with me especially as he knows the business in hand.

I had an audience of the Queen yesterday. She was looking better than I expected. We had a long conversation, and she was very kind in her manner. I am off on Wednesday night. Tomorrow my wife and I go to Bryanston Sq.

[*Postscript*] I *hope* not to be gone more than a month.

[*Postscript*] How very sad poor Elgin's illness, and, I fear, death is.[61]

36. Wodehouse to Russell   Berlin
    12 December 1863
    RlP 30/22/51, ff. 162–66

Private

I have just returned at six o'clock from an interview of three hours and a half with Bismarck,[62] and have only time to write you a few lines. He insists upon the Danes carrying out the common constitution projected after the German fashion that is to say by a representation not according to numbers.[63] This is the German interpretation of 'equal rights'. He does not however exclude any plan by which Schleswig shall not be more closely connected with Denmark than Holstein apart from the Federal ties. He insists on revocation of Constitution of October 18 as regards Schleswig. He looks upon the Execution as a 'buffer' between Germany and Denmark which may prevent war. If the execution was made illegal by Denmark giving to Diet the assurance that Holstein would have the same position as Luxembourg, occupation would be inevitable which he admits is war.

I pressed him strongly as to preventing the D. of Augustenburg[64] from raising the standard of rebellion under the protection of the Federal troops. His language was unsatisfactory on this point. He said the part of Rendsburg on Schleswig side of the Eider would not be occupied. He deplores the conduct of Austria in not receiving the Danish Envoy. The Austrians, he says, declare that the Treaty of 1852 would have no effect even as regards Kingdom of Denmark, if the engagements of 51–52[65] are not observed, because the renunciations were

---

[60] Philip Currie, Raikes Currie's fourth son.

[61] James Bruce, eighth Earl of Elgin (1811– 63), Viceroy of India, 1862–63; died November 20.

[62] Otto von Bismarck, President and Foreign Minister of the Prussian cabinet.

[63] The Common Constitution of 1855, generally unfavourable to German interests. Sandiford, *Great Britain and the Schleswig- Holstein Question*, pp. 37–45.

[64] Christian IX, the new Danish king in succession to Frederick VII.

[65] Austria and Prussia guaranteeing the integrity of Denmark in return for assurances that Schleswig and Holstein would be governed according to rules and traditions of the

given for the purpose of maintaining Danish dominions as a whole. Bismarck represents the King[66] whom I am to see tomorrow, as much inclined to war. He says he had great difficulty in carrying out his own views which he wishes to make out are pacific. He makes no secret that it is a race between Austria and Prussia for popularity in Germany. I fear he will not stick at anything to outbid Austria. He talks jauntily of a confederation of the Rhine as if it were a combination rather deplored than feared by Prussia. I need not say I pressed him strongly as to the iniquity of repudiating Treaty of 1852. It was of little use as he has evidently made up his mind not to be stopped by the Treaty. I will give you a full account of his conversation in a Despatch. I shall start for Copenhagen on Monday.

37. Wodehouse to Russell   Berlin
      13 December 1863
      RIP 30/22/51, ff. 167–72

Private

I had a long interview with the King today. His majesty is evidently much frightened but between his fears of revolution at home, and French aggression, he will I fear be drawn helplessly down the current of events without having power to take any decided line of his own.[67] My impression of the state of affairs here is very painful. Bismarck makes no concealment that he sticks at nothing if it will only save the purpose of the hour. At the same time it is evident that neither the King nor his Minister wish for war, and if the Danes can be persuaded to make immediate concessions war may perhaps be averted. I am glad to hear from Buchanan[68] that the Danish minister here has counselled concession, saying that the policy pursued hitherto by Denmark whether wise or not, must be abandoned, as Providence by removing the King has changed entirely the situation. I found him a very sensible moderate man.

I think something has been gained by getting the principle of the German demand on paper, namely that Schleswig must be as much separated from Denmark as Holstein is. This is very hard measure for Denmark, but it is better to know the uttermost of the German demand in a few words than to go on discussing interminable notes in the German 'Chancery Style' about the *gleichberechtigung* and the *gesamtstaat*.[69] I had a conversation this evening with the Russian. Russia seems to go very far on the German side. Buchanan will

German Bund. Sandiford, *Great Britain and the Schleswig-Holstein Question*, pp. 29–30.
[66] Wilhelm Friedrich Ludwig, King William I of Prussia.
[67] A great story which improved with age. Cf. Mountstuart Grant Duff, *Notes from a Diary, 1888–90*, 2 vols. (London: John Murray, 1901), 2:240.
[68] Sir Andrew Buchanan (1807–82), minister to Prussia since 1862; had previously served at Copenhagen, 1853–58.
[69] *Equalization* and *common state*.

write to you about the Congress. That is no affair of mine but both Bismarck and the King spoke to me about it and seemed most anxious to know what England would do. I said I had no authority to speak about such matters, but I was sure that England would join no coalition against France. They are trying all they can to get up a bad feeling between us and France. I took care to give them no encouragement.

Bismarck told me that the King was beset by his private friends and by the other German Princes with remonstrances against his anti-German policy. He said their letters were positively offensive in their terms.

Buchanan thinks it might still be possible to avert the Execution. I fear there is little chance of this. If it could be averted, it would no doubt be an immense gain, as there is the greatest danger of insurrectionary attempts when the Federal troops enter Holstein.

I start to-morrow morning for Copenhagen. I have sent my despatches home at once, as I think it is important that you should know without delay the result of my interviews with the King and Bismarck.

38. Wodehouse to Russell   Copenhagen
     22 December 1863
     RlP 30/22/51, ff. 177–83

Private

I am very much pleased to hear that you were satisfied with my language at Berlin. I am told that I left behind me the character of a *Danois furieux*; I am rapidly earning here the character of an *Allemand enragé*. The fact is that both parties are so blinded by passion, that they think all opinions extreme which are not their own. I wish for no better testimony to my impartiality. Meantime as you will see from my despatches, I am making no progress. The speech of the King closing the Rigsraad is a complete defiance to Germany, and a public rejection of our advice. I have only seen Hall[70] for a moment since our interview, but Paget's[71] interesting report of his conversation with him yesterday at dinner will show you how obstinate he is. I shall see him this evening with D'Ewers[72] at dinner and shall try him again but I see no way out of the 'impasse' with which he has deliberately led the King. The King, wisely I think, avoided speaking to D'Ewers and myself (except a few words of civility) yesterday at the Royal Dinner. I should have advised him (if I could have risked such a step) to insist upon the Rigsraad not being closed until they had received a communication making known to them the advice he had given, but I am so firmly persuaded that if he attempts to do anything at our instigation,

[70] Christian Carl Hall, Danish Prime Minister.
[71] Sir Augustus Berkeley Paget, British Minister to Denmark, 1859– 66.
[72] Special Russian envoy.

he will run the risk of losing his Throne that I cannot venture even to ask to see him.

Paget and I discussed last night every imaginable expedient to rescue the Danes from their impending ruin, but we could think of no advice which would not compromise the King too much....

I need hardly tell you that there is universal enthusiasm here for war. It is remarkable however that a deputation of Jutland peasants came here yesterday to express dissatisfaction with the Constitution. Their discontent however has reference only to their internal concerns. I shall try Hall this evening as to the possibility of his giving us some promise as to the Constitution which would enable us to get the matter adjourned over Jan. 1. There may perhaps be a chance yet.

39. Wodehouse to Raikes Currie   48 Bryanston Sq.
   9 April 1864
   KP1 3/1

I am exceedingly glad to hear that Whaites is actually disposed of. I forgot that besides the balance due to Barclay's on their £16,000, namely £5,000, there is a second sum of £4,000, which of course makes the £9,000 you mention.

I have a Railway Committee commencing on Monday, which will sit no doubt the whole week except Saturday, and as attendance is indispensable every day from 11 to 4, I cannot go to Cornhill[73] for our settlement till Saturday. Any hour on that day would suit me.

As far as I can make out I might have had some chance of the Duchy of Lancaster,[74] if there had not been dread of offending R. Peel and Lowe,[75] who have sworn eternal vengeance if any new man is put into the Cabinet. So Lord Clarendon was pressed to accept the office as a convenient way of avoiding all difficulties.[76] Besides no doubt his accession strengthens the Govt. as regards their foreign policy. It seems that Fortescue's ambition is satisfied by being made a P.C., and that he intends to remain.[77] I am rather glad of this, as it saves me from being offered his office, and prevents any new man coming in in the Lords.

[73] Currie's Surrey residence.

[74] Upon the succession of Cardwell to the Colonial Office following the resignation of the fifth Duke of Newcastle, 7 April 1864.

[75] Robert Peel (1822–95), Chief Secretary for Ireland; Robert Lowe (1811–92), Education Minister, both outside the cabinet.

[76] Clarendon had urged Palmerston 'most strongly' to appoint Wodehouse. Clarendon to Granville, 22 March 1864, in Herbert Maxwell, *The Life and Letters of George William Frederick, Fourth Earl of Clarendon*, 2 vols. (London: Edward Arnold, 1913), 2:287. See too Clarendon to Wodehouse, 9 October 1864, KP6 MS.eng.c.4475, f. 49.

[77] As Colonial Under- Secretary.

It is evidently supposed that I am very sore, as a great deal of soft soda is administered to me — which I take for what it is worth. As I *can't* do any harm if I wished it, they might save the trouble of trying to humbug me.

Postscript — What do you think of the Queen's Mem. in the 'Times'?[78] Delane[79] ought to be sworn of the Privy Council. It is a very foolish proceeding.

40. Wodehouse to Raikes Currie   Kimberley House
19 August 1864
KP1 3/1

.... I am glad to see you take the same view as I do of the Lord Lt., not that I think there is much probability of its being offered to me, but of course Delane's article set me thinking about it.[80] I have very little expectation of promotion whilst the present Govt. lasts.

Dufferin seems to me a likely man for the Ld. L.[81] He has pleasing manners, does no work whatever in Parliament, but is a favourite of Lord R. and is liked at Court.

41. Address to the Lord Mayor's Dinner   Mansion House, Dublin
24 November 1864
Dublin Evening Mail, 25 November 1864, [n.p.]

My Lord Mayor, my Lord Chancellor, and Gentlemen, I thank you most sincerely for the very cordial welcome which you have given my health, which has been proposed by the Lord Mayor in such very kind terms. I have no right to expect my health to be received more than as a matter of course, as the health of Her Majesty's representative is sure to be received at a banquet in the city of Dublin (hear, hear). My Lord Mayor, I feel that I am in one sense under a disadvantage, because you have been accustomed to hear in my place a nobleman, my predecessor, who is not only one of the most amiable and accomplished gentlemen in this country — indeed, I might say, in the United Kingdom — a most able and experienced statesman, but also one who is a most elegant and admirable orator (applause). It is impossible for me to supply his place as a speaker, but I shall do my best to supply his place in your affections (loud applause); and I have this encouragement, that the universal

---

[78] Refuting the prevailing idea that she was 'about again to hold levees and drawing-rooms in person, and to appear as before at Court balls, concerts, &c.' *The Times*, 6 April 1864, p. 9.

[79] John Thadeus Delane (1817–79), Editor of *The Times*.

[80] Delane observed that 'happily now and then a good man not placed so entirely to his liking as to shirk an untried burden. Lord Wodehouse is an Under-Secretary, and has been one for too long.' *The Times*, 12 August 1864, p. 6.

[81] Frederick Temple Hamilton-Temple-Blackwood (1826–1902), Under-Secretary for India, 1864–66. Cf. *DD1*, pp. 174, 176.

regrets which have been expressed at the retirement of Lord Carlisle[82] show that in this country, and, I believe I am warranted in saying, in all countries, a man who does his duty will be appreciated and fairly dealt with by all parties (hear, hear).[83] I have heard it said that a man in my position cannot do his duty, because he is necessarily a party man. I have no hesitation in avowing that I belong to a certain party. It is the inevitable law of our Constitution that there should be parties; and it is by means of these parties we preserve our freedom, and carry into effect those institutions which distinguish us amongst the nations of the world (hear, hear). I shall never be ashamed to avow that I belong to a party and I believe I can do my duty not the less well because I belong to that party (hear, hear); but, at the same time, I can say with truth, that there are duties which are superior to party ties, and I trust I shall never forget, as the representative of the Queen, and as the chief of the Executive in this country, that I owe to all parties and creeds the impartial administration of justice, without fear, favour, or affection (applause)....

Now, it so happens, and perhaps I may mention it as it may be an interesting circumstance, that the first public committee I sat on in Parliament was a committee on distress in Ireland. It so happened that in the year 1847 I sat on a committee which was engaged in the investigation of the state of Ireland. At that time I remember seeing some remarkable witnesses examined before that committee. Amongst others I saw a most remarkable man — one who is now departed, and to whom the citizens of Cork, to their great honor not long ago erected a monument — Father Mathew.[84] I saw that man at my first entrance into public life, and I heard him describe the then state of Ireland, and it made a great impression upon my mind.

We must look back some years, in order to estimate whether Ireland has made progress or not. We must go back six or seven years, and I say that comparing the state of Ireland then with the state of Ireland now, we have to bear testimony to undoubted progress. Gentlemen, I do not know that there is in the history, I was going to say of the world, but certainly not of the United Kingdom, a more signal instance of elasticity and recovery from a great calamity than the recovery which took place in Ireland after that most terrible calamity, the famine. Since that time, as was pointed out to me with perfect truth in the address presented by the Corporation, you have experienced no less than three bad seasons, which, in an agricultural country such as Ireland, could not fail to produce distress and

---

[82] George William Frederick Howard, seventh Earl of Carlisle (1802–64), Wodehouse's predecessor as Lord Lieutenant, 1855–58, 1859–64.

[83] An interesting juxtaposition to his private view, expressed to deGrey, that 'poor Lord Carlisle seems to have done his utmost to lower the character of his office and to have succeeded only too well...', 7 December 1864, RP Add. MS 43522, f.2.

[84] Theobald Mathew, joined the Capuchin Order in 1814, devoting himself to work among the poor until 1838, when he became principal leader of the temperance movement in Ireland.

difficulty. To me it is a matter of surprise, not that there should be distress, but that there should not be more distress. It is a matter of surprise to me that the country, being, as it is, an agricultural country, should pass through the crisis with no more distress than it has experienced. Happily, the last year, and still more this year, have been years of better harvests, and we experience now the commencement of recovery in the country; but gentlemen, the progress of an agricultural country is necessarily slow. The progress of agriculture in England has been exceedingly slow, and every man who has looked at the statistics of agriculture in England, and observed what has been the progress of agriculture as distinguished from commerce, manufactures, and navigation, will see that, notwithstanding all our labours and all our efforts, notwithstanding the large capital we have expended — notwithstanding the intelligence we have brought to bear on the land — and notwithstanding the confidence that exists between landlord and tenant — yet that agricultural progress has been exceedingly slow in England, and, therefore, it would be idle to expect that in Ireland it should be exceedingly rapid (hear, hear).Notwithstanding that, you see that great attention has been turned in this country to the breeding of cattle. That attention has now been turned to what my right hon. friend on my right so well spoke of the other night — the drainage of the country. As one who has dabbled somewhat in drainage myself, I can say, not that I know it to be not merely the most important, but the absolute, postulate to agricultural improvement, for without drainage it is impossible to cultivate with success (hear, hear)....

Gentlemen, I know very well that there is a reverse side to the picture — I hope the agreeable picture — which I have drawn. I would be but too glad if I had the wand of Prospero, and that with a wave of my hand I could banish misery, and poverty, and wretchedness from this country. But you know well that neither I nor any man, nor any government, have such a power. There are miracles wrought in our day, but they are not miracles wrought by magicians. They are the miracles of industry wrought by the hands of the labourer and artisan, directed by the intelligence of the manufacturer, the intelligence of the engineer, and the intelligence of the enterprising capitalist. Well, then, I say that I was justified in the answer I gave to the address that was presented to me by the Corporation of Dublin in appealing to the energy and industry of Irishmen to work these miracles (hear, hear).... We have awakened from that dream of commercial restriction, and we now know that the prosperity of other nations contributes to our own prosperity — that the loss of other nations is not our gain, but that the gain of other nations is our gain; and if this is true as regards foreign nations, much more is it true as regards our Irish fellow-countrymen; and I will undertake to say that at least the present generation of Englishmen desire nothing more heartily and more earnestly than to see established upon a firm, sound, and lasting basis, the manufacturing and the agricultural prosperity of Ireland. [His Excellency resumed his seat amidst loud applause.]

42. Wodehouse to Raikes Currie   Viceregal Lodge,
  2 December 1864   Dublin
  KP1 3/1

I am very glad you approve my speech.[85] It really seems to have produced a good effect here. I have very little faith in the 'popularis aura', but it is well to begin by making a good impression.

The main facts of which I am convinced as to this country, are that it will improve very slowly, and that it cannot for a long time be governed according to English principles. The last statement may startle you, as there are so many outward resemblances to English institutions. *That* is the outside. The 'inside' view is constant and minute interference of Govt. to keep matters tolerably straight between the bitter factions, who divide this people. By degrees just and moderate government will bear fruit here as elsewhere, but the results of the misgovernment and fierce religious hatred of centuries cannot be undone in a generation. A century is not too long for such an operation, and the difficulty is increased by the fact to which it is the custom of Irishmen to shut their eyes, that notwithstanding all the nonsense which has been talked about the 'gem of the British crown' &c., this is not a country of great natural resources.[86]

I enjoyed myself very much at Killarney, where the weather was better than we expected.[87]

43. Wodehouse to deGrey   Viceregal Lodge,
  7 December 1864   Dublin
  RP 43522, ff. 1-6

Private

I take advantage of a slight lull in my affairs to write you a line. I shan't attempt to give you an idea of the absurdities of my position.[88] They exceed all

---

[85] At the Lord Mayor's dinner at Mansion House on November 24. See item 41 above. For the complete text of Wodehouse's speech, see the *Dublin Evening Mail*, 25 November 1864, p. 3.

[86] Wodehouse later noted 'what intense pleasure' it always gave 'an Irishman to prove that his island (which he says is the most fertile land on earth) is the most miserable declining spot in the world!' Marginalia, [George Sigerson], *Modern Ireland, Its Vital Questions, Secret Societies and Government* (London: Longmans, Green, Reader, and Dyer, 1868), p. 136, in the author's possession.

[87] On Wodehouse's shooting trip with Lords Clanricarde, Cloncurry, and Castlerosse, see the *Dublin Evening Mail*, 1 December 1864, n.p.

[88] Lady Kimberley complained of 'the sham and rottenness of the Viceregal institution, of its costliness and uselessness, of her husband having at the "Drawing Rooms" to kiss some hundreds of ladies presented to him....' R. A. J. Walling, *The Diaries of John Bright* (New York: William Morrow, 1931), p. 325. See too Ernest Hamilton, *Forty Years On* (New York: George H. Doran, n.d.), pp. 15–16; *The Times*, 12 August 1864, p. 6; *Red Earl*, 1:73–74.

belief; but on no account even whisper that I regard my duties as comical. If such an idea once got abroad here, I should have nothing to do but to resign at once. I put on a very grave face, but it is a hard matter not to laugh, and I have by no means arrived at the acme of follies — the levees &c. in the 'Castle' season. Meantime I snatch a few minutes for business, and I am preparing to aid Peel in his assault on the Treasury about drainage works. I will write to you fully my ideas when they are matured and don't condemn [ill.] even though I appear in that used up character, the Irish beggar. Poor Lord Carlisle seems to have done his utmost to lower the character of his office and to have succeeded only too well, but whilst the office continues it ought to be administered as a real office, not treated as a pageant; I think I see my way to turning it to some useful account.

Larcom[89] is a keen-witted thorough-paced permanent official. I never met a better; but he is an out and out bureaucrat. I am sure I shall get on very well with him and I hope with Peel too, at all events we have started most amicably and cordially.[90]

I can't discern much signs of a friendly reaction amongst the Catholics, but I am told we have a fair chance of standing somewhat better at the next election. Lord Clancarty[91] has published a curious pamphlet, advocating the destruction of the national system of education and the adoption of the English denominational system, including the recognition of the Catholic University of Dublin. This is a bold bid for Catholic support, and if the Tories here adopt it, they will improve their position with the Catholics. We can't give way on that point. What I want to see and I am sure you agree with me, is the throwing open our old Universities to all religious creeds on equal terms. It would be ruinous to our chances of effecting this, to admit the denominational system here. I was sorry to find Archp. Trench[92] shaky on the question. I fear he is a poor creature, but I have not seen enough of him yet to judge of any confidence of his character.

The Catholic Bishops are getting up some new agitation Society, but they have not developed much of their plan yet. I fear they may have some more monster processions such as that to inaugurate O'Connell's statue. They like to show their power, and to 'trail their coat' before the Protestants.

It is very curious to observe how active the Fenians[93] are amongst the peasantry. This movement will come to nothing but it keeps alive the embers of disaffection. The police keep a quiet but sharp watch upon them. There is

[89] Major-General Thomas Larcom, Permanent Under-Secretary for Ireland from 1853.

[90] Upon leaving the Viceroyalty, Kimberley thanked Larcom for his '*invaluable* aid and support', without which he would have had 'little chance of success'. 27 June 1866, 20 July 1866, LcP 7591. Larcom continued to send Kimberley accounts of Irish affairs.

[91] Hon. William LePoer Trench (1837–1920), third son of the third Earl of Clancarty; M.P. for Galway County, 1872–74.

[92] Richard Chenevix Trench (1807–86), Archbishop of Dublin from 1864.

[93] Formed in New York in 1858 to aid in overthrowing British rule in Ireland.

no doubt they have been trying to tamper both with the constabulary and the soldiers but without success.

Don't get into a dispute with France about the missionaries.

44. Wodehouse to Grey   Viceregal Lodge,
   8 December 1864   Dublin
   RP1 43522, ff. 16-24

Copy

I have been anxiously considering the question of the arterial drainage of this country which has been pressed on my attention by an important deputation of landowners connected with the country near the Luck Rivers, one of the principal tributaries of the Shannon, who ask the Govt. to advance the money for the drainage of the Luck on the security of the adjoining lands. Under the act of the Session of 1863, they might obtain one moiety of the cost from the Govt. if they themselves advanced or borrowed the other moiety. They plead the magnitude of the work, its national character, and the difficulty of borrowing their share and they ask for the whole. This raises the whole question of advances for arterial drainage. I am strongly of opinion that the request for aid from the Imperial Treasury should under certain limitations be favourably considered. Everyone who has seen (as I have formerly) the centre of Ireland knows that it is of urgent necessity for the progress of agriculture and for the well being and health of the population that the great drainage outfall should be made thoroughly effective, so that the destructive floods may be prevented and the subsidiary land drainage may be extended to the large tracts now poisoned by water which has no outlet. Effective drainage is in fact an absolute *sine qua non* to the improvement of the country . . . .

I know how repulsive to English ears is a proposal to spend more money on the Shannon, yet I am convinced that good policy requires that we should not leave the principal river in Ireland in its present state unable to carry away the water. I have expressed my opinion with some confidence as this subject is not new to me (I was on the Commission on Irish Drainage bills in the HL in 1863), and I have carefully gone through the various reports which bear upon it and the correspondence with the Treasury at the beginning of the present year. I hope the Govt. will not refuse to entertain these proposals without full consideration.

They should be looked at from the social and political as well as from the purely economical side. If we decline to assist the Irish in sound schemes of improvement, they will from time to time force upon us some outrageous job like the Galway subsidy,[94] but if we aid them in real improvements we shall have some chance of resisting more assaults on the public purse. It is of great consequence also that Ireland should *feel* that she is fairly treated in the

[94] See *DD1*, pp. 171, 367 n. 29.

expenditure of public money. She pays now taxes equal to those borne by Great Britain. She is not the seat of great good establishments such as those which are maintained in England, and rightly or wrongly the Irish are persuaded that they don't get a fair share of the National expenditure. Now I think their demands are extravagant and many of their arguments fallacious, nevertheless I am sure we ought not to disregard them, if we wish to make this people contented with our rule. Moreover the undrained districts of their country are a blot which it is not to our credit as a nation to allow to remain.

Lastly altho' I am no advocate for spending public money for political purposes, it would be unwise to forget that if we reject all appeals to us for aid, we may render it easy for our political opponents to hold out promises and inducements which will materially help to destroy the remnant of the liberal party in Ireland. Sir R. Peel's views on the subject of public works are so well known that I need only say I consulted with him before he went over to England and that his views are generally in concurrence with mine. I know you will find him quite as strong as I am in recommending the prayer of the landowners for assistance, to your favourable consideration. He is also very anxious that grants should be made on a more extended scale for fishing piers, and I quite agree with him in the importance of these grants, as far as I understand their nature and objects.

I have written to you very freely my opinions, but pray do not suppose that I have held out any hopes or expectations in conversation or otherwise the grants will be made. I have carefully avoided all promises.

45. Gladstone to Wodehouse   Hawarden
  17 December 1864
  PP GC/GL/166

Copy

In returning to Sir Geo. Grey your recent letter to him,[95] I pointed out what I thought the proper course of proceeding officially.

There is little difficulty in the matter as long as we deal with loans for I do not think Great Britain would grudge to Ireland the benefit of low rates of interest, nor am I fearful of our being flooded with like demands for this country, which would (except in such very rare and special cases as Parliament has recognized) be most objectionable. These laws therefore have the effect and advantages of gifts without the dangers. The case becomes very different when we get to grants. Nothing can be more deplorable in my opinion than the effect of the granting system, as it has been known in former times, and as we found it springing up again in 1859, when we took office, in the forms of subsidy and otherwise.

---

[95] See letter 44, herein.

It would be most difficult, if not impossible, to reopen the practice of granting for local works in Ireland, without reviving demands for Gt. Britain, some of them on an enormous scale, and this in a dying Parliament, when men would be unusually keen in the desire to meet the wishes and various interests of their constituents.

The Paper you send me is of importance as coming from a high authority, and it sets forth clearly the conclusions at which Sir. R. Griffith[96] has arrived in his own mind; but it contains no argument or statement neutralising the dangers at which I point. I look upon the neutralisation of those dangers as an absolute preliminary to the opening of the door.

There are two points peculiar to the case of Ireland. First, establishments and expenditure are maintained there in certain pretty well known cases, in excess of all real wants, simply because they are Irish. Witness the present judicial establishment. Secondly, while we have laid upon Ireland every tax (with some few exceptions) that can affect the masses of the people which in that country are so poor, we maintain remarkable exemptions for the classes having property, though those classes are relatively richer in Ireland than in England, as a given sum of money goes farther in the former than in the latter country.

In my opinion the question ought to be looked at as a whole, and dealt with upon honest and consistent principles. It is true that if this epithet consistent[ly] were strictly interpreted it might lead us into matters which are far removed from the region of finance, and which are at present of hopeless difficulty. There are certainly some matters, not of finance, in which as I think present justice to Ireland is both desirable and attainable; but I have no title to a special voice on those questions.

I therefore confine myself in this letter to money in its various aspects and bearings. And I am very far from saying that there should be no consideration for Ireland, or that the measure of it should be unduly stinted, but I hold that it should be strictly guarded and marked by stout fences as exceptional, and also that it should be applied in the quarters which really need it.

You will perhaps show this letter to Sir R. Peel, and I should be glad if your Attorney General[97] were also to see it.

Pray accept my best congratulations on both your appointment and your *start*.

---

[96] Sir Richard John Griffith, Chairman of the Board of Works, 1850–64.
[97] Thomas O'Hagan.

46. Wodehouse to Somerset[98]   hfilViceregal Lodge,
23 May 1865   Dublin
RlP 30/22/26, f. 459

Copy

I quite agree with you that there are reasons why it would be better the French
should not visit any Irish Port.[99] We have a disaffected faction here who would
be sure to improve the occasion and say many foolish things. But on the other
hand if the French visit English ports and avoid Irish ports it will ooze out or
be guessed that we made objections, and their absence will do as much or more
harm than their presence. I think therefore it will be best on the whole that
they should visit Dublin (*certainly not Cork*). There has been some talk of E.
Napoleon[100] coming to the exhibition. If he does the squadron would probably
escort him. The exhibition would make it appear natural that the squadron
should come to Dublin in preference to any other port.

47. Wodehouse to Grey   Viceregal Lodge,
28 June 1865   Dublin[101]
BrP 216/a, Misc. Box 3, ff. 2–5

Copy

I have been in communication with several persons here respecting the University question, and although fuller information may possibly somewhat modify
my opinions, I will not delay longer writing to you on the points raised in your
letter. First as to the affiliation of new colleges to the Queen's University, or
the adoption of the present system of London University[102] by which all persons indiscriminately may under certain conditions be admitted to degrees: —
my own opinion on this point is that it would be decidedly better to adopt the
latter alternative. If degrees are to be conferred only on students from certain
colleges affiliated to the University, a grave difficulty must arise in determining
what colleges shall be affiliated.

This difficulty was, I believe, felt at the London University, but how much
more serious it would be in Ireland where the body who would decide, that is

---

[98] Edward Adolphus Seymour, twelfth Duke of Somerset (1804–85), First Lord of the
Admiralty, 1859–66.
[99] During the International Exhibition of Arts and Manufactures, Dublin, 9 May–10
November 1865.
[100] Louis Napoleon, Emperor of France, 1852–71.
[101] The final sentence of the letter suggests otherwise.
[102] Wodehouse had since 1859 served as a member of the Senate of the University of
London, eventually becoming its Chancellor, 1899–1902. For a full discussion of the
structure of the University of London at this time, see W.H. Allchin, *An Account of the
Reconstruction of the University of London*, 3 vols. (London: H.K. Lewis, 1905), vol.
1.

the Senate, must be composed of elements so discordant and so violently hostile both in religion and politics.

Obviously, the fewer questions are submitted to such a body the better. Further, as a matter of justice it is unfair to exclude from degrees those who may not happen to have been educated at particular colleges, or who may be privately educated. Besides, I think there is great advantage in adhering strictly to the precedent of the London University. We say we admit the claims of Irishmen to enjoy the same opportunities in Ireland of obtaining degrees, as we are afforded in England by the London University. As long as we stand upon this ground of simple justice, we are in an unassailable position, but once we abandon it and enter upon the considerations of the best form of University, we become involved in discussions of the most difficult character.

It is moreover impossible to conceal from oneself that the Ultramontane priesthood will use their utmost efforts to make the present measure subservient to their darling object of securing the monopoly of education of Roman Catholics .... Many Roman Catholics, though they will accept the present scheme as a stepping-stone, aim really at the establishment of the Belgium system, under which (four) several Universities existing separately from each other, are united under one general system of examination for conferring degrees. They would prefer therefore to have no interference with their University even to the extent of affiliation. I should hope therefore that by taking advantage of this view, and by urging the precedent of the London University we may obtain the acquiescence of the leading men in the open system....

The second point, namely the reconstitution of the Senate, is no doubt of still greater difficulty. From what O'Hagan[103] said I think the Roman Catholics will ask that certain dignitaries, e.g. the Roman Catholic Archbishop of Dublin, shall be ex-officio on the senate. To this I am altogether averse. It would be, I am sure, a grievous mistake to have any ex-officio members. We might by such an arrangement get men on the Senate utterly opposed to any reasonable system of education — or not possessing the confidence of the Roman Catholics themselves.

Besides we should be admitting the principle, which of all others I think the most radically vicious, namely that ecclesiastics as such have a right to control education.[104] Let them by all means have their fair share of influence, and let us not shrink from conciliating the feelings of the Ultramontanes by giving the Ultramontane Bishops, if they will act with us, a potential voice in the Senate, but let us not recognise any indefeasible claim on the part of certain ecclesiastics, whether they be fit persons or not, to determine the course of education....

I return to Dublin on Friday.

---

[103] Irish Attorney General.

[104] A constant concern. See, for instance, Kimberley to Fortescue, 18 June 1866, copy, KP6 MS.eng.d.4048, ff. 142–43.

48. Wodehouse to Palmerston   Viceregal Lodge,
    30 July 1865   Dublin
    PP GC/GR 2571, encl. 1

I am very glad to find that your views, as to the University Question coincide generally with the opinions I expressed in my letters to Sir G. Grey on that subject.[105] There is one point however which I should be glad if you would reconsider. You say if a Charter is granted to the R. Catholic College it should not convey the power of holding lands either by purchase grant or bequest. But I find that in the Charter of the London University *College*, power is given to hold lands not exceeding a limited yearly value in the whole. Would it not be better to give a similar *limited* power to the Roman Catholic College? It would seem invidious to refuse what has been given to others, and if duly limited, I do not see what harm could result. At all events it would be necessary to empower the Corporation to hold the land on which their College was built, and additions to the College might require the purchase of more land hereafter.

You may rely on my exercising great circumspection in this matter, and before anything is decided, I shall, as desired by Sir G. Grey, submit the details of the scheme through him to the Cabinet.

49. Wodehouse to Russell   Viceregal Lodge,
    1 September 1865   Dublin
    RIP 30/22/28, ff. 269–71

I entirely agree with you that the Fenians are not to be despised. They mean mischief and if they can get arms and leaders from America may attempt an outbreak which would cause bloodshed and confusion.[106] We have been most vigilantly watching them for months and if we can get, as I hope, evidence enough of their treasonable designs, we shall strike them a blow. But they are very *wary* and the difficulty is considerable of obtaining tangible proofs, tho' I am quite prepared to run some risk of exceeding the law, if necessary.

The Irish Law Officers[107] are both of them acute and courageous men, by whose advice I can be safely guided; and I have great confidence both in the Commander in Chief[108] and the Inspector General of Police,[109] so that I trust we shall be able to deal successfully with this conspiracy for such it undoubtedly is. I have written to the Duke of Somerset to suggest that two or three gun boats or other small armed vessels should be sent to Cork to cruise along the South and South Western coast. I see no reason why some Irish desperadoes

---

[105] 28 June, 9 July 1865, BrP 216/a, Misc. Box III, ff. 2, 7.

[106] For an eyewitness account of the procurement of these 'arms and leaders' see John Devoy, *Recollections of an Irish Rebel* (New York: Charles P. Young, 1929), chapt. 10.

[107] James A. Lawson and Edward Sullivan.

[108] General Hugh Henry Rose, Baron Strathnairn.

[109] Colonel John Stewart Wood.

who have been trained to arms in the American civil war should not run over in steamers with arms to some place like Skibbereen, and raise an insurrection in Cork and Kerry where the people are quite disposed for evil.

50. Wodehouse to Russell   Viceregal Lodge,
    17 September 1865   Dublin
    RIP 30/22/28, ff. 272–76

Amongst the persons arrested in Dublin on Friday night were two Americans, one an officer, it is stated, in the U.S. army.[110] No special orders were given to the police to arrest these men, but they were found with the suspected persons, and arrested by the police at the same time. The Attorney General[111] doubted whether there was conclusive evidence against them when I saw him this morning, but I hear he has discovered some further proofs. I desired him if he did not find satisfactory proof that they are implicated in the Fenian plot, to consider whether they should not be discharged. They call themselves Americans, but they are in all probability Irish-born. We had certainly good reasons for arresting the ringleaders here and at Cork, and the Americans were found in company with them. A mass of treasonable correspondence was seized at the *People* office which was the headquarters of the conspirators.

The Attorney General who has been busy examining it, tells me it shows that the conspiracy was widely spread and fully corroborates the reports of the police. It is only within the last few days, indeed not till just before we determined on the arrests that we obtained evidence in Cork against the leaders there, and we judged it essential to make simultaneous arrests in Dublin.[112]

If arrests had been made at Cork only we should have inevitably lost the opportunity of connecting the movements in the South with the chief plotters at Dublin. As it was necessary to act so promptly I could not communicate with the Government, but I am confident that no one responsible for the peace of this country with the proofs of intended mischief which I had before me, would have hesitated to take active measures to crush this conspiracy, which, idiotic as it is, was creating serious alarm throughout the South of Ireland.

---

[110] For a full account of Fenian plans and government response, see Desmond Ryan, *The Fenian Chief, A Biography of James Stephens* (Coral Gables: University of Miami Press, 1967), chapter 19; Leon Ó Broin, *Fenian Fever, An Anglo-American Dilemma* (New York: New York University Press, 1971), pp. 8– 29.

[111] James A. Lawson.

[112] Grey wrote to Palmerston that Wodehouse 'did not act a day too soon.' 27 September 1865, PP GC/GR/2582.

51. Wodehouse to Raikes Currie   Viceregal Lodge,
    23 December 1865   Dublin
    KP1 3/1

Private

I was very glad to see your handwriting again.

I find that 'uneasy lies the head that wears a Crown' is true of Viceregal as well as regal heads. I have really a very troublesome task on my hands. A foolish panic has seized many people and they imagine we are on the eve of a great rebellion. Xmas day is I am assured to be the signal for a general massacre.

There is no satisfying these alarmists. If the people are riotous, they say 'here is the beginning of the rebellion' — If they are quiet, they say a silent rebel is the most dangerous plotter of all. It would be amusing if it were not mournful, to see how all the incidents one has read of on such occasions reproduce themselves. Meantime there is *some* cause for uneasiness, tho' none for panic. There is no doubt a very widespread spirit of disaffection amongst the lower classes and a deep seated hatred of English rule, but the peaceful state of our relations with the U.S. has spoiled the game. I am beset with applications for troops from frightened magistrates, and occasionally stirred up by a threatening letter telling me that I am to prepare for death before Xmas, &c., or a warning letter begging me to go out always well guarded.[113] I believe the Fenians *do* hate me bitterly but I am not much afraid of their threats.

Lady Waldegrave was rather disturbed on asking Florence whether she thought there would be a rising, by the answer that she was not afraid of rebellion but assassination! Would they shoot Fortescue? My lady opined not — he had not been here long enough to be detested.[114] Observe however with all the vapouring and menaces the Fenians have as yet *done* nothing. I look to deeds rather than boasts.

I have written you a long gossip about our tiresome affairs. Give mine and everybody's kindest love to my aunt[115] and all at Minley.

[*Postscript*] A happy Xmas to you all.

---

[113] Wodehouse told Margot Asquith that he once received a letter which began: 'My Lord, Tomorrow we intend to kill you at the corner of Kildare Street; but we would like you to know there is nothing personal in it!' *The Autobiography of Margot Asquith*, ed. Mark Bonham Carter (London: Eyre and Spottiswoode, 1962), pp. 100–01; also, Wodehouse to Anne Wodehouse, 9 January 1866, KP1 15/K2/18.

[114] Fortescue having been appointed Chief Secretary on 7 December 1865.

[115] Sophia-Laura, Currie's wife.

52. Wodehouse to Gladstone   The Castle, Dublin
    12 February 1866
    GP 44224, ff. 31-42

Fortescue tells me that he has written to you on the subject of Irish measures, and it will therefore be convenient that I should give you my ideas which I believe agree in the main with his. There are three principal Irish questions, land tenure, the church, and education.

I am strongly in favour of a land bill being brought in this session. The Committee of last session recommended amendment of the present law, and no one acquainted with Ireland can pretend that the relations of landlord and tenant are satisfactory. Some however counter that no legal enactments can improve those relations, and that all that is needed will come naturally as the result of emigration and general improvement. I am not of that opinion. The tenants regard the law as their oppressor; we should gain immensely if we could induce them to look on the law as their protector against harsh and unfair dealing on the part of their landlords. When a man improves a hillside into an arable farm, fences the land, drains it, builds a house upon it, can it be wondered at that he thinks it a grievous hardship to be evicted or to have his rent raised without any account being taken of his expenditure? Of course the tenant ought not in prudence to undertake such improvements without a written contract securing them the enjoyment of the profits of their expenditure, but as a matter of fact they do, and the competition for land renders them helpless. It has been suggested that the tenants should be allowed to remove or destroy his improvements. This suggestion was made in some able articles by Prof. Cairnes in the *Economist*,[116] but this power would not be sufficient, as in many cases the tenant could not remove his improvements. Moreover, it is a loss to the national wealth that he should remove them. But could not this provision be supplemented by another *viz*: that in all cases where the landlord has not made an express stipulation in writing to the contrary, the tenant, if evicted, should have the right to compensation? This would throw the onus on the landlord of objecting instead of leaving it to the tenant to make an express bargain, or give notice under Cardwell's act. The idea is Fortescue's not mine. I think it an excellent one. The improvements for which the tenant could claim compensation would have to be carefully specified in the Act. Some are obvious enough such as houses and draining and I would confine the Act to those which are obvious. The compensation should be settled by two arbitrators appointed by landlord and tenant respectively, and in default of their agreement by an umpire appointed by the Chairman of Quarter Sessions. Perhaps also some alteration should be made in the law of distress but this is a very controvertible point.

---

[116] John Elliot Cairnes, Professor of Political Economy, Queen's College, Galway, 1859–65; University College, London, 1866–72; authored a series of eight articles between 9 September and 28 October 1865 under the general title 'Ireland in Transition'.

I have merely sketched out my notion of the sort of measure which might be attempted, but every detail would require the most careful consideration. *Any* measure worth passing will meet with fierce opposition and unless the Government take it up in earnest would not I think have a chance of passing. For my part I feel sure it is worth while to make a strong exertion and to run some risk rather than leave matters as they are now.

Next as to the Church. To maintain it as it stands seems to me contrary both to justice and policy. There are three courses open; to reduce the establishment to dimensions proportioned to the requirements of the actual church population; to endow the Roman Catholic Church as well, or to abolish the established church. The first expedient would leave the governance of the majority of the Irish population untouched, the second would be to my mind the most statesmanlike measure and the best for Ireland, but I fear it is but too certain that the opposition of the hot Church Protestants, combined with the dissenters who object to all endowments and the Scotch Presbyterians, would render it impossible; the third seems to be the alternative most likely to succeed.[117] Fortescue suggests a Commission of Inquiry but would not that be tantamount to embracing the first expedient? If the establishment were abolished I should like to see the tithe applied in relief of poor rate, but the appropriation of the revenues is one of the hardest parts of the problem.

Lastly as to National education. I agree with Fortescue that it would be best to agree to O'Reilly's[118] motion for an enquiry. I trust the govt. will adhere firmly, as they have announced their intention to do, to the principle of united education; but some modifications especially with regard to the model schools might probably be made with advantage to the general system. I will not go into questions of railway reform which you will have fully considered or into minor matters. The Irish people have conceived great hopes from the principles which, if I may venture to say so, you so well laid down in your speech on the address,[119] and I was anxious that you should know that whilst I am daily and hourly engaged in the repugnant task of repression and punishment, I am sensible that if we wish this country to become loyal and prosperous, we must deal with some of the questions to which I have alluded.

I am sorry to say the activity of the Fenians continues quite undiminished, and I cannot undertake to say that we shall not have an outbreak in the course of the spring. I have no doubt they are preparing for it. It is a very serious state of things and tho' I hope we have taken all due precautions, I cannot but feel great uneasiness, since, do what we will, if there is an outbreak there must be individual suffering, and probably many atrocities will be committed as in /98.

---

[117] Wodehouse considered the 'reasonable Presbyterian' cleric a 'rather rare' animal. Wodehouse to deGrey, 11 February 1865, RP 43522, f. 30.

[118] Myles William Patrick O'Reilly, M.P. for Longford, 1862–79.

[119] Urging treatment of Irish questions, as nearly as possible, 'in accordance with the views and sentiments of the natives.' 3 *Hansard*, 181 (8 February 1866): 265–73.

I must add that although I hope that remedial measures might lay the foundation of a better state of things, I am sure that the old hatred of English rule fomented by the Irish in America burns too strongly for any measures to cure under a long time. It can only die out slowly; and will I fear survive the present century whatever we may do.

53. Wodehouse, Notes on Books   Viceregal Lodge,
    April 1866   Dublin
    KP1 15/K2/6

Finished 'Life of Wolfe Tone' by himself,[120] This edition contains passages struck out of the edition published in England. It is a curious book, full of interesting information about the schemes of the rebels of 98/ the Bantry Bay Expedition and the expedition in which Tone was taken.[121] The Fenians of 66/ are the children of the Jacobin United Irishmen of 98/. The same ideas, the same ends. But the 66/ conspirators are far baser than those of 98/. American rowdyism has a large share in their present character. They have the violence and the boasting of Yankees without their shrewdness or pluck.

54. Kimberley to deGrey   48 Bryanston Sq.
    9 April 1867
    RP 43522, ff. 112–13

I will not fail to present your petitions, and am very sorry to hear the cause of your not being able to present them yourself.

What a total collapse last night.[122] I can't say I really regret that the move was made as it has showed us the weakness of our position and the force of the enemy. *Sham* strength is much worse than recognized weakness.

The only sound settlement, I am more and more convinced, is household suffrage pure and simple; and we must now arrive at it before long.[123]

---

[120] *Life of Theobald Wolfe Tone, Written by Himself and Continued by his Son*, 2 vols. (Washington: Gales and Seaton, 1826).

[121] Captured with a small French fleet off the coast of Ireland on 12 October 1798. Condemned to die by hanging, he committed suicide.

[122] Forty-five Liberals either pairing or voting against Gladstone's amendment to the Derby-Disraeli reform bill. See *DD1*, pp. 299–300; Matthew, *Gladstone*, pp. 140–41.

[123] Kimberley had written to Thomas Larcom in February that 'men's minds are wholly occupied with Reform.... Nothing can be more unsatisfactory than the whole situation. Unless the H. of Commons becomes suddenly converted to good sense and patriotism things will go from bad to worse, and the result will be a great gain to the Democratic party.' 18 February 1867, LcP 7593.

55. Kimberley to Grant Duff   Bryanston Square
17 July 1867
GDP, v.3, no. 23

I shall have much pleasure in taking charge of the Tests Abolition Bill, if
I find I can appoint the 2nd reading for some day next week. I shall appoint
it if possible for Thursday .... I have seen Dodson who has promised me full
information about the Bill.[124]

56. Kimberley to deGrey   Kimberley House
25 November 1867
RP 43522, ff. 120–24

I am extremely sorry that I am unable on account of engagements which
I have already made to accept your most hospitable invitation. Besides your
excellent shooting I should have liked the opportunity for some quiet talk with
you. I am not surprised to hear that the session is mortally dull. For my part
I don't think there will be much to do, apart from the Irish and Scotch Reform
bills, but to observe, till the new Parliament meets.

We are entering I believe on a new and unquiet era of politics which will
require very wary walking, especially for those who like ourselves are liberals by
conviction, and large landowners (if I may call myself 'large').[125] Our apparent
interests as a class will come into collision with our general views, unless I am
much mistaken, to an unusual extent. I am not afraid of saying this, because
you know how strongly liberal my sympathies are. Perhaps for that very reason
I am keenly sensible of the difficulties which await us.

I am heartily glad the Govt. had the firmness to hang the three Fenians
at Manchester.[126] I think it was a great mistake not to hang the Canadian
raiders and I also think (tho' I don't blame the Govt.) that English opinion was
mistaken in demanding that Burke should not be hung.[127] If I saw anything to
be gained by lenity, I should be only too glad, but the English notion that lenity

---

[124] The Lords defeated the measure eight days later. 3 *Hansard*, 189 (25 July 1867):
75–76. See Christopher Harvie, *The Lights of Liberalism, University Liberals and the
Challenge of Democracy, 1860–86* (London: Allen Lane, 1976), pp. 88–91.

[125] Kimberley owned some 11,000 acres; Ripon twice that amount. By comparison,
the Devonshire estate comprised 200,000 acres, and Argyll's highlands some 170,000.

[126] On 23 November 1867, for the murder of a policeman. While some saw widespread
Irish sympathy as indicative of broadening support for Fenian violence, Kimberley sug-
gested that it proved only widespread hatred. The Irish, he argued, were less disposed
to violence and that 'the executions have had their share in that result.' Marginalia,
[Sigerston], *Modern Ireland*, p. 51. See R. V. Comerford, *The Fenians in Context, Irish
Politics and Society, 1848– 82* (Dublin: Wolfhound Press, 1985), pp. 148–49; and Paul
Rose's sympathetic, *The Manchester Martyrs, The Story of a Fenian Tragedy* (London:
Lawrence and Wishart, 1970).

[127] The 'Canadian raiders' were American Fenians captured in a raid on Canada in
June 1866. Michael Burke was a leader in the March rising, convicted in May 1867 and

in these cases will conciliate our Irish enemies and severity exasperate them is I believe a delusion. If you study the history of Irish conspiracies, you will find that the Irish have been frequently coerced by fear, never conciliated by lenity. There is no chance whatever of the Fenians ceasing to hate England blindly in the present generation. We may however I am convinced deter new adherents from joining them, and we *may* (at all events I would try) lay the ground for reconciliation between the disaffected Irish and English at some distant day. Meantime we shall have to deal with an alliance of the 'Red' party in England with the Fenians, but I don't feel much alarm at this. The 'Red' party is weak here, and the Householder Parliament will give the Govt. the strong backing they now want.

What I dread is the unhealthy sentiment and the hair splitting refinements which are now the fashion, and which seems to me to be fast emasculating the once rough and ready English common sense.

57. Kimberley to Raikes Currie   Kimberley House
     5 August 1868
     KP1 3/1

I have not forgotten my promise to my Aunt to send you a haunch of venison, but I find it is useless to kill in this heat, as the venison won't keep. We lost the whole of one buck on the 3rd day, and half of another tho' we began to eat it very soon. The drought here is fearful. Scarcely a drop of rain since May 17! The grass, burnt brown, will I fear die entirely. The roots except a few mangel have not come up. Stock is quite unsaleable. The wheat harvest, now over, is very good; barley but indifferent; altogether the prospects of the farms very unpromising. I have all my lambs on hand, and am likely to have them. Young trees are dying generally. All this I naturally ascribe to a Tory Govt.!

E.W.[128] and R. Gurdon[129] have good prospects but a hard contest before them, and no one can say what Yarmouth with a fourth of the constituency may do.[130] I still adhere to my opinion that it is very uncertain whether Dizzy will be turned out. We shall have a majority no doubt, but whether they will support Gladstone in an attempt to force out the ministry I much doubt. Dizzy will have no hesitation in throwing over the Irish Church, and I shall not be surprised, if he carries enough of his own party, and of ours with him to enable him to

sentenced to death, whose sentence was reduced, on a technicality, to life imprisonment. Ó'Broin, *Fenian Fever*, pp. 177–80.

[128] Edmond Wodehouse, Kimberley's cousin and official private secretary, 1864–66; 1868–74.

[129] Robert Thornagh Gurdon, Kimberley's cousin.

[130] Both unsuccessfully contested North Norfolk for the Liberals, the Conservative candidates polling 2630 and 2563 votes, Wodehouse polling 2235 and Gurdon 2088. Both later became Liberal Unionists.

defy his enemies. The former will pardon him for the sake of office, the latter for their own purposes, arguing that he will be able to *carry* Radical measures which Gladstone can only pass through the H. of Commons.

If the moderate Liberals and moderate Tories too knew their own interests they would strain every nerve to put an honest man in the chief place; but they have neither earnestness nor energy nor pluck, and they will be ground to pieces in the end.

On the other hand there is the chance that warm from the elections a sufficient number of Liberals may unite at once in a want of confidence vote.

Florence is going to Cromer on the 17th, and I am thinking of going with Johnny[131] to Vienna.

58. Kimberley to Raikes Currie   24 Upper Brook St.
    8 December 1868
    KP1 3/1

Yesterday morning I received a telegram telling me that Gladstone wished to see me. I saw him in the afternoon, and he offered me the Privy Seal which I accepted. I am very much pleased at being at last in the Cabinet, and tho' the office itself is nothing, it puts me well on the road to promotion when the occasion offers.

Nothing could be handsomer than the terms in which the offer was made. Gladstone said I was perfectly fit for any of the more important offices, and that the number of other competitors was the only obstacle to my going higher.[132] The newspapers made me President of the Council, but with a colleague in the HC nominally subordinate but really more than an equal, the position is one I don't particularly covet.

At all events I shall now for once enjoy the 'otium cum dignitate'. I send you no news, as the 'Times' of this morning contains the latest intelligence. We are to be sworn in tomorrow at Windsor.

---

[131] His eldest son.

[132] According to Gladstone, he could give no more important offices to peers, prompting Kimberley's lament: 'What an obstacle it is to success in public life to be in the House of Lords!' *KJ*, p. 1. However, when Fortescue complained at being passed over in favour of Kimberley in the Colonial Office appointment of 1870, Gladstone argued that it was plain that the 'C. Secship should go to a Peer.' Gladstone to Granville, 29 June 1870, in Ramm, *Gladstone-Granville Corresp. 1*, 1:103–04.

3
The Charmed Circle

Having brought Kimberley into the Cabinet as Privy Seal in December 1868, Gladstone immediately set him to work on Irish policy, which was to be his principal occupation for eighteen months. He served on Cabinet committees studying Irish land, church and disturbance questions, and helped in drafting measures from the results, until Clarendon's death and Granville's transfer to the Foreign Office led to his appointment as Colonial Secretary on 6 July 1870.

Kimberley continued Granville's policy of withdrawing British troops and promoting self-government and fiscal responsibility in the settlement colonies, and expanded administrative reorganization of the Colonial Office. He reversed almost a decade of colonial retrenchment by sanctioning the annexation of Griqualand West, refusing further negotiations on the exchange of the Gambia, waging war on the invading Ashanti on the Gold Coast, and laying the foundation for British annexations in Fiji and the Malay Peninsula. While Kimberley's Cabinet responsibilities were primarily Irish and colonial, he continued to study the international questions which had occupied his professional career from the early 1850s. By the mid-1870s his competence in dealing with colonial, foreign and Irish problems was widely recognized, guaranteeing his claim to high office in future Liberal governments.

The Liberal defeat of February of 1874 brought welcome rest to Kimberley, who had been preoccupied, professionally since the summer of 1873 with the Ashanti invasion, and personally since 1871 with the financial irresponsibility of his elder son and the serious illness of his younger son. During Disraeli's ministry he attended shadow cabinets during sessions and spoke on foreign policy questions in the Lords, but otherwise retired to private life, reading widely, hunting and managing his estates in Cornwall and Norfolk, which, by 1879, were beginning to feel the effects of agricultural depression.

59. Kimberley to Spencer   Kimberley House
   12 January 1869
   SP K34

Private

   I think you are very fortunate in securing Roundell. I know him a little, and as far as I can judge, you could not have a better man[1] ....

I am unable to answer you as to the Registrarships. The whole question of patronage is in an uncertain position, as between the Ld. Lt. and the Chief Secretary. Nominally almost everything is in the gift of the Ld. Lt.; practically the Chief Secretary takes a large share of it. I hate having to give away places, and therefore did not care much what the Chief Secretary appropriated to himself. I think my policy was to leave to the C. S. all the minor appointments which in England would be disposed of by the Secretary to the Treasury. The Chief. Secy. is in constant communication with the Irish members and is best able to attend to their wishes. The more important appointments were a matter of consultation between the C. Secy. and me. The stipendiary magistrates we appointed alternately.

The question of the release of the Fenian prisoners is a very serious one.[2] It must of course come before the Cabinet, and I do not wish you to regard my opinions now given as my final opinions. At present I am decidedly adverse to their [Fenian prisoners] release. Nothing whatever will I believe be gained with the disloyal who will attribute their release entirely to fear and weakness; whilst all loyal Irishmen will be intensely disgusted and discouraged. I am convinced that a calm, impartial, and unbending justice is the only policy which in the long run answers with Irishmen. Even the men who clamour loudest, *respect* only the man who pays no attention to the clamour. They are so carried away with the feelings of the moment that they will ask for concessions which in calmer reflexion they themselves would condemn as imprudent.

For the instant some popularity might be gained by releasing the prisoners, but this popularity would not last three months. It will be wiser to content ourselves with not reversing the suspension of the Habeas Corpus Act, and to wait to see what the effect of that is. My remarks are directed against a general or extensive amnesty; but it is possible that a few prisoners (those who are old and in ill health or in favour of whom some mitigating circumstances can be urged,) might be properly released. I should be disposed to receive the Memorials if *loyally worded*. I don't see on what ground petitions for mercy can be rejected without being heard.

Pray forgive me if in the strictest confidence I venture to caution you against the atmosphere of intrigues and 'impulsive' statements into which you are about to launch. You and I are Englishmen and probably feel alike on most of these questions. I shall be surprised if you don't soon begin to fancy yourself, as I did, unusually cold-blooded, when you find how much you differ from the warmer blooded creatures with whom you will come into contact. I am vain enough to think, that the reason why Englishmen have governed Ireland for centuries, is

---

[1] Charles Savile Roundell (1827–1906), as private secretary. Kimberley probably had worked with him in the Tests repeal campaign of 1866–67. See letter 55 and note, herein.

[2] See Comerford, *Fenians in Context*, pp. 158–59.

just that coolness which we possess, and Irishmen do not as a rule.

Again asking you not to regard my advice as impertinent, and wishing you all possible success.

60. Kimberley Memorandum
18 February 1869
GP 44224, f. 56

I am inclined to think it would be wise to hold out greater inducements to commutation than are at present contemplated. Why not adopt the suggestion of the Dean of Cashel[3] that 'every incumbent should have a right within limited time to demand half the value of his life income in a lump sum, or an annuity of three fifths of his life income and be released thenceforward from all his duties as a clergyman'?

61. Kimberley Memorandum
4 April 1869
CfP DD/SH 324/CP1/44, C/1189

Ld. Clanricarde's bill[4] has some good points in it, and in the whole I believe it to be as Granville says, unobjectionable as far as it goes. But it does not really touch the questions involved in the 'tenant right' agitation, and I doubt whether if passed it would do anything to allay that agitation. Nor do I think it would have the slightest chance of being accepted by the Irish Liberal members as a settlement.

In the Committee on the bill last year Lord Grey moved a report strongly condemning all attempts to go beyond the provisions of the bill. I proposed to omit the controversial part of Ld. Grey's report, but was beaten by 9 to 5, Lords Devon, Clarendon, Bessborough and Dufferin voting with me.

Subsequently however the majority deserted Ld. Grey, and thought it more prudent to agree to a report simply recommending the bill to the House and describing its provisions. I drew up this report, which was carried unanimously.

As this report states that 'the Committee recommend that the Bill as now amended should be adopted by the House', I cannot of course now oppose the bill, and Clarendon, and Dufferin, who concurred in the report, are in the same position as myself. But I have always said, publickly and privately, that I thought the bill insufficient.

[3] J. C. McDonnell.
[4] Hubert George De Burgh Canning, second Marquess and fifteenth Earl of Clanricarde (1832–1916), Liberal M.P. County Galway, 1867–71; proposed a limited measure for substituting a 'written contract in cases of parole tenure'. For a full discussion, see E. D. Steele, *Irish Land and British Politics, Tenant Right and Nationality, 1865–70* (London: Cambridge University Press, 1974), pp. 83–87.

It seems to me best not to oppose the bill in the Lords, saying however that we regard it as insufficient, and in the Commons either to propose amendments or the rejection of the bill on the ground of its incompleteness, promising a bill next year.

[*Signed*] Mr. Fortescue [n.d.]
WEG, April 5

62. **Kimberley to Raikes Currie**   48 Bryanston Sq.
    16 July 1869
    KP1 3/1

I have desired a haunch of a very fine buck just killed to be sent to you. I have heard frequently from my cousins[5] and am glad to know you are well.

Our great political work verges on its conclusion. We don't know what the opposition will do in the Lords but I hardly think they can be foolhardy enough to risk the bill.[6]

Apart from the merit of the questions raised, the great feature of the Lord's doing is the open revolt of the Whig Lords against an advanced Liberal Govt. This will give trouble hereafter. Not only the votes but the feeling of the Lords is utterly averse to us. But the country is unmistakeably with us.

A whig regime and Household suffrage are incompatible.

63. **Kimberley to Clarendon**   Kimberley House
    1 October 1869
    ClP dep. c.499, ff. 163–65

Private

I rejoice to see by your speech at an agricultural meeting[7] that you are returned — better, I infer, for Wiesbaden. Your protest against the wild doctrines which fill the newspapers, on the Irish land question gave me particular satisfaction.

Each day I have read with increasing disgust the utterances of the patriots over the water, who exhort us to be bold, and confiscate every landlord's property without mercy. We shall need some courage, but I trust it will be exercised in withstanding, not promoting these schemes.

There are, as you justly said, real grievances to be redressed; but the sooner the Irish peasants know that we don't mean to hand over to them the *ownership* of the land the better.[8] Short of that we may have to go a long way, and we

---

[5] Currie's sons: Bertram, Maynard, George, and Philip.
[6] Irish Church Bill; see Morley, *Life of Gladstone*, 2: 270–80; *KJ*, pp. 6–7.
[7] At Watford.
[8] In sending his memorandum on the land question to Spencer, Kimberley contended similarly that nothing 'short of turning the landlord into a mere owner of a rent charge' would satisfy the Irish tenants. 29 November 1869, SP K110.

have the pleasure to know that nothing we can do will satisfy any mortal being in Ireland.

64. Kimberley to Gladstone
    17 December 1869
    GP 44224, ff. 71–75

On thinking over what passed today, I feel so much doubt on two points that I wish to state to you at once what occurs to me whilst the discussion is still fresh in my mind.

The first point is the right of a landlord to prohibit his tenant from executing any particular work. I call it 'work' advisedly instead of improvement because the word improvement seems to be to beg the question. I think on principle it is a very strong interference with the rights of property to enact that a landlord shall not have full power to prohibit any work to which he objects. In allowing the tenant compensation for improvements to which the landlord has not objected, we proceed on this sound basis, namely, that if the landlord tacitly acquiesces in the expenditure of money by the tenant, equity requires that the tenant if evicted shall be compensated. But if the landlord in letting the land forbids the tenant to do any particular thing, he is only exercising one of the primary rights of ownership and I do not see on what ground a tenant hiring on such conditions can complain of injury. I admit the force of the argument that a man like Ld. Leitrim[9] *might* schedule in his agreements every possible improvement and prohibit his tenants from doing anything which he might be called upon to pay for; but ought we to depart from sound principle in order to provide for very extreme cases? To provide as you propose that the landlord may bar improvement which would be inconsistent with the general advantage of his estate, would deprive the landlord of the right to determine what is for his own advantage, and place him at the mercy of his tenant and the court which might try the case; and he would never know with any certainty what his position was. Such a principle if extended to England and Scotland would deprive owners of a right most valuable (as I think) to the *good* landlord, and it is obviously a principle which might easily cross the channel. An agreement which on the face of it forbade the tenant to make necessary improvements is one which even in Ireland it would be very difficult to induce a tenant to sign, and unless the agreement were in writing, and part of the conditions of hiring, I would give no effect to it in law. You will see from what I have thus I fear very imperfectly expressed that I have come back on reflexion to Fortescue's view, which is the same as that embodied in the bill of 1866.

---

[9] William Sydney Clements, third Earl of Leitrim (1806–78), owned 55,000 acres in county Donegal, where he was eventually murdered. Kimberley had, during his viceroyalty, called Leitrim the 'curse of that part of this county'. Wodehouse to deGrey, 11 February 1865, RP 43522, f. 31.

If I am not mistaken the point is one of great importance and I think it should be carefully re-considered when we have the bill before us.

The other point is restriction of compensation for 'disturbance' outside custom, to tenancies created after the passing of the bill. I cannot see how this can be done without practically nullifying the bill as to all tenants who cannot prove some kind of custom. A tenancy from year to year is a continuing tenancy. It is subject to determination on six months notice but failing this notice, it has no termination. If then we exclude all existing tenancies from year to year from the operation of the act where no custom can be proved, I fear we shall leave outside the act a considerable number of tenants whose discontent will be greatly aggravated by the more fortunate lot of the other tenants. I am aware that this point is left undecided, but I wished to make these few observations upon it.

Pray don't think I am inclined to be impracticable. Far from desiring to object, I am earnestly desirous to support you in settling this question, but the subject causes me so much anxiety that you must excuse me for disburthening my mind. Pray don't answer me.

65. Kimberley to Gladstone   Travellers' Club
    12 March 1870
    GP 44224, ff. 77–79

I mentioned to the Cabinet your proposal that I should see Mr. Bright,[10] (or Mrs. Bright) for the purpose of letting him know our intended legislation for the repression of crime in Ireland.

The general (I think, unanimous) opinion was that it was better I should not go. It was argued that in his present condition it would not be fair to make him responsible for the measure in any way, that if he were made acquainted with its general substance, he would be in some degree responsible; that if he refused his assent, the position of the Govt. would be greatly embarrassed, also that a communication of this kind might have a prejudicial effect on his health. I must add that to my own judgement these reasons seem conclusive.

I should have preferred to tell you what passed by word of mouth, but as I have not been able to find you this afternoon, I write a line instead. If I do not hear from you tomorrow morning I shall assume that I am not to go to Norwood.

---

[10] John Bright (1811–99), Quaker M.P. for Birmingham, 1857–89, and President of the Board of Trade. On Bright's breakdown of March which forced his temporary retirement, see Keith Robbins, *John Bright* (London: Routledge and Kegan Paul, 1979), pp. 208–10.

66. Kimberley to Raikes Currie   Kimberley House
     15 April 1870
     KP1 3/1

.... We get on very unsatisfactorily with business this session. The dissensions sure to arise in so large a Liberal majority have begun to show themselves, and Bright is a great loss. I hear he is really better. Dizzy[11] is playing the game of obstruction. He does not care a straw for the merit or demerits of our measures. His influence with his party in the Commons is great and most mischievous to the country. Roundell Palmer[12] is our most dangerous opponent on the Land Bill. I greatly fear he may seriously mutilate the Bill. He is perfectly honest, and thoroughly English (that is ignorant) in his views about Ireland. It is strange that Englishmen can never be convinced that it is worse than useless to force English ideas on Ireland.[13] They expect too that the habits and temper of a nation are to be changed at once by Acts of Parliament. Laws however good can only very slowly mould national character. It is idle to expect much change in less than a generation. I hope you will pay Maynard and us a visit when he is installed.[14]

67. Kimberley to Raikes Currie   48 Bryanston Sq.
     23 July 1870
     KP 3/1

Private

I sent you a message of thanks through Edith for your kind letter. I did not need your note to assure me of your sympathy.[15] I know I always have it, and few things cheer me more in the hard struggle of life than that knowledge.

I have been so overwhelmed with work that I have not had a moment before to write to you.[16] But I begin to feel myself in the saddle, and am getting

[11] Benjamin Disraeli (1804–81), Conservative Prime Minister, 1868, 1874–80.

[12] Roundell Palmer, first Earl of Selborne (1812–95), entered parliament as a Conservative in 1847, gradually moving into the Liberal camp; Lord Chancellor, 1872–74, 1880–85.

[13] On an early source of this conviction, see the first two volumes of Archibald Alison's *History of Europe during the French Revolution*, which much impressed Kimberley when he read it in 1848. KP1 15/K2/6, p. 10; KP1 15/K2/7, pp. 25–27.

[14] Maynard Wodehouse Currie, son of Raikes Currie, who was being installed as Rector of Barnham Broom. Kimberley, patron of the living, wrote that the parsonage was good and the only drawbacks those 'common to Norfolk, that it is an out of the way corner of the world, and very cold in Spring....' Kimberley to Raikes Currie, 15 April 1870, KP 3/1.

[15] Probably related to Lord Wodehouse's financial irregularities, which led to his bankruptcy. In May 1870 Kimberley paid £11,000 in debts incurred by his son, principally at the racecourse. KP6 MS.eng.e.2792, p. 64; *KJ*, p. 35.

[16] Following his transfer to the Colonial Office, 6 July 1870. See *KJ*, p. 16.

my work under command. It is much more interesting and absorbing than I expected.

Pray read what I said last night about Canada.[17] The tremendous crisis on the Continent[18] naturally causes little attention to be given to colonial matters. So much the better. Our relations with the colonies will be all the better for being 'let alone' a little according to Melbourne's famous maxim.[19]

Some of my newspaper critics think my only talent is to get up Blue Books, but they will find themselves wrong there. I have a heart for the greatness of my country and I hope a cool head as well. Forgive this boasting. It is only to you. But there are times when 'sursum corda' is more than a mere sentiment.

Is not the patriotism of the Germans superb?

68. Kimberley to Henry Wodehouse	Kimberley House
    14 September 1870
    KP1 15/K2/18

I suppose you are not yet besieged,[20] and that at all events a letter will reach you. What a wonderful state of things you must be living in. Our newspapers seem to think now that Paris will really be defended, but I put no sort of trust in what they say, as they all write from some strongly biassed point of view. *If the fervour of revolution can really be got up to boiling point something might yet I suppose be done to prolong the struggle, and time is clearly in favour of France.* It is evidently the interest of all mankind that the Germans should receive some kind of check sufficient to induce them to consent to reasonable terms of peace. If the whole business were not so profoundly sad, it would be amusing to see how John Bull chafes under his policy of non-intervention, a wise policy, but one by no means suited to his temperament except when there is nothing with which he cares to meddle. It is lucky for Europe we are not armed to the teeth like the Continental powers....

[17] Arguing that its defence should 'to a very large extent' be left to Canadians. 3 *Hansard*, 203 (22 July 1870): 717. Six weeks later Kimberley wrote to the Governor-General: 'When I remember how long the Hudson's Bay Cy., with no force at their back, managed to keep the territory quiet, I can't believe that the Canadians with common prudence may not establish themselves firmly without quarrelling with the inhabitants white or red.' Kimberley to Young, 19 September 1870, KP4 A-314, PC/A/47.

[18] France having declared war on Prussia, 19 July 1870.

[19] A quarter-of-a-century later, a writer for the *Spectator* remarked that Melbourne was 'still remembered almost as much for his humour' as for his political ability. 'How often has his favourite though rather chilling question, "Can't you leave it alone?" been quoted as the English form of Talleyrand's political maxim, "Surtout, point de zèle," and how often has it not been favourably contrasted with Mr. Gladstone's superheated political enthusiasm?' 4 May 1895, p. 603.

[20] In Paris, where Wodehouse was serving as first secretary of the British legation. See *Letters from the Honourable Henry Wodehouse, 1870–71*, intro. Philip Currie (London: Privately Printed, 1874).

69. Kimberley to Cardwell[21]   Kimberley House
23 October 1870
CdP 30/48/31, ff. 77–78

I have read the Red River despatches, and my reluctance to assent to your proposals is, I confess, not thereby diminished.[22] Lindsay, and Wolseley are however settled as you have told them.[23] Colonel Fielden[24] as reward is concerned fairly deserves to be C. M. G. The other two Colonels[25] I should have been glad to have omitted, but as you press them so strongly I suppose I must give way. I admit it is difficult to leave one of them out if either is made. Assistant Controller Irvine[26] really seems to have distinguished himself. But my stomach rises at Surgeon Major Young, who made such excellent preparations for sick and wounded, if there had been any. Surely you will agree to leave him out.[27] Captain Huyshe[28] is also mentioned by Wolseley but left out, so you have a precedent.

70. Kimberley Memorandum
23 January 1871
GP 44760, f. 4

I think if this state of things continues in Westmeath, we ought to ask power

---

[21] Edward Cardwell (1813–86), Secretary of State for War, 1868–74.

[22] Recommending honours for troops involved in suppressing rebellious French-speaking citizens in the newly incorporated Canadian province of Manitoba. Between May 5 and August 24, Col. Garnet Wolseley (1833–1913) led an altogether successful expedition, particularly so by Liberal standards. According to Byron Farwell, 'it accomplished its objectives, not a life had been lost, it had exercised the troops, several good officers had gained invaluable experience, and it had not cost much money.' *Queen Victoria's Little Wars* (New York: Norton, 1972), p. 184. Wolseley had written on August 9 that there were no sick and that he had never seen the men 'looking healthier or in better spirits.' Wolseley despatch, 9 August 1870, in Young to Kimberley, 13 September 1870, CO42/688. See too WO 32/7585, particularly Wolseley's despatch of 26 September 1870. For a thorough study of the expedition, see George F.G. Stanley, *Toil and Trouble: Military Expeditions to Red River* (Toronto: Dundurn Press, 1989).

[23] Lieut.-Gen. James Lindsay, Commander in British North America, for the K. C. M. G.; Wolseley for the C. B. See Duke of Cambridge to Cardwell, 23 October 1870, CdP 30/48/3/14.

[24] Lieut.-Col. R.F. Fielden, Organiser of the two battalions of Canadian militia.

[25] Lt. Col. J.C. McNeill, secretary to the Governor-General; and Lt. Col. W.F. Bolton, senior British officer at Sault Ste. Marie.

[26] Matthew Bell Irvine.

[27] Kimberley here cites Wolseley's despatch, in which the commander had written that his 'Principal Medical Officer, made the fullest arrangements for the case of the sick and wounded (had there been any)....' On Kimberley's 'difficulty' about the honours, see Cardwell to the Duke of Cambridge, 21, 25 October 1870, CdP 30/48/3/14. Cf. letter 108, herein.

[28] Capt. G.L. Huyshe, Staff Officer to Wolseley.

from Parliament to suspend the Habeas Corpus Act in that county and the adjoining districts.[29]

[*Argyll minute*, n.d.] I quite agree.

[*Halifax minute*, n.d.] I think we should be unjustifiable if we hesitated to apply the most stringent measures of repression to such a state of things as described in Lord Spencer's letter.

71. Kimberley Memorandum
    24 January 1871
    GP 44224, f. 109

The expulsion of the Athanasian Creed from the Prayer Book would be most agreeable to my own feelings and wishes; but I agree with Lord de Grey that if we begin to pull to pieces the Prayer Book, we shall run great risk of pulling down the established Church.

72. Kimberley to de Grey   48 Bryanston Sq.
    20 February 1871
    RP 43522, ff. 180–84

Private

I hope this letter will find you comfortably installed in Washington.[30] Cardwell's army scheme[31] has been very well recd. The position of Childers and the Admiralty is unpleasant. Somerset made a fierce attack on him in the H of Lords and we were obliged to agree to a committee, which we had no power to resist.[32] For the rest Parliament is quiet. Gladstone made some imprudent statements in the HC about the Treaty of 1856 and Palmerston's and Clarendon's opinions thereupon.[33] If he does not take care, he will get us into trouble

---

[29] See Spencer to Gladstone, 10 January 1871, GP 44307, f. 1. See too J.P. Parry, *Democracy and Religion: Gladstone and the Liberal Party, 1867–1875*, (Cambridge: Cambridge University Press, 1986), pp. 317–18.

[30] As a British representative to the Anglo-American High Commission for settlement of the Alabama claims dispute.

[31] The Army Regulation Bill abolishing purchase of commissions and introducing short-term enlistment had been presented to Parliament on February 16. See Edward M. Spiers, *The Late Victorian Army, 1868–1902* (Manchester: Manchester University Press, 1992), chap. 1.

[32] The Duke of Somerset, former First Lord of the Admiralty (1859–66), moved that a committee of inquiry be formed to review 'changes in its constitution.' When Halifax requested delay because of Childers' illness, Somerset retorted that 'other people have feelings as well as [Childers].' 3 *Hansard*, 204 (11 February 1871): 295–304.

[33] In the address to the Queen, Gladstone recounted that he had 'been told' that Clarendon 'never attached value' to the neutralization of the Black Sea and that Palmerston considered it only a temporary arrangement. 3 *Hansard*, 204 (9 February 1871): 104–05.

about the Black Sea question. The country I believe does not agree with him ℚ
in his ultra-pacific, anti-Turkish policy. In the cabinet last Saturday, he was in
a state of great excitement about the cession of Alsace and Lorraine, harking
back to the proposal we rejected in the autumn to protest against the transfer
of territory without the consent of the inhabitants.[34] But the cabinet did not go
with him. However after much discussion agreed to ask Russia whether 'if we
receive an appeal from France as to the terms of peace she will consider such
appeal in common with us and the other neutrals.'[35] This I expect Russia will
decline civilly.

We also spent a great deal of time discussing Hartington's proposal to suspend the Habeas C. Act in Westmeath. Gladstone and Granville made a stout
resistance and it ended in our agreeing to propose a Secret Committee of the
H of Commons to inquire into Ribbonism in Westmeath, &c. O'Hagan[36] is for
this and I think it is perhaps the best course, as we were told by the stipendiary
magistrate of the worst district, whom we had over to consult, that the act may
have to be suspended for two or three years, and afterwards from time to time to
do real good, and it is not easy to produce in a mere speech evidence necessary
to justify so extreme a measure....

The news today by tel. from Canada shows, I fear, that we shall have trouble
in that quarter.[37] But of course we can't allow Canada to dictate to us, however ready we may be to give her all reasonable support. Still I am not sure
that Canadian bumptiousness may not be a convenient set off against Yankee
buncomb. It will show the U.S. that they can't have everything their own way
in North America, and that we are the promoters of moderate counsels.

[*Postscript*] Stork's return for Ripon is an excellent stroke of business.[38]

---

73. Kimberley to Raikes Currie   48 Bryanston Sq.
     10 May 1871
     KP1 3/1

A great calamity has alas! befallen us in the sudden and alarming illness
of dear Army. He went to school at Hendon the week before last and on last
Thursday he was seized with an illness commencing with acute ear-ache, and
a terrible convulsive attack lasting three hours. Florence brought him home in

---

[34] Kimberley's immediate reaction to the proceedings of this Cabinet were carefully
modified in preparing his journal for possible publication. Contrast *KJ*, p. 20 with his
original journal entry, KP6 MS.eng.e.2792, pp. 122–24.

[35] See *Gladstone Diaries*, 7:450.

[36] Thomas O'Hagan, Lord Chancellor of Ireland.

[37] See Lisgar's Secret and Confidential telegram noting his council's deprecation of
Rose as a commissioner on the Alabama claims enquiry, because his firm 'depends on
the American Government.' Supplemental Correspondence/Canada 1871, CO537/102, f.
38.

[38] Sir Henry Knight Stork, Major-General from 1862 and M.P. for Ripon, 1871–74.

the carriage after the fit. Since then he has had several fits tho' not so violent. Farre[39] attends him and we have had a consultation with Sir Wm. Jenner.[40] They think it a very grave case, tho' they have hopes of recovery. The disease is in the membrane of the brain, and the spinal cord. He cannot sit up and has partially lost power over his legs. His brain is entirely unaffected, even during the fits. The malady is connected with an attack (but without fits) which he had when three years old, which gave us then great anxiety. It is *conjectured* that it is connected with derangement of his digestive organs, and over excited nerves. Today he seems a little better but we dare not hope much yet. Need I say that I fear all hopes of our happy visit to you are gone.

It was indeed with an aching heart that I sat thro' seven hours debate on the Tests Bill. I am glad you like my reply to Salisbury.[41] I was very ill reported, but I think the reply really was successful. A kind of desperation stirred me up more than usual.

[*Postscript*] The doctors are *certain* it is not epilepsy.

74. Kimberley to Gladstone   Colonial Office
    28 June 1871
    GP 44224, ff. 154–170

Private

After reading the mem: of your conversation with the Queen on the subject of the Irish Govt.,[42] it occurred to me that it would be convenient that I should put my ideas on paper. I am, as I said in Cabinet, decidedly in favour of abolishing the Ld. Lt. It does not seem to me to command respect as regards its ceremonial duties, and as an executive office the disadvantages of maintaining it are in my opinion greater than the advantages.[43]

The advantages are that in the absence of the Chief Secretary, there is a political head of the local administration who on an emergency can give orders,

---

[39] Probably Frederic Farre, physician to the Royal London Ophthalmic Hospital.

[40] Sir William Jenner, physician to University College Hospital, 1854-76; established separate identities of typhus and typhoid fevers.

[41] Salisbury's amendment, requiring university faculty to subscribe to the test of teaching nothing 'contrary to the teaching or divine authority of the Holy Scripture', prompted Kimberley to argue that such a test was ambiguous, unenforceable, and unnecessary. 'I do not believe in hothouse religion. I believe men are fortified by the frank and careful study of all the best thinkers on all sides, and I have sufficient confidence in the truth and vigour of religion to think that, at all events, the majority...will in the afterlife bear testimony to the soundness of the principles of Christianity.' 3 *Hansard*, 206 (8 May 1871): 349–50. Cf. Kimberley's Eighty Club speech of 1898, still combatting Salisbury's 'clericalism'. *Eighty Club Yearbook, 1899*, 26 February 1898, pp. 20–21.

[42] *Gladstone Diaries*, 7:514–16.

[43] Kimberley had long held this opinion. See his letter to Palmerston accepting the Viceroyalty, 27 September 1864, PP GC/WO/2/1.

and that from constant residence in Ireland and intercourse with the Irish, the Lord Lieut. is to some extent the representative and exponent of Irish feelings and opinions. The disadvantages to my mind are these. The existence of a Viceroy keeps up the notion that the Govt. of Ireland is separate from the Govt. of the rest of the Kingdom, and that Ireland is in some sort of dependency upon Great Britain.

It interferes with the unity of the administration. If the Lord Lieut. is a man of considerable personal weight, and political position, he will naturally exercise a great influence in the Irish Govt.; but the presence of the Chief Secretary in the Cabinet really places the Ld. Lt. in a subordinate position. Hence when you have an active Lord Lieut., the Chief Secretary has been often excluded from the Cabinet. I remember Lord Clarendon telling me, when I was appointed Lord Lt., that he never would have consented to hold the office with his Chief Secretary in the Cabinet. But I think it essential that the Irish Govt. should be represented in the Cabinet, and that the Cabinet Minister entrusted with this important office should have as regards his own department supreme and undivided authority and responsibility.

If measures are adopted by the Cabinet on the recommendations of the Lord Lieutenant, they are accepted without the opportunity of hearing the Ld. Lieuts. reasons and discussing them with him. The Chief Secretary, however well he may work with his nominal Chief, cannot be an adequate exponent of his views. Moreover if the Lord Lieut. has some better opportunities of gauging local feeling in Ireland, he has much worse opportunities of knowing the views of the Irish members, and the opinions of parliamentary men. A Secretary of State for Ireland, residing in Ireland when Parlt. is not sitting, would obtain a far more complete knowledge of the whole subject and the more so that he would not be hampered by the absurd ceremonies of the Lord Lieutenancy.[44]

An objection is made to the change on the ground that when the Irish Secretary was attending Parliament, the business would fall into the hands of the Under Secretary. But to a large extent this is the case already. I don't know how Lord Spencer manages the business, but I certainly found that it had been the custom of those who preceded me to leave the business very much to the Under Secretary. I believe I went much more into the details than was usual, but still I had not the same constant control over the office which the head of an ordinary department has. It was always a question how far the Chief Secy. must be consulted. In short there are two kings of Brentford, and all the inconveniences of divided rule; and the Under Secretary is in the proverbial difficulty of having two masters.

In the Fenian affair I practically passed over the Chief Secretary altogether. Peel with great good sense and good feeling acquiesced in this, but if he had chosen to kick, the greatest embarrassment must have resulted, probably dissen-

---

[44] See letter 43, herein.

sion which would have been fatal to the swift and secret action which enabled us to paralyse the rebellious party. In an emergency there would be no difficulty in the Secy. of State going to Ireland during the session. In all this I think we agree, but as I know many persons have other opinions, I thought it might be useful to state the arguments pro and con.

Now as to the residence of the P. of Wales in Ireland. I think it would be useful that he should discharge the Court ceremonial duties now performed by the Viceroy. This he could easily do by residing in Dublin for a couple of months at the beginning of the year, say from the beginning or middle of January till St. Patrick's day. He could hold levees and drawing rooms and attend public dinners and important gatherings of societies, &c. But (and this is the point where I think we do not quite agree), I should fear great inconvenience if HRH were to take part in the actual administration. Ireland is full of intrigues, and flatterers, and a clique would be sure to gather round the Prince, and endeavour to make use of him for the purpose of thwarting the responsible advisers of the Crown. To some extent this evil would be unavoidable, but if it were known that the Prince took an active share in business, this evil would be greatly aggravated, however prudently he might conduct himself.

Of course my view is not inconsistent with the Secretary of State giving to the Prince information of what was going on, and in this way H.R.H. himself might acquire much useful knowledge of affairs, and might by using his knowledge judiciously guide himself in public speeches, and conversation with important men in such a manner as to strengthen the authority of the Crown and of the executive Govt., but I should strongly deprecate any ostensible and avowed interference on his part in the actual business of Government. Perhaps an exception might be made as to the Privy Council. The business of the Privy Council is chiefly formal, and it is perfectly understood that the Council is not to oppose the measures of the responsible Minister. At the same time it must be remembered that in the eyes of the public the functions of the Privy Council have a certain importance.

I think Hartington was quite right in pointing out that we must carefully consider the probable effects of the abolition of the Lord Lieutenancy on the Home Rule agitation. I see nothing in that agitation which should deter us from proceeding, even if the measure should be regarded by the agitators as a direct challenge. This home rule agitation is merely one of the phases of the anti English feeling which has prevailed in Ireland for centuries. Sometimes this feeling takes the form of an appeal to physical force, sometimes it clothes itself in the garb of peaceful and constitutional agitation, but it is at bottom one and the same. The volunteer movement in 1783 was the peaceful form; stimulated by the French revolution that movement ended in the rebellion of 1798. When the country began to recover from the exhaustion caused by the rebellion, 'peaceful' agitation recommenced, culminating in O'Connell's repeal movement.[45] The hollowness of that becoming apparent, and revolution in Europe stirring up men's passions, the 'physical force' men under Smith O'Brien came to the front.[46] As soon as Ireland began to breath again after the famine, the agitators reared their heads, and the movement terminated in the Fenian outbreak, the American Fenians giving the agitators the impulse to open rebellion.

Now that the Fenians are out of the running, the 'peaceful' phase reappears. Our healing measures cannot have their full effect for many years, and in the interval we shall have to deal with the old disaffection in one shape or other. Persuaded as I am that in no circumstances whatever should England permit the withdrawal of Ireland from its connexion with her, that we must treat the question of separation as the North did the question of breaking up the American union, I should not hesitate to meet the Home Rule agitation by a measure for a closer administrative connexion between the two countries.[47]

75. Kimberley to Dodson   Kimberley House
     4 September 1871
     MBP

.... The task you have undertaken of defending the Govt. is difficult not merely because no doubt we have made mistakes, but because there is an un- reasoning cry against us. In the main if we had to begin the session over again, I don't think we would very differently. What could we have done about the army? In the face of the absurdly panic struck feeling which prevailed last autumn and winter and which continued when the session began, we could not avoid increased army estimates, nor altho' I think the panic utterly despicable, am I of the opinion that we were wrong in proposing a moderate increase. An army without artillery is powerless and we had only 180 field guns, sufficient for 60,000 men at most. Now we have over 300 guns. Fortifications without guns are useless; we took a large vote for arming them. The Belgian treaty[48] which the country approved, might at any time involve us in war. We augmented the infantry by 20,000 men, which would have enabled us to send respectable aid to Antwerp. We also made up the Cavalry to a number proportionate to the other augmentations. I see nothing to regret in all this. But we deeply offended

---

[45] Daniel O'Connell, leading force behind Catholic emancipation in the 1820s and attempts to repeal the Union in the 1830s and 1840s; averse to bloodshed, utilizing massive peaceful protest instead.

[46] William Smith O'Brien, ardent repealer who joined Young Irelanders and led an abortive rising in 1848.

[47] This letter, excepting the final sentence, was circulated in the Cabinet. J. L. Ham- mond, *Gladstone and the Irish Nation* (London: Longmans, Green and Co., 1938), p. 116. See Spencer's memorandum in response, *Red Earl*, 1: 93–95.

[48] Actually two treaties with France and Prussia, 9 and 11 August 1870, guaranteeing Belgian neutrality during the Franco-Prussian War.

the radicals by our increased estimates, and before they were passed we had the 'cold fit' on the nation, which instantly turned round with its usual folly when peace was made on the Continent. This was our misfortune, not our fault. As to the Army Bill, I hold we were right in abolishing purchase. The truth about not doing it till we had provided a perfect substitute is nonsense....

I have neither space nor patience to go through all the rest which would require an essay, but except *entre nous* the Licensing Bill which I always thought a blunder,[49] I could make a defence, plausible at least, on the other points. But our difficulties lie deeper than casual mistakes and Parliamentary squabbling. We have a radical tail which naturally becomes more and more exacting. It is a monster which cannot be contented and by which we shall irretrievably be driven to distraction. The country won't go the lengths of Fawcett and Co.[50] Our party will not let us govern by help of the Tories. We shall fall by a combination of the left with the right. Still by good management and with good fortune we might frustrate this combination for some time and keep the nation with the left centre which is about our position. Much will depend on finance, and if peace continues on the Continent with a fair harvest and a growing trade, it *may* be possible to have a popular budget.

I don't think you and I should differ much as to the programme.

76. **Kimberley to Dodson**   Kimberley House
    27 September 1871
    MBP

....I think I never read such nonsense in my life, as has been written in the newspapers about our army. Gladstone has most properly and opportunely set his foot down about Irish 'Home Rule' at Aberdeen.[51] Home Rule simply means separation from England, and when we are such fools as to assent to that, we deserve to be kicked by every nation in the world.

77. **Kimberley to Gladstone**
    12 March 1872
    GP 44224, ff. 270–72

Since our last discussion in the Cabinet I have anxiously reconsidered the Australian Tariff Question, and I was inclining to the conclusion that it would

[49] See 27 April 1871, *KJ*, p. 22. Ironically, a year later Kimberley became responsible for drafting a licensing measure for the Lords. See 20 April 1872, *KJ*, p. 30.

[50] Cf. *KJ*, p. 36. Henry Fawcett (1833–84), Professor of Political Economy at Cambridge, 1863–84; Radical M.P. for Brighton, 1865–74; urged proportional representation from 1860. Kimberley first met Fawcett at a meeting of the Political Economy Club in 1863. Kimberley Journal, KP6 MS.eng.e.2790, p. 156.

[51] In a speech of 26 September 1871.

be better, looking to the great gravity of the issues involved, and the differences of opinion which exist amongst us, to discuss the matter further with the colonies before taking a decision, when I received the despatch which I send you from New Zealand.[52]

The perusal of the mem. of the N.Z. minutes convinces me that it is impossible to proceed without further communication with the colonies. The tone of the mem. is friendly, but its demands most alarming.

1. It assumes that the colonies (generally) should be at liberty to make reciprocal tariff arrangements, not merely a group of colonies geographically connected.

2. It contemplates the establishment of a system under which differential duties shall be established throughout the Empire, including the United Kingdom, in favour of the produce of the empire as against foreign countries, that is to say a revival of the old colonial monopoly in a new form.

It is noticeable that Sir J. Macdonald[53] (see a current despatch of Lord Lisgar[54]) has put forward a similar doctrine on behalf of Canada.

3. It points distinctly to reciprocity treaties between the Australasian colonies and the United States, and other foreign states.

4. It maintains that if the Imperial Govt. asserts the right to control colonies tariffs, it follows that the colonies must enjoy some share 'either by *representation* or consultation in deciding the policy by which they would be affected'. 'In short' Gt. Britain must logically do one of two things — either leave the colonies unfettered discretion — or if she is to regulate Tariffs or reciprocal Tariff arrangements, *or to make Treaties affecting the colonies* — give to the Colonies representation affecting the Empire. In other words, either federation of the whole empire, or independence in commercial matters. I need not pursue the subject further now. The whole paper is worth reading, and we owe a debt of gratitude to the N. Zealand govt. for at all events boldly stating to what the consequences their policy leads instead of veiling them in ambiguities, and equivocally worded resolutions like those of the Australian governments. When we have discussed the question of the Zollverein Treaty with the Law Officers I should propose to circulate the New Zealand Despatch to the Cabinet. If it is agreed that the discussion should be continued with the colonies, it will be necessary to carefully prepare a Despatch stating our general views. There are several points in the N.Z. Memorandum which I have not noticed in this letter, requiring attention. But the main propositions to which I have adverted, raise the whole question of the connection between this country, and colonies, having 'responsible' governments.

---

[52] See *Gladstone Diaries*, 7:xlviii–l; C. D. Allin, *Australasian Preferential Tariffs and Imperial Free Trade* (Minneapolis: University of Minnesota Press, 1929).

[53] John Alexander Macdonald, Canadian Prime Minister, 1867–73; 1878–91.

[54] Sir John Young, Baron Lisgar, Governor-General of Canada, 1869–72.

It would not surprise me if the separation of the colonies were to result from differences on commercial policy, and if the present discussion were to prove the turning point from which this separation commenced.[55] So much the more reason for the greatest circumspection and deliberation in the first steps which may lead to such momentous consequences. I send the printed paper which contains my Despatch (at page 6) to which the N.Z. Mem: is answer for convenience of reference.

78. Kimberley to Gladstone   Colonial Office
    7 May 1872
    GP 44224, ff. 294–95

Private

I am delighted to hear that you have proposed the Duchy to Childers,[56] and there is no one to whom I should be glad to do a service; but on reflection I have come to the conclusion that there are serious objections to his going to Victoria.

He is now agent to the colony, that is to say, the servant of the colonial Government. This, in the eyes of the colonial public, identifies him to some extent with the views of the local ministers.

Besides having held formerly the office of a responsible minister in the colony he has been connected with a party there, and he receives a pension from the colony. No one can doubt that he would do the work well, but his antecedents as regards this particular colony seem to me to be such as might greatly impair his influence as a constitutional Governor who ought to be perfectly impartial, and unconnected with local interests and factions. I think therefore it will be better to say nothing to him as to Victoria.[57]

79. Kimberley to Northbrook[58]   48 Bryanston Sq.
    20 June 1872
    NP MSS Eur. C 144/20, pp. XLVII–XLVIII

I was very glad to receive your letter of May 23rd, and to learn from it that you find India not disagreeable. I knew Major Burne[59] in Ireland, and have

---

[55] Cf. letter 89, herein.

[56] Hugh Culling Childers (1827–96), who had resigned the Admiralty in March 1871. He returned as Chancellor of the Duchy of Lancaster in August 1872.

[57] Kimberley had in February met with George Verdon, Victoria's agent-general in Britain, 1868–72. On Childers in Victoria see Spencer Childers, *Life and Correspondence of Hugh C. E. Childers, 1827–1896*, 2 vols. (London: John Murray, 1901), 1:23–78.

[58] Thomas George Baring, first Earl of Northbrook (1826–1904), Viceroy of India, 1872–76; First Lord of the Admiralty, 1880-85.

[59] Owen Tudor Burne, political aide-de-camp to the Secretary of State for India.

always heard him well spoken of. He would probably make a good Governor in some small Colony, or a Colonial Secretary in a big one. I will put him down on my List, though the chances of my being able to offer him any employment are slender.

One is always pleased when one finds another man, whose opinion is weighty, agreeing with oneself, and I am, therefore, pleased to find that your views of Indian affairs exactly coincide with mine. The India Office send me their excellent printed summary of despatches which I have read regularly since we have been in office, and I have, for a long time, had a strong impression that we have been driving the coach too fast in India, and that what is wanted is quiet. If you can give the Natives confidence that they have no rude changes to fear, and can get rid of the Income tax, I believe you will have a successful reign.

We have been in very hot water here. Badgered about the treaty night after night, *we* have had no rest.[60] I believe now we shall pull the treaty through, and generally our prospects look brighter. I expect that the violent amendments of the Lords in the Ballot bill will end in the acceptance by both Houses of the system of Hartington's Bill of 1870. The Scotch Education Bill has nearly passed through Committee, and the other bills in hand contain nothing which can be dangerous to us. I, therefore, anticipate that we shall get through the Session. Your successor Lansdowne[61] does his work well in the House.

Thanks very much for your kind inquiries after my boy.[62] He took a sudden change for the better yesterday, but I cannot bring myself to hope that the improvement will be permanent. Meantime, however, it is a great relief to us, and though I feel sure he will relapse, I feel more sanguine of possible ultimate recovery.

[*Postscript*] I shall always welcome any news from you.

80. Kimberley to Ripon   Colonial Office
    13 March 1873
    RPD 18-H

Private

Let me first say how glad I have been to hear that your son is going on well.[63] Every day now must I should hope greatly diminish your and Lady Ripon's anxiety.

---

[60] Treaty of Washington, 8 May 1871, which provided for settlement of the *Alabama* claims by an international commission. The *Alabama* dispute so overshadowed other matters that Kimberley wrote in his journal, 'as to the ballot and other minor matters, are not the debates written in the pages of Hansard? There is nothing worth recording about them'. *KJ*, pp. 30–33 and notes.

[61] Henry Charles Petty-Fitzmaurice, fifth Marquess of Lansdowne (1845–1927), Under-Secretary of State for War, 1872–74.

[62] See letter 73, herein.

[63] In Cannes, where he was recovering from a 'severe accident'.

Long before this gets to you you will know we are out.[64] It was evident from the first we should be beaten, and the majority against us was until the last moment expected to be greater. On Saturday the Cabinet except Forster seemed to be for dissolution if we were beaten. On Wednesday the morning after our defeat, it was evident the Cabinet was inclining to resignation. [Ill.] altho' the decision was postponed till to day I looked on it as virtually taken. Today every one was for resignation except Lowe, Goschen, and myself who were, as we had been all along, for immediate (that is as early as possible) dissolution.[65] Cardwell said nothing but I suppose he was for resignation. Bruce said nothing but I think he was for dissolution. No other alternative was regarded as possible by any member of the Cabinet. I expect to see Dizzy soon at his old tricks governing by the aid of the Extreme Radicals: to my mind a very unpleasant prospect.

81. Kimberley to Gladstone   Colonial Office
   13 August 1873
   GP 44225, ff. 73–76

Cardwell and I after consultation with the Duke of Cambridge came to the conclusion that in the present state of affairs on the Gold Coast it is essential that the whole civil and military power should be concentrated in the hands of one person, and that the person selected should be a man of high military reputation. We accordingly offered the post to Sir Garnet Wolseley who has accepted it.[66] I don't think a better man could be selected. He managed the Red River Expedition admirably. I have submitted his name to the Queen as Governor and when HM has approved, H.R.H. will submit his name for the command of the troops. The civil authority will of course only be held by him for the time necessary to deal effectually with the Ashantees, as he is far too valuable a man to remain long on the coast.

Whatever we do must be done quickly, and if possible in such a manner as to deter the Ashantees from attacks upon our settlements for a long time to come. It is not likely that any permanent peace can be secured unless we can get to Coomassie, an operation which when the rains cease in November does not seem to present any insuperable difficulty. Captain Glover by operating on the

---

[64] A premature observation. Disraeli refused to form a government and Gladstone continued in office until February 1874. See *KJ*, p. 37; Morley, *Life of Gladstone*, 2:446–56; *Gladstone Diaries*, 8:299–302.

[65] Gladstone reported that the Cabinet, 'without any marked difference, or at least any positive assertion to the contrary, determined on tendering their resignation.' *Gladstone Diaries*, 8:300.

[66] For the circumstances see W. D. McIntyre, 'British Policy in West Africa: The Ashanti Expedition of 1873–74', *Historical Journal* 5 (1962), pp. 19–46; John Keegan, 'The Ashanti Campaign, 1873– 4', in *Victorian Military Campaigns*, ed. Brian Bond (New York: Praeger, 1967), pp. 163–98.

flank of the Ashantees by way of the Volta will create a powerful diversion even
if he should not get to Coomassie which he may very possibly find himself able
to do.[67] We shall take care that Capt. Glover has regular legal powers given
to him by a colonial ordinance so that the expedition may not be in any way a
'filibustering' one. Capt. Glover will have, if he can collect them, a force of
natives of 10,000 men including 800 or a 1000 trained Haussas.

The natives will as usual be under their chiefs subject to his general authority. The Principal cost of the expedition will be in the first place arms and
ammunition for the force, a steamer to transport stores &c. up the Volta, three
steam launches, and subsidies to the chiefs (not large amounts), also some small
pay will probably be required by the natives when they get into the Ashantee
country. The expedition will have, in addition to Capt. Glover, six European
officers, besides two doctors, and a central officer to keep accounts. It is impossible to estimate with any precision the cost of the expedition. It cannot I
should think cost less than £100,000. It is very provoking to have to spend
such large sums of money on these savages, but we cannot leave the matter as
it is, and I know of no possible plan which promises such considerable effects
at anything like so small (comparatively) a cost.

As the present administrator Colonel Harley will be superseded by Sir G.
Wolseley through no fault of his own, but because he cannot hold the military
with the civil command (being no longer in the army) we shall have to give
him pay till some other post is found for him, and Sir G. Wolseley will require
a special salary.

Time is of so much importance that Cardwell and I agreed that we ought to
proceed with Sir G. Wolseley's appt. at once without waiting to communicate
with you, and I have no doubt you will approve what we have done.

Now I envy you the country. I do not know when I shall get away, as I have
a child very ill with typhoid fever which is epidemic in my part of London.

82. Kimberley to Granville[68]   Colonial Office
     2 September 1873
     BP 43387, ff. 83–84

Private

If the 'Economist'[69] is inspired it is not by me. I think its views and those

---

[67] John Hawley Glover, explorer and administrator of Lagos, 1863, 1866–67. See
Kimberley's instructions of 18 August 1872 in G. E. Metcalfe, ed. *Great Britain and
Ghana, Documents of Ghana History, 1807–1957* (London: University of Ghana and
Thomas Nelson, 1969), pp. 350–51.
[68] Enclosed in Granville to Bright, 3 September 1873, BP 43387, f. 81.
[69] In an article generally supporting the government, but concerned that English 'fear
of responsibility' might be so deep as to preclude orders for securing 'absolute security'
on the coast. 23 August 1873, pp. 1018–19.

of nearly all the newspaper articles I have read (and they are not few) on this wretched Ashantee War are most extravagant. As we must repel the invasion, the only question is how can we do it most effectually, quickly, and at least expense of lives and money. The talk about an African Empire, &c. &c. is simply 'bosh'.

Mr. Clarke's plan of abandoning the Fantees to the tender mercies of the Ashantees is not new.[70] It might answer *provided* the British public was content to see the coast the scene for some years of all the horrible barbarities, human sacrifices &c. which accompany Ashantee rule. In time contact with Europeans might soften this as in the case of other tribes; but I don't believe people here would ever let the experiment be fairly tried, and I dare say Mr. Clarke himself would not be thoroughly satisfied with the strong native power.[71]

83. Kimberley to Gladstone   Kimberley House
10 September 1873
GP 44225, ff. 103–04

I am very sorry to trouble you with more business; but I think you ought to see this draft. The condition of the Malay Peninsula is becoming very serious. It is the old story of misgovernment of Asiatic States. This might go on without any very serious consequences except the stoppage of trade, were it not that European and Chinese capitalists stimulated by the great riches in tin mines which exist in some of the Malay States are suggesting to the native Princes that they should seek the aid of Europeans to enable them to put down the disorder which prevails. We are the paramount power on the Peninsula up to the limit of the states tributary to Siam, and looking to the vicinity of India and our whole position in the East I apprehend that it would be a serious matter if any other European power were to obtain a footing in the peninsula. Ever since the mutual Cessions in 1825 by the treaty between us and Holland, it has been recognized that whilst Dutch influence was paramount South, our influence was paramount north of the Straits of Malacca. Our treaties with the native states are enumerated in a mem: sent herewith. These proposed instructions to the new government, who is going out soon do not actually pledge us to anything but they simply imply that some attempt is to be made to produce a better state of things.[72]

---

[70] W. H. Clarke. See James L. Sturgis, *John Bright and the Empire* (London: Athlone Press, 1969), pp. 108–09.

[71] Kimberley informed Goschen on September 12 that the government were not 'deluded by the talk about the Ashantees being an interesting nation of traders whom we have only to treat reasonably in order to make them fast friends and excellent consumers of cotton and hardware.' Arthur D. Elliot, *Life of Goschen, 1831–1907*, 2 vols. (London: Longmans, Green, and Co., 1911), 1:122-23.

[72] On the development of Kimberley's Malay initiative, see W. D. McIntyre, 'Britain's

84. Kimberley to Halifax   Kimberley House
  24 December 1873
  HfP A4/151

Private

.... As to the Gold Coast my view is what, as you remind me, I stated in the Cabinet, that we must either do more or give the whole thing up. I confess my mind inclines more than it did to the latter course. The grand obstacle is the *climate*. Were it even a tolerable climate such as the West Indies or Labuan or Hong Kong none of them paradises of health for Europeans, I should see no difficulty which could not be surmounted in governing the country effectually. Besides however the climate there is another serious obstacle, the institution of domestic slavery. You cannot make the natives British subjects unless they cease to be slaveholders. Even if you could abolish slavery within the Protectorate, you would not be out of trouble, for you would immediately be face to face with the fugitive slave question with all your neighbours. Lagos (the inland) is British territory, and small as it is, we have interminable and very serious disputes with our neighbours about fugitive slaves. What would it be along a land frontier of three or four hundred miles?

I have mentioned two points but there are many others. Do not however suppose I have made up my mind to recommend abandonment. This question must be reserved till after the war, and I wish to keep myself quite free. But a *half-measure* is what I am most afraid of. The half measures recommended by the Committee of 1864 were I believe a great mistake; and I wish the policy of that Committee had never been adopted.[73] I pursued the path I found chalked out and carried the policy fairly on the same line as Carnarvon, Cardwell, and Granville had done. Advice and arms the natives had freely, but the whole thing broke down for a simple reason, that the natives of the Protectorate without European aid are no match for the Ashantees. Every day proves this and *ad nauseam*, and if I had known this sooner I might perhaps have shown myself wiser than my predecessors.

85. Kimberley to Raikes Currie   Colonial Office
  13 February 1874
  KP1 3/1

You must be interested in this Liberal 'debacle'. I confess I thought with many others that we should have a small majority. Toryism is now triumphant.

Intervention in Malaya: The Origin of Lord Kimberley's Instructions to Sir Andrew Clarke in 1873', *Journal of South East Asian History* 2 (1961): 47–69; E. Chew, 'The Reason for British Intervention in Malaya: Review and Reconsideration', *Journal of South East Asian History* 6 (1965): 81–93; McIntyre, *Imperial Frontier*, pp. 185–210.

[73] Forbidding new settlements but allowing consolidation, or 'non-intervention — except in special cases'. McIntyre, *Imperial Frontier*, pp. 80–103.

It will very likely I think become rampant in which case its triumph will be brief; but if the new govt. is prudent, it may have a long reign. Our best chance is in my opinion Disraeli. A man cannot change his whole nature because he becomes First Minister with a majority.

For myself I am *really* glad of rest. I want it, and it is fortunate for me that I must take it whether I like it or not, tho' I cannot plead the difficulty or responsibility of an office which I see the D. of Buckingham is thought a very fit man to undertake. 'Either the D. of Buckingham *or* Lord Carnarvon.'!! a flattering conjunction for the latter.[74]

We have got into 35 Lowndes Sq. If you are in town any day, I hope you will look in.

86. Kimberley to Gladstone   Penzance
    27 May 1874
    GP 44225, ff. 150–53

I will certainly look at the publications to which you refer and I am much obliged to you for calling my attention to them.[75] I am however I confess not much concerned about the foreign criticism. The English 'monster of cruelty' is about as like the original as the 'Godam Anglais' of the 15th cent. or the 'Milord of Anglais' of the 19th[76] —

War is a measure which cannot be divested of its horrors and the burning of Coomassie though an act of severity which everyone must wish to have avoided, seems to me as justifiable as killing an enemy in battle. If we had retreated from Coomassie without signing a treaty with the King, leaving the town untouched, the effect would have been that the African tribes would have believed that we were practically defeated. We should have made no permanent impression. The king would probably have not made any submission and the whole expedition would have been to a great extent a failure. Wolseley was much pressed to stay another day and to burn the 'Bintoma', the burial place of the Ashantee Kings, which is a little way off from Coomassie. He refused and I think it is much to his credit that he did so. Desecration of tombs has a peculiarly repulsive character, and would have been a proceeding unworthy of a civilized Christian people. Still I have seen this censured as a weakness on the part of the General.

---

[74] Henry Howard Herbert, fourth Earl of Carnarvon (1831–90), had been Colonial Secretary for eight months in 1866–67 before resigning in opposition to the 1867 Reform Act, at which time he was succeeded by Richard Grenville, third Duke of Buckingham and Chandos (1823–99). Disraeli always considered Buckingham a poor second, and Carnarvon was reappointed in 1874. Monypenny and Buckle, *Life of Disraeli*, 4:504–05.

[75] In Gladstone's letter of May 25. The publications are untraced, but may have been among the 'diverse pamphlets' which he noted on May 21. *Gladstone Diaries*, 7:494.

[76] See Beaumarchais, *Le Mariage de Figaro*, Act 3, Scene 5.

I am making a little tour of Cornwall but return to town on Monday. I have changed my house which is now 35 Lowndes Sq. next door to Lowe.[77]

87. Kimberley to Northbrook   Kimberley House
    9 August 1874
    NP MSS Eur C 144/22, pp. 181–82.

Private

You have had far too heavy a work on your hands for one to wish to give you the trouble to read a private letter; but now that you seem to be getting near smoother water, I must write you a line to assure you that I have watched with the deepest interest your manner of dealing with the great crisis of the famine, and congratulate you most warmly on the success of your measures. My opinion on Indian affairs is worth very little indeed; but, as far as I was called upon, before we left office, to examine what you were doing by way of preparation, and your wise abstinence from the rash measure of prohibiting the grain exports, I thoroughly approved your policy. All this is mere ancient history, and it matters to nobody what I think or thought; but you may perhaps like to know how much I admired your firm resistance to the ridiculous outcry made by the Press here. It says much for the good sense of the English people that all the writing of the Press could not stir them into unnecessary panic.

We have had a fine display of the admirable management of our strong Government at the close of the Session.[78] We were not in such a sorry plight after five years' campaigning.

On the other hand, the Opposition are not in a much better plight, if indeed we are not in a worse. Ecclesiastical questions, on which Gladstone is at issue with the great mass of our party, have come to the front.[79] It almost looks as if we should have a break up of parties; next session will show.

[77] Robert Lowe (1811–98), Secretary of State for Home Affairs, 1873–74. On the nature of the friendship between Lowe and Kimberley, see letters in KP6 MS.eng.c.4471, ff. 99– 101; KP1 15/K2/10, p. 27.

[78] On Tory divisions over the Public Worship Regulation Bill, see Monypenny and Buckle, *Life of Disraeli*, 5:313–28.

[79] Northbrook wondered how Gladstone could lead 'if the main questions are church questions' in which he commanded no confidence. Northbrook to Kimberley, 8 September 1874, KP6 MS.eng.c.4472, f. 21. See Parry, *Democracy and Religion*, pp. 411–28; Kimberley journal, KP6 MS.eng.e.2791, pp. 334–35, 343–54.

88. Kimberley, Notes on Books   Lowndes Sq.
    [June 1875]
    KP1 15/K2/10

Read *Sir H. Rawlinson's* volume on *Central Asia* (England and Russia),[80] 1
vol. A mine of information on this subject. I disagree from the policy of Sir
H. R. No good could come to us from the premature advance to Herat which
he advises.

89. Kimberley to Musgrave[81]   35 Lowndes Sq.
    19 July 1875
    MgP 22-G, Box 8

I have to thank you for your pamphlet on 'Economic Fallacies'.[82] I am
afraid I must say that I am too steady an adherent to the pure Free Trade theory to become a convert to your views. I see you adduce our recent Treaties
of Commerce, and the Act authorizing special customs arrangements between
Australian colonies, as examples of our readiness to discard our free trade opinions, when it suits our convenience. I think you are fairly entitled to the benefit
of the first. It has always seemed to me that the French Treaty was a departure
from sound principles, and I doubt whether for that reason it will not in the long
run be found to have done more harm than good.[83] The second example I do
not admit. We never pretended for a moment to believe that the Australian Act
was consistent with sound economical views. We passed it solely on political
grounds, considering that having given the Australian colonies full control of
their domestic affairs, even to the point of allowing them as in Victoria to lay
protective duties on our goods, we could not prudently refuse them the further
liberty they asked for. You will forgive a Freetrader[84] for regretting that the
Australian protectionists will be able to quote the authority of so able a Governor as yourself, in favour of a policy which is so antagonistic to the policy

---

[80] *England and Russia in the East* (London: John Murray, 1875), by Sir Henry
Creswicke Rawlinson (1810–95), soldier, diplomat, and archaeologist in India, Afghanistan, Persia, and Mesopotamia, 1827–55, 1859–60; member of the Council of India,
1858–59, 1868–95.

[81] Sir Anthony Musgrave (1828–88); Governor of Newfoundland, 1864–69, of British
Columbia, 1869–71; Lieutenant Governor of Natal, 1872–73; Governor of South Australia, 1873–77.

[82] Probably *Studies in Political Economy* (1875).

[83] Treaty of Commerce of 1860, reducing tariffs on a wide variety of goods. Cf.
Kimberley's public rationale of 1860, arguing that an agreement for ten years with
'mutual advantage' would go far toward increasing trade and bettering relations between
France and England. 3 *Hansard*, 157 (15 March 1860): 579–84.

[84] Kimberley was stigmatized by some colonials as 'rather behind the age'. Sir John
Macdonald, chafing under imperial restrictions, called him 'a Free Trade doctrinaire of
the most restrictive and illiberal kind'. Quoted in David M. L. Farr, *The Colonial Office
and Canada, 1867–1887* (Toronto: University of Toronto Press, 1955), p. 207, n. 86.

of the Imperial government. Apart from the mere commercial question, I look upon the Protectionist tendency of some of our colonies as peculiarly dangerous to the permanence of their connexion with this country.

90. Kimberley to Northbrook   Kimberley House
    5 September 1875
    NP MSS Eur C 144/23, p. 231.

Private

.... It is impossible to conceive anything duller than home politics. A great torpor has come over the nation, and, as far as any cne can judge, seems likely to continue. Hartington did well last Session,[85] but our party is so demoralised that, were he a heaven-born Leader, he could do little at present to mend our fortunes. Meantime the Government have made blunder on blunder in conducting the business of Parliament. But the nation, like Gallio, cares for none of these things.[86]

91. Kimberley to Halifax   Kimberley House
    10 December 1875
    HfP A4/151

I should much like to know what you think about this Suez Canal business.[87] No doubt it is a palpable hit for the Govt., but this does not prove they are right. John Bull has been sulky at cutting a poor figure in the world ever since the Alabama affair,[88] and he is delighted at this opportunity of making a dash. It is obvious that he is deluded in supposing that 170,000 deferred shares give us control of the canal. Nothing but naval supremacy in the Mediterranean can give that. It is obvious also that this purchase commits us to a larger and indefinite future expenditure, to probable quarrels with the Company and the French shareholders, to complications with the French Govt., and to constant interference in the affairs of Egypt. On the other hand, I always thought that Palmerston made a great mistake in opposing Lesseps.[89] If he had not done

---

[85] Following Gladstone's resignation as Liberal party leader.

[86] Junius Annaeus Gallio, Roman proconsul of Achaia, who refused to settle what seemed to him unimportant internal disputes among the Jews. 'Then all the Greeks took Sosthenes, the chief ruler of the synagogue, and beat him before the judgement seat. And Gallio cared for none of those things'. *Acts* xviii: 12–17 (KJV).

[87] On the circumstances surrounding Disraeli's purchase from the Khedive of 176,602 shares in the Suez Canal Company for £4,000,000, see Robert Blake, *Disraeli* (New York: St. Martin's Press, 1968), pp. 581–87.

[88] Payment of £3,250,000 to the United States for damages caused by the Confederate frigate *Alabama*, which had been built in England during the American Civil War.

[89] Ferdinand de Lesseps, French diplomat instrumental in forming the company which constructed the Suez Canal, 1859–69.

so we should have had our due share of influence in the enterprise from the beginning. The present move gives us a large share in the concern, and for ever displaces exclusive French influence — so far a decided gain. And in the present more than ever decaying conditions of Turkey it may be expedient to announce to Europe in a manner not to be mistaken, that we are resolved at all hazards to prevent Egypt and the canal from falling under the control of any Power but ourselves —

Assuming, as I do for my part, that as long as we hold India, this is a wise and necessary resolution, I am inclined on the whole to think that the Govt. have acted rightly, though the objections to their course are weighty.[90] I say nothing as to the details of the transaction, because it seems to me that the broad grounds of general policy are those on which its approval or condemnation must be rested.

---

92. Kimberley to Harcourt   35 Lowndes Sq.
       2 June 1876
       HP MS. Harcourt dep. 49, f. 1

I entirely agree with your letter to the 'Times' [91] — I can't conceive what can have possessed the 'Times' with notions so utterly repugnant to all received opinion as to the relations between Parliament and the colonies.

---

93. Kimberley to Halifax   Kimberley House
       25 September 1876
       HfP A4/151

Private

What do you think of this hurricane of passion about Turkey?[92] What is it to end in? The Govt. has managed by a series of blunders to put itself out of sympathy with large masses of people. Just when they needed all the support they could get in dealing with a most thorny question, they have aroused one of those bursts of popular frenzy which now and then from Titus Oates' plot[93] downwards seize on our countrymen. I myself detest the Turks, and wish

---

[90] Cf. his journal entry, MS.eng.e.2792, p. 386.

[91] Arguing the folly of 'squandering our fighting fleet about the world among our distant possessions'. Gardiner, *Life of Harcourt*, 1:303.

[92] The British public's horrified reaction to Turkish atrocities in Bulgaria, where up to 30,000 men, women, and children were reported to have been massacred. See R. T. Shannon, *Gladstone and the Bulgarian Agitation 1876* (London: Thomas Nelson, 1963), chaps. 2–4.

[93] Accusing Queen Catherine among others of plotting to murder Charles II and restore Roman Catholicism to England. In the ensuing panic, ten men were tried and executed, although Oates's 'fertile and unscrupulous mind invented the whole thing.' Lacey Baldwin Smith, *This Realm of England*, 3rd ed. (London: D. C. Heath, 1976), pp. 283–86.

them with all my heart replaced by decent civilized communities. I think the Palmerston policy is played out, and that we should look to the gradual increase of the self governing Christian communities. But a mere statement of such an opinion is not in itself sufficient foundation for a plan of operations in the present crisis. Excellent principles are no use unless you can transmute them into action. How can this be done? I can conceive an arrangement of Bosnian and Herzegovinan affairs based on the detachment of these provinces from direct Turkish rule, and placing them under a Christian prince. But Austria's consent and active co-operation are essential to such a scheme. With her aid success wd. be difficult, without it impossible.

As to Bulgaria I can't see how it could be wrested from Turkish rule without Russian intervention. Are we then to invite Russia to intervene? The more I turn these questions over in my mind, the less possibility I see of any great changes being effected except by war —

Do we then really wish our government to push the matter to the extremity of war? If there were an organized opposition which could hope to upset the Ministry and form a sufficiently strong administration in its place, I should say that every effort should be made to bring about such a catastrophe as soon as possible. But there is nothing of the kind. Possibly Derby[94] may yet be able to patch up some arrangement if Russia and Austria really desire a patching up. But it is mere delusion to suppose that Downing Street is master of the situation.

Perhaps after all that is the most consolatory reflexion in my letter.

94. Kimberley, Notes on Books   Kimberley House
  October 1876
  KP1 15/K2/10

Read 'Through Bosnia and Herzegovina' by Arthur J. Evans,[95] 1 vol. A useful book to run through at this juncture of Eastern affairs. The style of composition is of the 'smart' order and therefore detestable. Mr. Evans would make a good 'Daily Telegraph' correspondent, if he is not one already.[96]

---

[94] Edward Henry Stanley (1826–93), fifteenth Earl of Derby; Secretary of State for Foreign Affairs, 1866–68, 1874–78.

[95] Arthur John Evans, *Through Bosnia and Herzegovina, on Foot during the Insurrection, August and September 1875* (London: Longmans, Green, and Co., 1876). Evans was a student of Balkan culture who later became Keeper of the Ashmolean Museum, 1884-1908, and after 1894 distinguished himself as an archaeologist in Crete.

[96] Most of his work was in fact for the *Manchester Guardian*.

95. Kimberley to Halifax   Kimberley House
    5 November 1876
    HfP A4/151

Many thanks for your letter. I am sceptical as to the foreign agents in Bulgaria. It is a very old mode of excuse on the part of those who provoke rebellion by mis-government. But no doubt the absence of any defined line between 'Bulgarian horrors' and C[onstantino]ple is as Forster[97] points out an immense difficulty. Indeed one does not know where to stop. The Turks are a curse everywhere, as much in Asia Minor, as in Turkey in Europe. For all that I think something may be gained if a sort of autonomy could be established in Bosnia and Herzegov. and the province called Bulgaria, the Turks retaining the fortresses as they did Belgrade formerly. I am for a patched up peace if it can be got, and not for heroic remedies. A 'thorough' policy is only wise when you see your way pretty clearly — Now no one can pretend that he sees his way clearly through this business. I wish Gladstone had not written the article in the 'Contemporary'[98] — He does himself and his cause infinite harm by bandying hard words with such an antagonist as the 'Pall Mall' —

I agree entirely in what Hartington said at Keighley[99] — It seems that there is a chance now of avoiding a great war. Will the govt. have the sense to try to work with Russia in endeavouring to make an arrangement, or will they allow the popular Russophobia to blind their eyes? I am very much afraid they will still be aiming at 'checkmating' Russia — Meantime so far Gladstone has gained his point that a thorough pro-Turkish policy is impossible, and in this I rejoice.

[97] W.E. Forster (1818–86), Liberal M.P. for Bradford since 1861. From August 15 until early October, he had travelled through eastern Europe, including stops in Prague, Krakow, Pesth, Belgrade, Bucharest and Constantinople, making a controversial speech to his constituents upon his return. Wemyss Reid, *Life of Forster*, 2:141–52.

[98] Condemning the veracity of the *Pall Mall Gazette*'s account of Russian atrocities in Turkestan. 'Russian Policy and Deeds in Turkestan', *Contemporary Review*, 28 (November 1876): 873–91.

[99] 3 November 1876. After several weeks in Vienna, Pesth, and Constantinople during September and October, Hartington concluded that 'the root of the mischief was the incapacity of the Turks for good administration', and therefore accepted that 'some degree of external influence' might become necessary. Bernard Holland, *Life of Spencer Compton, Eight Duke of Devonshire*, 2 vols. (London: Longmans, Green and Co., 1911), 1:182. On the political implications of both Hartington's and Forster's speeches, see Patrick Jackson, *The Last of the Whigs: A Political Biography of Lord Hartington, Later Eighth Duke of Devonshire, 1833–1908* (London: Associated University Presses, 1994), pp. 77–79.

96. Kimberley, Notes on Books Lowndes Square
     April 1877
     KP2 15/K2/10, pp. 40–41

Read the new volume (5) of the Wellington correspondence.[100] Extremely curious details of the "Eastern Question" in 1829–30. Some of the Duke's memoranda might with changes of names and dates have been written now. Will history repeat itself in another treaty of Adrianople? Not improbably I think.

97. Kimberley to Dodson Kimberley House
     30 September 1879
     MBP

Many thanks for your inquiry about my leg.[101] I get on very slowly. Still I do improve and now can crawl about the room and garden. I am assured I shall be sound, but I don't expect to be so for 6 mo. from the accident. Meantime I have lost no shooting for we have nothing to shoot. Not only are there no young birds but most of the old ones are dead. Our harvest is generally over, though I saw two fields of wheat, not carried, today. Wheat is a miserable crop; barley pretty good and carried here about in fair condition. Farmers are really in a bad way. I have my largest farm (500 acres) thrown on my hands this Michaelmas. It is a pleasant thing to have to spend £5,000 at once to stock it, and more hereafter with the almost certain prospect of losing part of it. It is true I was not fairly treated about this farm, as the tenant, whose 20 year lease is just out, agreed to go on, and then two months ago, informed me that he found himself without the necessary means, which was only too true. If I had had six months notice, I think I could have let it, as I have let four other farms, 2 at 10 per cent reduction, two at the same rents, and the farm is in excellent order. Altogether our prospects here are very disagreeable. I have refused all general percentage reductions of rent which I look on as unbusinesslike and unequal, and prefer to deal with each case on its merits. I have made very inconsiderable reductions. My rents were mostly fixed 15 or 20 years ago, some more than 20 years. I thought you might like to know how these matters stand here.

As to politics I agree with you. The government are going to the dogs, and will fare badly at the general election; and what is called the Liberal party consists of fragments. They will however coalesce here for a time if there is a change of government, as far as England and Scotland are concerned. But Ireland? Things are running their usual course there. The hatred of England is deep-seated and the only consolation is that we are so far better off than our

[100] 2nd Duke of Wellington, ed. *Despatches, Correspondence and Memoranda of Field Marshal Arthur Duke of Wellington... from 1818 to 1832*, 8 vols. (London, 1867–80).
[101] Injured playing tennis on July 16. Kimberley was unable to walk until the end of the year. Kimberley journal, KP6 MS.eng.e.2792.

ancestors, that we have a tolerably clear conscience as to our mode of governing them.

We must be degenerate indeed if we cannot keep them under control without much strain on our resources. But we may look forward to a renewal of agrarian crime and perhaps some fresh rebellious organizations.

A new coercive bill will probably be one of the first measures of a new Liberal govt.

4

The Loyal Lieutenant

A vigorous assault on Tory foreign policy lifted the Liberals back into power in May 1880, and with the new government came Gladstone's offer of the Indian Viceroyalty. Kimberley's refusal 'stunned' Gladstone, who then offered the Colonial Office, which was accepted. By 1880, colonial and foreign policy were becoming inextricably tangled, necessitating a close working relationship between Granville and Kimberley, particularly in African affairs. Kimberley's second term at the Colonial Office was dominated by affairs in southern Africa. The Liberal government's decision to pursue Carnarvon's confederation policy was widely condemned by Liberals and thus easily turned against them when the Boers revolted in December 1880. Kimberley and the Liberals were widely taunted by the Tories for signing an armistice in March 1881 before redeeming the minor military defeat at Majuba. Between 1880 and 1882 he pursued a policy of imperial consolidation, promoting self-government generally, but protecting Britain's strategic position in Cape Colony. Nevertheless, he refused to annex Namaqualand and Damaraland in southwest Africa, and the Cameroon in west Africa.

With Gladstone relinquishing the Exchequer to Childers in December 1882, Hartington was transferred to the War Office, and Kimberley to the India Office. There, his first year was dominated by events surrounding Lord Ripon's aggressive promotion of local self-government and native judicial control, which Kimberley supported in principle, but the specific measures for implementation of which he frequently felt compelled to curb in the interests of 'sound administration'. From February 1884, Russian aggression in Central Asia became the fulcrum upon which all Indian policy decisions were balanced, a situation which led to the brink of war in the spring of 1885. As colonial, Indian, and other foreign questions steadily became more entwined, and foreign affairs a more troublesome issue in domestic campaigning, Kimberley's long experience heightened his value as a minister, with Gladstone and Granville routinely consulting him on matters relating to international issues.

Throughout Gladstone's second ministry, Kimberley's role in domestic politics steadily declined, first because of the extraordinary increase in the pace of colonial and Indian affairs since 1874, and second, due to the consolidation of Conservative power in the House of Lords. Still, as a former Lord-Lieutenant who had managed Ireland with considerable success, his opinions were regularly sought on Irish coercion and land purchase. Knowing there would be many desertions over Home Rule, Gladstone sought Kimberley's support, which was at last reluctantly given. Having decided that some form of Home Rule was a practical necessity, however, he remained one of Gladstone's staunchest supporters during the opposition between 1886 and 1892.

98. Kimberley to Hicks Beach[1]   Colonial Office
24 May 1880
HBP D2455/PCC95

Private

I quite agree with you as to Governors' private letters as a general rule. Bowen is an old private acquaintance of mine,[2] and on Victorian affairs on which he wrote to me, I happened to be in accordance with your views; so no harm came of the letters I recd., but such a correspondence might become very embarrassing.[3] You will have seen our announcement as to South Africa in the Queen's Speech.[4] We are threatened with attack from our own side for not having immediately recalled Frere.[5] I hope very soon to present some papers containing your recent correspondence, and a few despatches of my own. We shall endeavour to carry through Confederation and if we can do this, we shall I hope be able to give the Transvaal a free provincial Constitution.[6] This I think was your intention also.

I am anxious that the Conference should meet. We shall then see whether there is any real chance of Confederation. But the Cape colonists as you know are difficult to deal with, and I shall not indulge in too sanguine expectations.

[1] Sir Michael Hicks Beach (1837–1916), Secretary of State for the Colonies, 1878–80.

[2] Sir George Ferguson Bowen (1821–99), Governor of New Zealand, 1867–73; of Victoria, 1873–79; of Mauritius, 1879–82. Bowen recalled 'Kimberley's steady support', especially during the 'manifold difficulties' encountered as Governor of New Zealand. *Thirty Years of Colonial Government*, 2 vols. (London: Longman, Green and Co., 1889), 1:403; 2:202–04; see too Bowen to Kimberley, 13 December 1889, KP6 MS.eng.c.4468, ff. 11–12.

[3] In Bowen's letter of 13 January 1880, however: 'To return to Mauritius, "Sir Hitch Bitch" (as he is always called here because the French so pronounce his name) has raised a political hurricane. . . .' KP6 MS.eng.c.4135, ff. 24–29.

[4] Announcing Liberal intention to pursue the Conservative government's initiative in promoting confederation of the South African colonies. 3 *Hansard*, 252 (20 May 1880): 108.

[5] Sir Bartle Frere (1815–84), Governor of Cape Colony and High Commissioner for South Africa, 1877–80.

[6] For a brief summary, see D. M. Schreuder, *Gladstone and Kruger, Liberal Government and Colonial 'Home Rule', 1880–85* (London: Routledge and Kegan Paul, 1969), pp. 24–29, 60–80.

S. Africa has always been a most perplexing problem, and will I fear long remain so.

99. Kimberley to Gladstone   Colonial Office
    24 May 1880
    GP 44225, ff. 167–169

I hardly think we can lay much stress on the financial questions which Frere has in hand. Any one else in his place could probably do all that can be done for us and that I fear will turn out to be but little. I see a great deal written about 'Frere's native policy'[7] — I don't admit that a Governor can have a native policy of his own. The responsible colonial minister may of course have their own policy, but the governor in giving advice to them must conform to our views, and still more as High Commissioner, and the instructions which have been and will be sent to him will clearly explain what these views are.

I think this should be clearly brought out in debate. I shall send you tonight the instructions to Colley.[8] Carnarvon[9] is I believe going to say something to night in the Lords which will give me an opportunity of speaking about S. Africa.

I send the Mem: you asked for as to the Basutos. That about disarmament can be laid before Parliament immediately.

[*Postscript*] I will answer you about the hares.[10]

100. Kimberley to Granville   Colonial Office
    8 June 1880
    GrP 30/29/135, ff. 1–2

The treaty[11] is important as a means of reconciling the Boers, and to secure free transit thro' Delagoa Bay. I am told the Slave Trade clauses are the chief obstacle, as wounding Portuguese pride. Might we not dis-connect them from this Treaty? I am very much averse to concessions of territory to Portugal on the west coast. It would never do to let her extend her 'dead hand' over the

---

[7] Schreuder, *Gladstone and Kruger*, pp. 68–78. As early as February 1879 Kimberley was convinced that Frere was 'to blame for the Zulu War'. John P. Rossi, 'The Ripon Diary, 1878–80: I', *Recusant History*, 12 (January 1973): 30.

[8] Major-General George Pomeroy Colley, Governor of Natal.

[9] Henry Howard Molyneux Herbert, fourth Earl of Carnarvon (1831–90), Secretary of State for the Colonies, 1874– 78.

[10] On Kimberley and the Ground Game Bill, see letter 102, herein.

[11] Lourenço Marques Treaty, providing free navigation of the Zambesi, the building of rail and telegraph lines to the Transvaal border, and suppression of the slave trade along the coast. Never ratified by Portugal. On the development and demise of the treaty see Schreuder, *Gladstone and Kruger*, pp. 192–94; Agatha Ramm, *Sir Robert Morier, Envoy and Ambassador in the Age of Imperialism, 1876–1893* (Oxford: Clarendon Press, 1973), chap. 3; Extracts, Kimberley memoir, RsP 10186, p. 266.

great Congo waterway. I fear Morier has held out hopes of this. I think I should give the Portuguese to understand that we shall regard it as a very unfriendly act if they refuse to ratify, adding (if you would be disposed to omit the Slave Trade clauses) that we should be ready to consider whether any modifications can be made to soothe the susceptibilities of the Cortes.

101. Kimberley to Gladstone   Colonial Office
    20 July 1880
    GP 44225, ff. 192–93

I want to make a tiny annexation, namely the island of Rotumah. It is 150 miles N. of Fiji. Its whole length is six miles and breadth 2 1/2 miles; population 3000. The inhabitants have been Christianised, some (a majority) R. Catholics, the rest Protestants.

At page 2 of the annexed mem: (passage marked) will be found Sir A. Gordon's reasons for acceding to the petition of the chiefs to be placed under British rule.[12] The late Govt. left the question undecided and Sir A. Gordon writes strongly pressing that the question which has been long under discussion should be decided at once. I have consulted Granville concerning some scruples which were felt lest offence should be given to some foreign powers by annexing the island, and he says he has no objection.

The matter is so small that I would not have troubled you, were it not that it is an actual addition to the British dominions. The printed mem: if you care to look at it, gives full particulars.

102. Kimberley to Ripon   Kimberley House
    4 October 1880
    RP 43522, ff. 257–62

Private

I have been *going* to write you for weeks and have never found the moment. I was so weary with our eternal session[13] that I could not bring myself for long time to do any but indispensible work, and that is tolerably heavy, for the colonial office work has increased about 1/3rd since I was there before and I am about to take over that most *damnosa hereditas*, Cyprus from the F.O.

Our session ended much better than it began. Our dogged perseverance told at last, and Hartington in the chief's absence did admirably[14] —

---

[12] Arthur Gordon (1829–1912), Governor of Fiji, cited proximity, prospect of financial return, and morality as his reasons. W. J., 'Memorandum respecting the proposed Rectification of the Boundaries of the Fijian Group so as to Include the Island of Rotumah', 6 July 1880, GP 44225, ff. 194–96.

[13] Sitting 29 April to 7 September 1880.

[14] Gladstone having taken a voyage of recuperation with Donald Currie on the *Grantally Castle* between August 26 and September 3.

The Game Bill was accepted with very long faces indeed, but sensible men on both sides admitted that on the whole it was the least disagreeable thing we could have done.[15] Here in Norfolk it seems to have given great satisfaction, and the repeal of the Malt Tax has been a grand Coup for us. I really believe our farmers will turn Liberal.

We now have four weighty affairs on hand: 1. India 2. Ireland 3. Basuto War and South Africa 4. FA in the East. As to India I congratulate you. We seem to be getting out of our difficulties — You know my opinion about Candahar — I will only say that I am personally strongly in favour of not remaining there an hour longer than we can help.

2. Ireland — This is the worst business by far. I am in despair about it. We shall have to go the old weary round — coercion and all the rest of it, as we have done any time these 300 years past.

3. Basuto War — This is a horrible mess caused by the wanton folly of the Cape Govt., backed by Frere, who thank heavens is fairly out of S. Africa, where he has done an untold amount of mischief. I shall keep out of it if possible and leave the colonists to fight their own battle, but there will be presently a hideous outcry, if, as I expect, the war drags on interminably.

4. Last but far from least, Turkish affairs– Here we are I fear making no progress. Granville has driven his incongruous European team with great skill, but the coach may upset at any moment. What will happen there, God only knows.

As to domestic measures I have sedulously abstained from asking anything about them. Sufficient and more than sufficient for the day is the evil thereof. November cabinets will bring all that bother only too soon. Altogether, as you see, I do not think the prospect agreeable.

We have a fair harvest here, and first rate roots. Farmers however are generally in a bad way and likely to be worse. Bankers here say they never knew so little money in the district, and the sales of retiring or broken farmers are immeasurable. Still there is a better feeling on the whole than last year.

As to game, partridges are very thin all over this county, pheasants I suppose pretty good.

103. Kimberley to Courtney   Kimberley House
   25 December 1880
   CtP IV, item 18

I return with thanks Mr. Jorissen's letter.[16] I am afraid there is little chance

---

[15] Ground Game Bill, allowing concurrent hunting privileges for owners and occupiers in order to prevent destruction of crops. Received Royal assent on September 7. On the contemporary debate over 'sporting rights', see George C. Brodrick, *English Land and English Landlords* (London: Cassell, Petter, Gelpin, and Company, 1881), pp. 285–89.

[16] Edward Jorissen, Hollander State-Attorney to the South African Republic, who

of agreement between you and me as to South African affairs, but I shall always listen with attention to your views as I know how much you have studied that tangled web. A man must indeed be self confident who is not glad to get light wherever it is offered to him.[17]

104. Kimberley to Gladstone
20 January 1881
GP 44226, ff. 9–10

After looking carefully at your printed heads of Land Bill by the light of the explanation you gave me to day, I offer the following criticisms.

If *I* (present adjustment of rents)

II (perpetuity with free sale by consent)

III (Preference to cont. at option of either party)

are adjusted, and in all three I am disposed to concur, is number *V* necessary or expedient?

Will not every tenant who does not agree with his landlord for perpetuity under (2), resort to (3)? And will not the Court put (3) in force in every case, and ought it not to put it in force in every case except where there has been management on the English system? I would add some words to the first head of clause 9 of III to cover grass or other lands where tenant has made no permanent improvement, and I think I would omit the other head (want of general consent &c.) as unnecessary refinement, and as being likely to work hardship on individual tenants.

If however you are of the opinion that II and III will not cover all the cases which must be provided for, I do not know any better way of dealing with the residue than by some such method as is provided by V.

The advantage of omitting *V* would be the increased simplicity of the scheme. On the other hand you would lose the continuity between the Act of 1870, and the new law, and the landlord would have no power of determining the tenancy except by consent of the court.

But my contention is that every tenant would take advantage of *III*, and if he did not get a decrees of the court in his favour, is there any good reason for giving him the increased privileges conferred by *V*?

In the case of 'custom' especially, would it not be best to enable the Court to determine all cases of rent on changes of tenancy? Practically I believe this is done to a considerable extent already.

Apart however from these observations which I do not put forward as formed

argued that compromise was possible. Courtney wrote to Kimberley that the 'terror of civil war ensuing was a "phantom".' Courtney to Kimberley, 24 December 1880, KP6 MS.eng.c.4141, ff. 1–2.

[17] Courtney was then leading a Liberal cabal to immediately reverse Carnarvon's federation policy. See Schreuder, *Gladstone and Kruger*, pp. 68–72.

conclusions but only for what they are worth, I like much the method of alternatives which is the basis of your proposals.[18]

105. Kimberley to Granville   Lowndes Sq.
     7 April 1881
     GrP 30/29/135, f. 35

Private

I enclose a letter from Lorne.[19] It would be a very serious thing for our trade if the U.S. close the Isthmus to all trade but their own. They are quite capable of such a measure, and they are now so powerful that I suppose they would pay little heed to remonstrances. I hope you are better notwithstanding the keen wind.

[*Postscript*] Does the *Standard* get its information I wonder *gratis* or how?

106. Kimberley to Ripon   Colonial Office
     12 April 1881
     RP 43522, ff. 263–67

Private

It is a long time since I have written to you and many things have happened in the interval. First and foremost I rejoice to hear that you are well and I hope quite well again. The clouds seem to be clearing in India, and you will reap the fruit of the wise policy of quitting Afghanistan in, I trust, a period of comparative tranquility.

My affairs are as you will have seen in a terrible mess. That we were right in not going on with the war in the Transvaal, I have no doubt.[20] Every day the danger increased of the war extending. It must have soon drawn in the Orange Free State and the state of Dutch feeling in the Cape Colony was becoming very alarming. The worst of it all was that if we had to fight the Dutch population throughout Africa, we should have been practically unable to hold the country after having conquered them, not to mention the loss of blood and treasure which would have been enormous. Nevertheless there is no denying that it is very unpleasant to make peace after a series of defeats, small tho' they were;

---

[18] See Gladstone's reply of 21 January 1881, *Gladstone Diaries*, 10:10.

[19] John Douglas Campbell, Marquess of Lorne (1845–1914), Governor-General of Canada, 1878–83; urging that the newly formed American administration be warned of British opposition to 'American fortification of the projected Panama Canal'. Lorne to Kimberley, 24 March 1881, KP4 A-313, PC/B/57c.

[20] The humiliating but minor British defeat at Majuba on 27 February 1881 followed tentative Boer acceptance of peace terms. See Schreuder, *Gladstone and Kruger*, chapter 3.

and it is personally most disagreeable to be associated with a 'caving in' — Poor Colley's imprudence was most disastrous. We sent him abundant reinforcements and if he had not so grievously underestimated his enemy, he would have waited for them. We are far from the end yet. Of course everything in the Transvaal is in the utmost confusion, and a very little spark would set everything on fire again.

To turn to home affairs, Argyll's retirement tho' greatly to be lamented was no surprise.[21] I cannot yet cast the horoscope of the Land Bill. The country has not taken it in yet. When it is understood it will be seen to be a very drastic measure.[22] Will it succeed if passed in pacifying Ireland? That is the real question. I am not hopeful about anything Irish, and cannot therefore pretend to be sanguine as to this Bill. But I know of nothing better. To leave matters as they are is simply impossible.

Foreign affairs drag their slow length along. Goschen[23] does all and more than man can do with that wretched Turk who is still alive enough to give endless trouble. I think it must end in Greece accepting what she can get.

With my kind regard to Lady Ripon.

107. Kimberley Memorandum   Colonial Office
      6 May 1881
      DkP 43891, ff. 241–42

I hope we shall not threaten retaliatory duties. It would be the first and an irreversible step towards the abandonment of our free trade policy.

It may unfortunately prove true, as Mr. Chamberlain[24] fears, that class interests will outweigh the general interest of the nation. The more necessary does it seem to give no encouragement to so pernicious an agitation. If once we enter on the well trodden path of reciprocity we shall soon be landed in the old system of protection. There are many classes of producers besides the cotton and woollen manufactures who object to what they call one sided free trade.

---

[21] *Gladstone Diaries*, 10:lv, 41.

[22] According to Morley, 'few British members understood it, none mastered it'. *Life of Gladstone*, 3:54.

[23] George Joachim Goschen (1831–1907), serving as Ambassador Extraordinary to Constantinople, 1880–81.

[24] Joseph Chamberlain (1836–1914), President of the Board of Trade, 1880–85.

108. Kimberley to Lorne   Colonial Office
   19 May 1881
   KP4 PC/B/51a

Copy

I am glad Sir A. MacDonald[25] takes a sensible view of the Panama canal.
I sent his note[26] to Lord Granville. Honours are as you say a great difficulty.
Indeed as to orders I have always a difficulty in seeing why everyone who
has not done anything discreditable, should not have one. In Russia this is
as regards official people, practically the rule, and you will remember the old
Prussian saying that there are only two things no man can escape 'death and the
3rd class of the Red Eagle'. Seriously the only thing to do is to distribute them
sparingly unless they are to be of no value.[27] I should be afraid of a Canadian
order. It would I fear soon fall into disrepute, more especially as we should
soon have to grant an 'order' to every considerable colony. The local order
would have to be given locally, and would be certain to be jobbed....

109. Minutes on Wood[28] to Kimberley
   23 August 1881
   CO179/138

Herbert[29], 30 September 1881 — I would express concurrence in the opinion
that the consideration of Dunn's Railway and harbour proposals should be for the
minute postponed.[30] Hereafter it will become a very serious question for Natal
whether its railway, the longest and most difficult route to the Transvaal can be
pushed much further beyond the point to which it is now being constructed.
   Kimberley, 2 October 1881 — I agree as to the railway and harbour. We shall
however have to let them be made, if capitalists can be found to make them.

[25] Sir John Alexander Macdonald (1815–91), Prime Minister of Canada, 1867–73;
1878–91.
[26] Agreeing with Granville that a British remonstrance might stimulate 'the Americans
to act contrary to our wishes rather than that of deterring them'. Macdonald to Lorne,
28 April 1881, GrP 30/29/135, ff. 40–41.
[27] On Kimberley's reluctance to grant honours, see letter 69, herein; Extracts, Kimberley memoir, RsP 10186, p. 255; Godley, *Reminiscences*, p. 203; Kimberley to Ripon,
24 January 1883, RP 43523, f. 22.
[28] Sir Henry Evelyn Wood, army officer; served in the Crimean War, Indian Mutiny,
Ashanti campaign and Zulu War; Royal Commissioner for the Settlement of the Transvaal, 1881.
[29] Robert George Herbert (1831–1905), Permanent Under-Secretary for the Colonies,
1871–92.
[30] John Dunn, an Englishman who had been 'for many years a chief of high rank in
Zululand', was appointed by Sir Garnet Wolseley to govern an important Zulu district
bordering Natal. According to Wolseley, Dunn had 'completely adopted the life of
a Kaffir', but was 'in intelligence, sympathy, and demeanour wholly an Englishman.'
Memorandum of 7 May 1880. African no. 218, CO879/17.

We cannot prevent useful lines from being made for the purpose of cockering up Natal lines. The whole question must be considered in connection with the general arrangements in Zululand. These papers like all recent ones show that the Zulu will not long continue to respect the Resident. Send the draft.

---

110. Kimberley to Ripon   Kimberley House
3 September 1881
RP 43522, ff. 274–78

Private

.... Apart from the Transvaal, which has excited a good deal of interest, Ireland has absorbed Parliament almost entirely. I will not venture to prophesy as to the Land Bill. There are some rather encouraging signs. I fear however that hatred of the English is too strong a passion in the mass of the Irish to permit fair play to any measure passed by an English Govt. and Parliament. If I am right, it is a gloomy prospect.

In the House of Lords our weakness is quite ridiculous. There has been nothing like it since Melbourne's Govt. I don't believe there are 40 men, not placemen, who support us. Salisbury[31] in my opinion did not manage badly in the Land Bill discussions except on one night (when we considered the Commons' amendments). On that night he was insolent and defiant to the H. of Commons, and if Gladstone had not behaved with admirable tact and temper he might have brought on a serious conflict between the houses. Granville was unluckily absent from the greater part of the debates from a sharp fit of gout, and it devolved upon me to fill his place as well as I could. You may imagine what a pleasant time I had of it, more especially as I was just then not at all well, having had a sharp feverish attack from the great heat which made me very weak, tho' I soon got over it. Our majority in the H. of Commons remains most faithful. How we stand in the country it is not so easy to say. Incessant rain is destroying the harvest, and the prospects for the next winter are not cheering.

The probable breakdown of the French Commercial Treaty[32] is bringing about a certain agitation for 'fair trade' i.e. our old friend Protection.[33] The farmers will vote for this to a man, not caring a rap for the Radical shibboleths about free land, abolition of primogeniture, &c. &c. &c. &c. I am not at all sure some of the artisans won't join them and the Tories are already beginning to coquet with this anti Free Trade movement. However, what Demos may do, I

---

[31] Robert Arthur Gascoyne-Cecil, third Marquess of Salisbury (1830–1903), Conservative Secretary of State for Foreign Affairs, 1878–80; 1885–86; 1887–92; 1895–1900; Prime Minister, 1885–86; 1886–92; 1895–1902.

[32] Of 1860; renounced by France from 1 January 1880, but prolonged until 15 May 1882 by various declarations.

[33] See letters 89, 107, herein.

think the wisest man cannot foretell. What seems pretty certain is that he is sure before long to veer round entirely. Uncertainty and instability are a growing danger in English politics.

I have said nothing as to the H. of Commons. You can judge from the newspapers the pitch of impotence which it has reached. Clôture might be of some use, but it cannot be adopted without the cooperation of the opposition which we are not likely to get.

Give my kind regards to Lady Ripon.

111. Kimberley to Gladstone
　　　2 January 1882
　　　GrP 30/29/135, ff. 97–98

The Cameroon River is in the Bight of Biafra far away from any British settlement. I think there can be no question of acquiring territory there. We have already quite enough territory on the West Coast of Africa and it would be very unwise in my opinion to increase our already heavy responsibilities in that part of the world. I would suggest that King Bell and King Akua receive a civil answer saying that we appreciate their desire for good government, and for the abolition of heathen customs but that we cannot advise the Queen to increase her territorial possessions in that part of the world, especially as the Cameroon River is far distant from any country ruled over or protected by Her Majesty. It would be well I think to refer to the F.O.[34] — who I think have more information as to the Cameroon people than the Col. Office.

112. Kimberley to Spencer　　　　　　　　　　35 Lowndes Square
　　　14 May 1882
　　　SP K35

Private

I have not written to you since the horrible tragedy,[35] as I felt you must be overwhelmed with letters and urgent work. I will say no more on the past except

---

[34] Dilke and Granville pressed for further enquiry, doubting that anything could be done without the consent of the Colonial Office. After reviewing the Foreign Office case, on 14 June 1882 Kimberley wrote to Granville confirming his opposition to annexation, and arguing 'I hardly know where we are to stop, if we are to annex territory on the W. African coast in order to keep out the French. Upon that principle there are several places in the vicinity of our settlements which should at all events have the preference before we establish settlement in new districts.' GrP 30/29/135, ff. 111–14.

[35] The May 6 murder in Phoenix Park, Dublin, of Henry Burke, Under-Secretary for Ireland, and Lord Frederick Cavendish, Chief Secretary for Ireland. Matthew terms it 'the Cabinet's Majuba in Irish policy: a disaster, but one essentially irrelevant to the flow of policy.' *Gladstone Diaries*, 10:cxxii.

that when Harcourt put into my hands the telegram at the Austrian Embassy where we were dining I felt for the moment quite stunned.

We are all united and of one mind as to the necessity of stern repression whilst we do not recede from our other policy, but I fear there are some who do not fully appreciate the difficulties of the situation. They exaggerate I think the value of the lip demonstration of horror in Ireland, and they overestimate the power of the Govt. to deal with the secret associations of assassins. I shall believe in the demonstration against the murders, when I hear of any real active cooperation with the police to discover the murderers. I hope I may be wrong, but I expect that cowardice in some and sympathy with the crime in others will prevent any real aid being given by the general population to bring the guilty to punishment. Nor do I put much if any faith in the offer of rewards. Perhaps the most valuable weapon which one will put in your hands will be expulsion of aliens.

I am alarmed at the outcry which is being raised here against the Irish police. New heads and energetic administration are evidently wanted to secure its thorough efficiency and you have taken steps to supply these: but the cry against the police is fomented by the anti-English agitation whose deliberate policy it is to break down, if possible, the only strictly Irish organized body which is staunch to the Government.

The Radicals from ignorance blindly play into their hands. I am sure you will not fall into this trap, but it is a serious danger in my opinion, and some of our colleagues take, what I conceive to be, very hasty and erroneous views on this subject.

As to feeling in the country, it is as far as I can make out resolute and calm; distrustful of the Government, although ready to give us fair support if we are firm.

I do not know anything else which I could write, worth your reading. I will only add that at all times if I can be of any use to you, you may command my services to the utmost.

Don't trouble yourself to acknowledge my letter.

113. Kimberley Memorandum   Lowndes Sq.
   21 May 1882
   ChP 8/5

I agree generally with the Chancellor: and most earnestly desire that we should adhere firmly to all the main provisions of the bill,[36] admitting of course any amendments which may be improvements but not in the direction of weakening its powers. I should regret the shortening the time. Lord Spencer proposed

---

[36] Prevention of Crime Bill. On Chamberlain's opposition, see J.L. Garvin, *The Life of Joseph Chamberlain*, 3 vols. (London: Macmillan, 1933–35), 1:370; *Red Earl*, 1:200–03.

five years, which would have been better I think than three. It seems to me most unwise to run the chance of having to go through all the labour of reviewing the bill two years hence.

I trust that before any important amendments are agreed to we shall have a Cabinet to consider them. No more fatal course could in my opinion be taken either for the good govt. of Ireland or our own credit than after having brought in a bill which we have declared to be necessary to meet a grave peril of the country, to shrink before the opposition of Parnell and his friends and, as I said before, to 'whittle away' the bill by concessions to them.

114. Kimberley to Halifax
17 June 1882
HfP A4/51

Private

I can write nothing satisfactory about public affairs. Things do not mend in Ireland; our bill moves at a snail's pace in the H. of Commons: and we are in a great difficulty in Egypt. I don't regret the release of Parnell and Co. — we have not gained much by it, but his release must have taken place soon, and it is better that he should be in the House during the discussion of the Crime and Arrears bills.[37]

It would have been disastrous if he had remained in prison till the Act expired, and then walked out, defying the Government. Now at all events we had a decent excuse for releasing him. This is not putting the matter very high; but when all the wordy conflict about the 'Kilmainham Treaty' is set aside, not much more in my opinion remains than what I have said.

Egypt is a most serious complication. Araby Pasha[38] is master of the situation, and it is not at all apparent how he is to be dislodged. Worse still, we have been obliged to look on whilst British subjects have been insulted and murdered in Alexandria, and it is not at all clear how we are to obtain reparation and security for the future. The policy now is to get the Turk to interfere. The Turk who has got the ball at his feet, is by no means anxious to send his troops. He does not like to put down Mussulman fanatics to please European Powers. He is afraid of an Arab movement. He is intriguing this way and that for his own corrupt purposes. France is growing very lukewarm about the whole business.

[37] Charles Stewart Parnell (1846–91), Irish Land League president; jailed in October 1881 for inciting agrarian violence, but released in April under the 'Kilmainham Treaty' — the May 2 agreement by which the government released Irish activists and paid arrears in rent of 100,000 Irish tenants in return for Parnell's cooperation in suppressing agrarian crime.

[38] Egyptian Under-Secretary for War; led a successful military revolt in September 1881, leaving the Khedive with only nominal power.

The other Powers are 'united' with us, but really I suspect not at all anxious to help us out of the mess.

Altogether an uncomfortable prospect.

---

115. Kimberley to Derby   Kimberley House
       31 December 1882
       DP 920 Der (15) 20

Meade[39] came to me when I was in London to mention the subject of the Congo. Altho this is more directly the business of F.O., Granville has referred the matter to the Col. Office and I have been in consultation with him.

You will have observed the proceedings of the French in the Congo and the de Brazza Treaty.[40] Our merchants are much alarmed at the prospect of France controlling this great water-way. Granville decided to come to terms with Portugal as to her old Congo claims, and by recognizing under stringent stipulations as to trade her territorial claims he hopes to check-mate France.

Now, as Meade told me, our traders are beginning to fear similar French attempts on the Niger, and they apprehend that if the French designs in the Congo are frustrated, efforts will be immediately made to deliver a counter blow in the Niger district. Our Congo trade is at present comparatively small, our Niger trade very important. The Foreign Office have long been very uncomfortable about the Niger and the 'oil rivers' — They proposed to me to take possession of the whole coast from Lagos to the Gaboon River! This I entirely declined to do. But I am well aware that our position is not satisfactory. Meade seemed to think we ought to try to come to some agreement with France as to this region.

In the present state of French feeling this, even if desirable, would, I think, be hopeless. On the whole I see nothing better to be done than to go on with the agreement with Portugal.[41] But I commend the whole question to your consideration.

[*Postscript*] Meade told me that the difficulty with the Treasury about Zulu expenses had been got over for the moment.

---

[39] Robert Henry Meade (1835–98), Assistant Under-Secretary of State, 1871–92; Permanent Under-Secretary of State, 1892–96, at the Colonial Office.

[40] 1880 treaty establishing a protectorate on the north bank of the Congo River.

[41] On the evolution of Anglo-Portuguese relations in West Africa, see G.N. Sanderson, 'British Informal Empire, Imperial Ambition, Defensive Strategies, and the Anglo-Portuguese Congo Treaty of February 1884', in Stig Forster, Wolfgang J. Mommsen, and Ronald Robinson, eds. *Bismarck, Europe, and Africa: The Berlin Africa Conference 1884–1885 and the Onset of Partition* (Oxford: Oxford University Press, 1988), pp. 189–214.

116. Kimberley to Ripon   Kimberley House
    n.d.
    RP 43523, ff. 1–3

Private and Confidential

Your very kind telegram was most welcome. It gives me the greatest pleasure
to find myself working with you again. My translation to the India office was
very unexpected. I left London fully believing Derby was to go there. At the
last moment almost, it was found that difficulties (you may guess where, not of
course with Derby) existed which could not be overcome,[42] and I was asked if
I should object to change in order to facilitate the arrangements. Of course I
could not do otherwise than consent. I had no wish to leave the Colonial Office
especially as several questions are approaching completion there which I have
had long in hand, but the India Office is rather more important and certainly
not less interesting. The time of change is very inconvenient just at the Xmas
holidays.

We stand very firm as a government. The procedure session was, thanks to
Gladstone's wonderful exertions, a complete success; and the quick termination
of the Egyptian campaign was a great piece of luck.[43] The liberal party in the
country did not half like the war, and if it had been prolonged, we might have
expected discontent amongst our supporters.

Ireland too tho' still far from pacified, is more hopeful.

I shall not attempt in this letter to write anything on Indian questions. Pray
give my best regards to Lady Ripon.

117. Kimberley to Ripon   India Office
    14 February 1883
    RP 43523, ff. 36–40

Private

Though I do not invite long letters, pray don't think I am impatient of them.
I had many Colonial correspondents, and the aggregate of the letters I wrote
and received every week more than equalled any Indian correspondence I am
likely to have....

I entirely agree in what you say of the impolicy of showing sensitiveness about
Russia. This however is of course consistent with the exercise of watchfulness

---

[42] Hartington, the previous Indian Secretary, wrote to Spencer that 'Her Majesty would
not have Derby at the India Office. She said he could never make up his mind, either for
peace or war, and that the Russians would immediately come to India.' 16 December
1882, *Red Earl*, 1:231; *EHJ1*, 1:375–76. See also, *CJ*, pp. 61–62.

[43] British and French fleets had been sent in May 1882 to safeguard law and order
following the Arabi *putsch* of April. Granville issued a circular note on 3 January 1883,
stating Britain's intention to retire from Egypt as soon as the powers recognized her
paramountcy and guaranteed free navigation of the Suez Canal.

as to her proceedings, and counteracting her designs in any way which may be prudent. I had a conversation a few days ago with Granville, Hartington, Northbrook and Dilke on this subject, and we are all agreed that the rapid advance of Russia towards the Afghan frontier is assuming a serious character and that it is necessary carefully to consider our position. The Queen as you know is very sensitive on this point and she is not unnaturally anxious that our attention should be given to the intelligence which reaches us from the Persian and Afghan frontier. Do not for a moment suppose that I am an alarmist. I have paid close attention to this subject ever since I was Minister to Russia (25 years ago) and I am too familiar with Russian intrigues and Russian modes of action, to be seized with any sudden panic because I hear that Cossack parties are pressing upon the Turcoman tribes. Nevertheless I cannot shut my eyes to the fact that very soon the Russians will exercise authority up to the Northwestern Afghan border, and that we shall have an entirely new state of things to deal with before long.

The question therefore is what, if anything, ought we to do to prepare ourselves to meet the emergencies which may arise. I will put aside at once interference in Afghanistan. It is unnecessary I should assure you that I utterly disapproved of Lytton's policy, and entirely approved our retirement from Candahar.[44] Your policy is to leave the Afghans alone, and I heartily concur in it. But we have given the Amir a distinct assurance of support against foreign attack provided he follows our advice in his foreign relations, and we may be called on to redeem our pledge.

I expect no immediate difficulties, nor any distinctly aggressive move on the part of Russia. On the other hand I have not the slightest doubt that it is her deliberate policy to advance near enough to India to be able to give us serious trouble whenever it suits her to do so.

I am sorry that I cannot agree with you as to the advantage of an understanding with Russia, embodied in a public diplomatic instrument. This plan of action has been repeatedly discussed since we have been in office and after giving it my best consideration, I remain of the opinion (1) that it is not practicable; (2) that if it were practicable, we should derive not benefit from it, but the contrary....

What then remains? Two things in my opinion: 1) we ought to secure the means of accurate and trustworthy information of the state of affairs on the Afghan border. Nothing is so conducive to panic and party measures as want of real knowledge of what is going on. With this view I am with your consent (if our minister in Persia[45] sees no objection) about to send Colonel Stewart[46] back for another year. 2) We should make our position on our frontier strong.

---

[44] Edward Robert Bulwer Lytton, as Indian Viceroy, 1876–80, pursued a 'forward' policy of protecting India by occupying Afghan territory, including the fortress of Kandahar.

[45] R. F. Thompson.

[46] Charles Edward Stewart, Indian army; political agent in Persia, 1880–85; Assistant Commissioner in the Perso-Afghan boundary demarcation, 1885.

It is most satisfactory that your communication with Peshawer will shortly be completed by the opening of the bridge over the Indus, the absence of which always seemed to me a serious evil. But on the other side, our communications with Quetta are far from perfect. You have recently proposed to improve the road from Sibi, of which I entirely approved. Ought we not to proceed also with the railway from Sibi to Quetta?

It appears to me to be contrary to sound principles to hold an advanced post such as Quetta and not to have the best possible means of communication with it. Besides the military advantages of an extension of the railway, there is the subsidiary benefit to our trade, which benefit must I apprehend be not unimportant.

My colleagues, whom I mentioned above, all agreed that the time had arrived for considering the extension of the Railway. Of course the question of expense is a serious element of the case. I shall be glad to know your views confidentially, and if you are in favour of making the line, I will consult the cabinet upon the question.

118. Kimberley to Gladstone　　　　　　　　　　　35 Lowndes Sq.
　　3 March 1883
　　GP 44228, f. 57

....I want to mention to the Cabinet on Tuesday[47] a matter which the Queen strongly presses, and on which I have obtained Ripon's opinion, the establishment of a small Indian Body Guard (some 20 men) in this country. Ripon does not object and Hartington and Northbrook agree with me that we must humour HMy. with this toy. She is very eager for it.

119. Kimberley to Ripon　　　　　　　　　　　　Kimberley House
　　29 March 1883
　　RP 43523, ff. 80–81

Private

I am much obliged to you for your letter of March 4 on the Criminal Procedure Bill.[48] You make an excellent case, and I hope I may be able to do justice to it on Lytton's motion.[49] It is evident that the feeling of the European opponents of

---

[47] Actually Monday. *Gladstone Diaries*, 10:412.

[48] Introduced into the Viceroy's council on 2 February 1883 by legal member, Sir Courtenay Ilbert, enabling Indian district magistrates and sessions judges in country districts to serve in cases involving Europeans. Widely known as the Ilbert Bill. For a full study, see Edwin Hirschmann, *'White Mutiny': The Ilbert Bill Crisis in India and the Genesis of the Indian National Congress* (Delhi: Heritage Publishers, 1980).

[49] Purposely vague, but designed to give 'timely expression to the fears ... which ha[d] been aroused' by Ripon's alteration of the Indian criminal justice system. Kimberley

the bill goes much deeper than this particular measure. They are really opposed to the whole policy of giving the natives a share in administrative appointments. Probably however many of them are not aware of the real consequences which necessarily flow from their views, and are only actuated by a vague jealousy and dislike of anything which tends to the treatment of natives on an equal footing with European British subjects.

Colonists generally throughout the British Empire are strongly imbued with similar feelings, and the chief difficulty of a Col. Minister is to avoid a collision between the Liberal policy towards coloured races which is now on the whole firmly established at home as the only just policy, and the narrowminded views of most of the colonial communities; Canada is perhaps the only exception....

120. Kimberley Memorandum   35 Lowndes Sq.
    26 April 1883
    DP Der 920 (15) 20

The difficulty in this case is that all parties want to force the Imperial Govt. to take the responsibility of governing Basutoland.[50] The colonists, very naturally, want to be relieved of the expense and risk of managing their unsettled frontiers, and to recur to the old plan of their frontiers being under the High Commissioner. Past experience shows that this means a Caffir war from time to time at Imperial expense.

The missionaries want the Basutos who are their especial pets, to be under the Imperial Government because they hope that we shall keep the colonists out of the country and preserve Basutoland exclusively for the Basutos. This has a very tempting look, but I have no belief in the permanence of any system which closes the country to white colonisation.

The strong feeling which now exists among the Basutos against being under the colonial Govt., has been sedulously fostered by the missionaries.

121. Kimberley to Ripon   India Office
    15 June 1883
    RP 43523, ff. 148–55

Private

I have read your letter of May 21 with great care and attention, and I hope in our despatch on the Bengal Bill I may be able so to express myself as to remove

---

agreed with Lytton as to the 'necessity of caution', minutely reviewed the circumstances, then concluded: 'for the ultimate safety and security that there should be a gradual introduction of Natives into our services' in order to avoid a 'high autocratic policy'. 3 *Hansard*, 277 (9 April 1883): 1736, 1767.

[50] On the Cape parliament's move to disannex Basutoland, see Schreuder, *Gladstone and Kruger*, pp. 337–42.

at all events to a considerable extent the annoyance which the Desp: of April 19 has given you. I freely admit that in assuring you that I would support your Local Govt. policy I did not conceive that I was committing myself to approval of all the details of your memorandum, concerning which indeed at the time I wrote I was not in a position to form definite conclusions.[51] I intended to convey to you that I fully concurred in the general principles of your policy, namely, cautious but real and substantial advance in the grant of local self- government.... The only question in my mind is, whether the measures we are taking will in the long run conduce to good administration, and strengthen the foundation of the government. In speaking of govt. I do not mean merely British rule. I believe indeed that the possibilities of good government in India are inseparably bound up at the present time with the maintenance of British rule, but we have to look to the permanent security of peaceful and civilized govt., and we should not be furthering this all important end, if from any desire to please the educated natives, we were to impair the vigour of the main supports of the whole fabric of our administration. We have in short to reconcile two objects, the extension of the native share in local management, and the maintenance of the full strength of our general political system. My anxiety is that both should receive equal attention.

With what you say, as to the danger of allowing it to be supposed that the Govt. at home are withholding its support from your policy I cordially concur. I shall endeavour so to word any Bengal Despatch as to make it quite clear that there is no ground for any such supposition.

With what you say as to your personal position at the close of your letter, I can only express my sorrow that you should have found in the substance of my views on your local gt. policy or the manner in which those views were conveyed to you, cause for the difficulty in which you feel yourself placed. The weapon which you wield when you say that you doubt whether you can conduct the administration with advantage, is so powerful with me both on personal and political grounds that I hope you will use it mercifully: as I might be sorely tempted to depart from what I believe to be my line of duty rather than view so great a misfortune as your secession from us. You may be sure that I shall do my best to support you, altho' I may be compelled sometimes to criticise and even disagree....

You must forgive me for not adopting your suggestion that Cross should deny the story in the 'Englishman'[52]— I have the greatest objection to taking

---

[51] On tensions within the Liberal party over Indian policy, see Sarvepalli Gopal, *The Viceroyalty of Lord Ripon, 1880–1884* (London: Oxford University Press, 1953); R.J. Moore, *Liberalism and Indian Politics, 1872–1922* (London: Edward Arnold, 1966), chaps. 3-5; John Powell, 'A Whig Facade: Indian Policy Development under the Liberals during 1883', *Quarterly Review of Historical Studies*, 30 (Oct.–March 1990–91): 70–86.

[52] Of 28 April 1883, suggesting that the Ilbert Bill was the first of a series of measures to rapidly turn over to Indians the whole administration of the country. Christine Dobbin,

any notice of the innumerable lies set about by newspapers.[53] The usual result is that people believe that after all there was something in the statement.

122. Kimberley to Gladstone   Privy Council Office
      11 August 1883
      GP 44228, f. 96

There *is* an amendment in the bill[54] which does rather savour of Balfour's amendment, that the value shall not take into account anything which is justly due to any cause other than the *skill & outlay* of the tenant.

123. Kimberley to Gladstone   Kimberley House
      26 September 1883
      GP 44228, ff. 113–14

I have today received the enclosed letter (wh. please return) from Ripon. His recommendation that the 'Ilbert' bill should be postponed deserves the most serious consideration. Nevertheless I still think it is better to proceed with it at once.

If the bill is postponed, it will have the appearance of weakness, and the agitation will be encouraged. It will not be necessary that I should assent to the Bill till after Parliament meets, so that an opportunity will still remain for considering it. But the point is a nice one, and I feel that your judgement in the matter, as especially affecting the HC and our position here must be far better than mine.[55]

124. Kimberley to Derby   Kimberley House
      26 September 1883
      DP 920 DER (15) 20

I have been asked to recommend to you Lord Canterbury for a colonial Governorship. His father as you will remember, was a long time in the Colonial service, which may constitute some claim for consideration.[56] He is very popular in this county where he has some property and has an agreeable wife (a Walpole).

'The Ilbert Bill: A Study of Anglo-Indian Opinion in India, 1883', *Historical Studies: Australia and New Zealand*, 45 (October 1965): 91–95.

[53] Kimberley generally disdained the press. See for instance letters 22, 87, 105, 259, 278, herein.

[54] Earlier in the day, Gladstone had spoken with Kimberley, presumably about the Agricultural Holdings Bill. *Gladstone Diaries*, 11:16.

[55] See Gladstone to Granville, 28 September 1883, *Gladstone–Granville Corresp. 2*, 2:91.

[56] John Henry Thomas Manners-Sutton had served as Governor of Trinidad, 1864–66; and of Victoria, 1866–73. His son was not appointed.

Whether he has much ability I do not know him well enough to say. He has however at all events the usual qualification, that he is poor, and I must not omit that he is a good Liberal.

125. Kimberley to Ripon   Kimberley House
     3 October 1883
     RP 43524, ff. 41–44

Private

I am in communication with Gladstone and other of my colleagues about the Crim. Proc. Bill and can write nothing definite by this mail, but I may say that I think it improbable that we shall be in favour of postponement.

With regard to the statement about Eden[57] in the Calcutta Memorial I will consider when it reaches me whether anything should be done. I expect however that Eden will not be for withdrawal of the bill, and if he is officially with us, we had better not press him as to his private sentiments.

I am afraid the evil of private letters of which you complain is irremediable. You must remember that the Council is composed, as a body of men who do not sympathise with the policy of a Liberal Govt. They are not really under our control except so far as the Secretary of State has legal powers to restrain them, and they do not possess the traditional loyalty of the civil service to whatever party is in power. At the same time I do not think they mean to be disloyal or that they are capable of doing anything deliberately to injure the Government. They are men of high and honourable character as far as I am acquainted with them, and this makes it the more difficult to make them understand that with the best intentions they may do harm, I mean difficult in this sense, that they would naturally resent any attempt to curtail their freedom of correspondence[58] .... I have no doubt that it will be convenient that you should make as few speeches as possible just now, and your trip to Cashmere will be a convenient way of avoiding them. I always feel a wish to avoid them altogether, but they are one of the duties in public life with which unfortunately one cannot dispense, and I am sorry to say in this country 'going to the stump' has become a recognized part of the business of politics, and will become more and more indispensable every year, as the democracy gains in strength.[59] The one thing which I admired in Lord Beaconsfield was his abstinence from platform oratory. I have written to

---

[57] Sir Ashley Eden, member of the Council of India.

[58] On the nature of the council, see Kaminsky, *The India Office*, chap. 3.

[59] A point not lost on others, and frequently cited as a detriment to good governance. Rosebery wrote in 1899 that no Prime Minister could exercise such control as Peel had had for 'a minister of these days would be preparing or delivering a speech in the country when Peel would be writing minutes of policy for the various departments.' *Sir Robert Peel* (London: Cassell and Company, 1899), p. 29.

the Duke of Connaught about his time of arrival in India and other arrangements and shall let you know by telegraph as soon as I have his answer.

P.S.—Mallet[60] has given up his office and Godley[61] reigns in his stead. I am exceedingly sorry to lose Mallet not only on account of his great knowledge of the business of the office, but because he is a man of thoroughly enlightened views, and most pleasant to work with.

126. Kimberley to Halifax   Kimberley House
   27 October 1883
   HfP A4/151

Private

I am very glad to learn your opinion about the Ilbert Bill, tho' I never doubted what it would be. To withdraw the Bill would, as you say, for the Govt. of India [be] simple suicide.

Apart from the trouble the agitation about this Bill gives, things are going on well in India. No apprehension now of famine, and consequently very good financial prospects for next year.

I note what you say in favour of Mr. Forjett.[62] But the vacancies in the Star of India are few and far between, and the candidates perfectly endless....

I should wish the Tory leaders were always on the 'stump' if they fared as they did in Ulster.[63] What folly to stump at all, when every one wants to be as quiet as mice, as far as present politics are concerned. In due time we shall all get hot again, and the Tories will not want for opportunities to stir us up.

127. Kimberley to Hartington   35 Lowndes Sq.
   10 February 1884
   DvP 340.1414

If we are resolved not in any circumstances to send a soldier into the interior of the Soudan, it is of no use to ask Genl. Gordon questions about an expedition to Suakim such as Ld. Wolseley suggests; but if we think that such an expedition is admissible, I do not see why we should not ask him in plain terms.[64] The

---

[60] Sir Louis Mallet (1823–90), Permanent Under-Secretary of State for India, 1874–83; member of the Political Economy Club.

[61] Arthur Godley (1847–1932), Principal Private Secretary to Gladstone, 1880–82; Permanent Under-Secretary of State for India, 1883–1909.

[62] Charles Forjett, Commissioner of Police and Chief Municipal Commissioner, Bombay, from 1855; according to Buckland's *Dictionary of Indian Biography*, he 'saved Bombay' from Sepoy mutiny in 1857. Deserving but never decorated, he retired considering himself slighted.

[63] In Monaghan, where Home Ruler Tim Healy won a bye-election on June 30.

[64] See Holland, *Life of Devonshire*, 1:418–19.

quotation, made by Mr. Gladstone shows that Gordon's mind was so much against fighting that there is no risk of a leading question having too much influence with him.[65]

It is evident that the newspapers know all about Wolseley's plan.

128. Kimberley to Ripon
15 February 1884
RP 43524, ff. 165–66

Private

.... As far as I can see we are getting the best of our party fight about the Soudan. Gladstone made a magnificent speech demolishing Northcote.[66] The strongest speech yet made against us is Forster's. I am very sorry for the line he has taken, not on this occasion only.[67]

Meantime everything points to a prolonged occupation of Egypt; and here comes to my mind the most serious difficulty, the want of sufficient British soldiers. People here clamour for the maintenance and extension of British 'prestige' as they call it all over the world. This means force, and force must be supported by more taxes, for the old taxes have ceased in these unprosperous years to be 'elastic' as they used to be.

Nothing strikes me more than the decline of the Bright school. The neo-Radical is more often a 'jingo' than not.[68] It is very important to take note of this change of feeling, which will ere long, I anticipate, produce far-reaching consequences.

129. Kimberley Memorandum[69]   India Office
13 May 1884
GP 44228, f. 141

The real question seems to me to be, whether we consider it to be a paramount object of policy in Ireland to create a large number of peasant proprietors in the place of the present landlords.

If we do so consider it, and are prepared to advance the money of the State for the purpose, we must run some risks. Lord Spencer's objection is mainly

---

[65] Morley, *Life of Gladstone*, 3: 147–52.

[66] 3 *Hansard*, 284 (12 February 1884): 700–27.

[67] Former Liberal Chief Secretary for Ireland, 1880–82, who in arguing against the vote of censure admitted that the government did not 'quickly enough realize the true policy'. 3 *Hansard*, 284 (14 February 1884): 935–47. On Kimberley's early diffidence regarding Forster's policies, see Kimberley journal, 5 September 1880, KP6 MS.eng.e.2793, pp. 487–88.

[68] See letter 132, herein.

[69] In response to Spencer's note and letter on the Irish purchase clauses, *Red Earl*, 1:269–70; *Gladstone Diaries*, 11:146.

that the debtors of the state will possibly refuse to pay, and he therefore prefers a plan which will create comparatively few such debtors.

Be it so; but then the operation must fail as a scheme for creating a peasant proprietary in any large sense. The scheme will be reduced to one for somewhat facilitating the working of the purchase clauses. Will this satisfy any one, whether landlords or tenants? and may it not practically fail as previous attempts in the same direction have failed? and be followed by a Conservative scheme giving large concessions to the landlord with the effect of alienating from us all parties in Ireland?

Lord Spencer seems to contemplate with some satisfaction the possibility that the tenants may not choose to buy. In that case what will become of the landlords who want to sell? and is it safe that the present deadlock in the land market should continue?

As to the local guarantee, I have no particular preference for the county over the general guarantee.

130. Kimberley to Halifax   10 Downing St.
    18 July 1884
    HfP A4/151

Private

....As to the franchise, Salisbury is evidently determined on war. It was impossible to make a more provocative speech than he did last night.[70] If our mere party interests were at stake it would be difficult to invent anything more advantageous to us than his proceedings.

In all other aspects they are lamentable.

131. Kimberley to Derby   Witton Park, Norfolk
    17 September 1884
    DP 920 Der (15) 20

Private

....As to the Nile expedition the chief has been gradually edged on till he is fairly embarked on an enterprise he hates.[71] I hate it too, but there is no

---

[70] 3 *Hansard*, 290 (17 July 1884):1368, 1374. For an equally provocative study of the reform bill of 1884, see Andrew Jones, *The Politics of Reform, 1884* (Cambridge: Cambridge University Press, 1972); also, *Gladstone Diaries*, 10:cvi–cviii.

[71] The expedition to relieve Gordon in Khartoum. See Gladstone to Hartington, 13 September 1884, in *Gladstone Diaries*, 11:207; Derby to Kimberley, 13 September 1884, KP6 MS.eng.d.4242, f. 121; Adrian Preston, *In Relief of Gordon, Lord Wolseley's Campaign Journal of the Khartoum Relief Expedition, 1884–1885* (London: Hutchinson, 1967), pp. 3-10.

avoiding it. From the moment we made the fatal mistake of sending Gordon, we were inextricably involved in the Soudan affair.[72] Probably sending *any* English officer to Khartoum would have had the same effect. It is however now no use to lament over our initial mistake.

You have exhausted all the possible alternatives about the franchise bill. The H. of Lords will certainly not give way. The Queen would in all probability refuse to make peers. Resignation would in my opinion be folly. Remains dissolution after autumn session or to re-present the bill in the ordinary session.

I thought we were pretty well certain to adopt the former course; but after the speeches at Edinbro'[73] I hardly see how we can now. Else I should have said, with you, if Egypt looks well in December, dissolve. I fear however that we shall be still in the thick of it in the Soudan, when the end of the year arrives.

Like you I should have no objection to consider any practicable plan of reforming the H. of Lords — only I have never yet seen such a plan. Unless it is such a plan as would put an end to Tory ascendancy in the House, it will do little or no good. What is wanted is the infusion of a more or less permanent Liberal element, sufficient to counter-balance to some extent the landowning Toryism which is now predominant. A limited number of life Peers might be of some use. How would it be to have a certain number like the Scotch peers sit for Parliament only? This would enable a Govt. having a Liberal majority in the H. of Commons to add to its strength in the Lords.

132. Kimberley to Ripon   Kimberley House
     24 September 1884
     RP 43525, f. 180.

Private

.... Our affairs in the Soudan are brightening wonderfully, and it is now proved that our belief that Gordon was in no serious danger, was fully justified.

Parnell and Co. threaten serious trouble next session. The worst symptom to my mind in public affairs is the increase of the 'Jingo' spirit, which I fear is taking hold of our party as well as the Tories. One comfort is that if the Radicals turn Jingo, the Tories are sure to take the other side soon.

---

[72] According to Sir Robert Meade, Kimberley believed that he could 'have shown Gordon to be unfit for the work' had he met with Granville, Hartington, Northbrook, and Dilke on January 18. It is impossible to say how far he would have persisted in the face of Hartington's and Granville's recommendations. Edmond Fitzmaurice, *Life of George Leveson Gower: Second Earl of Granville*, 2 vols. (London: Longmans, 1905), 2:400–01. On Kimberley's earlier mistrust of Gordon, see Schreuder, *Gladstone and Kruger*, p. 294 and note 3.

[73] Gladstone's of late August. See Morley, *Life of Gladstone*, 3:126–30; Jones, *Politics of Reform*, pp. 162–66, 170–71.

133. Kimberley to Chamberlain   Kimberley House
    25 September 1884
    ChP 9/1/1/5

I was much surprised as you were at the German annexation of the Cameroons. After the decision of the Committee I thought the matter was settled and as I have more than enough to do with India, I gave it no further thought.[74] I am quite ignorant of the reasons why our decision was not acted upon. 'Too late' I fear may be the explanation.

I entirely agree as to the Niger and I would add, all what are termed the 'oil rivers'. We have an immense trade there, and it would be folly to let any other Power get a footing there.

I am also much of your opinion about Zululand and Bechuanaland. You will remember I supported Derby's proposal to annex Zululand as far as the black Umfolosi.[75] The Cabinet declined this and it was evident, as Derby and I said at the time, that, if we did not interfere, the Boers would. We made our choice, and I would abide the result and leave Zululand beyond the reserve to its fate.

I wish I could resist the conclusion that we must interfere by force in Bechuanaland, but I see no other way out of that miserable business. Our credit and our good faith is at stake, and we must stand the hazard of the die. The latest telegram brings an offer from the Cape Govt. to cooperate with us. This is very important, especially considering the Dutch tendencies of the present Cape Government. If the colony heartily joins with us, our task will be comparatively easy. The Soudan looks much more hopeful.

134. Kimberley to Ripon   India Office
    24 October 1884
    RP 43525, ff. 202–05

Private

I do not deny the evils which you point out in your letter of September 26 of 'burning the candle at both ends'. I would not 'burn the candle' at all, if I could help it, but unfortunately the questions involved are not dependent solely on our own actions. You underrate the aggressiveness of France, over whose policy there has come during the last year a remarkable change.

---

[74] The cabinet committee on West Africa, including Derby, Kimberley, Northbrook, Chamberlain, and Granville, recommended annexation in November 1883, which was approved by the Cabinet. GP 44644, f. 109; Derby diaries, 16–22 November 1883, DP; *Gladstone Diaries*, 11:63; Chamberlain to Granville, 28 September 1884, GrP 30/24/120. See too D. M. Schreuder, *The Scramble for Southern Africa, 1877–1895, The Politics of Partition Reappraised* (Cambridge: Cambridge University Press, 1980), pp. 139–40.

[75] The Umfolozi River. For diplomatic circumstances, see Schreuder, *The Scramble for Southern Africa*, chap. 4.

I have been reading the minutes appended to your frontier railway Despatch. They would have been more instructive (I am not of course referring to your minutes), if they had given some information as to the ways and means for the payment of the additional European troops. Your councillors of course feel themselves relieved from the obligation of *finding* these additional men. At present unfortunately we are not able to keep the army up to its strength either at home or in India as now fixed. I should be curious to see the practical plans for permanently raising 15,000 additional men. We have not yet provided for the increase of force which will be inevitable if the occupation of Egypt continues.

I have sent Sir C. Macgregor's alarmist book[76] to Hartington for his consideration. My own inclination is, if possible, not to make too much of the scandal. It may however be difficult to avoid notice of it, since the 'confidential' document is practically public. I shall do nothing hastily.

I have read Sir R. Garth's[77] minute. As your despatch raises the question I will not anticipate our decision upon it. No class of man is more difficult to deal with than a wrong-headed Indian or colonial judge. The public always thinks that any rebuke of a Judge means interference with his judicial independence, altho' his proceedings may be anything but judicial.

I suffered many things at the Colonial Office at the hands of indiscreet judges, of whom we had there a more than ample supply, and tho' we had also some excellent judicial officers.

As to home politics, we have no indication yet that the Tories will not fight us on the franchise to the bitter end. I believe Salisbury to be quite indifferent to the consequences to the House of Lords, and in fact rather to look forward with satisfaction to its possible abolition.

If that should happen, it will be a greater shake to our Constitution than those who speak so lightly of it suppose, and might lead eventually to the establishment of a Republican form of govt. When Salisbury has abolished our House, you will no doubt return to the commons. I am afraid I shall be too old to begin there. Whatever happens, you will find politics exciting enough when you come home.[78]

---

[76] Sir Charles Metcalfe Macgregor, Indian Quartermaster-General and head of the Intelligence Department in 1884 had written 'The Defence of India, A Strategical Study', suggesting formation of an Indian army of 340,000 men, including 120,000 British troops. He also urged the partition of Russia by a 'grand coalition' of England, Germany, Austria, Turkey, Persia, Turkestan, China and Afghanistan. Although confidentially printed, it 'had a circulation which practically amounted to publication.' Gopal, *Viceroyalty of Ripon*, p. 43 n.

[77] Sir Richard Garth, Chief Justice of Bengal.

[78] Although Ripon's term as Viceroy was not complete, it had been decided in July for political reasons that he should be replaced before the end of 1884. Kimberley to Gladstone, 23 July 1884, GP 44228, ff. 144–46; *Gladstone Diaries*, 11:178.

135. Kimberley to Dufferin   Kimberley House
11 December 1884
DfP MSS Eur. 130/3, ff. 5–6

Private

This letter will I trust find you comfortably installed in your Viceregal chair after a prosperous journey. I enclose a copy of an interesting letter from Lumsden.[79] His presence with the rest of the expedition on the frontier is causing much annoyance to the Russian military authorities, who are doing all they can to frustrate the objects of the Commission....

We on our side have certainly strong motives for avoiding a quarrel. Our position in regard to Egyptian affairs is, if possible, more embarrassing than ever. We are making no progress with the financial settlement, and Bismarck, who is animated by an extraordinary feeling of bitterness against this country, the cause of which it is not easy to explain, will do his utmost apparently to prevent any settlement, with the object evidently of embroiling us with France.

A combination between Germany and France against us seemed to be the most improbable of events, but it exists to a certain extent already, and in Bismarck's present temper of mind one cannot be sure whether it may not any day assume a formidable aspect. In short, as long as we are in Egypt, we have a millstone tied round our necks, and no one sees how or when we are to get out of it. A pleasant prospect!

136. Kimberley to Hartington
18 April 1885
DvP 340.1738

I think we should adhere to our decision.[80] It would not be safe to base our policy on the varying rumours from distant places, the truth of which we have no means of testing.

The fundamental objection to the attempt to reconquer the Soudan remains the same, namely, that when we have reconquered it we shall not know what to do with it, unless (which would be madness) we are determined to hold it ourselves; and apart from the Soudan difficulty itself I feel strongly the urgency for what I may call imperial reasons, of disentangling ourselves from the expedition.[81]

---

[79] Sir Peter Stark Lumsden, Major-General, Indian Army; member of the Council of India, 1883–93. His letter of 29 October 1884 reported Russian perfidy in failing to abide by the boundary agreement. DfP MSS Eur. 130/3, ff. 6–8.

[80] Of 13 April 1885, to abandon Khartoum to the Mahdi. See Morley, *Life of Gladstone*, 3:555–59.

[81] Cf. Lieutenant-General Edward Hamley's assertion that 'national preservation transcends in importance national pride.' *The Times*, 17 February 1885, p. 8; also, Greaves, *Persia and the Defence of India*, pp. 64–65.

137. Kimberley to Halifax 35 Lowndes Sq.
10 May 1885
HfP A4/151

Private

The press of business upon me during the last week has been so severe that I was quite unable to find a moment to answer your letter.[82] To take your questions seriatim —

1. The Russians have behaved as badly as possible. The fact is Giers,[83] who, with the civil element at St. Petersburg generally, does not want war, suggested to us after the occupation of Merv a delimitation of the frontier. We readily agreed. Then the military party cried out against him as having made a great mistake in bringing us to the frontier, where they preferred being left alone to their own devices. Hence, after the appointment of Genl. Zelenoi as their Commissioner, the Russian Govt. suddenly found out various reasons, his illness &c. &c. &c. &c. &c. why he could not join Lumsden. Meantime the soldiers had their way and in spite of our remonstrances occupied nearly all the disputed territory except Penjdeh. That remained, until Komaroff's fight,[84] to the Afghans. A singularly opportune 'misunderstanding' of the agreement with us that the Russian and Afghan troops should remain where they were till the delimitation was made, enabled Komaroff to expel the Afghans from the Penjdeh valley.

2. Before this 'unhappy incident', our officers had examined and roughly mapped out the country from the Heri Rud to Khoja Saleh on the Oxus, so that we are in possession of full information: and the interview of Dufferin with the Amir put us in possession of his views.[85] It was impossible to get at them through our Mahommedan Agents at Cabul. The Amir trusts no one, and will speak his mind to no subordinate officer. We found that he was indifferent as to Penjdeh: indeed he showed plainly that he was aware he could not usefully hold it. He has practically no hold on the Saryk Turcomans who inhabit it. It is different, as he told us, with the Aimak tribes further South, over whom he can exercise control. He mentioned certain points, the Zulfagar Pass especially, to which he attached importance: and those points he will retain. It would have been absurd to fight for territory to which he is indifferent and the possession of which it is clear would be a source of weakness rather than strength to him. The

---

[82] In preparation for possible war with Russia. Kimberley to Dufferin, 14 May 1885, DfP MSS Eur. F 130/3, f. 70. On the Penjdeh incident generally, see Greaves, *Persia and the Defence of India, 1884–1892* , chap. 5 and appendix 1.

[83] Nikolai Karlovich de Giers, Russian Foreign Minister.

[84] General A. V. Komarov, Russian Chief of the Transcaspian Region. For accounts see Kimberley to Dufferin, 10 April 1885, DfP MSS Eur. F 130/3, ff. 48–49; Firuz Kazemzadek, *Russia and Britain in Persia, 1864–1914, a Study in Imperialism* (London: Yale University Press, 1968), pp. 94–97.

[85] *CJ* , pp. 84–85.

only objection to the line of frontier will be that it will bring the Russians two or three marches nearer to Herat than a line running to near Saraks. No Afghan has for years been in the district which will be Russian, except at Penjdeh where they had a certain amount of footing, varying according to circumstances. They had till last year no troops there — Whether the Amir is honest or not who can tell? He is an Afghan. He speaks us fair, and has just given a real proof of confidence by allowing two of our officers to go to Herat.

On the whole I think and so does Dufferin, the presumption is that he means to stick to our alliance. As to holding Herat as an Indian fortress I entirely agree with you. Lytton's policy has done a world of harm, and although the Amir is friendly it will take years to efface its effects on the Afghan people.

The Amir tells us fairly that we cannot expect that they will become at once our cordial friends. Give me four or five years, he said, and I will do my best to 'innoculate' them with a friendly feeling towards the English.

The recent 'incident' at Penjdeh will help us, as it is the first time the Russians have shed Afghan blood, and I have reason to believe that some even of the Russians regret it as *contrary to their own interests* but of course our stupid Jingoes think it has been a masterpiece of Russian policy.

138. Kimberley to Spencer   10 Downing St.
    21 June 1885
    SP K35

Private

In the present state of affairs might you not come over at once, deferring your leave taking.[86] It is impossible to say with any certainty what will happen, but it is, to say the least by no means improbable that Salisbury will throw up and Mr. Gladstone be called back. If this happens, the pivot on which everything will turn is the Irish question, and whatever course is taken you ought to be on the spot to state your views and hear the view of others —

Every moment will be precious as in the condition of our relations with Russia, it is of most serious importance that no time should be lost in forming some Govt.

P. S. — If after all Salisbury goes on, you can go back to take formal leave. Of course this is very inconvenient, but the conjuncture is grave and extraordinary.

---

[86] On the political turmoil requiring Spencer's return, see Cooke and Vincent, *Governing Passion*, pp. 261–69; *EHJ1*, 2:891–92; *CJ*, p. 120.

139.   Kimberley to Grant Duff[87]   India Office
      23 June 1885
      GDP MSS Eur. F234, v. 1, no. 47

Private

Salisbury has at last made up his mind to take office, and we give up the seals tomorrow. He has passed ten days in trying to extract from us assurances, that we could not possibly give, of support to his finance. I can't think what he has expected to gain, or why he did not, if he meant to come in, go on at once, trusting to the common sense of the H of Commons not to prevent him from carrying on the Govt. till the Dissolution.

I shall be very curious to see the official performance of my successor, R. Churchill.[88] If he is as erratic in office as opposition, you will have queer times, but he is probably too clever not to adapt himself to his new circumstances.... We should have lively times between this and Xmas.

140.   Kimberley to Grant Duff   Kimberley House
      23 July 1885
      GDP MSS Eur. F 234, v. 1, no. 50

Private

I have fled to the country and fresh air. Nothing really remains to be done at Westminster. It is not our cue to oppose, and the sooner the session ends the better. R. Churchill evidently rules the roost, and will, I suppose, oust Beach in due course.[89] The bargain with Parnell is I doubt not his making, and he had to pay earnest the other night on the Maamtrasna murder business.[90] His mean tone about Spencer has disgusted many people, and Salisbury tried the other night to get rid of some of the nasty taste by eulogising Spencer. But this won't have much effect, as the motive power is in the Commons. I am not sure however that Tory democracy and truckling to Irish nationalists will pay in the long run with English and Scotch people. For the moment it will answer its purpose.

---

[87] Mountstuart Grant Duff (1829–1906), Governor of Madras, 1881–86.

[88] Randolph Churchill (1849–95), Secretary of State for India, 1885–86.

[89] As leader in the House of Commons.

[90] During 1882 the murder of a family in Galway led to the hanging of three men, including one who continued to proclaim his innocence. Beginning in October 1884, Churchill took up the cause of those accused during the previous administration, supporting on 17 July 1885 Parnell's motion to reopen the case. Bucking Conservative cabinet decisions and breaching parliamentary etiquette, Churchill was widely criticised on both sides. On this and its relation to the 'bargain with Parnell', see Hammond, *Gladstone and the Irish Nation*, pp. 315–337; Foster, *Lord Randolph Churchill*, pp. 221–29.

Prophecy is busy about the elections. The case stands thus. New House will have 670 members. Say now (at least) 250 Tories. If they neither gain nor lose then   250 plus 80 Parnellites= 330

      Liberals   = 340

      Majority   10[91]

I am not at all sure the Tories will not gain some seats. The *old* boroughs will probably go round: still their prospects in the counties seem bad enough to counteract this. Lancashire however is I hear Tory, and we shall have the whole Irish vote wh. was with us last time, against us. This must lose us several seats. If we have a near balance, and Radicals and Tory Democrats bid against each other, we may look out for squalls.

The Russian difficulty remains apparently *in statu quo*. I should not be surprised to see Salisbury back down in some way. The nation will be angry if there is war about Zulficar and angry if he gives way, so I don't envy him his task.

As far as I can learn, the democracy shows no care for foreign politics. It is interested on the home questions about which its demagogues preach to it. If this temper continues, it will become increasingly difficult to maintain an Empire. But the most menacing question is Ireland, and as usual the problem is utterly perplexing.

141. Kimberley to Gladstone   Witton Park,
     13 September 1885[92]   North Walsham
     GP 44228, ff. 205–11

I am very much obliged by your letter received this morning. I need not say how rejoiced I am to hear that you have decided to seek reelection. No one but yourself could steer the party in an even course between our right and left wings, and the future of this country will largely depend upon the impulse given at the commencement of the new political era. To give that impulse will be the fitting crown of your political life.

I see no reason why we should split up. Chamberlain has made some imprudent speeches but his speech at Glasgow was admirable, and in all his speeches the matter has been much less open to objection than the form.

Our prospects in this county are good, except that in one division, that in which I am at this moment, we are without a candidate. The manifestation here in favour of disestablishment is very striking; and it is somewhat difficult to account for.

---

[91] In the final poll, Liberals won 334 seats; Conservatives, 250; and Irish Nationalists, 86, prompting Grant Duff to observe, 'for the purposes of your biographer that you have a fair claim to the title of a prophet.' 16 December 1885, KP6 MS.eng.c.4222, ff. 144–45.

[92] Probably misdated. See Matthew, *Gladstone Diaries*, 11:401, n. 1.

As far as I can judge, apart from the genuine Nonconformist opposition to Church Establishments in general, it is due to the narrow Toryism of the country clergy, and their utter want of sympathy with the aspirations of the people. The Squire, Tory though he now usually is, is less narrow minded than the parson, and by no means so unpopular — a great calamity to the church and in itself, it cannot be denied, an argument in favour of disestablishment. Taken as a whole, however, I believe the Church to be stronger than its hot adversaries suppose.

As to the land question, the ideas floating about seem to be very hazy. Surely there is nothing distinct or practical in the proposals I have heard put forward in this part of the world. It is very easy to declaim on the subject — very hard to discover practical remedies.[93] For my part I shall want to examine each particular proposal. Allotments to labourers, of which I have had a good many always in my Estate, are useful things in their way, but will do but little to solve the problems of giving the rural population a more direct interest in the land.

I have run to an inordinate length, and will only end by an earnest wish that your health may carry you through your labours.

142. Kimberley to Ripon   Kimberley House
        10 October 1885
        RP 43526, ff. 10–11

Since I telegraphed to you, further conversation with Packe (who went home this morning) makes me think he may possibly be persuaded to stand for Lincolnshire, if no other candidate can be found.[94]

Our prospects in this county seem to be favourable if one can judge from meetings and demonstrations. There is a marked feeling for Disestablishment of the Church, stronger I am told than in perhaps any other English county. The non-conformists have evidently got the hearts of the labourers with them.

143. Kimberley to Derby   Kimberley House
        14 December 1885
        DP 920 Der (15) 20

Private

I know nothing down here of what is going on amongst our friends, but the state of things you describe is exactly what I should have guessed.[95] I agree

---

[93] Cf. his journal entry of 31 March 1886: 'Harcourt violent and ridiculous; declaimed against bill and never made a single suggestion for amending it.' KP6 MS.eng.c.2793, p. 185.

[94] Hussey Packe, Kimberley's son-in-law, of Prestwold Hall, Loughborough; unsuccessfully contested Northern Division of Leicestershire, 1874 and 1880; did not stand in 1885.

[95] Derby to Kimberley, 13 December 1885, KP6 MS.eng.c.4469, ff. 15–20; *DD3*, p. 45.

with you that *nothing* which any English Ministry can propose will satisfy the Irish Nationalists — They hate us, and wish to get entirely free of all connection with Gt. Britain with the intention of, when free, doing us all the harm in their power. But the problem we have to solve is not how to satisfy the Nationalists, but how to carry on the Govt. of the Empire.

It is simply impossible to work our Parliamentary system unless some *modus vivendi* is arrived at with Parnell and his 85 followers. Holding then as I do that *some* transaction with the Nationalists is unavoidable, the question in my mind is, ought we, the opposition, to make any move in that direction now? My inclination would be to wait. We are not in office. Let those who turned us out by the help of the Parnellites try their hand. If they can manage to govern by means of any arrangement (and without some arrangement with Parnell they cannot exist) we escape the odium of being the party responsible for what cannot be popular in any circumstances. If they fail, which is pretty sure to happen, we have a clearer stage for action; and I shall have a much better hope of success than if we show our hand at once.

It might however happen, tho it seems to me improbable, that Parnell might make some unexpectedly reasonable overture to us, which would require consideration.

The long and short of my thoughts is this — No satisfactory arrangement with the Irish is possible; some arrangement *must* be made; we are not *now* responsible; better therefore wait as long as we can and let the other two parties show their hands. At the same time I have not any belief in this govt. going on long. Three hundred and Thirty three Scotch and English Liberal members will not long permit 249 Tories to govern by the grace of Parnell, even if Watkin[96] and the other 'Independent' should support them; and I think we should make a mistake, if we played into the hands of the Radicals who want to wait till Gladstone is gone and then break up our party in order to reconstruct it on a Radical basis.[97]

This House of Commons is not Radical, and if the Irish difficulty could be tided over would support a Liberal Cabinet in settling many urgent questions in a reasonable manner.

If this settlement is postponed, the new voters will get angry and may become revolutionary.

As to Houghton, I wish some man like Cadogan would buy it.[98] He could I

---

[96] Edward William Watkin (1819–1901), Liberal M. P. for Hythe, prior to his defection in the fall of 1885.

[97] In this vein, see *DD3*, p. 85.

[98] George Henry Cadogan (1840–1915), Under-Secretary of State for the Colonies, 1878–80; Lord Privy Seal, 1886–92; whose daughter was married to Kimberley's cousin. Houghton was the Norfolk seat of the Marquess of Cholmondeley, whose principal residence was Cholmondeley Castle, Nantwich, Cheshire. Inherited from Horace Walpole, Houghton was put up for sale on several occasions as its lands were inadequate to support

imagine afford to live there and he has no country house.

144. Kimberley to Granville   Kimberley House
    28 December 1885
    GrP 30/22A/5, ff. 291–94

Do you know what is to be the course of events when Parliament meets? Will there be business, as soon as members are sworn and when is the Queen's Speech likely to be?

I hope we shall avoid premature moves, and declarations of policy about Ireland. It is the business of Government, not Opposition to propound policy, and where the difficulties are so immense, it is better to wait and get as much light thrown on the situation as possible.

It will puzzle the wisest heads to steer a tolerably safe course. All the alternatives are bad, and yet worse may be in store for us, if in despair, we commit ourselves either to Home Rule, or absolute refusal to consider the Irish grievance.[99]

145. Kimberley to Gladstone
    21 January 1886
    GP 44228, f. 212

I send you extracts from Carnarvon's Speech.[100] Nothing is said in his speech of the failure of the late Govt. to put down the National League, which is now to be the plea for the failure of Carnarvon. On the contrary the Crimes Act was said to have produced its effects, and special legislation to be no longer required.

146. Kimberley to Grant Duff   35 Lowndes Sq.
    22 January 1886
    GDP MSS Eur. F 234, v. 1, no. 38

Private

. . . . We have just embarked in what every one expects will be a most eventful session. The Govt. is of course in a very weak position, and can hardly stand long. They spread a net for us about Ireland in the Queen's speech, but never

the house. It did not find a buyer in 1885, however, and today remains in Cholmondeley hands. See Constance Battersea, *Reminiscences* (London: Macmillan, 1922), p. 125.

[99] Forwarded to Gladstone who remarked, 'what a mass of good sense compressed into a very small compass without a wasted word.' Ramm, *Gladstone–Granville Corresp. 2*, 2:421.

[100] Of 6 July 1885, in preparation for the Queen's Speech; see KP6 MS.eng.c.4470, ff. 66–68.

was the adage 'in vain is the net, &c.' better exemplified than last night. Gladstone made an admirable speech, and I must do Parnell justice to say that he showed great tact and discretion.[101] This it is which makes him so dangerous. If he were a frothy Celt, he would be easy to deal with. We have really all London newspapers so violently hostile to us that I warn you against accepting statements about us on any subject.

The Govt. of India is to be overhauled by Committees of both houses. This may have the good effect of preventing the House of Commons from meddling with affairs it does not understand, for an enormous Blue Book is a wonderful damper to discussion, and of that result, I mean this production of a gigantic mass of print which no one will read, we are certain at all events.[102]

I suppose you are beginning to think of your return home, and are not sorry at the prospect.

147. Kimberley to Grant Duff   India Office
5 March 1886
KP6 MS.eng.c.4223, ff. 19–21

Private/copy

.... Now a word as to home politics. I do not think we shall incur just reproach for being a weak government. I certainly hope our policy will be decided. As to its wisdom, there will of course be two opinions, as usual in human affairs. A steady policy of coercion of Ireland would be intelligible, perhaps in time successful. A see-saw between coercion and relaxations is hopeless.

We managed with much difficulty, and incurring much obloquy to get Ireland tolerably in hand, thanks to Lord Spencer's courage and ability. Then came a turn in our faction fights in Parliament, and down went the edifice of order we had so laboriously reared, like a pack of cards.

Our opponents, neither worse nor better in this respect than the average English party men on either side, let Ireland drift until they had got the benefit of the Irish vote at the Elections. Then, when it was evident that Irish support would not avail to keep them in office, they threw themselves in their dying gasps into the arms of the coercion party and they are now stirring up the passions of Orangemen. Need I pursue the matter further?

---

[101] On Gladstone's refusal to be forced into a premature declaration on coercion, see Cooke and Vincent, *Governing Passion*, p. 332.

[102] On the results of committee deliberations, see R. J. Moore, 'The Twilight of the Whigs and the Reform of the Indian Councils, 1886–1892', *Historical Journal*, 10 (1967): 400–14. The growing democracy increasingly demanded the kind of involvement which Kimberley wished to avoid. The *Spectator* some years later attacked such delaying tactics as 'Blue Book intrigues'. See 'The Forlorn Hope of the Government', 5 January 1895, p. 5.

Ugly symptoms shew themselves of coming wide-spread distress amongst the working classes. The long continued depression of trade is beginning to tell and it looks as if we might be on the eve of troublous times such as England has not known these forty years and more.

The disgraceful riot in London was an accident for which not the smallest responsibility attaches to the present government. It was the work of thieves not of the 'unemployed'. But the struggles against the inevitable fall of wages, and the sinking of respectable labourers into the class of the indigent must undoubtedly strengthen the elements of discontent and disorder, and we shall need steady hands, if the clouds continue to thicken.

148. Kimberley to Gladstone[103]   35 Lowndes Sq.
       15 March 1886
       GP 44228, f. 225–27

I incline to a second Irish House, because

1. Two houses are the general rule in our colonies.

2. They exist in most political constitutions elsewhere, which creates a strong presumption of utility in their favour on the ground of experience.

3. A second house would furnish in Ireland a means of giving the educated minority some weight, apart from numbers.

4. It would tend to impede the passing of measures which the crown might be imperatively called on by public opinion here to veto.

The danger of sudden rash votes will be peculiarly great in an inexperienced Irish (single) house, especially also must we take into account the impulsive Irish character.

What would you think of such a house as the following?

The 28 Irish representative peers — 28 members elected by provinces on the 'scrutin de liste' system[104], each province sending so many of the 28, as is proportionate to its population, and the franchise for this purpose to be confined to electors with a certain qualification as in the colony of Victoria.

When vacancies occur in the 28 Peers, the same constituency as above to elect a peer. A certain proportion of the second house to retire at fixed periods. Power nevertheless to dissolve at any time?

Another point, might not the American system be introduced as regards the House of Representatives, so as to have a self-adjusting machinery of representation to population, and thus avoid future 'Reform' Bills? I only throw this out as an idea which occurred to me.

---

[103] In response to Gladstone's circular of March 14. See *Gladstone Diaries*, 10:cl.

[104] Representatives elected by province, on the French model.

149. Kimberley to Gladstone   India Office
20 March 1886
GP 44228, f. 232

Pease's Opium motion.[105] See the written mem.[106] and the printed mem.[107] herewith from where I have marked it on *page 5*.[108] Our recent convention with China enables a much higher duty to be levied at the Treaty Ports (see passage marked *page 4*. We and China really both desire to levy the highest duty (consistent with not being defeated by smuggling) and by the same means to keep the consumption within bounds. Prohibition they know as well as we do, to be impracticable. Unless the House of Commons is prepared to vote money to meet the loss to the Indian Treasury, what sense is there in an abstract resolution such as Pease's?

Some part of the void might be filled up by raising the salt duties, a grievous burden, and by reimposing customs duties on Manchester goods. I know no other considerable source of revenue available; but this would still leave a heavy deficit, and no one would really advocate having recourse to such financial shifts. I am afraid this H of Commons is quite capable of passing the resolution all this notwithstanding. Giving effect to it is a very different matter.

150. Kimberley to Grant Duff   India Office
9 April 1886
KP6 MS.eng.c.4223, ff. 70–71

Private/copy

.... What will you say to our Home Rule Scheme? There are now the proverbial three courses: 1. Coercion 2. A Local Govt scheme, Educn. Gen. 3. Our scheme

The first if applied steadily and severely for a considerable time might possibly answer. Fitful coercion which all experience shows is all that can be expected, will never succeed.

The second has most of the disadvantages, none of the advantages of the first.

Remains the third. Observe Grattan's Parliament was a sovereign Parliament. Ours will not be.

The Rockingham Govt. wished to limit its powers but dared not. They made a faint attempt *after* concession, which of course failed. With the Army and

---

[105] Sir Joseph Pease (1828–1903), Quaker businessman and M.P. for South Durham, 1865–85; Barnard Castle, 1885–1903. Moved prohibition of opium cultivation except for medicinal purposes. 3 *Hansard*, 305 (1886): 278.

[106] W.G. Pedder, memorandum, 18 March 1886, GP 44228, f. 234.

[107] 'Opium Revenue, 1875- 1884', GP 44228, f. 235; and W.G. Pedder, 'Note on the Opium Revenue', 7 February 1882, GP 44228, ff. 236–41.

[108] Outlining possible means of limiting the opium trade between China and India.

Foreign Affairs in the hands of the Imperial Government, the essential unity of
the Empire is not lost; not to mention the Customs and other points reserved.

Mr. G's speech was I am told a splendid effort of oratory, and I think
convincing in argument.[109] I have just come from a Cabinet where he seemed
as fresh as if he was not in his 77th year and had not spoken last night for 3
hours and 1/2.

151. Kimberley Memorandum[110]   House of Lords
      12 April 1886
      GP 44228, f. 243–44

I agree in all Granville's arguments and objections. I would not say with
him however that I should *not* object even to a small representation as he
describes.[111] But if it is thought necessary to say something which leaves open
to the Government to possibly admit some extension of the power of summoning
Irish members to Westminster I should not see any harm in showing that we do
not absolutely close the door.[112]

152. Kimberley to Grant Duff   Kimberley House
      28 April 1886
      KP6 MS.eng.c. 4223, ff. 81–82

Private/copy

I was much interested by your address, enclosed in your letter to me of March
29 and I trust your Dravidians will profit by your good advice.[113] I have also
received yours of the 31st.

Our political situation here is very curious. The Liberal constituencies are
evidently more favourable to Home Rule than their members, many of whom
are embarrassed by strong election speeches, denouncing Parnell and all his
works. Have you in your remembrance the scathing denunciations of the Union
by Fox and other Whig luminaries and their prophecies of the failure of the
measure? They would be not a little amused at the fierceness against Home

---

[109] Of the previous day, introducing the Irish Home Rule Bill.

[110] Enclosed in Granville to Gladstone, 12 April 1886, in Ramm, *Gladstone–Granville
Corresp. 2*, 2:441.

[111] Granville had written that he would not object 'to a small representation either of
the Irish Parliament or of the 2 orders, or of the 4 provinces, if the number is small enough
to prevent their obstructing business, or upsetting Govts. Anything like 20 appears to
me to be fatal.' Ramm, *Gladstone–Granville Corresp. 2*, 2:441.

[112] See Kimberley's journal for a fuller explanation of his tactical flexibility. 17 April
1886, KP6 MS.eng.e.2793, pp. 186–88; cf. his later regret, Extracts, Kimberley memoir,
RsP 10186, p. 273.

[113] *An Address Delivered to the Graduates... of the University of Madras* (Madras:
Higginbotham and Co., 1886).

Rule of the members of the Fox Club of the present day. But although many of our friends cannot bring themselves to let the Irish manage their own affairs in their own way they are, wonderful to say, equally unable to make up their minds to compel the Irish to submit to their affairs being managed by us in our way. They halt between two opinions. Home Rule and coercion are equally hateful to them.

Surely, they say, there must be a middle way. Unfortunately as they will find out, whether they like it or not, there is not a middle way. Meantime the Tories look on and remain quiet which shows good sense.

153. Kimberley to Grant Duff　　　　　　　　　　　　　India Office
　　　14 May 1886
　　　KP6 MS.eng.c.4223, f. 91

Private/copy

. . . . Our great political struggle here still continues. In spite of the confidence of our opponents, our Irish policy has more life in it than they imagine: but it takes time for the constituencies to understand and appreciate it.

154. Kimberley to Monk Bretton　　　　　　　　　　Kimberley House
　　　4 October 1886
　　　MBP Box 37

It is refreshing to read of your designs on India. It makes one feel quite young. I have had some thoughts of a tour abroad, but I have grown very lazy about travelling, and my curiosity is grown dull about foreign parts. What I should like to see are the people and how they live and move and have their being (but one must be stationary and in the culture, &c.) I have ceased to care for churches, pictures, &c.

Florence and Rome I saw thoroughly (years ago) and most of the famous Italian towns. They will repay you your trouble better than any part of Europe which I know. Get Ruskin's Traveller's guide (or some such name) to Venice,[114] an abridgement of the 'Stones of Venice', if you care for art. I don't at all swear by said Ruskin, but he is very instructive, and interesting.

I should take the tall hat. A hat box is not much incumbrance. If you want to see princes and other swells, which probably you do not, take a uniform. I have utterly lost the power of speaking Italian tho' I often read it.

As to India, the thing is too big for me. I should not care just to run over a lot of country by rail, and then one knows no Indian language. However so many educated Indians speak English that this is perhaps not a very serious drawback.

---

[114] *The Stones of Venice: Introductory Chapters and Local Indices for the Use of Travellers, while staying in Venice and Verona*, 2 vols. (London, 1879–81).

As to Parlt. meeting in the autumn, I doubt it; but the Govt. *may* be compelled to come for coercive power. If so, there would be the devil of a row. I agree with you as to Randolph. He has made a very good start.[115] I suppose their programme for Ireland will be: extensive facilities for tenants buying their holdings — and considerable extension of local Govt.— the last will simply increase the power of the Parnellites and give them a fresh and powerful lever to work for Home Rule.[116]

But it will suit the British public, who have to make two bites of a cherry. The really curious thing is to see what Chamberlain will do. Our Radicals here at present hate him like poison.

Nothing but old partridges in this county, but as we had many left from last year, they will bear some thinning.

155. Kimberley to Monk Bretton   Kimberley House
   17 October 1886
   MBP Box 37

Many thanks for your kind congratulations on the birth of my second grandson.[117] Mother and infant are doing as well as possible. His elder brother[118] said it (the babe) was very nice, but suggested it should be given to the coachman's wife! Not quite so severe as two young owls bred in a cage, who as their owner told me, enlarged their elbow room as soon as they were fledged, by killing and eating their brother, the third.

I suppose you will not kiss the Pope's toe; that honour is, I believe, reserved for the faithful.

Hannibal was a very great man indeed, but the Carthaginians were a people with whom I have little sympathy. Read the accounts of their horrible doings in Sicily. They were barbarians to the core, and it was happy for the world that the Romans got the best of them.[119] I think we can move elephants in India, but they are swam across rivers there. Why did not Hannibal take them over the Rhone in that way? Perhaps he thought it was too cold. I suppose you have read Livy's account of Hannibal's march to Italy. It is wonderfully graphic but of course Polybius is the authority for the Punic war.

I have read some of him but he is very dry, and his Greek not being 'classic' sometimes puzzling. However I have that great desideratum a good Latin crib

---

[115] On Churchill's good start at the India Office see Foster, *Churchill*, pp. 281–82.
[116] Cf. Kimberley's annotations on 'The Condition of Ireland: A Sketch of Unionist Policy, 1888', KP6 MS.eng.d.2454/14.
[117] Philip, born to John and Isabel Wodehouse on October 1.
[118] John Wodehouse, b. 11 November 1883.
[119] In reading Bosworth Smith's *Carthage and the Carthaginians*, Kimberley noted that it was somewhat disfigured by 'fine writing about the great "Phoenician" meaning Hannibal which is as absurd as it would be to call Washington a great Englishman.' Notes on Books, KP1 15/K2/10, p. 61.

at the bottom of the page. Did you ever get through Goethe's Dichtung und Warheit? I am determined to read it through, having only dipped into it hitherto; but it is terribly long.[120]

A propos of books, have you got John Morley's Essays, just published in a very neat form, 9/O volumes?[121] They are very pleasant reading, and told me a great deal about Rousseau, Diderot, &c. which I did not know.

156. Kimberley to Gladstone   Kimberley House
    5 November 1886
    GrP 22A/5, ff. 383–86

Your ideas and mine concur entirely, our policy is to stick to our colours but to wait to let the Tories develop their policy. After the beating we got at the elections, it would be the worst possible tactics to be in a hurry. I saw nothing to take exception to in Morley and Harcourt's speeches; and they were clever and telling for an occasion such as the Leeds meeting.[122]

I disliked what Rosebery said. I am for letting the Dissentients alone but making no overtures to them at the present time.[123]

[*Postscript*] Liberals in this part of the country are furious against Chamberlain who *was* an idol here.

---

[120] During December Kimberley 'at last' finished *Dichtung und Warheit*, 'an interminable book, but indispensable for understanding Goethe's character and works.' He had completed for a second time *Faust* in September and went on to read Lewes's *Life of Goethe* in February 1887 and *Wilhelm Meister* during January 1888. KP1 15/K2/10, pp. 89, 90, 98.

[121] Which Kimberley had completed in September. KP1 15/K2/10, p. 88.

[122] On November 3, see Gardiner, *Life of Harcourt*, 2:10–11; Morley, *Recollections*, 1:303–11.

[123] Cf. Granville to Spencer, 3 November 1886, in *Red Earl*, 2:136.

5
A Radical Indeed

During the opposition between July 1886 and August 1892, Kimberley continued to support Irish Home Rule, though he thought it best to say little while the Conservatives had their turn, which was bound to end in failure. Although staying in touch with Derby and other Liberal Unionists, he believed that they should not be courted. Having served on Dilke's committee of 1883–84 which had laid the foundation for the Conservative Local Government Bill of 1888, Kimberley played an active role in its implementation in Norfolk.

When the Liberals were returned to office in 1892, Kimberley was offered the India Office and asked to take the Lord Presidency of the Council as well. The principal issue facing the government of India was an unstable economy. Kimberley appointed a committee of inquiry and after a year of deliberation, and intense debate both in England and in India, the gold standard was adopted and the rupee stabilized. In foreign affairs, Kimberley and Rosebery worked in almost complete agreement.

With fewer urgent departmental issues than at any time between 1880 and 1886, Kimberley assumed greater parliamentary responsibility. On Granville's death in 1891, he became Liberal leader in the Lords, began speaking on a wide variety of issues and organized the Liberal rump in the upper house. He was widely praised for piloting the intricate Parish Councils Bill through the Lords in 1894, the only non-departmental measure ever clearly associated with his name. Sorely disappointed that some measure of Home Rule still had not been enacted, he nevertheless agreed that Gladstone ought to resign when he refused to bow to the will of the Cabinet over Spencer's naval estimates.[1] After weeks of anxious negotiation, Gladstone offered his resignation to the Cabinet on 27 February 1894, paving the way for Rosebery's ministry and Kimberley's elevation to the Foreign Office.

---

[1] Hutchinson, *Private Diaries of West*, p. 271.

153. Kimberley to Ripon   Kimberley House
        8 January 1887
        RP 43526, ff. 17–18

What do you hear about the prospect of an arrangement with Chamberlain? We shall not I hope 'climb down' far to meet him.[2]

The Tories are cutting a pitiful figure, and if we are patient and persevering, we shall get the country round to us.[3] At the same time it would be an immense advantage to divide the 'Unionists' if we can do it on really fair terms.

Things seem to be going decidedly better in Burmah, thanks to Roberts' energy;[4] and I hope our relations with the Chinese on the frontier are satisfactory, as I hear nothing to the contrary.

154. Kimberley to Grant Duff   35 Lowndes Sq.
        9 June 1887
        GDP MSS Eur. F 234/18, no. 2

Thanks for your speech.[5] I am glad you found the passages.[6] Very pretty, are they not? both of them, as well in form as sentiment. I am fond of Italian poetry; who would not be who can read Dante?

In my boyhood we learnt no modern languages at school, but I have managed to get a fair knowledge of German and Italian since my school days, and enough Spanish to read, though not without difficulty, *Don Quixote* in the original. So you see I am so flattered by your letters, as to follow St. Paul's example, and take to boasting![7]

---

[2] Ripon responded that he fully shared Kimberley's view of Chamberlain; that he felt 'entire confidence' in John Morley 'refusing to be a party to any abandonment of principle', but could not have 'equal confidence in Harcourt' and was 'ever inclined to be doubtful about Herschell' who always seemed a 'lukewarm supporter of our policy.' RP 43526, f. 19.

[3] Kimberley confided in Derby that he believed the Conservative reaction to Home Rule beneficial insofar as it interposed 'an interval for consideration before other questions came on. Without some such check, the radical movement would have been too rapid.' *DD3*, p. 85.

[4] General Frederick Sleigh Roberts (1832– 1914), Indian Commander-in-Chief, 1885– 93; in suppressing pro- French rebels following British declaration of a protectorate on 24 July 1886.

[5] Probably of May 25 to the Northbrook Club. See Grant Duff, *Notes from a Diary, 1886–1888*, 2:109–18.

[6] From Tasso's *Gerusalemme liberata*, Canto xvi, 14; and Spenser's *Faerie Queene*, Book 2, canto xii, 74. Kimberley was particularly interested in Spenser's unattributed 'translations' from Tasso. See Grant Duff, *Notes from a Diary, 1886–1888*, 1:124–25; Commonplace Book, KP1 15/K2/12, pp. 1–2.

[7] As in 'I exhort you therefore, be imitators of me.' I Cor. 4:16 (KJV).

155. Kimberley to Ripon 35 Lowndes Sq.
 7 July 1888
 RP 43526, ff. 31–32

Private

You are terribly pugnacious.[8] In this depressing town atmosphere we are but feeble creatures I fear.

We discussed Argyll's motion yesterday,[9] and the opinion was not to divide, but to treat the motion with some gentle contempt, as embodying a truism to which every one can agree. We must all be in favour of securing 'personal freedom &c.' The Question is as to the proper means of securing it. The motion is a trap set to catch us, if we vote against it, as we should then appear to be the supporters of *unlawful* combination, and the opponents of security for personal freedom, in other words anarchists. If the trap is not deliberately laid for us, we can treat it as such and decline to walk into it.

Besides is it not desirable to treat abstract motions by the 'portentous pedagogue' as little seriously as possible? These are my sentiments and our proposed course seems to be the right one. But I hope you will come up, and speak if the debate goes on. Some short chaffy speeches on our side will be appropriate to counteract the solemn Ducal rhetoric.

156. Kimberley to Monk Bretton Kimberley House
 8 February 1889
 MBP 37

You will have seen in the 'Times' the result of the first meeting of the Provisional Council,[10] but it may perhaps interest you to know some further particulars.

Our councillors (57) are composed of 25 Tories, 21 Liberals, 11 Libl. Unionists. Of these, 27 are magistrates. The Liberals were determined to propose me as Provisional Chairman.[11] Of course I did not particularly wish to be, as there is some trouble and no glory in the office; but I said if the council should elect me, I should think it my duty to accept. There was however no chance of such

---

[8] In 'going up' to London for a discussion of the Government's Irish policy.

[9] 'That in the opinion of this house Her Majesty's Government deserves the support of Parliament in securing for the subjects of the Queen in Ireland the full enjoyment of personal freedom in all their lawful transactions, and in protecting them from the coercion of unlawful combinations.' Motion agreed to *nemine contradicente*. 3 *Hansard*, 328 (12 July 1888): 1053–70.

[10] 8 February 1889, p. 10.

[11] Of the Norfolk County Council, created by the Local Government Act (1888), which Kimberley had helped to prepare prior to the formation of Salisbury's government. See V. D. Lipman, *Local Government Areas, 1834–1945* (Oxford: Basil Blackwell, 1949), pp. 142– 56; Kimberley to Spencer, 4 & 7 August 1888, SP.

a result.[12] Lord Walsingham (Tory), proposed R. Gurdon (Lib. Unionist) and we had practically a pure party vote. Of our 21, one voted against me because he thought I should be in office again and it was no use to elect me; one, (I guess) because he is elected on the anti-workhouse ticket and dislikes me as a strict Poor Law guardian; and one who is a 'faddist' for reasons that I can guess. One Tory farmer voted for me and I did not vote myself. This left me 18 with 37 against me, a handsome beating. No J.P. voted for me except my son. I expect on the election of chairman next Saturday the same vote will be repeated as I hear the Liberals are determined to challenge Gurdon's election.

The list of aldermen was settled practically at a caucus of Tory and Lib. Unionist magistrates. I was present as a go-between. The list settled by the Caucus (the whole of which was carried) comprised 11 Tories, 2 Lib. Unionists and 6 Liberals. Two of the latter would probably have been omitted if I had not pressed them on the Caucus. The Liberals held their Caucus, but their opponents would not take the names they most wished for.

The list adopted is on the whole a good one as regards the qualifications of the men. Twelve of the aldermen are magistrates making a total of 39 J.P.s, a clear majority of the whole Council 76. It is evident that, as I expected, we shall be divided into political parties. Most of our elections were fought on political issues, and all of them will be so fought, I have little doubt next time. Meantime the magistrates will have the whole thing in their hands, if, as seems certain, many of the non-magistrates being busy men, attend but seldom. In short matters will go on very much as before. Such at least is my forecast.

[*Postscript*] All our aldermen were elected from outside.

157. Kimberley to Ripon   35 Lowndes Sq.
    23 July 1889
    RP 43526, ff. 40–43

Private

There is a pretty kettle of fish here about the 'Royal Grants.' You probably know we had a meeting to discuss them. Every one agreed that no grandchildren of the Sovereign should have grants except children of the heir apparent; beyond this we were agreed on nothing.

A majority I think were for a grant to Prince Albt. Victor. Gladstone and two or three men, myself among the number, were for grants to all the P. of Wales' children. The proposal to give a sum to the Prince of Wales out of which he should provide for his children was however favourably received by several and this is the proposal, as you know, which carried in the Committee.

---

[12] Kimberley was nevertheless elected to both the Finance and Joint Committees. For a helpful 'study' of the Norfolk County Council elections, see William Carr's copy of the 'Local Government Act, 1888', annotated and interleaved with related press clippings. KP7.

Now it is said, the large part of our people will desert Gladstone and vote with Labouchere.[13] You have seen in the newspapers the point in dispute. It seems to me a rather fine point on which to split the party. The Queen has really given up the grants to grandchildren other than the Prince of Wales' children. She may have refused to make a bargain *totidem verbis*, but such grants are dead henceforth.

The part I fear is that our M.P.s, knowing that there is a strong feeling amongst the working men against all further grants, have eagerly caught at an excuse for voting against them.

It is an ugly sign for the future, as it was but too evident that there was scarcely an M.P. at our meeting who ventured to have an opinion of his own. I am very sorry that G. should be deserted.[14] He has fought our fight well and deserved more generous treatment, if ever [a] leader did. If Labouchere is to be leader, I for one can't follow him, and as I don't mean to turn Tory, I shall have to retire into private life.

Seriously, I fear the signs of the times are not encouraging for the future of the Liberal party. If they won't follow G., who can possibly lead them.

[*Postscript*] I hear there are attempts to compose the differences, but I am afraid hitherto without success.

158. Kimberley to Gladstone   Kimberley House
   19 October 1889
   GP 44229, ff. 4-5

I hope in some speech you will say a strong word for the amendment of the Allotments Act. We sadly want some lever to stir up the agricultural votes and almost the only thing the labourers really care about is the Allotments question.

The compulsory powers of the act are hedged in by so many expensive formalities that they are practically useless. The whole matter should (subject perhaps to some limitations as to amount) be put into the hands of the County Councils to deal with finally.

I dare say you have all this fully present in your mind, but I am so anxious on the point that I am sure you will forgive me for troubling you with a line.

---

[13] Henry Labouchere, founder and editor of *Truth*; Radical M.P. for Northampton, 1880–1906.

[14] On radical separatism, see Hamer, *Liberal Politics*, 149–51; L. A. Atherley-Jones, 'The New Liberalism', *Nineteenth Century*, 26 (August 1889): 186–93; 'The Government and the Disintegration of the Opposition', *Spectator*, 3 August 1889, p. 132.

159. Kimberley to Gladstone   Kimberley House
     22 October 1889
     GP 44229, f. 6

Private

Many thanks for your letter.[15] I am glad to hear that there will be no further disclosures at present of the Home Rule plan.[16] I feel sure that such disclosures would only help the enemy.

Your expressions about myself are most kind. I do not esteem highly my powers or usefulness as a platform speaker, but I should speak oftener, but for particular reasons (unconnected with politics) which make it difficult for me at the present time to absent myself from home.[17]

160. Kimberley to Spencer   Kimberley House
     18 December 1890
     SP K327

What do you think of the crisis in Irish affairs.[18] To me it seems that English and Scotch people will be so disgusted with the exhibition of folly and violence now going on in Ireland that no Home Rule majority will be possible.

As to the split, the separation of the Irish into many factions would in some sense render Home Rule all the safer as far as England is concerned, as there would be less chance of a combination against us, and it would put Ulster in a much stronger position. But logic never governs nations, and people will say (and justly) what manner of man is Parnell to whom we were about to entrust the destinies of Ireland! I make every allowance for the childishness of the Irish to whom a shindy is an irresistable attraction, but the sober staid English and Scotch voter will make no allowances. It will renew all his old feelings of contemptuous dislike of the Irish nationalists.

I am deeply sorry for Gladstone, whose unwearied labours for Ireland deserved a better destiny.

---

[15] Of 21 October 1889, marked 'Secrct', indicating that Gladstone intended to 'speak in your sense,' and requesting the advantage of 'your great knowledge and ability by speaking in public.' KP6 MS.eng.c.4470, f. 12.

[16] Cf. *Red Earl*, 2:162.

[17] At the end of 1889, Lady Kimberley wrote to her daughter Alice that it had been 'the unhappiest year' in her life. She suffered physically from severe rheumatism and emotionally from the loss of her youngest son, Armine, who had married Eleanor Arnold in June. Florence Wodehouse to Alice Packe, 14 October, 31 December 1889, PP DE1749 38/21, 33; John Powell, 'Parenthood and Politics: Some Reflections on the Shared Values of Matthew and Eleanor Arnold', *Nineteenth-Century Prose*, 16 (1988–89): 35–46; KP6 MS.eng.e.2793, p. 257.

[18] The most immediate cause being Parnell's divorce case. See Morley, *Life of Gladstone*, 3:428–59; *Red Earl*, 2:165–68.

161. Kimberley to Spencer   Kimberley House
   20 December 1890
   SP K327

Very many thanks for your interesting letter.[19] I agree with all you say. But
how are the English people to be persuaded to pursue a rational and consistent
policy towards Ireland? I fear they will never have the courage and patience to
leave the Irish to themselves, and let them work representative institutions in
their own way.[20] Unless they do so, the old weary round may go on for ever,
for anything I see.

I wish I could have more faith in the effect of a transfer of the land to the
peasant farmers in pacifying the country. But that and local Govt. (if at all
democratic) will I believe increase the power of worrying the English Govt.
and not diminish the desire to do so which arises from hatred of the 'Saxon'
rule.

162. Kimberley to Rosebery   35 Lowndes Sq.
   14 April 1891
   RsP 10068, ff. 6–7

I have seen your letter to Mr. Gladstone[21] and I should like to explain to you
what has been done with regard to appointing a successor to Granville.

I quite agree in all you say of the importance of keeping our small party
together, and I should have most willingly served under whatever leader had
been selected if a selection had been made; but the arguments for not appointing
any one at this *particular juncture* of affairs, seemed to me very strong, and I do
not think any real inconvenience will result. It is understood that I am to go on
attending to the business as I did in Granville's absence, an arrangement which
can be terminated at any time and prejudices nothing for the future. We must
have a dissolution soon, and we may possibly have a change of government.
In such circumstances, apart from any other reasons, Mr G's wishes that no
definite leader should be chosen deserves the utmost consideration.[22] I can do
what is necessary to keep our little party from falling to pieces meanwhile.

[19] Of October 19, lamenting the effect of Parnell's personal difficulties on the cause
of Home Rule. 'My answer to enemies when they bait us about Parnell would be that
I admit his incapacity for Government, but that I did not know he was a lunatic.' KP6
MS.eng.c.4474, ff. 40–43.

[20] Twenty years earlier Kimberley had noted that the Irish had 'not the slightest fitness
for a republic, nor any *real* republican feeling.... he [the Irishman] is democratic in the
sense that a Frenchman is, but a "republican" he can never be but in name.' Marginalia,
[Sigerson], *Modern Ireland*, pp. 15, 19, (in author's possession).

[21] Of April 12 from Biarritz, reviewing options regarding leadership in the Lords
following Granville's death on March 31. GP 44289, ff. 135–6.

[22] Gladstone wrote to his wife three days earlier that he had 'been lucky about the
affair of leadership in the Lords.' A. Tilney Bassett, ed. *Gladstone to his Wife* (London:
Methuen and Co., 1936), pp. 255–56.

I am very sorry you could not be here to give us your advice. We had a meeting of such Liberal peers as are in London (sending notice to *all* our supporters) and they seemed to be well satisfied with our course.[23]

I hope whilst you are away, if anything occurs to you about public business, you will let me know.

163. Gladstone to Kimberley   [Hawarden]
    2 November 1891
    KP2 10244, f. 35

Postcard

I have only to thank and express my decided concurrence in your excellent statement.

[*Kimberley memorandum*], n.d. — As to Mombasa Ry. Mr. G's subsequent speech was founded on my letter.[24]

164. Kimberley to Spencer   Kimberley House
    15 December 1891
    SP K330

It is very kind of you to send me an account of what passed at Mr. G's visit to you.[25] Like you, I do not feel myself competent to criticize Goschen's one pound note scheme.[26] But I distrust, perhaps from party bias,[27] Goschen's finance, clever as he is.

As to the Home Rule Bill, I do not think we can carry the matters of detail much further than the provisional conclusion which Mr. G laid down last year after his discussion with Parnell.[28] If we had nothing more serious to decide than the future status of the Irish peers, I should feel easy in my mind. Why not leave them as they are? As there are to be Irish members still in the Imperial

[23] Kimberley, Spencer, Ripon, Oxenbridge and Gladstone were present. Bassett, *Gladstone to his Wife*, pp. 255–56.

[24] Kimberley's statement has not been traced; see Gladstone's speech criticizing the Government for inadequate preparation, 4 *Hansard*, 1 (3 March 1892): 1868–80.

[25] 13 December 1891, KP6 MS.eng.c.4474, ff. 44–45; also Lady Spencer's account in *Red Earl*, 2:176–78.

[26] In the wake of the Baring crisis, George Joachim Goschen (1831–1907), Unionist Chancellor of the Exchequer, 1886–92, suggested that one-pound notes be issued against gold reserves in order to protect the bullion supply in times of crisis. Cf. Robin Harcourt Williams, ed. *The Salisbury-Balfour Correspondence, 1869–1892* (Hertfordshire Record Society, 1988), p. 384.

[27] Perhaps based in part upon conversations with his cousin, Bertram Wodehouse Currie, who had on occasion been consulted by Goschen. See Currie to Goschen, 11 January 1888, Currie Papers, Royal Bank of Scotland Archives; Roger Fulford, *Glyn's 1753–1953, Six Generations in Lombard Street* (London: Macmillan, 1953), pp. 213-14.

[28] See Hammond, *Gladstone and the Irish Nation*, pp. 602–05, 619–21.

Parliament, the Irish representative peers may fitly remain in the House of Lords. If there is a second House at Dublin, the Irish peers might elect to it a certain number of their body, to sit with such other members or may be component parts of the new body.

I hope Rosebery will make up his mind soon to take part again in public affairs.[29] Both for him and for us it will be hurtful if he remains aloof.

If the D. of Devonshire dies,[30] the translation of Hartington to the H. of Lords must weaken the Dissentient Liberals. Old Whig members of the H. of Commons cannot in their hearts be devoted followers of Chamberlain who will be their leader.[31]

165. Kimberley to Monk Bretton   Kimberley House
20 December 1891
MBP 37

We are just beginning a sharp frost after repeated hurricanes of wind and rain. I hate frost! So I envy you the climate of Tenerife.[32] Nothing very extraordinary is happening here. The Teck marriage[33] and the illness of the D. of Devonshire are the principal events. The usual dreary round of platform speeches goes on. I do as little as I can but I have alas! three in prospect. I doubt if I were beginning life, I should embark in public affairs.

The 'stump' will predominate more and more.[34] Rosebery has written a smart little book on Pitt.[35] Some parts of it are very good, but the style has too much straining after picturesque sayings. Salt is excellent, if not used too freely. Still with all drawbacks the book is very clever.[36]

[29] Following the death of his wife. James, *Rosebery*, pp. 227–33.

[30] As he did on 21 December 1891.

[31] Cf. *DD3*, pp. 76–79.

[32] For an instructive contemporary perception of the value of subtropical climes, see 'Health-Seeking in Tenerife and Madeira', *Nineteenth Century*, 26 (July 1889), pp. 120–35.

[33] Engagement of Albert Victor, Duke of Clarence, to Princess Mary of Teck, the daughter of Queen Victoria's first cousin.

[34] Cf. letter 125, herein; Morley to Kimberley, 12 February 1889, KP6 MS.eng.c.4471, f. 131.

[35] *Pitt*, published in November as a part of Macmillan's 'Twelve English Statesmen' series. George Grove had first suggested Gladstone as author. Charles Morgan, *The House of Macmillan (1843–1943)* (New York: Macmillan, 1944), p. 115.

[36] James argues that Rosebery's 'principal defect as a historian was an excessive preoccupation with the interesting and vivid, and with the polish of the final portrait rather than the meticulous accuracy of that portrait.' *Rosebery*, p. 215.

166. Kimberley to Grant Duff   35 Lowndes Sq.
    1 March 1892
    GDP MSS Eur. F 234, v. 1, no. 19

I agree in almost all you say in your interesting historical lecture.[37] But your address to the girls is really a gem.[38] What a fervent Anglican you are! Henry the 8th would assuredly have given you a handsome slice of Monastery lands. Your joke however about the next world (an excellent one) must I fear have shocked your pious hearers, or were they females of the epicene and 'strong minded' class?

I especially like what you say about mathematics, (having no aptitude for them myself).[39] I never could see what good it could do to any one without such an aptitude to study more mathematics than is necessary to make him understand the difference between mathematical reasoning and probable reasoning.

167. Kimberley to Gladstone   35 Lowndes Sq.
    5 April 1892
    GP 44229, ff. 23–27

Private

I have thought much, since I last saw you, about the Irish Home Rule Bill, and the more I reflect upon it the more anxious I am that the Irish members should be debarred from voting in the Imperial Parliament on questions over which if Irish, the Irish legislature will have exclusive control.

I cannot see what answers we can give without such a limitation to the objection that we Englishmen and Scotchmen shall be placed on a footing of inequality with Irishmen. The objection is one which will tell heavily on the platform, it is obvious, broad, easily to be understood by the humblest voter. To leave such a weapon in the hands of our opponents would it seems to me, if it can by any means be avoided, be a fatal mistake.

Can it be avoided? To me it appears not to be impossible, if we adopt the plan of the Canada Act, and delegate specific powers to the Irish Legislature and reserve everything not so delegated to the Imperial Parliament. It may be said that this is an impracticable plan because an exhaustive enumeration of powers to be delegated cannot be framed. But is this a *very* serious objection? The enumeration could not fail to include all the really prominent and indispensible

[37] Urging a greater role for history as an academic discipline. Address to the Royal Historical Society, 18 February 1892.

[38] 'Address to the Oxford Girls High School', 23 May 1891, published in Grant Duff, *Notes from a Diary, 1889–1891*, 2:239–50.

[39] Suggesting that girls not be taught arithmetic, 'except insofar as those rules are concerned which you will have to use more or less every week of your lives.' Thirty years earlier, Kimberley had noted his son's good report from Eton, 'except as to arithmetic in which I fear he is as stupid as his father.' 1 August 1862, KP6 MS.eng.e.2791, p. 52v.

matters. If there were a defect in the enumeration the error would not be unremediable, and such a danger is surely not comparable to the risk of the bill failing altogether from the unpopularity of leaving our domestic affairs open to Irish interference whilst we are shut out from all control over similar Irish affairs. The Speaker might have power to determine whether on a given matter the Irish members would take part.

Now let us test this plan by some particular cases. English or Scotch Education or Local Govt. would be examples of subjects obviously excluded from Irish participation. Any matter on the other hand touching the Army or Navy, the colonies, India, Foreign affairs, and commercial tariffs, would be within the scope of Irish votes.

You mentioned votes of confidence. From direct votes of this kind I presume in no case could the Irish be excluded. But of course a question may be treated by a Govt. as involving its existence though no direct vote of want of confidence be moved. If this arose on a matter on which Irish members could vote there would be no difficulty; if on some question from which they were excluded, the Govt. must judge according to all the circms. whether they would be warranted in refusing to yield to the British majority on the ground that on imperial questions they had a majority.

I fully recognise that no system can be framed in which holes cannot be pricked, but I return to my point, namely, that it is of paramount importance not to expose ourselves to the argument of injustice to Great Britain. This is I fear a very imperfect statement, but I think it will be enough to explain my view.

168. Gladstone to Kimberley   1 Carlton Gardens
     6 April 1892
     GP 44229, ff. 29–30

Private/Copy

I am very glad to have your letter. We cannot sift too thoroughly the inconveniences attaching to the several modes in which an Irish representation may be retained at Westminster. And I fully admit the inconveniences which you state. But on the other hand it seems to me that your remedy is inefficacious, if as I am disposed to think, you retain the vote of the Irish members on the very points where there would be the greatest objection to it.

You would not allow them to vote on a question (say) of English Education. But if in consequence of the proceedings of the Govt. on this question of education a vote of want of confidence were moved the Irish members would vote. I think that if this were so you would have gained nothing by excluding them from particular subjects: you would close the wicket and leave open the great gate.

Of a case like this I do not see that you take cognisance.

The distinction of subjects can no doubt be drawn; at least I assume this.

In your House you have little except legislative subjects apart from judicature. But in the House of Commons the business of Inquest, Control, and calling to account is almost measureless; and the difficulty thus raised is one which I have never seen any means of surmounting.

Parnell like you was disposed to let the Speaker allow or disallow the Irish vote; but I am persuaded that his authority could not suffice for such a purpose and would break down under the attempt.

By all means let us continue our efforts to crack the nut.

169. Kimberley to Ripon   35 Lowndes Sq.
      14 May 1892
      RP 43526, ff. 67–68

Private

I have not written to you because there has really been nothing to report. The vote in the House of Commons about women's suffrage caused a little excitement,[40] and I suppose the disappointed women will do us some harm at the elections. Harm or not, I am utterly opposed to women's suffrage, and am heartily glad Mr. G spoke out against it.[41]

I am not so sure he was right in refusing to receive a deputation on the eight hours question. I think Salisbury and Balfour who received a deputation and spoke very sensibly on the subject, scored against us here. Salisbury's speech about Ulster is the topic of the moment.[42] The election fever is getting strong when the Prime Minister not obscurely preaches rebellion.

You will have seen, I hope, Rosebery's speech at Edinburgh. He vigorously attacked Salisbury, but otherwise gave Ireland a back place:[43] a sign of the future, worth noting.

As to dissolution no one knows anything. It may be in July, it may be in the autumn, it may be next year. The Hackney election has put the Tories in spirits:[44] perhaps this may encourage them to make the plunge. It is lucky there is a septennial Act, or Tories wd. never dissolve as long as they have a majority.

My son Armine writes that he met you and Lady Ripon, who I hope is better, at Como.

---

[40] Discharging the measure on its second reading. 4 *Hansard*, 2 (22 March 1892): 1435.

[41] See too his *Female Suffrage: A Letter from the Right Hon. W. E. Gladstone, M.P. to Samuel Smith, M.P.* (London: John Murray, 1892). On Kimberley's attitude and surprising change of heart, see letter 205, herein; Frances Balfour, *Ne Obliviscaris, Dinna Forget* (London: Hodder and Stoughton, [1930]), pp. 155–56.

[42] 4 *Hansard*, 4 (6 May 1892): 335.

[43] The Queen perceived otherwise, considering Rosebery after the Edinburgh speech 'as violent as anyone' regarding Home Rule. James, *Rosebery*, p. 234.

[44] W. R. Bousfield defeating T. A. Meates, 4460 to 3491 in a bye-election.

170. Kimberley to Ripon
   19 July 1892
   RP 43526, ff. 69– 71

Private

I suppose you will be coming to town soon and I shall be anxious to talk with you. The Tories are fairly beaten[45] and can't stay in office, but our position is full of difficulties. I have not heard what the temper of the Irish nationalists is. Everything really depends on this. What little has reached me in the way of rumour about the feeling in the Liberal Party tends to show that there is no enthusiasm for Home Rule, and a desire to put forward at once other measures. Of course Home Rule *must* be brought forward. Besides our position and repeated pledges, the Irish Nationalists hold us in the hollow of their hand.

But *if* the Nationalists are reasonable (a large assumption), they may allow us free hand enough to enable us to do something at once to satisfy our party. I am afraid J. Morley is in a very awkward situation. The labour party, I am told, is making a dead set at him.[46] Altogether what a kettle of fish! I see the late returns just in reduce our majority to 42. At this I conclude it will remain as we are not likely to lose Orkney. None too many considering that nine are Parnellites, our bitter enemies in heart, and several more are disaffected Labour members.

171. Kimberley to Spencer   35 Lowndes Sq.
   29 July 1892
   SP K336

Private

I wrote a short note to Mr. G. telling him I would not add to his troubles by calling on him unless he wanted me for anything, and I had a note from him telling me briefly what[47] was going on. From Ripon, whom I saw to day, I gathered that Harcourt is pressing for postponement of the Home Rule Bill. I hope this will not be attempted. Whatever the difficulties of carrying a Home Rule Bill and they are manifest enough, I feel sure that we should gain nothing, but much the contrary, by postponement. I won't go into the arguments because they are perfectly familiar to you, and I am sure you will be for facing the question next session. Of course *if* the Irish Nationalists were themselves

---

[45] In the final poll, Liberals won 273 seats, Irish Nationalists 81, and Independent Labour, 1; Conservatives 269, and Liberals Unionists, 46.

[46] Morley eventually was elected by a comfortable margin. D.A. Hamer, *John Morley, Liberal Intellectual in Politics* (Oxford: Clarendon University Press, 1968), pp. 278–79.

[47] Gladstone's note, marked 'Secret', indicated that he was buried in 'a preliminary but indispensable' business, determining the views of Irish members on 'questions of confidence.' KP6 MS.eng.c.4470, f. 22.

convinced that postponement was the best policy and cordially agreed in it, the case would be quite altered, but this I regard as quite inconceivable, and therefore not worth discussing.

You know our friend well enough to feel pretty certain that if Mr G. puts his foot down he will in due time get calm and very probably fully convinced of the wisdom of not following his present advice.

Ripon says why not have another important measure in the same session as Home Rule, some measure which would give satisfaction to the English and Scotch Liberals? I agree with him: why not? In 1870 we carried both the Land Act and the Education Act, both measures of the highest importance.

All this will no doubt have occurred to you, but I thought you might like to know my opinion.

I feel very anxious that Mr G. should not now be worried to death with this [ill.] controversy: meantime I put my trust in you and J. Morley.

I am going into the country to morrow afternoon to Hussey Packe's Prestwold, Loughboro', and I shall be back on Tuesday.

172. Kimberley to Spencer   Prestwold Hall,
       1 August 1892   Loughborough
       SP K336

Private

Very many thanks for your letter, which I received this morning.[48] Don't think for a moment that I am jealous of your consultations with Mr G. You and J. Morley are for every reason the best persons to give advice on the questions under discussion.

Your letter quite reassures me as to the course Mr G. will take on the Home Rule Bill, which is the chief matter: and I cannot doubt that before next session it will be found possible to agree on measures wh. will be acceptable to the Liberal members.

It is so pleasant here that I have been persuaded to stay till Wednesday morning. I shall be in Lowndes Sqr. by 12.30, if my train is punctual.

173. Kimberley to Gladstone   Kimberley House
       31 August 1892
       GP 44229, ff. 34–38

I send you herewith a copy of a despatch from the Govt. of India.... urg[ing] in the strongest manner that if we do not adopt bimetallism, they should be allowed to take immediate steps for the introduction of a gold standard into

---

[48] Of July 30, KP6 MS.eng.c.4474, ff. 46–47.

India.[49]   Now I apprehend there is no chance of our adopting bimetallism,[50] (I should be very sorry if I thought there were any) and when the bimetallic conference has ended, as no doubt it will, without any result we must be prepared to decide whether the proposals of the Govt. of India for establishing a gold standard are to be sanctioned....

Whilst I have frankly expressed my *predisposition*,[51] I must own I am shaken by finding that Bertram Currie, who has he told me written to you, has come to the opinion that the Govt. of India ought to be allowed a free hand.[52] I feel that his opinion must carry great weight. Godley too has I think arrived at the same conclusion. He suggests what occurred to me, that it would be desirable to appoint a special committee[53] to consider the proposals of the Govt. of India.

If you can approve of this idea, I will communicate with him as to the nature of the Committee, and write to you further on that point.

P.S. — Of course Harcourt would have to be consulted, but as he is abroad, I write first to you.[54]

---

174. Kimberley Memorandum   India Office
   21 September 1892
   RsP 10068, ff. 20–22

You have sent us a nice nut to crack in Uganda.[55] I feel much difficulty in forming an opinion without knowing what measures would be necessary if we remain there. The railway being put aside, the immediate expenditure would I suppose not be very large. Probably we should have to enlist permanently the best of the Soudanese who are now with Lugard[56] and a certain number of English officers would have to be appointed to command them.

[49] For Gladstone's response of September 2, see *Gladstone Diaries*, 13:70–71.

[50] On the bimetallic debate, see Arnold P. Kaminsky, '"Lombard Street" and India: Currency Problems in the Late Nineteenth Century', *Indian Economic and Social History Review*, 17 (1980): 307–27. For the larger context see E. H. H. Green, 'Rentiers versus Producers? The Political Economy of the Bimetallic Controversy C. 1880–1898', *English Historical Review*, 103 (July 1988): 588–612; A. C. Howe, 'Bimetallism, c. 1880–1898: A Controversy Reopened?' *English Historical Review*, 105 (April 1990): 377–91; E. H. H. Green, 'The Bimetallic Controversy: Empiricism Believed or the Case for the Issues' *English Historical Review*, 105 (July 1990): 673– 683.

[51] Against tampering with the silver currency.

[52] See his memorandum of August 19, KP6 MS.eng.c.4357, ff. 8–9.

[53] Subsequently chaired by Herschell and including Sir Richard Strachey, Currie, Reginald Welby, Sir Thomas Farrer, Arthur Godley, and Leonard Courtney.

[54] The day after the despatch arrived, Kimberley wrote to inform Harcourt that, after it had been carefully considered, he would 'consult Mr. G.', August 22, HP 49, f. 13.

[55] Whether or not to evacuate Uganda following the bankruptcy of the Imperial British East Africa Company. See Martel, *Imperial Diplomacy*, pp. 80–87.

[56] Frederick Lugard, soldier and Administrator of Uganda in the service of the Imperial British East Africa Company, 1890–92.

The Houssa regiments on the Gold Coast which are very successful would be a model. Eventually natives of the country would supply materials for the necessary armed force. Some but not large expenditure for civil government would also have to be incurred.

On the other side, what revenue may be expected?

The most serious danger will be from the Arabs. Shall we secure from an organized attack by them from the North? Our Sudan experience shows how formidable the Arabs are, and if any reverses were to happen to our native force, we should be unable for many months to send any reinforcements. Unless therefore our local force was strong enough to maintain itself against all comers, might we not have the Gordon catastrophe over again?

Lastly, how shall we fare in the House of Commons where we propose a vote for Uganda? Shall we not be abandoned by a considerable number of our own party, and carry the vote only by the help of the Tories?

You have I doubt not considered all these points, but the question is so grave and difficult that I send you my thoughts for what they are worth.[57]

---

175. Kimberley to Harcourt   Kimberley House
   6 October 1892
   HP MS Harcourt dep. 49, f. 52

Private

Thanks for the articles. There have been a series of them, no doubt by Giffen, I take in the 'Statist'.[58] On consulting Herschell as to the composition of the Committee, I found him *very* strongly in favour of having Courtney[59] ....

I am afraid we shall find it extremely difficult to get out of Uganda, when the three months expire. The British public is easily stirred by the cry of extension of the Gospel of peace to the blacks with its attendant blessing of fire water and bellicose missionaries. Throw in the Anti-Slavery crusaders, and the 'Empire' Jingoes, and you have a formidable body of agitation.[60] 'Empire' on the cheap is so very attractive till soldiers have to be found to defend it, and the bill comes in.

---

[57] The following day Rosebery informed Gladstone that Kimberley had sent him this 'short useful paper .... Harcourt writes volumes. Elsewhere a vast silence.' GP 44289, f. 203. Kimberley was originally against retention. Kimberley journal, KP6 MS.eng.2793.p. 406.

[58] Sir Robert Giffen, assistant editor of the *Economist*, 1868–76; edited *Journal of Royal Statistical Society*, 1876–91; chief of statistical department to the Board of Trade, 1876–97. See *Statist*, 30:326–29, 381–84.

[59] Leonard Henry Courtney (1832–1918), Liberal M.P. for Liskeard from 1876; Financial Secretary to the Treasury, 1882–84; deputy speaker, 1886–92.

[60] See Anthony Low, 'British Public Opinion and the Uganda Question: October–December 1892', *Uganda Journal*, 18 (September 1954): 81–100.

176. Kimberley to Campbell-Bannerman   Kimberley House
    7 October 1892
    CBP 41221, ff. 103–04

Private

In writing to you the other day, I overlooked a letter to me from Lord Lansdowne recently received in which he gives his reasons for wishing Roberts' term to be prolonged. I enclose copy of the passage in his letter, which refers to the matter.[61] Now I may tell you in *strict confidence* that I do not wish Roberts to stay longer in India. He is no doubt a very able man and he has done excellent work . . . . but he is the powerful representation of a forward policy which has gone very far already and if it goes on, may involve us in serious dangers. More especially is his continued presence undesirable, because he has, I believe, got command of the Indian frontier policy and carries the F.O. (Indian) and Lansdowne too much with him. In these circumstances what is wanted is some good *military* reason, which I can give to Lansdowne for not complying with his request. Will you think it over.[62]

177. Kimberley to Gladstone   35 Lowndes Sq.
    12 November 1892
    GP 44229, f. 58

I know how strongly you feel the objections to limiting the right of Irish members to vote in the Imperial Parlt., but is it really impossible to mark off the questions on which they should be restrained from voting? I am not competent to draw one myself, but surely Jenkyns[63] could put the proposal into a suitable form of words.

Forgive me for again pressing this point. The more I think of it the more I fear that our Bill will be wrecked in the Commons, if the Irish are allowed to vote on all questions. Labouchere has in 'Truth' declared himself unequivocally opposed to any such provision, and determined to prevent its passing. Will he not get members enough from our side to follow him to secure with the help of the Tories our defeat?[64]

---

[61] Lansdowne, Indian Viceroy, 1888–94, argued for the extension of General Frederick Sleigh Roberts' tenure as Commander-in-Chief in India, pleading difficulties of transition, imminent delicate negotiations with the Amir, and, failing their success, the possibility of a quarrel with Russia or the Amir. Lansdowne to Kimberley, 30 August 1892, CBP 41221, f. 105.

[62] Roberts was succeeded by Major-General George Stuart White, whom Dufferin characterized as 'a larger man' than Roberts, and 'less inclined to inflate the purely military programme'. Dufferin to Kimberley, 20 December 1892, KP1 10248, f. 33.

[63] Sir Henry Jenkyns, Parliamentary Counsel to the Treasury, 1886–99.

[64] On the nature of Labouchere's influence, see Gladstone to Bertram Currie, secret, 13 August 1892, GP 44515, ff. 143–44; Currie to Algernon West, 25 August 1892, GP 44515, f. 284 and enclosure.

178. Kimberley to Gladstone   35 Lowndes Sq.
    13 November 1892
    GP 44229, ff. 60–61

Your letter[65] crossed mine. I feel the greatest hesitation in setting any opinion of mine against yours in a matter of HC procedure; but I do not feel the insurmountable difficulty which presents itself to you with reference to the Irish voting on questions of want of confidence.

The fact that it is not necessary to state any particular considerations in support of such a motion seems to me to lighten the difficulty. Different members may vote on different grounds, the Irish on grounds specially affecting Ireland, the English for specially English reasons, and so on, but all would have a just claim to record their votes. The objection to the Irish voting on questions arising on British matters, when the British members are debarred from voting on similar matters, does not it seem to me rest on the importance or unimportance of the matters themselves, but on the inequality of rights. The British members by such a provision are placed in a position of inferiority as regards Parliamentary functions from the Irish members. I cannot believe they will submit to such inferiority. The Jew or Parsee has no subjects specially reserved to him, and if he is chosen by a constituency, he must be able to vote on every question: otherwise the constituency would be possibly disfranchised.

Reduction of the number of Irish members would palliate the inequality, but it is open to the charge of unfairness to Ireland which has a just claim to be as fully represented as Gt. Britain on all Imperial questions. Scotch and Welsh members who look to obtaining powers analogous to those which we propose to give to an Irish Parliament, will kick at such a precedent.

179. Gladstone to Kimberley   10 Downing St.
    14 November 1892
    KP2 10244, f. 38

Cadit quaestio. You admit that in her highest of all matters the cleavage cannot be made. Other matters are open and all or mostly practicable, but I should like the power to remain in *its* hands.

180. Kimberley to Spencer   Kimberley House
    3 December 1892
    SP K336

Private and Confidential

Last week at Windsor Rosebery returned to the subject of the leadership of the House of Lords and said he *must* decline it. Work was too heavy at the

---

[65] Of November 12, suggesting the complexity of Irish participation in votes of confidence in the Commons. KP2 10244, ff. 36–37; also *Gladstone Diaries*, 13:141.

F.O. &c. I strongly pressed him to undertake it but he persisted and begged me to tell you. This is most provoking. It is really essential that he should be leader. He has great influence in the country and is an admirable speaker. I have neither of these advantages. Of course I *can* do the business, and probably without any serious discredit to myself. But in the interest of the Govt. I feel most strongly that Rosebery must be leader. I should be altogether in a false position which will be disagreeable to myself and bad for everybody concerned. It must be settled when we meet again in January and meantime I see no use in mooting the matter. I expect that Mr. G will have influence enough with R. to make him give way, and we can, if needful, bring the Cabinet to bear on him.[66]

Mr G told me you had made good progress with the Irish bill.

What a scene Harcourt made at the last Cabinet! It was really too bad.[67]

181. Kimberley to Gladstone   India Office
       2 May 1893
       KP2 10244, f. 57

Copy

I return your list of names. Farrer is excellent.[68] Vivian I see no objection to, tho I doubt his remaining long on our side.[69] Gordon's long and varied services in the colonies constitute a fair claim, but some jealousy will be excited in the breasts of other distinguished colonial governors.[70] Are you sure he will support us? I think this should be clearly ascertained.

[66] Five weeks later Gladstone formally requested Kimberley to lead in the Lords. 11 January 1893, KP2 10244, f. 42; cf. *Gladstone Diaries*, 13:175–76, from Gladstone's copybook, which suggests January 5, but see diary for January 11, and note Kimberley's response of January 12.

[67] Cf. Rosebery's comment on the cabinet of November 23, Extracts, Kimberley memoir, RsP 10186, p. 277.

[68] Thomas Henry Farrer, Permanent Secretary to the Board of Trade, 1865–86; recommended to Gladstone in 1842 by Coleridge of Eton as a potential private secretary at the Board of Trade. Created Baron Farrer of Abinger, 1893.

[69] Henry Hussey Vivian, industrialist and Liberal M.P. for Truro, 1852–57; Glamorganshire, 1857–85; Swansea, 1885, 1886, 1892–93. Created Baron Swansea in 1893. On Vivian's 'commitment' to Home Rule, see *Red Earl*, 2:119, n.4. In McCalmont's *Parliamentary Poll Book*, he is listed as a Liberal Unionist in 1886, a Gladstonian Liberal in 1892.

[70] Arthur Hamilton Gordon, Lt. Governor of New Brunswick, 1861; Governor of Trinidad, 1866–70; of Mauritius, 1871–74; of Fiji, 1875–80; of New Zealand, 1880–83; of Ceylon, 1883–90; family friend of the Gladstones. Gordon was created first Baron Stanmore in 1893. On Stanmore's political reticence and Gladstone's disappointment, see Stanmore to Kimberley, 26 August, 3 September 1893, KP2 10248, ff. 93–95; *Letters of Queen Victoria*, 3rd ser., 2:313–14; J. K. Chapman, *The Career of Arthur Hamilton Gordon, First Lord Stanmore, 1829–1912* (Toronto: University of Toronto Press, 1964), pp. 355–62; *EHJ2*, p. 174.

182. Kimberley to Lansdowne   India Office
      9 June 1893
      LP MSS Eur. D 558/6, no. 31

Private

.... You will see by the newspapers that we were beaten in the House of Commons on a motion by Mr. Paul,[71] (a very clever young Member), in favour of establishing simultaneous examinations for the Civil Service in India and at home. Every effort was made to prevent our supporters from voting for the motion, and many abstained in consequence.[72] Otherwise we should have been much more heavily beaten, as there is a strong feeling on the subject in our party. We could not of course expect much support from our opponents, as party animosity runs breast high at the present time.

We considered the matter carefully in the Cabinet and came to the conclusion that the best course to take was to send the motion out to you for the observations of your Government.

As the Despatch will have to go before my Council in the usual way, you will not receive it immediately, and the subject is so difficult and important that you will no doubt take some time to consider it before you send us an answer. It will be a good thing to give time for reflection before any final decision is arrived at.

I need not say that I am fully alive to the grave objections to a simultaneous examination in India.[73] Mr. Russell[74] stated the case very well in his speech against the motion.

On the other hand, we have to deal with a formidable pressure for equality (as it is argued) of treatment for Indian and European candidates. This pressure is part of the general movement here about Indian affairs.

It is sad to see the House of Commons swayed by such men as those who lead this movement; but the fact is there, and we have to deal with it as best we can. Every day shows that there will be extreme difficulty in carrying on the Government of India in the face of the constant attempts to interfere, not only with its general principles, but with the minute details of your administration.

In the present case it seems to me that two cardinal points have to be borne

---

[71] Herbert Woodfield Paul (1853–1935), Liberal M.P. South Edinburgh, 1892–95, who 'was not aware that our Secretary of State, the distinguished gentlemen who in this country were responsible for the affairs of India, were always subjected to the preliminary test of visiting that country. Lord Kimberley had been in many places .... but he did not know that he had ever been to India.' 4 *Hansard*, 13 (2 June 1893): 102– 11.

[72] See *Gladstone Diaries*, 13:245–46.

[73] See Kimberley's cabinet circular, in which he argued that the holding of simultaneous examinations would 'endanger the whole fabric of our administration.' KP6 MS.eng.c.4366, ff. 29–31.

[74] George W. E. Russell, Liberal M.P. for Bedfordshire; Under-Secretary of State for India.

in mind: (1) that it is absolutely essential for the maintenance of our supremacy in India that there shall be a sufficient number of European members of your Civil Service; (2) that in whatever mode the native members of the service are selected, provision should be made for a fair distribution of the appointments between Mohamedans and Hindoos, and for preventing weak but clever races like the Bengalis from obtaining an undue share of the offices....

What I wish is that you should present your view of the motion fully in a form suitable to be laid before Parliament. Whatever may be your objections, pray present them in such a manner as to show that you do not resort to simple *non possumus*, and that you sympathise generally with the desire of the natives to have access on equal terms to the Civil Service. Such a tone will facilitate dealing with the matter here, and will add weight to your opinion.

I cannot write to you anything definite on the Currency question. My own opinion is in favour of closing the Mints at all events. The question of fixing a ratio is open to more doubt. Currie's arguments are weighty, but the course recommended by the majority of the Committee would probably conciliate opposition here, and allay the fears of those who dread a sudden large rise of exchange and its consequences. I do not feel at liberty to indicate the opinion of the Cabinet, as thus far we have only had preliminary discussion, and we shall not decide till we receive your official opinion on the recommendations of the Committee.

I fear we shall have Parliamentary trouble. Already there is a heavy pressure from the Opposition for the production of the Report before we act, the objections to which are obvious.

The news from America that Cleveland intends to summon Congress in the autumn to consider the Silver question will help us very materially.

183. Kimberley to Lansdowne   India Office
   17 June 1893
   LP MSS Eur. D 558/6, no. 33

Private

I am glad you wrote to Russell the letter about the 'Contagious' diseases, copy of which you sent me in your letter of May 23rd.

Nothing can be more odious to me than the agitation for the protection of venereal disease, for I can call it nothing else. We mass together a number of young single men. We know that we cannot in any way interfere with their inevitable illicit intercourse with women, and on 'moral' grounds we decline to interfere to prevent the diseases which are a cruel injury to both the men and women, not to speak of the consequences to innocent persons and the heavy diminution of the efficiency of our troops. Anything more *immoral* than such a course of action I cannot imagine. But I am sorry to say we are powerless, and the responsibility must rest on the misguided agitators.

The anti-Opium party have at last got a day (the 30th instant) for their motion.[75] Our position is not a pleasant one. No less than six of the present Cabinet and eleven other Members of the Government voted for the motion of April 10, 1891. G. Russell has also given strong pledges to his constituents on the subject; and there is a large increase of Members who have given similar pledges.[76] I can think of no better way out of our difficulties than the appointment of a Commission. The matter must soon be decided by the Cabinet. The agitators are, I fear, for the most part, impervious to argument, but there are probably a good many Members on our side, who, although they have made anti-Opium speeches to their constituents, would be glad to find some way by which to avoid voting for the Resolution....

184. Kimberley to Gladstone   House of Lords
    30 June 1893
    GP 44229, ff. 126–27

I am sorry that I have been kept here by a Scotch Home Rule debate, still going on, and unable to go to you at the H. of Commons; but I explained fully my view to Harcourt. It is in my opinion essential that the Commission should inquire '*whether*' the opium production and sale could be prohibited, not '*when*', which would imply that the principle of prohibition was admitted. I could not reconcile it my [sic] sense of duty to India to prejudice this question which is according to my view the proper subject for inquiry.[77]

185. Kimberley to Gladstone   35 Lowndes Sq.
    1 July 1893
    GP 44229, f. 128

I cannot say how grateful I am to you for your support of the Opium amendment last night and for the admirable and conclusive speech in which you showed that the only proper mode of dealing with the question in its present

---

[75] To prohibit poppy cultivation in India except for medicinal purposes.

[76] Virginia Berridge and Griffith Edwards estimate that there were 240 supporters of the anti-opium cause in the House of Commons, including Asquith, Campbell-Bannerman, and Grey, and that Gladstone was sympathetic. *Opium and the People, Opiate Use in Nineteenth-Century England* (London: Allen Lane, 1981), p. 185.

[77] After Kimberley's threat to resign, passed verbally through George Russell, Gladstone responded: 'I have no option after the communication from you but to proceed along your lines though I am truly sorry that in Pease's last concession you do not find a means of the final accommodation to which you had yourself, I must allow, largely contributed.' 30 June 1893, GP 44549, f. 100. For accounts of the exchange, see Russell, *Half-Lengths*, pp. 151–57; *Gladstone Diaries*, 13:256. Cf. Cooke and Vincent, *Governing Passion*, p. 460, n. 11.

place is by a full and unrestricted inquiry into the whole subject.[78]

I am convinced that no better course could be adopted.

Rosebery made a capital reply to Argyll on Scottish Home Rule, or rather on Irish Home Rule, for that was the principal theme of Argyll's discursive remarks.[79]

186. Kimberley to Lansdowne
21 July 1893
LP MSS Eur. D 558/6, no. 39

Private

.... Siam is a very nasty affair.[80] The French Government has completely broken its word to us; this is, however, we believe, caused by their weakness and their dread of the Chauvinists, and not by any deliberate bad faith. Rosebery thinks that Develle[81] has throughout wished to act in a moderate and conciliatory spirit, but circumstances have been too strong for him.

The Siamese will, I fear, play the French game by prolonging the affair in the vain hope of being able to resist, and our position may become a very difficult one, if it should result in a war between France and Siam, as the French might then attempt to seize the whole country. There are rumours that the Chinese are disposed to interfere. This may alarm the French, who have never forgotten their Tongking experience....

187. Kimberley to Campbell-Bannerman   35 Lowndes Sq.
1 August 1893
CBP 41221, ff. 137–138

As the Irish Bill is now through Committee I am beginning to be anxious about the fate of the Indian Armies Bill.[82] It would be a great misfortune if it did not pass this year, as whilst it is pending, all military reforms in India are hung up, except urgent matters.

I have mentioned the bill to Mr. G and I hope you will help to get it forward. I cannot think there will be any serious obstruction to it. This however may be

---

[78] On the tactical outmanoeuvring of the anti-opium movement, see Berridge and Edwards, *Opium and the People*, pp. 185–88.

[79] See 4 *Hansard*, 14 (30 June 1893): 522–29.

[80] Martel, *Imperial Diplomacy*, pp. 125–136.

[81] Jules Develle, French Foreign Minister.

[82] Madras and Bombay Armies Bill, introduced in the Lords in April 1893; abolished military control of Madras and Bombay governments and eliminated the position of Commander-in-Chief of the presidency armies; received royal assent on 5 December 1893. For a concise discussion of Indian obstruction, see Hira Lal Singh, *Problems and Policies of the British in India, 1885– 1898* (Bombay: Asia Publishing House, 1963), pp. 152–59.

an Utopian view, and as I have no right to presume that it would care anything about so trifling and uninteresting a subject as Indian armies. But I will still *hope*.

188. Kimberley to Ripon   India Office
     19 September 1893
     RP 43526, ff. 167–68

Private

I was brought up here by Harcourt who is in a terrible state of fuss about the Indian budget. On my arrival I was presented with Norman's telegram.[83]

Pleasant! I can think of nothing better than to ask Lansdowne to stay on another year. But failing that? Affairs look very unpleasant in India. Lansdowne and the Govn. of the Punjab and North W. Provinces are seriously alarmed at the proceedings of the anti-cow killing association. They say the movement is really political and they fear there may be grave events. I have not time to explain further, but we sadly need a really strong man. Ought not Spencer to go. I feel almost sure he would if it was put to him as a public duty.[84] Even his support of Home Rule seems to me less important than the stability of our Indian Empire.... [85]

189. Wolseley to Kimberley   3 Green Street,
     4 October 1893   Park Lane
     KP2 10248, ff. 107–10

Please forgive me for recommending myself to your notice as one who would very gladly go to India to succeed Lansdowne. My views upon India are I believe well known to those who were my colleagues on the India Council. Briefly they are as follows:

We have far more to dread in India from the difficulty of making Revenue and Expenditure balance than we have from Russia; to keep down expenditure

[83] Withdrawing acceptance of the Indian Viceroyalty. For subsequent events, see J. Chandran, 'Victoria, Gladstone and the Indian Viceroyalty, 1893–1894', *New Zealand Journal of History*, 3 (October 1969): 175–89.

[84] Precisely the appeal which Gladstone had made to Kimberley in 1880. *Gladstone Diaries*, 9:508–09.

[85] Cf. Gladstone's view. Gladstone to Kimberley, 26 July 1893, KP6 MS.eng.c.4329, f. 2. As early as 1 August 1893, Kimberley had provisionally offered the Viceroyalty which Spencer refused, ostensibly on medical grounds but also for political reasons at Gladstone's request. Kimberley once again proposed Spencer to Gladstone on September 19. Kimberley to Gladstone, Secret, 2 August 1893, GP 44229, f. 142; Hutchinson, *Private Diaries of West*, pp. 185, 197; Spencer to Kimberley, Secret, 6 August 1893, KP2 10247, f. 53; Kimberley to Gladstone, 19, 21 September 1893, GP 44229, ff. 156–62; *Gladstone Diaries*, 13:302–03. Cf. Chandran, 'Indian Viceroyalty', pp. 176, 181–82.

ought I think to be the Viceroy's first aim; the chief if not the only item upon which retrenchment can be effected is the military budget; to keep it down and within bounds can only be well done by a soldier. The military craze in India is towards military extravagance, and when the Comdr. in Chief puts forward urgent demands for new items, he is so supported by the Viceroy's council that he finds it difficult to resist. A soldier of experience as Viceroy could not have this pressure put upon him, for he being able to review the military arguments as well as the Comdr. in Chief, would be able to turn a deaf ear to all such applications. I have always thought that you will never have real economy in military expenditure in India until you have a soldier at the head of affairs there.

Then again there is that old bogey of the 'forward policy' which has cost millions and still weighs heavily upon our revenue. Our generals are always preparing for what I believe to be an impossible campaign in Central Asia, and forever scheme for sending an army to Herat. If we ever attempt to send our army to meet the Russians at Herat we shall lose India. I believe it was a most unwise measure to increase the infantry in India by three battalions of British troops, as we did some four years ago; we then added 10,000 English soldiers to our garrison of India. I don't think anyone but a soldier opposed to this fatal 'forward policy' will ever be able to redress all these mistakes.

If your views are different from mine, I have nothing to say in my own favour that would recommend me to your favourable consideration. But if retrenchment and a peace policy be objects you think well of, I believe a soldier — because he can hold his own with soldiers — is more likely to effect those objects than a non military man could.

Please forgive me for my presumption in thus writing to you.

190. Harcourt to Kimberley   11 Downing Street
      31 December 1893
      KP2 10245, ff. 27–29

I am sorry that you don't see your way to letting people know what is the fact, that under no circumstances will an import duty upon silver into India be allowed.[86] I spoke to Mr. Gladstone the other day on the subject and he treated the thing as a proposal that could never be entertained. It is quite certain therefore that the cabinet would never consent to it.

I have not spoken to anyone whose opinion is worth having who does not regard such a proceeding as altogether intolerable.[87] It is only a desperate

---

[86] Kimberley, opposed to an import duty, informed Harcourt that 'as Currie the Chairman of my Finance Committee is strongly of the other opinion it is essential that he should be consulted before any step is taken...'. Copy, 2 January 1894, KP2 10245, f. 31; cf. Kimberley to Herschell, 4 January 1894, WP VIII, f. 41.

[87] After meeting with Currie, Harcourt modified his view: 'I cannot find any person, whose opinion is worth having, except Currie, who is in favour of an import duty.'

resource of incapable financiers to prop up a broken down experiment. I have not the smallest reliance upon the financial intelligence or prudence of the Indian Govt.....Is it not at once the most honest and the wisest policy to put an end to an uncertainty which is operating most unfavourably to Indian Finance.

191. Kimberley to Gladstone   Kimberley House
      21 January 1894
      GP 44229, ff. 208–11

Secret

.... Now in all deference to my colleagues, I think I am better able to judge of this than they are (excepting of course Ripon).[88] Lansdowne's career ought to be judged as a whole, and I consider that as a whole it has been successful.[89]

He made one great blunder about the juries,[90] but *between ourselves* I do not think it was a worse one (if as bad) than Ripon made about the Ilbert Bill,[91] tho' it was of a very different kind.

His other fault was that he was far too much, in his conduct of frontier affairs, under the control of Roberts.[92] On the other hand, Roberts being removed, he took a most wise step in proposing to send Durand to Cabul, and to send him without any escort. The instructions to Durand,[93] based no doubt on a despatch from me, were judicious, and the success of the mission complete.

The rest of his Viceroyalty was marked by no great event, but is not a reign of five years of peace, unbroken except by the inevitable small frontier trouble, in itself no small credit, be it due to policy or fortune.[94]

Lastly, I must say he has always acted cordially with me, notwithstanding differences of opinion on certain points.

Harcourt to Kimberley, 3 January 1894, KP2 10245, ff. 33–35; cf. Gardiner, *Life of Harcourt*, 2:205.

[88] See *Gladstone Diaries*, 13: 363.

[89] And this despite his estimation of Lansdowne as 'decidedly the weakest' of the viceroys with whom he had worked. Extracts, Kimberley memoir, RsP 10186, p. 277. As early as April 1893 Kimberley had recommended that Derby's vacant Garter be reserved for Lansdowne. On the context of the debate, see Hutchinson, *Private Diaries of West*, p. 155; Gopal, *British Policy in India*, pp. 206–10; Kaminsky, *India Office*, pp. 96–101.

[90] Sanctioning the withdrawal in Bengal of jury trials in cases of murder and culpable homicide. Lord Newton, *Lord Lansdowne, A Biography* (London: Macmillan, 1929), pp. 110–12.

[91] See letter 119, herein.

[92] See letter 180, herein.

[93] Henry Mortimer Durand, foreign secretary to the Government of India, 1884–94.

[94] For a predictably similar assessment of Lansdowne's viceroyalty, see Newton, *Lord Lansdowne*, pp. 124–26.

You will see from this terribly long epistle that I am much better. I hope to go to town early next week.

192. Kimberley to Monkswell[95]   Kimberley House
      24 January 1894
      KP6 MS.eng.c.4471, ff. 124–26

Private/Copy

I am not at all surprised at your annoyance at the Local Government Bill being taken out of your hands. I am myself extremely vexed at what has happened. I was very ill at the time when the Bill was put into your hands, and was not aware that it was thought to be essential that the bill sd. be in the hands of a Cabinet Minister.

As you know I had intended to take it myself. Had I been less ill, I should have taken care to ascertain whether it was necessary to give the Bill to some other member of the Cabinet. The blame must rest on my shoulders for what must I feel be a mortification to you.

Will you take a piece of advice from an old stager? If I were in your place, I should certainly speak on the 2nd reading. It is never politic to put the dots on the i's for the benefit of the public. If you speak, you will be in my opinion in a better position than if you are silent.[96]

This will not at all affect your desire to be relieved of further connexion with L.G.B. business. Any way, whether you speak or not, I will as soon as I am able to attend the House, consult with you as to your wishes, and make the best arrangement I can for you.

I beg you however to take no step till we meet, which I hope will be next week.

193. Kimberley to Gladstone   35 Lowndes Sq.
      11 February 1894
      KP1 15/K2/22

Secret/Copy

The Queen approves the offer of the next K.G. to Lansdowne.[97] She does not like the reservation.[98] Is it necessary? Our peers are but a tiny band, and there is no probable K.G. among them. It would diminish the grace of the offer.

---

[95] Robert Collier, second Lord Monkswell (1845–1909), Lord in Waiting, 1892–95; Under-Secretary to the War Office, 1895.

[96] Monkswell wrote to thank Kimberley and say that he would take his advice. 25 January 1894, KP6 MS.eng.c.4471, ff. 128–29.

[97] See Queen Victoria to Kimberley, 5 February 1894, KP1 15/K2/22

[98] That in the event of 'some strong political claim' arising 'before there is a vacancy', the offer might be reconsidered. Cited in Kaminsky, *India Office*, p. 101.

194. John Morley to Kimberley   Dublin Castle
        25 February 1894
        KP6 MS.eng.c.4471, ff. 150–51

Secret

In reference to the confidence which you were kind enough to make to me on Friday as to your intention in a certain contingency, it seems very important to me that you should not give the advice proposed, unless it is clearly and definitely understood beforehand that R. would go on with the business.[99]

It is obviously of the very first importance that plans should be ready and not half a day lost — both on account of the pressing demands of parliamentary business, and in order to put an extinguisher at the earliest possible moment on the excitement, gossip, and general distraction and clamour which is sure to arise, and to go on swelling until definite solution is known.

I know the difficulty of ascertaining the *Irish* view of the best personal solution, and until that is known, you will all be somewhat in the dark. I am writing to Mr. Gladstone to ask if some communication should not be made to McCarthy. They ought not to find it out from the evening papers.

However, I only write now to press that R. should make up his mind *now*, and I shall probably send him a copy of this epistle.

Do not trouble to answer, as I shall be on the wing, until I reach home on Tuesday night.

[99] See Stansky, *Ambitions and Strategies*, pp. 74–78.

6
At the Foreign Office

Gladstone's retirement in February 1894 marked the beginning of a new and uncertain era in Liberal Party politics. Without an obvious leader or clear domestic program, chances for harmony were slim. From the beginning there was dissension over constitution of the new Liberal cabinet, Harcourt coveting the prime-ministership, Morley the foreign secretaryship. However, the Queen called for Rosebery, who insisted on Kimberley for the Foreign Office. Harcourt agreed in the general feeling that Kimberley was, next to Rosebery, best fitted for the office, but argued that the Prime Minister and the Foreign Secretary should not sit simultaneously in the House of Lords. He and Morley finally acquiesced in the arrangement, with Harcourt going to the Exchequer and Morley to the Home Office. Harcourt nevertheless continued to complain of the arrangement and consistently promoted a 'little Englandism' which was uncongenial to both the Prime Minister and his Foreign Secretary.

Kimberley and Rosebery had worked together harmoniously during Gladstone's third and fourth governments. During Rosebery's brief ministry, they generally agreed in a foreign policy of maintenance, though they were more aggressive when southern Africa appeared threatened. Kimberley was, however, more cautious than the Prime Minister, and less interested in direct involvement in secondary arenas such as Uganda, the horn of Africa and northern China. Given Rosebery's elegant mastery of the Foreign Office and Kimberley's long experience, the cabinet apart from Harcourt remained virtually silent. With the ill-conceived Anglo–Belgian Treaty of April 1894, initiated by Rosebery but concluded under Kimberley, they managed immediately both to irritate France and Germany, and to ruffle the hypersensitive susceptibilities of the vociferous Harcourt. Talks with both French and German representatives smoothed immediate difficulties but proved inconclusive during the following fifteen months in settling broader international tensions, which were exacerbated by the Sino-Japanese War (August 1894–April 1895). Kimberley and Rosebery refused to join Russia, Germany and France in forcing Japan to moderate its settlement with China, reinforcing Britain's diplomatic isolation while laying the foundation for better relations with Japan in East Asia. Though successful in protecting Britain's paramount interests, Kimberley and Rosebery were not able during their short tenure to clarify Britain's international role *vis-à-vis* the other European powers.

At home, diplomatic missteps undermined public confidence in the already fissiparous government, and aggravated differences among members of the cabinet. Although the government pushed the landmark budget of 1894 through the Lords, and successfully passed a series of smaller measures, Liberals lacked a coherent Irish policy, were divided over reform of the House of Lords, and were politically damaged by Harcourt's dogged attempt to pass a Licensing Bill for which there was little enthusiasm. In June elections of 1895, the Liberal Party was soundly defeated (Conservatives 340, Liberal Unionists 71, Liberals 177, Irish Nationalists 82), sending it into a decade of confused opposition.

199. Kimberley to Ripon   35 Lowndes Sq.
23 March 1894
RP 43526, ff. 179–80

We are writing to you about a request of the German Govt. to be allowed to recruit 500 coolies at Singapore. I should be particularly glad if you could comply with this request. Count Metternich[1] told me that the Emperor took a very special interest in it, and he said it was an affair almost of life and death for their colony to get this supply of labour as soon as possible. Compliance with this request would much help to smooth other colonial questions in Africa with the Germans. You might, if you think it necessary, say that no further applications of this kind can be entertained.

200. Kimberley to Rosebery   35 Lowndes Sq.
27 March 1894
RsP 10068, ff. 83–84

I propose to proceed at once on the lines suggested by Anderson.[2] There is evidently no time to be lost.

Must we not let Harcourt know of this negotiation? He ought not to kick at it as it really tends to narrow our responsibilities. If we leave him in ignorance, we shall have trouble I fear worse than by letting him know early.

Pray don't apologise for sending me suggestions.[3] I am most thankful for them. It is always difficult at first to know whether and how to make any move, and you who know the ground, are sure to see quicker than I can at present, what should be noticed.

---

[1] Paul von Wolff Metternich, German Minister to London.

[2] Sir Percy Anderson, Assistant Under-Secretary to the Foreign Office, 1893–96. On details of the Anglo-Belgian Treaty, see Martel, *Imperial Diplomacy*, chap. 6.

[3] On Kimberley's Cabinet memorandum regarding the Anglo-Belgian Treaty, KP6 MS.eng.c.4412, ff. 5–12, 77.

201. Kimberley to Harcourt   35 Lowndes Sq.
      28 March 1894
      RsP 10143, f. 5

Typescript Copy

I think you ought to know that we are engaged in secret negotiations with the King of the Belgians with a view to transfer to him under a long lease our 'sphere of influence' on the Upper Nile. The object is to prevent the French, who are about to send an expedition across Africa to that region, from establishing themselves there, and to settle with the Belgians, who are there already, the questions arising out of our claims to a sphere of influence in that quarter.

The arrangement, if we can carry it through, appears to me to present many advantages. We shall have a friendly neighbour; we shall not be under pressure to extend our operations in that district; we shall prevent the French from interfering. The presence of the French there would be a serious danger to Egypt, and might easily involve us in complications with them. I can at any time give you verbally any further explanations you may desire. The matter is *very* secret.[4]

202. Kimberley to Rosebery   Foreign Office
      2 May 1894
      RsP 10068, ff. 120–21

Secret

Sanderson[5] is alarmed at what may happen when an agreement with the King of the Belgians is published. He thinks the French will be furious and that the King may then ask us on account of the danger to relations between France and Belgium to withdraw or modify the agreement. I am not as alarmed at this, as I doubt the French pushing the matter to extremities with Belgium however angered they may be. They may insist on concessions at the Congo State limits, but I do not expect they will care on account of this matter, to raise an European question.

But I am alarmed at the position we shall be in toward the cabinet if we have not communicated to it the despatches from Plunkett.[6] If anything serious were to happen, we should be in a very awkward position if we keep them in ignorance, and I do not think we could justify ourselves.

---

[4] The final sentence was omitted by Gardiner in his *Life of Harcourt*, 2:313, reinforcing Harcourt's unfounded pretension that he had had only a 'slight hint' of the negotiations. See Martel, *Imperial Diplomacy*, pp. 204–05.

[5] Thomas Henry Sanderson, Assistant Under-Secretary for Foreign Affairs, 1889–94; Permanent Under-Secretary for Foreign Affairs, 1894–1906.

[6] Sir Francis Richard Plunkett, Minister to Belgium, 1893–1900. Rosebery agreed to their distribution. Rosebery to Kimberley, 7 May 1894, KP6 MS.eng.c.4412, f. 28.

No doubt we shall have a very unpleasant *quart d'heure* when we produce them but we will be better to face that at once, than the much more serious danger if we keep the despatches back. I am having them printed and would circulate them tomorrow. Please telegraph to me whether you concur....

I repeat I am convinced that if we keep back the despatches, we should run a very serious risk.

[*Postscript*] I am sending this by messenger so that it will not be necessary to telegraph unless you simply concur in which case a telegram would save time.

203. Kimberley to Ripon   35 Lowndes Square
       6 May 1894
       RP 43526, ff. 186–87

Secret

A discussion in Cabinet and subsequent consideration by a few of us as to the best mode of carrying into effect the Cabinet's decision resulted in a telegram sent last night proposing to cancel the agreement and substitute something in which will practically come to the same thing (in my opinion). But it is thought that this device will lighten the wrath of the French, and I think myself it is a good move looking to all the circms.

Harcourt wrote me an absurd letter full of 'blood and thunder' which I need hardly tell you had not the slightest effect on us: I mean the violent language.[7] His *opinions* I of course pay due regard to: only if they were expressed in rational terms, they would be more likely to carry weight with me.

However, all that, tho' rather wearisome, is of no real consequence. I will call at your home this afternoon on the chance that you may be able to see me, as I should much like to have a talk with you on this and another matter.

---

[7] Harcourt wrote that he had 'just read with astonishment, and I must say indignation, the correspondence which has been going on for the last fortnight....', Harcourt to Kimberley, 3 May 1894, copy, RsP 10143, f. 24. Asquith later recalled the 'unflagging industry and unfailing copiousness' of Harcourt's attack. 'I can speak with the more freedom because on the merits of most of the points at issue I was disposed to side with Harcourt; but his lack of any sense of proportion, his incapacity for self-restraint, and his perverse delight in inflaming and embittering every controversy, made cooperation with him always difficult and often impossible.' *Fifty Years of British Parliament*, 2 vols. (Boston: Little, Brown, and Co., 1926), 1:252.

204. Kimberley to Rosebery   Foreign Office
       15 May 1894
       RsP 10068, ff. 146–47

Private

More from Harcourt as to the instruction to Portal.[8] He demands from me
your mem: of which he says I am in charge! Please send it to him, as you are
in possession of it. I have explained the true meaning of the mystic words 'not
to be printed' which merely indicate that the document is not to be included in
the printed papers sent to our principal missions, and has nothing to do with the
Cabinet. But no explanations on this portentous matter seem to be any use. I
am getting very tired of the correspondence.

With regard to Harcourt's complaint that he is absolutely without knowledge
of the view of the Foreign Office upon the question of Uganda, I have made
more than one futile attempt to get the cabinet to come to close quarters with
the points which must be decided before the discussion comes on in the House
of Commons, and I feel strongly the necessity of a clear understanding as to
our policy.

I would propose to circulate the Departmental Report with the annexed mem:
which, subject to your observations, express my views.

205. Kimberley Memorandum   Foreign Office
       29 May 1894
       RsP 10146, f. 48

I most sincerely hope that the unanimous prayer of the 70,000 women will
not be granted to them.[9]

206. Kimberley to Malet[10]
       19 June 1894
       MP FO 343/3, ff. 293-94

Private

I have to thank you for your letter of June 16.

You will have seen that we have adopted the course which you recommend.
It was manifest that it would be most impolitic for the sake of the acquisition

---

[8] Sir Gerald Portal, Special Commissioner to Uganda, 1892–93. Rosebery had as
Foreign Secretary in 1892 commissioned Portal with the task of arranging the 'best
means of administering Uganda', while Harcourt and others wished for withdrawal. See
Martel, *Imperial Diplomacy*, pp. 86–88.

[9] Seeking the vote. In response to Rosalind Carlisle, President of the Women's Liberal
Federation, to Rosebery, 20 May 1894, RsP 10146, ff. 43–45. See letter 173, herein.

[10] Sir Edward Baldwin Malet (1837–1908), Ambassador to Berlin, 1884–95.

of a strip of land for a road and a telegraph to embroil ourselves with Germany and to encounter all the dangers which would follow from the common action of Germany with France in African questions. Indeed the consequences would be of far wider impact as has been clearly seen by the alarm of the other parties to the Triple Alliance. Both the Austrian and Italian Ambassadors have spoken to me on the subject and have not concealed their serious apprehensions.

I have just learned that the Porte will protest against the Agreement, but if we succeed in satisfying Germany, this will not add, I think, much to our difficulties. I hope the Germans will not object to the form of our declaration. Hatzfeldt[11] wanted me to refer to the objection to the Lease as being equivalent to a cession as one of the grounds of the declaration, but this would it is clear strengthen the grounds of the French objection to the rest of the agreement.

As to the German argument that the agreement infringes the right of Germany that no cession of territory shall be made without her consent, no such right, as far as we can see, exists. On the contrary their treaty with the Congo State distinctly provides for the case of cession, and only stipulates that in such case all the obligations of the Congo State shall remain applicable to the new possessor. On the other hand the two objections of Germany on which we have based the declaration are not unreasonable and may fairly be recognised by us as sufficient.

207. Kimberley to Rosebery   35 Lowndes Sq.
        30 July 1894
        RsP 10068, ff. 207–09

Private

I should be glad to know what you think about the China and Japan quarrel. We have confined ourselves thus far strictly to friendly advice to both parties. This may be said to have failed in its object. Japan is bent on war, and the Chinese, tho' they hesitate to formally declare war, are in practice accepting the challenge.

The question is, ought we to interfere more decisively?, or shall we let matters take their course? In the present state of affairs, interference must take the form of armed mediation, and will really be directed against Japan, who is the aggressor. If we take this step, it must be in conjunction with Russia who I expect would not be sorry to coerce Japan. The Japanese are very uppish and would probably not be very easy to bring to reason, but they could not resist the presence of ourselves and Russia if applied in earnest and other powers would no doubt more or less support our action.

On the other hand the result would be that we and Russia should have to settle the affairs of Corea, and once having done this we should become permanently

---

[11] Count Paul von Hatzfeldt, German ambassador to Great Britain.

responsible for them; a very disagreeable prospect.

On the whole I incline to leaving the Chinese and Japanese alone as the least of two evils provided the Russians abstain from active interference.... [12]

I have got a bad cold, which, tho' somewhat better, obliges me to stay at home.

---

208. Kimberley to Rosebery   35 Lowndes Sq.
20 August 1894
RsP 10068, ff. 237–38

Private

I differ from Cromer,[13] because I am not in favour of 'continued occupation' of Egypt if (which I understand to be Cromer's real meaning) continued occupation is to be construed 'perpetual' occupation. I therefore think the balance of argument is in favour of concluding the Convention with the Sultan, so far as the first article goes. The other articles seem to me more doubtful.

There is however one objection which may be worth considering, namely, that the French may take strong objection to the 'five years' term as inconsistent with our promises to go as soon as Egypt is in a position which will admit our retirement.

They may take advantage of this as an excuse for remaining at Chantaboun.[14]

---

209. Kimberley to Ripon   Kimberley House
9 September 1894
RP 43526, ff. 225–26

Private

A despatch from Phipps[15] has gone to the Col. Office, recording a conversation with the French Govt. of the Ivory Coast, to which I invite your particular attention. He has also written a private letter to Sir P. Anderson, which will be sent to you.... If your colonial officials are like our Consuls, I have no doubt our interests suffer from undue suspicion and jealousy of the French, and readiness to believe and report every story to their disadvantage. You know what

---

[12] Kimberley's letter served as the basis of the Prime Minister's memorandum of 30 July 1894, printed in Kenneth Bourne, *The Foreign Policy of Victorian England, 1830–1902* (Oxford: Clarendon Press, 1970), p. 433. Rosebery composed the memorandum 'hastily' upon receipt of Kimberley's *note*, rather than *box* as indicated in Bourne. See KP2 10243, ff. 53–55.

[13] Evelyn Baring, first Baron Cromer, Agent and Consul-General in Egypt, 1883–1907.

[14] On Siamese policy, see Martel, *Imperial Diplomacy*, pp. 126–36; Nigel Brailey, ed. *Two Views of Siam on the Eve of the Chakri Reformation* (Whiting Way, Scotland: Kiscadale Publications, 1989).

[15] Edmund Phipps, Acting Minister of the British legation in Paris.

Indian officials think of Russians, and in Africa the same thing happens, only the *'bête noire'* there is France. Phipps' first conversation with Hanotaux[16] is on the whole encouraging.

210. Kimberley to Rosebery   35 Lowndes Sq.
    11 November 1894
    RsP 10069, ff. 90–91

Private

Here is a long jeremiad from Cromer[17] all arising from my telling him privately that he had better avoid 'burning boats' in the matter of the appointment of an English adviser to the Ministry of the Interior. I am not at all moved by his arguments. It would never do, that every time he wants some reform in the Egyptian government, he is to be at liberty to commit us to go to extremities. Such heroic policy should be reserved for really great occasions.

The only two reforms lately of any consequence in Egypt have been the appointment of an English head of the Khedive school, and this question as to the minister of the interior. In both instances we have carried our point. Cromer's letter shows, it seems to me, a certain amount of nervousness or lack of confidence which I should not have ascribed to him. Of course his position is and must always be extremely difficult and trying.

As to the reduction of our force in Egypt, his argument really is that the difference between the present Khedive and Tewfik requires a permanent addition to the garrison. No doubt this is an important consideration. The rest of his arguments appear to me to apply as much to Tewfik's time as the present. But as we shall receive Cromer's official reply to my despatch, it is unnecessary now to discuss the question.

[*Postscript*] Of course I shall write him a soothing letter.

211. Kimberley to Rosebery   Foreign Office
    20 November 1894
    RsP 10069, f. 98

Will you look at these memoranda by Anderson. Rhodes is very anxious for a decision, as he is to leave shortly.[18] I propose to take the course suggested by Anderson, and *specially* to declare a protectorate over the Chartered Territory either now or when Rhodes takes over the administration. I incline to the latter.

[16] Gabriel Hanotaux, French Foreign Minister.

[17] Noting that the government's vague and indefinite policy required Cromer to make local decisions, which were then weakly supported by the Foreign Office. Cromer to Kimberley, 3 November 1894, Cairo, Cromer Papers FO 633/6, pp. 234–37.

[18] Cecil John Rhodes, Prime Minister of Cape Colony, 1890–96; in London for a meeting of the board of directors of the British South Africa Company.

212. Kimberley Memorandum   Kimberley House
30 December 1894
RsP 10147, f. 13

Exactly the same view is taken here in the two divisions (Mid: and East
Norfolk) with which I am immediately connected.[19]

I am told[20] that if we have a bye Election in Mid Norfolk from which our
member (Higgins)[21] threatens to retire, it is very doubtful if we could win, for
the same reasons as are given in this letter for the loss of Brigg, though at a
general Election we should almost certainly keep the seat.[22] We have a good
local candidate in the field.

213. Kimberley to Rosebery   Kimberley House
3 January 1895
RsP 10069, ff. 135–37

Private

I doubt whether anything can properly be said 'to soothe the feelings' of the
Sultan.[23] It would be more appropriate if he were to do something to soothe the
feelings of those who are indignant at his proceedings. From Block's report[24] it
is clear that the Sultan himself is the author of the merciless measures against
the Armenians, and the signal honours conferred upon Zekki Pasha[25] are a
deliberate affront to us and the other powers. I did not think so at first, but
recent information leaves I fear no doubt of this.[26] However the question as far

---

[19] That the Local Veto Bill 'goes beyond public opinion and at the poll the temperance
men are as nothing.' Henry Spring to Rosebery, 20 December 1894, RsP 10146, ff.
216–17. On the growing electoral strength of the drink trade, see David W. Gutzke,
Protecting the Pub: Brewers and Publicans against Temperance (London: The Royal
Historical Society, 1989).

[20] By John Wodehouse, Liberal agent in the district. See their correspondence. KP1
3/2.

[21] Clement Higgins, Liberal M.P. for Mid Norfolk from 1892 until April 1895, when
he became a Liberal Unionist and resigned his seat.

[22] On the loss of Brigg Division, Lincolnshire, see *EHJ2*, pp. 195–96. According
to Spring, as long as 'wealthy organizations'— the drink trade, in this instance— were
allowed 'to expend money without stint, such not being reckoned as part of their candidate's expenses, hardly any bye election can be won. . .' Spring to Rosebery, 20
December 1894, RsP 10146, f. 216. The April bye-election was lost by 216 votes, while
Frederick Wilson regained the seat for the Liberals in July by a margin of 134 votes.

[23] Abdul Hamid II, Sultan of the Ottoman Empire, 1876–1909.

[24] Adam Block, Commissioner of Inquiry into the Sassoon Massacres; report of 25
December 1894, in Kenneth Bourne and D. Cameron Watt, gen. eds., *British Documents
on Foreign Affairs, Reports and Papers from the Foreign Office Confidential Print*, pt.1,
ser. B, 19:140–41.

[25] Ottoman general in charge of Armenian repression.

[26] See, for instance, the report in the *Spectator*, 8 December 1894, p. 1.

as we are concerned is simple enough. We have asked for an inquiry and we have neither said nor done anything which can indicate that we have prejudiced the result of the inquiry. It is not our business as a government to explain or defend Mr. Gladstone's speeches (if they need any defence) and I am sure we could do nothing more unwise than to seek to diminish the effect of his speech the other day.[27]

I am inclined either to give no answer to Said Pasha,[28] or to tell Currie[29] that he should point out that the only way by which the Sultan can meet attacks upon himself and his Govt. is to take every measure to secure that the inquiry is thorough and impartial and further to assure complete indemnity and protection to every witness who may come forward.

The latter course seems to me on the whole the best, but you may be able to suggest something better.

214. Kimberley Memorandum   35 Lowndes Sq.
    8 January 1895
    RsP 10069, f. 139

The Italians naturally want us to cooperate with them, but their advance on Kassala was not made after consultation with us, and we have never led them to expect support from us in their forward movement. I am for steadfastly resisting all attempts to draw us in and I propose therefore to tell Cromer that we cannot countenance any movement of Egyptian troops.

215. Kimberley to Gladstone   35 Lowndes Sq.
    12 January 1895
    GP 44229, ff. 230–31

Private

Your letter of the 7th[30] for which many thanks did not reach me till after you had started, as I only returned to London on the 8th. I should be greatly obliged if at your leisure you could give me an account of what passed in 1881 or 2.

The Sultan has made loud complaints of your speech at Hawarden, and I should wish you to know what has passed on the subject. In answer to a telegram from Currie, reporting the complaints made on behalf of the Sultan by Said Pasha, the Turkish Minst. for Foreign Affairs, I replied that you are not a

[27] Addressing an Armenian deputation at Hawarden on December 29; reported in *The Times*, 31 December 1894.

[28] Grand Vizier of Turkey.

[29] Philip Currie, Ambassador to Turkey, 1893–98.

[30] Which Kimberley had shown to Rosebery, who agreed that Gladstone's account should be obtained without delay. Gladstone to Kimberley, 7 January 1895, KP6 MS.eng.c.4470, ff. 30–31.

Minister, and we have no control or responsibility for your sayings but that as the Sultan raised the subject, we could not disguise from H. My. that in this matter you had expressed the general public feeling here which would only be satisfied by a real and searching investigation followed by *condign* punishment of those who might be proved to be guilty.

Rustem Pasha[31] came to me subsequently with a despatch complaining of your 'insulting' language about the Sultan, to which I returned a similar answer. I am really sorry for Rustem who is a good creature, and most anxious to preserve friendly relations between us and the Porte. The poor man takes to heart the Armenian business and has persuaded himself that it is nothing but the result of a revolutionary movement against the authority of the Sultan.

I hope you did not suffer from your long journey and that you have better weather than we have here, where it is bitterly cold.

216. Kimberley to Rosebery   Foreign Office
  26 January 1895
  RsP 10069, f. 158

These papers show what the Italians want. I see no possibility of meeting their views by giving up Zeyla to them, and the idea of a common occupation seems to me ludicrous. As to the exchange suggested, the territory to the east of our protectorate extending to Cape Guardafui is absolutely worthless. We might have occupied it but it was considered to be perfectly useless to us. The French were angry with us for making the 'Somali Agreement' with the Italians.[32] I do not think they had just cause for their anger. If however we now let the Italians into Zeyla, they would be furious with us, and not without cause. They would probably denounce the agreement by which we are mutually bound not to establish a protectorate over Harrar. The result would be to open Harrar to them, and a serious quarrel might arise between them and Italy. Moreover, such a proceeding on our part could not fail to have a prejudicial effect on our negotiations with France on other African questions.

We have done all we can for Italy in this question by concluding the Somali agreement delineating our respective spheres, and recognizing their protectorate. It is unreasonable to press us further, and a due regard for our own interests requires that we should not weaken our own position and embroil ourselves with France for the purpose of supporting this shadowy Italian protectorate, which they have not, and never had any means of enforcing.

I am sorry we cannot meet their wishes, but I see no way of doing so in this matter.

---

[31] Chimelli de Marini, Ottoman ambassador to Great Britain.
[32] Protocols of 1891, defining Red Sea frontiers and confirming Italian claims in Abyssinia.

217. Kimberley to Rosebery   Foreign Office
    19 February 1895
    RsP 10069, ff. 188–90

Private and Confidential

You have always been so kind to me and our relations have been so invariably cordial in official matters that, you will I am sure forgive me for most earnestly entreating you not to persevere in the determination you announced to us today.[33] My sympathies are entirely with you, and I fully admit that you have a right to expect hearty support in the Commons. Your strong remonstrance will clear the air, and I have no doubt, at all events for a time, improve your position and strengthen your authority. With this I think you may be satisfied. You know how I have suffered ('tis lately there has been a cessation of the insolent letters with which I was flooded.) I only bore with them because I felt it a duty not to do anything which could embarrass the government, or give you trouble. Pray consider how extremely serious the consequences of such a step as you contemplate must be to our whole party and to yourself. We are not likely as a government to last long, and however irksome your position may be, I cannot believe that on reflection on what passed today, you will not feel that it would be perfectly honourable to yourself to yield to what you must have seen was the strong and unanimous wish of all your colleagues.

I may call myself now an old friend, and it is in that capacity and in the most sincere wish for your happiness and reputation that I have ventured to write to you my whole mind.[34]

218. Kimberley to Rosebery   Foreign Office
    26 March 1895
    RsP 10069, ff. 211–13

Your criticism on the Siam draft is just. Another and I hope more impressive draft is preparing.

General Ferrero[35] asked me the other day if I had recd. answer from Indian Govt. as to Italian agent at Zeyla. I said that the official answer from India Office had not yet reached me but I believed the opinion of the Govt. of India was adverse to the appointment. I have in fact seen the telegram which expresses a strong opinion against it. Hatzfeldt told me that Ferrero was 'furious' at the prospect of our refusal. Ferrero said very little to me and I told him we had taken no final decision. This matter, small in itself, is very troublesome. The French are excessively jealous in that quarter, and it is most undesirable if it

---

[33] To resign.
[34] Not quite. For Kimberley's private thoughts, see Kimberley journal, KP6 MS.eng.c. 2793, pp. 419-426.
[35] Annibale Ferrero, Italian ambassador to Great Britain.

can be avoided, to disturb the status quo there.

Hatzfeldt suggested that if we have to give an unfavourable answer we should put it off as long as possible. This seems to be prudent.

P.S. — I met Mr. G at Grillion's last night. He spoke to me about Armenia. His language was moderate and he quite agreed that we should avoid raising the 'Eastern question' in an acute form, the danger of which I impressed upon him. Stevenson[36] he said had pressed him to make a speech in the H of Commons but he had declined. He was in great force and spirits.

219. Kimberley to Gladstone   35 Lowndes Sq.
    27 March 1895
    GP 44229, ff. 232–33

I think if you would put your recollections on paper as you propose, it would be very convenient.

As you justly say fear is the only motive which stirs the Sultan to action. His great hope is to play off the different powers against each other. At present the game fails, but if we should be unable to maintain our common action, I should not have much hope of a successful result; and it must not be forgotten that at this moment, the Russians are not so stirred up, as our English public, on the subject of the Armenians. The French merely follow suit with the Russians whose very humble and devoted servants they are at present.

220. Kimberley to Rosebery   Foreign Office
    29 March 1895
    RsP 10069, ff. 221–22

Private

I hear that Harcourt is furious at Grey's speech,[37] and that his fury will be expended at the cabinet. For my part I think his speech was excellent, combining firmness with prudence of language in a remarkable degree. I have not had time yet to read the other speeches, except Chamberlain's which was very temperate, but you will see from the enclosed note from de Courcel[38] that he is much disturbed at them. I shall send him a short and conciliatory answer. I enclose my rough minute of the remarks which passed between us on the Nile Sphere.

[36] Francis Seymour Stevenson, Liberal M.P. for Suffolk N.E. from 1885.

[37] In the House of Commons on March 28, Foreign Under-Secretary Edward Grey warned that a French expedition to the Nile valley would be regarded by England as an unfriendly act. Harcourt feared that it would end 'all hopes of a friendly settlement' with France. According to Edward Hamilton, Grey's speech gave 'general satisfaction' in England 'except to Harcourt and John Morley, the solitary "Dodos" of Cobdenism.' See Martel, *Imperial Diplomacy*, pp. 237–41; Gardiner, *Life of Harcourt*, 2: 335; *EHJ2*, p. 234.

[38] Alphonse Chodron, Baron de Courcel, French Ambassador to Great Britain.

Considering the language used about us quite recently in the French Chambers in the debate on their Colonial budget, it is not surprising if some strong things are said in our House of Commons. Of course they are apt to do harm on whichever side of the water they are said by exciting angry passions, but I am not sure that the time had not come for a little plain speaking.

My Armenian deputation this morning went off quietly.

[*Postscript*] My conversation with de Courcel was quite *par parenthèse* and by way of 'illustration', I send you copy of my answer to de Courcel.

221. Kimberley to Rosebery   35 Lowndes Sq.
   31 March 1895
   RsP 10069, ff. 225–26

I am afraid you will think me very pertinacious in returning to the point, whether Harcourt ought not to be informed that it is proposed to appoint a Committee of Experts to consider the Uganda railway, but the more I reflect on it, the more necessary it seems to me to be to let him know.[39] If he is not told he will make it a great grievance, and it will prejudice the question, when we come to the actual point.

[*Postscript*] We propose to ask the India Office to suggest experts. Their experience of small gauge lines will be most valuable.

222. Kimberley to Rosebery[40]   Foreign Office
   1 April 1895
   RsP 10070, ff. 1–4

I have told Harcourt that I would communicate with you before answering this letter from him. I have no objection to letting him see proposed answers on important questions. Indeed I have I think usually done so when the questions were really important, and I can extend the practice somewhat.

As to his undertaking important statements on behalf of the Cabinet, I apprehend that this is the ordinary course. Mr. Gladstone used to undertake such statements when Dilke was Under-Secretary and when the Under-Secretary is not a strong man, it is always done.

But it would be to the last degree unjust to do anything which would cast any slur upon Grey, or imply any (the least) withdrawal of confidence from him, and if anything of the kind were done, he would, I have little doubt, resign.

[39] Rosebery responded, 'By all means tell Harcourt.... I have no objection — quite the reverse. I only did not think it *necessary* at this stage'. 1 April 1895, KP2 10243, f. 187.

[40] Written after receiving Harcourt's demand to 'see all answers on important questions of foreign policy before they are given in the House of Commons' and to 'make, on behalf of the Cabinet, all important statements in debate on foreign affairs.' Gardiner, *Life of Harcourt*, 2:336.

I should be disposed to agree that the leader of the House ought to make statements on behalf of the cabinet where it has been decided by the cabinet that such a statement is to be made.

In cases where a debate arises without notice, as on Thursday last, it is the duty of the undersecy. to consult the leader who can give such advice to him as he thinks best, and can himself take such part in the debate as he deems right.

If Harcourt had not gone away and stayed away, when he was told that Chamberlain was going to speak on the Nile question the 'unfortunate difficulties' would probably have been much diminished.

John Morley came to see me yesterday. I hope I made some impression on him. He admitted that Grey's correction quite met his particular arguments about the water-way.[41]

223. Rosebery to Kimberley
    2 April 1895
    NLS 10070, f. 7

Most Confidential

Your letter with regard to answers and statements on For: Aff: is precisely on the right lines. Important answers should be shown to the leader of the House. Statements directly drawn up or resolved upon in Cabinet shd. be made by him. But nothing should be done to diminish, impair, or reflect upon the present position of E. Grey. He is one of the most important members of the Govt.; for his being outside the Cabinet is the direct result not of his failure, but of his great success as Reptve. of the F.O. Moreover he is a *persona gratissima* to the H. of C., popular, admired, and respected. Any attempt therefore to take out of his hands what he has been doing with such consummate skill wd. be resented by many besides himself, by none more than Yrs.,
    AP

224. Kimberley to Rosebery   Foreign Office
    3 April 1895
    RsP 10070, f. 12

Harcourt has sent me the enclosed memorandum. I send it to you before I reply. The concluding paragraph should I think be omitted. It is in fact covered by the first paragraph, and might be taken as reflecting on Grey.

---

[41] Grey restoring the word 'Egyptian', which had been omitted, in description of the sphere of influence. See Martel, *Imperial Diplomacy*, pp. 240–41, and notes. Cf. Kimberley journal, KP6 MS.eng.c.2793, pp. 437–38.

[*Enclosed*]:
[Harcourt, *Memorandum*[42], 3 April 1895, HP MS Harcourt dep. 52, ff. 86–87.]
  I had a conversation today with Lord Kimberley on the subject of my request that all answers to questions of importance relating to Foreign Affairs[43] should be submitted to me before they were made in the House of Commons and secondly that all announcements on important questions of policy relating to foreign affairs should be made in the House of Commons by the Leader of the House *on behalf of the Cabinet*.
  Ld. Kimberley said that after consultation with Lord Rosebery he assented to the general principle embodied in my request.
  It was quite understood that in the application of this principle the greatest regard should be had to the position of the Under Secy. for Foreign Affairs and that the matter must be largely governed by the circumstances of the case as they arise.

It was also agreed that it was not desirable that elaborate and definite declarations of policy, which might have serious consequences should be made on the occasion of desultory debates without previous consultations between the Leader of the House and the Foreign Office.

225. Rosebery to Kimberley   10 Downing Street
    4 April 1895
    KP2 10243, f. 185

Confidential

  The memorandum certainly does not represent my views; I do not know if it correctly reports the conversations that took place.
  The memorandum should run that 'all arrangements on important questions of foreign policy *which have been decided upon by the Cabinet* should be &c. &c.[44] Omit then 'on behalf of the cabinet', which is superfluous. So is the last paragraph. I regard the underlined passage as essential for obvious reasons.

226. Kimberley to Harcourt   35 Lowndes Sq.
    4 April 1895
    RsP 10143, f. 240

Copy

  I sent your proposed mem: to Rosebery. He agrees, with the pencil alterations which I have inserted.
  He also thinks with me that the last paragraph should be omitted as it is not needed, being in fact included in the previous paragraphs.

---

[42] Returned to Harcourt with deletions enclosed by marks — '*' — in Kimberley's hand, 4 April, after receipt of letter 225, herein, from Rosebery.

[43] Kimberley inserts 'which have been decided upon by the Cabinet'.

[44] Kimberley had earlier suggested this. See letter 222, herein.

227. Harcourt to Kimberley   11 Downing Street
5 *April 1895*
RsP 10143, ff. 243–44[45]

Copy

I cannot by any means assent to the proposed alteration in my Memorandum which would entirely defeat its whole object.

The words as suggested by you would limit my action to important questions of Foreign Policy which have been decided by the Cabinet, but the whole difficulty and danger arises in the case of important questions of Foreign policy on which the Cabinet has not decided because it has not been consulted.

The Anglo-Belgian Convention was a striking example of which unfortunately there have been too many in this Govt and the whole question of the policy with regard to the Nile Valley is in the same condition.

This arises from the fact (the great objections to which I have always felt) of the Prime Minister and the Foreign Secretary being in the H. of Lords and determining vital questions of Foreign policy without reference either to the Cabinet or to the Leader of the House of Commons.

What is absolutely necessary that I should insist upon (as I have done from the first) is that no announcement of an important character should be made in the H. of Commons except by me or with previous consultation with and assent from me, whether the matter has been brought before the Cabinet or not, in which case I should be able to judge whether or not in my opinion the Cabinet should be consulted upon it.

I understood distinctly from you in our conversation after the Cabinet, and also at the Levee, that you assented to this view as expressed in the first part of my memo. and I cannot agree to its now being revoked by Rosebery.

I must therefore adhere to the text of my memo. the object of which is to establish the position of the Leader of the H. of Commons as the organ of the Govt in that House on important questions of Foreign Policy.

As to the last paragraph which you propose to omit, it represents only that to which you expressly assented in our conversation.

I cannot agree that it is advisable or safe that formal and far-reaching declarations of policy involving questions of Peace and War should be fired off at random on the occasional interpellation of some unimportant member without previous consultation with the Leader of the H. of Commons.

If the positions I have thus laid down are seriously disputed I must request that they should be submitted to the Cabinet as I regard them as absolutely vital.

---

[45] The original is in HP MS. Harcourt dep. 52; see too Gardiner, *Life of Harcourt*, 2:337.

234 Liberal by Principle 5 April 1895

228. Kimberley to Harcourt   Foreign Office
5 April 1895
HP MS. Harcourt dep. 52, ff. 101–02

There could be no question of Rosebery revoking my understanding with
you, as the words I proposed to insert in your memorandum are in accordance
with my view as much as with his.... I must have failed to convey to you my
meaning and I need take blame to myself for not having been sufficiently clear
and precise in my language, for which I am very sorry....

229. Rosebery to Kimberley   10 Downing Street
6 April 1895
KP2 10243, ff. 189–90

Confidential

It is of course impossible to prevent the leader of the House of Commons
from making statements on any subject that he chooses. But of course if he
makes them on foreign policy without consulting with you, me or the cabinet,
they represent no opinion but his own.

Under ordinary circumstances this would not matter. But it is impossible to
conceal from members, or at any rate it is impossible for me to conceal from
myself that there is a deepseated and radical difference between Harcourt and
myself on questions of foreign policy. His view is broadly that in questions
between Great Britain and foreign countries, foreign countries alone are in the
right and Great Britain always in the wrong.[46] Therefore if he speaks his own
views on the questions at issue — say between this country and France he might
bring about the instant disruption or fall of the government.

In view of this delicate state of affairs it would not, I think, be fair or proper
for Harcourt to make statements on foreign policy without consulting you or
me or the Cabinet, and I think he himself will see this. It is true that Grey
made his statement without consultation from me. But that was *unnecessary* as
he knows the views I hold and the policy I maintain, and has known them for
two years past. Harcourt knows them too, but the difference between him and
Edward Grey is that Grey shares them and Harcourt does not!

But it is probable that I am mistaken and that Harcourt does not contemplate
statements on Foreign affairs without consultation with you or me or the Cabinet.
That case *cadit quaestio*.

I may remark that he is wrong in thinking that the evil arises from the First
and Foreign Ministers being in the House of Lords, for were either in the House

---

[46] When Harcourt insisted that France served England as an example of 'temper and
good sense', Kimberley characteristically retorted that such was 'of course. . . a matter
of opinion'. Kimberley to Harcourt, 31 March 1895, HP MS. Harcourt dep. 52, f. 76;
see too *CJ*, p. 92.

of Commons, there would be no question of his making statements on Foreign Affairs. The evil arises from the fact that he is wholly and entirely opposed to the foreign policy which I at any rate favour and pursue.

230. Kimberley to Harcourt   ·   Foreign Office
     6 April 1895
     HP MS. Harcourt dep. 52, f. 109

I do not think it would be of any advantage that I should prolong the correspondence about the 'understanding'. I will only say that I in no way repudiate the condition that you are to be consulted in important questions of foreign policy.

I will tell Rosebery that you wish a cabinet to be called.

231. Kimberley to Rosebery   Foreign Office
     6 April 1895
     RsP 10070, ff. 23–24

Confidential

I agree with all you say in your letter of yesterday about Harcourt. The position is really almost impossible. I do my best (with small success) to smooth matters, but there is a far more serious question than my personal relations with him. How is the business of the country to be carried on successfully under such conditions?

I have just received a ridiculous letter from him on the affairs of China and Japan which displays in its worst form his combined ignorance and arrogance in relation to foreign affairs.[47] You know how difficult my task is and how heavy the work and still more the responsibility.

I feel that at present on almost all the most important questions of the present moment we are really without any definite policy. Everything is at a deadlock. Now there is nothing so unsatisfactory and dangerous as more drifting. Unfortunately there are many questions in different parts of the world, notably in the Far East and in Africa, which require firm handling and that we should know our minds as a government. Armenia, China and Japan, Siam and above all Africa, all present questions in which interests of this country are largely involved. Harcourt practically insists upon playing the part of joint Prime Minister.

---

[47] Probably of April 5, complaining of all the 'bugbears constantly cooked up in the F.O.' RsP 10143, ff. 241–42. Harcourt's ignorance had long invited the contempt of colleagues. Ten years earlier Fortescue had noted a 'long discussion of the situation with Russia. W. Harcourt very vociferous and unreasonable. Hartington said to him "Now I bet a 100 to 1 you haven't read any of the papers" which he could not deny.' *CJ*, p. 80. By 1895, few Liberals took Harcourt's foreign policy pronouncements seriously. See Meade to Ripon, 26 December 1894, RP 43558, ff. 53–54; *EHJ2*, pp. 240–41.

How can I serve two masters with one of whom happily I have no differences, tho' of course there may be details in which we do not take exactly the same view, but with the other of whom I have, to put the matter mildly, little in common?

I send you Harcourt's last effusion[48] to which I have replied that I will make known to you his request that a cabinet should be summoned. I think that is the best solution.

P.S. — I enclose my last note to Harcourt.[49]

---

232. Rosebery to Kimberley   The Durdans
        6 April 1895
        KP2 10243, f. 194

Secret

I return your box at once with only a line, because I wish to point out that it is a fatal mistake to allow a cabinet to be called on the false issue raised by Harcourt's note. I think before a cabinet is called that you should send a temperate reply to Harcourt recapitulating the case as we view it;[50] and then, on that, if he wishes a cabinet called, I am ready to call one. But I really cannot ask our colleagues to assemble and consider his last letter as a serious production.

---

233. Rosebery to Kimberley
        7 April 1895
        RsP 10070, f. 33

Secret

I must write you a line in answer to your almost pathetic letter of last night.[51] You must not think that I do not sympathise with and understand your difficulties and almost intolerable position as regards Harcourt, but last night I only had the bare time necessary to answer your most pressing questions. I warmly appreciate your rare patience and self control and I thank you warmly for them. And I agree with you that the position with regard to foreign affairs is almost intolerable. Had it not been that on the whole we have had our way, I shd. have thought it my duty to make way patriotically for a homogeneous government that could carry out an efficient foreign policy. That is my answer to what you say about our having no policy. So far our policy has prevailed and has been satisfactory and sufficient.

---

[48] Letter 227, herein.
[49] Letter 230, herein.
[50] Kimberley to Harcourt, 7 April 1895, HP 52, ff. 114– 16.
[51] Letter 231, herein.

But I do not disguise from myself that we are approaching the parting of the ways because I cannot compromise on these vital matters and I confess that I view the approach of the critical moment with a certain sense of relief. So I suspect do you.

234. Kimberley to Harcourt   Witton Park
   13 April 1895
   RsP 10143, f. 259

Copy/Typescript

Colville[52] whom I saw for the first time a few days ago was very discreet in his conversation with me. I was much surprised on reading the report of the interview. But you must make some allowance for the inexperience of such matters which is natural in a man who has been passing his time in the centre of Africa. The F.O. is not, as I know from other examples of the results of the pestilent practice of interviewing, the office [sic] which suffers from imprudent utterances to newspaper touts.

We are doing nothing which indicates a forward policy in Uganda or the Upper Nile, and nothing will be done without your previous knowledge. As I had understood from Rosebery that he had written to you and that the examination of the railway question might proceed, I have taken steps accordingly. The collection of the best information which can be procured is surely indispensable for the proper consideration of the question, and must be (of) advantage to us all when we have to come to a decision whatever our views may be.

The essential point I take it is that nothing shall be either said or done which can prejudice the question, and this condition you may absolutely rely on my observing.

I beg of you to let the matter now rest till we meet again. I am sure that nothing will be done by inquiry which will undermine or injure the position you take and I shall carefully abstain from expressing any opinion until it is necessary to decide on the policy to be pursued.

It is clear that eventually the question must be decided one way or other, so far as to enable a line to be taken when the vote comes up for the sum of £50,000 which is to be paid to the I.B.E.A. Company.

---

[52] Sir Henry Edward Colville (1852–1907), acting Commissioner of Uganda, 1893; commander of the Unyoro expedition, 1894.

235. Kimberley to Rosebery   Foreign Office
16 April 1895
RsP 10070, ff. 64–65

It is all very well for Harcourt to treat this matter by offhand platitudes about arbitration — The question is not so easy to dispose of.[53] If whenever one of these petty South American countries ill treats British subjects we submit the question of redress to arbitration, we shall have no end of trouble. The insolence of these wretched little states is beyond bearing, and Nicaragua is perhaps the worst of them. Nothing but a sharp lesson from time to time will keep them in order, or secure decent treatment for foreigners.

We have an arbitration going on in Colombia but we cannot get anything done. We have another question as to the ill treatment of our police on the Venezuela border, which must be dealt with shortly. Even the United States government shows no sympathy with the Nicaraguans in their ill treatment of British subjects. Bayard[54] has never in our conversations said a word in their favour. On the contrary he speaks of them as an unbearable set of people.

P.S. — I send an article from the *Siècle*, which is worth reading. The last sentence in it shows what Frenchmen think of the matter.

236. Rosebery to Kimberley   10 Downing St.
8 May 1895
KP1 15/K2/22

I could not get to you yesterday.[55] Bigge[56] came from the Queen and kept me till 7.30.

But I shall be with you in spirit during this terrible day, the blackness of which I know too well.[57] But I know that your splendid manfulness will carry you through.

---

[53] The expulsion of the British vice-consul from Nicaragua and subsequent attempts at settlement. For circumstances, see Robert A. Naylor, *Penny Ante Imperialism: The Mosquito Shore and the Bay of Honduras, 1600– 1914* (London: Associated University Presses, 1989), pp. 204–08; *Red Earl*, 2:253. Harcourt had written to Kimberley confessing 'an invincible repugnance to using force in a case of small indemnities like the present', where 'we are always making loud professions of our readiness to adopt arbitration in place of force and if we refuse it in a case of this kind which is trumpery enough the hypocrisy of such pretences will become apparent.' RsP 10143, f. 258.

[54] Thomas Francis Bayard, American ambassador to Great Britain.

[55] Before Kimberley left London for the funeral of Lady Kimberley, who had died on May 4. Rosebery did, however, send a wreath.

[56] Arthur John Bigge, Queen Victoria's private secretary.

[57] The early death of his wife, Hannah, in 1890 having largely contributed to his political diffidence. See James, *Rosebery*, pp. 225–30.

237. Kimberley to Ripon   35 Lowndes Sq.
      10 June 1895
      RP 43527, f. 52

Private

Read what is said in this letter from Howard, our Secy. of Embassy at Paris
(who was in China some time) about Hong Kong.[58] If the Russians grab some
territory and get a powerful hold on China (which seems not unlikely) we may
look out for squalls.

Ought we not to take any good opportunity to get the strip of the mainland?

238. Kimberley to Rosebery   Foreign Office
      22 June 1895
      RsP 10070, f. 154

Secret

If you dissolve, you will dissolve as leader of the party. Ought not this to
have some weight, looking to the future. Further, if we dissolve we shall go as
a 'united' body to the country. If not, will not our dissensions become apparent
when the Tories dissolve, to the great injury of the party? Forgive me troubling
you with this but I could not say this in the cabinet.

Rosebery Minute, 22 June 1895 — Written and received between the two
cabinets on this day.[59]

239. Rosebery to Kimberley
      24 June 1895
      RsP 10070, f. 157

Do not think I was unmoved by the note you wrote me between the two
cabinets on Saturday. Its personal kindness and solicitude for my future were
of a piece with your constant generosity to one so much younger than yourself
whom accident placed over you. But I have not the same feeling that you
express for my leadership. On that point I shall have something to say to my
colleagues a little later. I must take this opportunity however of thanking you
once for all for your unwavering loyalty, helpfulness, and friendliness. — I
know what you have had to bear — largely for my sake and I shall never forget
your behaviour to me.

---

[58] Henry Howard, Secretary of the British legation in China, 1887–90, and Secretary
of the embassy in Russia, 1890–94, before going to Paris.

[59] See *EHJ2*, pp. 255–256.

7

Uncle Kim in the Wilderness

As Kimberley neared seventy in the summer of 1895, he might well have retired with his memories. His wife of forty-seven years had died in May, and the Liberals were badly beaten at the polls in July. Nevertheless, during the following seven years he maintained a spirited opposition, feeling that Liberal disorganization was an 'utter misfortune' to the proper working of the British constitution. He regularly criticized Conservative measures, though frequently he ended by supporting them, as in the Workmen's Compensation Act of 1897 and in prosecution of the Boer War, 1899–1902. On the whole, Kimberley believed in continuity of foreign policy and admired Salisbury's moderation and respect of diplomatic traditions. The largest policy difference, vigorously pursued in 1897–98, involved Conservative commitment to the integrity of the Ottoman Empire. His outspoken declarations in opposition earned him an unusual measure of popular Liberal support, especially in the wake of a new wave of Turkish atrocities against the Armenians in 1895–96.

Within the Liberal Party, Kimberley guarded the growing no man's land between Gladstonian Liberals and emerging Liberal Imperialists, each trying to define and reinforce positions in the absence of Gladstone's commanding authority. He succeeded Rosebery, who retired as Liberal leader in the Lords in October 1896, and managed to remain on good terms with Harcourt, who retired as Liberal leader in the Commons in December 1898. During the turbulent Rosebery/Harcourt dispute Kimberley carefully managed the tiny Liberal contingent, resisting all quasi-official attempts to restructure the party. He preached the necessity of Home Rule in parliament and around the country, and applauded Campbell-Bannerman's emergence as leader in 1899. Although they sometimes disagreed over opposition tactics during the Boer War, both were committed foremost to freedom of expression within the party and thus worked well together. Kimberley criticized Conservative lack of foresight, but supported the government's contention that the Boers must be defeated before negotiations could begin. His stolid conservatism on this point, in conjunction with staunch support for Liberal domestic policy, minimized the negative impact of 'pro-Boer' activity within the party, providing a patriotic shield as the Liberals began to reorganize under Campbell-Bannerman. After a recurring illness of more than a year, Kimberley died of heart failure in London on 8 April 1902.

240. Kimberley, Notes on Books   35 Lowndes Sq.
    June 1895
    KP1 15/K2/10, p. 153

I also read Arthur Balfour's book on the foundations of Belief.[1] 1 vol. Very clever, and not at all convincing like all arguments about the 'Unknowable'.

241. Kimberley to Spencer   35 Lowndes Sq.
    20 July 1895
    SP K349

I am very sorry for your brother's defeat.[2] What a smash we have had! I put it down mainly to beer and agricultural distress. Asquith's triumphant return is some comfort.[3]

242. Kimberley to Ripon   Kimberley House
    30 July 1895
    RP 43527, ff. 62–63

Private

Shall you go up for the meeting of Parliament. There will be nothing in the Lords except perhaps Chitral,[4] as I take for granted the Govt. will announce no programme till next year. But what are we to do as to the leadership of our small flock? I fear there is no possibility of Rosebery and Harcourt working together, and what trust can one put in Harcourt? His folly about local veto[5] is in itself proof of his utter want of judgement. Was ever man in such a fool's paradise!

He can handle questions in the Commons with dexterity and make a slashing speech. These are qualities by no means to be underrated; but there is *praeterea nihil* or rather the rest is nothing but weakness and bluster.

It is very unfortunate for us. I suppose we shall do best to be guided by the wishes of the remnant of our late colleagues in the Commons. We represent in

---

[1] Arthur James Balfour (1848–1930), Conservative leader in the Commons and First Lord of the Treasury. *The Foundations of Belief* (London: Longmans, Green, and Co., 1895).

[2] C. R. Spencer in the Mid Northamptonshire election. See *Red Earl*, 2: 258–259.

[3] In the sweeping Conservative victory — Conservatives, 340; Liberals, 177; Irish Nationalists, 82; Liberal Unionists, 71 — the election of Herbert Henry Asquith (1852–1928), Secretary of State for Home Affairs, 1892–95 and M.P. for Fifeshire East since 1886, was some comfort, as both Morley and Harcourt had lost their seats.

[4] On the uneasy peace following a victorious spring campaign only minor questions were in fact put. 4 *Hansard*, 36 (19, 22 August 1895): 258–59, 531–32.

[5] Abortive bill of 1893, which would have allowed prohibition of public houses in specific areas following referendum. On this and the subsequent Local Option Bill, see *EHJ2*, pp. 86–87.

the H. of Lords not much more than our own selves, so we cannot claim much voice.

I hope you observed that in the *county* of Norfolk we lost *no* seats and regained one. I am rather proud that in the three places with which I am connected, Mid- and East Norfolk and Falmouth, Liberals were returned.

[*Postscript*] How curious the reversal of the bye elections.

---

243. Kimberley to Monk Bretton   Kimberley House
    3 August 1895
    MBP Box 37

My leg is getting well tho' slowly. I am able now to walk about, provided I don't go fast. I fear the weather is broken up, and that to crown our agricultural bad luck we shall have a wet harvest. Corn crops are tolerably promising here as far as I have heard. I have just had that most disagreeable of things, an interview with my agent. The further reductions I will have to make will amount to 50 pr. ct on the rents as they stood in 1878. I need not say I am in the street called 'short'. The worst of it is that even with these reductions I may not be able to keep my tenants. Nor do I see any prospect of improvement. But I forgot; the new Govt. is to put us all straight again. I wonder how. Shall we get a handsome subsidy from the state? This with old age pensions will be a nice problem for Hicks Beach[6] to solve. Here in Norfolk as you may have observed, we suffer from a want of faith, as we have returned as many radical county members as we did in 1892 and more than in 1885. Is it not curious that the bye elections were reversed in so many places.

P.S. — I hear that the increase of Arch's[7] majority was due to many Tory farmers exerting themselves to get their labourers to vote for Arch, because they find that he keeps quite quiet whilst he is an M.P. and gives them no trouble. This is very amusing *if* true. Number one is after all 'the first law of nature'.

---

244. Kimberley to Spencer   Kimberley House
    8 August 1895
    SP K349

Private

I agree in all you say in your letter.[8] The outlook is bad. I have turned the matter over in my mind in every way, and I can think of no solution of the

---

[6] Sir Michael Hicks Beach (1837–1916), Conservative Chancellor of the Exchequer.

[7] Joseph Arch, Secretary and President of the National Agricultural Labourers Union from 1872; Liberal M.P. for North-West Norfolk, 1885–86, 1892–1902.

[8] Untraced, however see Spencer to Kimberley, 11 August 1895, KP6 MS.eng.c.4474, f. 48.

difficulty as to the leadership. R[osebery] and H[arcourt] will inevitably lead a cat and dog life, and in H. I have no confidence whatever.

J. Morley is wise in resolving to wait awhile before returning to the H. of Commons, since he as you know well, has an invincible dislike to acting with H. If H. were out of the way, C. Bannerman or Asquith could lead. But H. is there and he will remain, tho' there are I hear not a few in our ranks, who have found him out. My conclusion, a very lame one, is that we must let things drift for the present, unless our late colleagues in the Commons have anything to suggest. *Their* opinion must necessarily have great weight.

The Armenian news looks as if Salisbury would act with vigour. As to Chitral I doubt if we have heard the last word. I incline to the belief that the present arrangements are provisional.

---

245. Kimberley to Monk Bretton   Kimberley House
23 November 1895
MBP Box 37

Private

I am sorry to hear you are apprehensive as to your health. I feel London fog so much and generally detest that grimy town, that I rejoice to be able, now I am out of office, to remain in the country. I am quite well, though very sad and lonely.[9]

I admire your energy in beginning Hebrew. I have passed most of my time in reading various novels, amongst others one called 'Nero' by a German, which I do not recommend.[10] It is in the main a reproduction of all the historical accounts of Nero's atrocities and I prefer the history to the novel. I amuse myself somewhat by reading Gibbon and referring to his authorities, most of which I have here. He is certainly a wonderful writer. I hope you will like your bishop. *Our* new bishop[11] is remarkable only for his long beard and his seventeen children.

I was greatly edified by the Brighton insurrection against Salisbury.[12] He has

---

[9] Florence, Lady Kimberley having died in May. See letter 236, herein.

[10] In the midst of an uncharacteristic concentration of fiction reading, during the fall Kimberley read William Morris, *The Wood Beyond the World*; H.G. Wells, *The Time Machine*; Charlotte Brontë, *Shirley*; Gustave Flaubert, *Salambo*; E. Werner (Elisabeth Burstenbinder), *Gesprengte Fesseln*; Mrs. Humphrey Ward, *Bessie Costrell*; and Ernst Eckstein, *Nero*, with only the first volume of Samuel Gardiner's *History of the Commonwealth* intruding. KP1 15/K2/10.

[11] Rev. John Sheepshanks, appointed Bishop of Norwich, 1893.

[12] The Conservative cabinet refusing to sanction independent naval action against the Ottoman Empire following the Sultan's brutal suppression of the Armenian Revolutionary Movement. C.J. Lowe, *Salisbury and the Mediterranean, 1886–1896* (London: Routledge and Kegan Paul, 1965), pp. 103–05; Robert Taylor, *Lord Salisbury* (London: Allen Lane, 1975), pp. 168–71.

got a most awkward business to deal with in Turkey. The real source of the evil is that the Sultan will trust no one and has surrounded himself by a set of corrupt useless parasites.... Said Pasha[13] and Kiamil Pasha,[14] if he would have followed the advice of either of them, might have saved him, but he quickly dismissed them. It is the same in the provinces. If a governor shows some capacity and honesty, he is sure to be dismissed and replaced by some corrupt Court minion incapable of governing even if he would let them try, and pernicious advisers. The few honest and capable Turkish statesmen he will not employ, because they show independence.

What is the use of reform in such a state of things? Poor old Rustem,[15] whilst officially he stood up like a man for the Sultan, privately could not deny that the root of the evil was what I have described. Poor old fellow, he was quite broken hearted about the whole business and almost wept when speaking about it. He was a very able and a really honest man. It was impossible not to like him. Meanwhile the powers are united, but in which policy? They have all not excluding Russia an intense dread of raising the 'Eastern' question, but I fear the 'Eastern' question may raise itself in spite of them. It is a good sign that Germany is acting with the other Powers. She has been very lukewarm, and her union with the other powers will certainly alarm the Sultan who counted on her standing aloof.

I don't envy the govt. in having to 'do something for agriculture'. They can do but little and they will get small thanks for that little. Fancy our wiseacres at the Norfolk Agricultural Chamber resolving that a duty ought to be levied on foreign barley and the proceeds applied to a bounty on home grown wheat! Could folly go further? I don't wonder that Salisbury declined to receive a deputation from them....

246. Kimberley to Rosebery   Kimberley House
     14 December 1895
     RsP 10070, ff. 162–63

Your sympathy is most welcome to me. As you justly say, too justly, alas! there is a vacant place which can never be filled. I am well and have nothing to complain of but of lost happiness which can never return to me in this world. I live a peaceful life here and my children are a great comfort to me.

I should like much to pay you a visit. About the second week in Jan. would suit me best if convenient to you. In any case however I will endeavour to avail myself of your hospitality at whatever time you fix.[16] The paeans about Salisbury's wonderful management of foreign affairs are ridiculous; still it will

---

[13] Grand Vizier of Turkey.
[14] Vizier of Turkey.
[15] See letter 215, herein.
[16] James, *Rosebery*, pp. 387– 88.

only be fair not to condemn him till we know exactly with what difficulties he has had to contend.

I am no sentimentalist, but on mere grounds of policy I believe we shall make a great mistake if the Armenians are left to the tender mercies of the Sultan. Why do not the powers, who are rightly anxious to avoid raising the Eastern question, see that if this matter is allowed to drift, the 'Eastern question' may be raised whether they like it or not? A little timely vigour might postpone the evil day.

Hoping you are enjoying your tour.

247. Kimberley to Ripon   Kimberley House
   31 December 1895
   RP 43527, ff. 75–77

I return Gladstone's letter[17] which I am very glad to have seen. By all means send it to Rosebery. In a recent letter to me he says 'I shall try and collect some of our political friends at Mentmore before the meeting of Parliament.' I think his letter on Armenian affairs an excellent one. I wrote much to the same effect some time ago to John Morley, who replied that he entirely agreed with me. McColl[18] and the hysterical pro-Armenians entirely misunderstand the attitude of Russia, unless it is much changed since I was at the F. O. Both Labonoff[19] and Staal[20] declared in unmistakeable language that Russia would not take *any* forcible measures against the Sultan. The fact is the Russians have not much sympathy with the Armenians. They have a large number of them in their own Caucasian provinces, whom they find extremely troublesome. France follows suit as a matter of course.

Do you observe how hostile Germany is about the Transvaal. We shall have trouble with here there, and she will pay us off in European affairs for our resistance to her unwarrantable pretension in South Africa.

As to Venezuela we shall have to support Salisbury.[21] We cannot submit to be bullied by the United States. What bosh the gush about the friendship of our American 'cousins' is! I never saw any practical proof of their friendship.[22]

---

[17] Of 27 December 1895, urging Ripon to encourage the Liberal leadership to present a united front in the face of President Cleveland's Venezuelan policy. See Wolf, *Life of Ripon*, 2:240-41.

[18] Malcolm MacColl, Canon of Ripon.

[19] Prince Aleksei Borisovich Lobanov-Rostovski, Russian Foreign Minister.

[20] Baron Georgi de Staal, Russian Ambassador to Great Britain.

[21] Following President Grover Cleveland's special message to Congress, 17 December 1895, insisting that the United States independently determine the disputed boundary between Venezuela and British Guiana because of British delay.

[22] See letter 262, herein.

248. Kimberley to Ripon   Kimberley House
8 January 1896
RP 43527, ff. 81–84

Confidential

Rosebery has asked me also to Mentmore on Feb: 8 and I have accepted.

The South African imbroglio is very serious.[23] I agree in the view you take of Rhodes' probable course of action. I think Jameson's preparations could not have been made without his knowledge and authority but that he did not order Jameson to advance.

What I cannot understand is the apparent ignorance at the Colonial Office of what was brewing. Letters received before Jameson's advance by relatives here (whom I know) of a young man who had joined the Chartered Company forces spoke of those preparations and of a probable advance on Johannesburg.[24] I shall see these letters and know exactly their date and what they contain, but my informant is my own son who has seen them. I understand that other similar letters had reached this country. Is it conceivable that Robinson[25] did not know what was going on? Or that if he did know, he never telegraphed to Chamberlain?[26] I do not concur with Rosebery that the importance of the German Emperor's telegram is exaggerated. If it was merely a personal outbreak, it might not signify so much, but it is part of a settled policy, as was shown most unmistakeably in the communications which passed both between Hatzfeldt and me, and Malet and the Berlin foreign office. Moreover, German public opinion has been constantly hostile to us for some time past.

I hope our government will give the Emperor plainly to understand that we shall offer a firm and uncompromising resistance to his interference in South Africa. I am glad to see that ships are reported to be ordered to Delagoa Bay. A display of our naval force may cause the Germans to reflect on their utter impotency to get at us anywhere, if they were to quarrel with us.

---

[23] On 29 December 1895 Leander Starr Jameson led 660 South African Company men into the Transvaal hoping to raise an insurrection among Uitlanders in Johannesburg, but was defeated and forced to surrender on January 2. The German emperor telegraphed congratulations to Kruger the following day. Three days later Cecil Rhodes was forced to resign as Prime Minister of the Cape, having financed the raid.

[24] 'We were glad to see that a young Grimes who was with Dr. Jameson is not reported hurt and also Foley's brother', Kimberley had written to his daughter, Alice. 7 January 1896, PkP DE 1749 38/27.

[25] Hercules Robinson, Governor of Cape Colony, 1895–97.

[26] For a concise account of who knew what and when, see Robert I. Rotberg, *The Founder, Cecil Rhodes and the Pursuit of Power* (New York: Oxford University Press, 1988), chapter 9.

249. Kimberley to Spencer   Kimberley House
    30 September 1896
    SP K351

I wish you and Lady Spencer could have come today. Everything looks so bright and cheerful in the sun. The only day next week when I am free is Friday, but in the following week I can arrange to be at home on any day, which will suit you, if you will give me fair notice.

I don't at all like the aspect of European affairs or the excessive sentimentalism which possesses our public. The treatment of the Armenians is horrible, and the Sultan is personally responsible for it, but the policy of a great country cannot be safely based on mere sentiment, however just and laudable, and a breakup of the Turkish Empire must raise most momentous questions, deeply affecting the welfare and future of Europe. It is of course a truism that *if* we can agree with Russia we can do what we please, as Russia would carry France with her; and if Russia is prepared to take Constantinople, and we are ready to acquiesce, an agreement might be arrived at. But then as to Egypt? The French will never agree with us as long as we remain in Egypt, and a bargain with Russia would probably be impossible without satisfying France as to Egypt. Then further are we prepared to give up our position in the Mediterranean? You are a better judge than I am of our naval strength, but I cannot think we could permanently hold our own in that sea against France and Russia combined.[27]

The problem is most serious and difficult and requires to be treated with cool and cautious deliberation and not in a paroxysm of philanthropic passion. I entirely agree with Rosebery's views as expressed in his recent letters except his first letter which I did not altogether like.[28]

If we meet, as I hope we shall, I shall be very glad to talk over the knotty points which I have briefly touched above.

250. Kimberley to Ripon   Kimberley House
    9 October 1896
    RP 43527, ff. 104–06

Secret

All *I* know about Rosebery's state of mind was that he was vexed at Gladstone's proceedings but I had not the slightest idea of his resignation till I got a letter from him yesterday letting me know that he had determined to resign and had written the letter to Ellis.[29]

---

[27] As early as 1883 Kimberley agreed with Ripon that 'a Russian occupation of Constantinople would not threaten India; but it would altogether change the position in the Mediterranean.' RP 43523, f. 97.

[28] In support of the Government's policy. See Stansky, *Ambitions and Strategies*, pp. 208–09.

[29] Informing Tom Ellis, chief whip, of his resignation as Liberal Party leader. James,

Spencer, who has been here today, had heard nothing. I am afraid he consulted nobody because he knew very well that we should all have advised him not to resign.

The moment too is ill chosen, for on the burning question of the day, the line he has taken has been generally approved. There was nothing in Harcourt's speech about Armenia which could cause him any embarrassment, nor do I think that Gladstone's action was a sufficient reason for resigning, though of course it is not pleasant to have the wind taken out of your sails by the former leader.

As you say we are handed over body and soul to Harcourt, if we continue to take an active part in public life.[30] It is too soon to form a decision on so sudden a crisis. I do not feel sure that any member of the party in the Commons will refuse to follow Harcourt now that Rosebery has abdicated, and it is possible therefore that a fresh split may not take place. No time to write more.

251. Kimberley to Ripon   Kimberley House
        16 October 1896
        RP 43527, ff. 114–15

Confidential

I think Rosebery was in a real difficulty. A man of his abilities which are undoubtedly great, could never be satisfied unless he was a real leader. In our party this is almost impossible for a peer, especially a peer who has not previously made his mark in the Commons. It can only be at all possible if the leader in the Commons has the most cordial relations with him, and looks up to him as his leader. In all the circumstances I am not disposed to be angry with Rosebery for seizing an opportunity to get out of an intolerable situation. It must be remembered too that he was *most* reluctant to take the post of Prime Minister, and he only did so because he felt as we all did, that it would be discreditable to us and the whole party, if we had been unable to continue the Government after G's retirement.[31] It seems to be clear that no step will be taken now to choose a leader of the party and this, I feel sure, is the best course.

It appears to me incredible that Mr. G. should return to Parliament, but he is such a wonderful old man that there is no telling what he may be able to do.

Rosebery, pp. 391-93; Rosebery to Kimberley, 6 October 1896, KP2 10247, ff. 26–28; cf. Stansky, *Ambitions and Strategies*, pp. 212– 13.

[30] Ripon had written that Rosebery's resignation 'hands us over to Harcourt, unless we prefer, as I in all probability shall, to retire from public life altogether. I do not want to be hard on him, for he has destroyed himself, even surer than he has destroyed us. But I can see no justification for the course which he has adopted.' Ripon to Kimberley, 8 October 1896, KP3 10246, f. 75.

[31] See Kimberley journal, KP6 MS.eng.e.2793, pp. 394–97.

252. Morley to Kimberley   57 Elm Park Gardens
     2 November 1896
     KP2 10245, ff. 137–39

Confidential

I have to make a speech in Glasgow on Friday.[32] Following Rosebery in his own country, I understand that I shall be the object of rather close scrutiny. Of course I will skate rapidly and as lightly as I can over the ice of his retirement, of which, however, I have exceedingly strong opinions.

On Armenia I suppose I may say that England is not able to apply coercion military or naval, to the Turk, unless the Powers agree? It seems clear that our ships would have some trouble to get up to Stambul, and that they would find the Russian there before them. But what earthly good are we likely to get out of the concert of Europe [ill.]. You wanted to send ships, if I remember right, but that was before Russia had shown her teeth.

If you can find time to give me any indication of your notions, I need not say how grateful I should be .... I think I must say something about *Egypt*. But *what*?[33]

253. Kimberley to Rosebery   Kimberley House
     14 November 1896
     RsP 10070, ff. 182–84

Private

The Chinese Minister here told me that the Chinese government would be willing to surrender Formosa to us; and I declined the offer. I cannot remember exactly in what terms he made the offer, and how far it might be regarded as a formal and definite proposal. But my impression certainly was that it was seriously made.[34]

I have not read *Diplomaticus*.[35] I will send for the Review. Thanks for telling me about the Jerningham letters.[36]

---

[32] See *Liberal Magazine*, 4 (38) (November 1896), pp. 494–96.

[33] Kimberley's letter is untraced, but two days later Morley thanked him for his 'valuable epistle'. KP2 10245, f. 140.

[34] See F. Q. Quo, 'British Diplomacy and the Cession of Formosa, 1894–95', *Modern Asian Studies*, 11 (1968), pp. 148–49.

[35] 'Lord Rosebery's Second Thoughts', *Fortnightly Review*, new ser. 359 (1 November 1896): 615–25, in which Lucien Wolf ('Diplomaticus') castigated Rosebery's and, implicitly, Kimberley's, proposed policy of 'single-handed interference' in Turkey.

[36] *The Jerningham Letters (1780–1843). Excerpts from the Correspondence and Diaries of the Hon. Lady Jerningham and her Daughter Lady Bedingfield*. ed. Egerton Castue, 2 vols. (London: Richard Bentley and Son, 1896). 'Charming gossiping letters and specially interesting' to Kimberley for references to various relatives. KP1 15/K2/10.

What do you think about the Venezuela settlement with the U. S.?[37] It seems to me that its merits (apart from the undoubted advantage of avoiding further dispute with the U. S.) depend upon how far the 60 (or 50?) years prescription covers our *bona fide* settlements.

The recognition of a quasi U. S. Protectorate over the whole of America (which is the obvious result of admitting their claim to interfere in our quarrel with Venezuela) is a step which must have very far-reaching consequences, but I incline to think that on the whole it will not be to our disadvantage. I wonder what the other European powers think of this move. I see that the French newspapers are rather disquieted about it.

254. Kimberley to Ripon   Kimberley House
       1 January 1897
       RP 43527, ff. 130–31

Confidential/copy

I enclose Rosebery's letter to you which I ought to have returned before.

I have just come back from staying two nights at Mentmore. I had a long talk with R. I asked him whether there was any foundation for the 'Pall Mall' Statement that he had opposed Harcourt's budget. I never heard of any thing of the kind, but I thought it was just possible that something might have taken place behind the scenes which I did not know. As I expected R. said there was never any opposition on his part to the budget. The only suggestion R. made was that the maximum duty should be 8 instead of 10 pr. ct, and you will remember it was settled at 8 pr. ct after a slight discussion in the Cabinet.[38] Fowler was there for a night. He explained to me very weirdly the Irish financial question on wh. I am not surprised he does not see his way. I wonder who [ill.] the P. Mall the lie about R's opposition to H's budget. Labouchere? and if so from what source did his information come or did he concoct it?

255. Kimberley to Harcourt   35 Lowndes Sq.
       23 January 1897
       HP MS. Harcourt dep. 53, ff. 9–10

Private

I quite agree that Thursday will be best for our meeting and I will give notice to our Peers accordingly for 3 o'clock at your home. I have read the Turkish

---

[37] Rosebery responded that though 'the honour of the situation' might be saved in words, the victory rested almost entirely with the United States. 28 November 1896, RsP 10070, ff. 186–87.

[38] Cf. James, *Rosebery*, pp. 341–47.

despatches of which I take the same view as you do.[39] The cardinal point is agreement on the measures to be taken if the Sultan refuses, *before* the demand is made upon him. The Russians still 'wobble' tho' they have come much nearer to Salisbury. Goluchovsky seems to have been most cordial and to have pursued a straight course throughout.[40] Hanotaux makes a poor figure. He merely sits on the fence till he gets his *mot d'ordre* from St. Petersburg.

I wonder, as you do, what happened between Nov. 17 and 25. Who put the pressure on the Tsar which caused him to suddenly change his mind.[41] Salisbury I think deserves much credit for having succeeded in bringing the Powers this far together. But the end is not yet. Everything depends upon Russia.

256. Kimberley to Herschell[42]   35 Lowndes Sq.
25 January 1897
KP2 10245, ff. 109–10

Private and Confidential/Copy

I am much disturbed at your disapproval of the meeting of the ex-cabinet. Our colleagues in the Lords are decidedly in favour of such meetings being occasionally held, and I am myself strongly of opinion that they are for many reasons desirable. As to the custom, Mr. Gladstone no doubt summoned very few such meetings after 1886, but this was in fact a departure from the earlier and I think better practice. As to the place of meeting, Harcourt suggested either his house or mine. I did not think it would be convenient to bring everyone up to this end of the town at three o'clock, (the H. of Commons meeting at 3.30).

Leaving these details, I come to the real objection raised by you, namely the serious difficulty of working with Harcourt. You will easily believe me when I say that no one can feel this more acutely than I do, and feeling this, I should gladly have avoided being placed in the position of a sort of joint leader (if I may use the expression), and only accepted the position because I thought it my duty not to refuse my services to our supporters in the Lords.

But whatever we may think of Harcourt, he as leader of the party in the Commons, occupies a position of such importance that the fortunes of party

[39] Harcourt had written that they appeared 'on the whole very creditable to Salisbury. The having obtained the assent of Russia to the *principle* of coercion is a great step in advance.' KP2 10245, f. 46.

[40] Count Agenor Goluchowski, Austro-Hungarian Foreign Minister. Shortly before his death, Kimberley advised Edmond Fitzmaurice that there should be no quarrelling with Austria. 'She has been the only steady friend we have had in Europe — I mean since 1866.' Gwynn and Tuckwell, *Life of Dilke*, 2:509 note.

[41] In agreeing to an ambassadorial conference regarding Turkish reform. See J.A.S. Grenville, *Lord Salisbury and Foreign Policy: the Close of the Nineteenth Century* (London: Athlone Press, 1964), pp. 86–88.

[42] Farrer, first Baron Herschell (1837–99), Liberal M.P. for Durham City, 1874–85; Lord Chancellor, 1886; 1892–95.

must greatly depend on his action. Is it not clearly the best policy to endeavour to exercise our influence on that action, and to prevent him from committing the party to steps of which we disapprove? Now this cannot be done unless we have free intercourse with him and know what he is about. If we do not meet him and our colleagues in the H. of Commons from time to time we shall inevitably lose touch of each other and be unable to exercise any moderating influence. More than this, there are, I know, not a few numbers of our party in the Commons who, not trusting Harcourt, look to us (who are in the Lords) to exercise influence.

Nothing could be more disastrous than the absence of all communications between Rosebery and Harcourt, and Rosebery himself, who wished me to succeed him as leader in the Lords, told me that he believed I might be able to do useful service in dealing with Harcourt. I cannot however be of much use, if I cannot carry my colleagues in the Lords with me, and I still hope notwithstanding your letter[43] that you will put in an appearance on Thursday.

No doubt we shall have to endure a good deal from Harcourt, but you know as well as I do that, if resolutely faced, he is by no means irresistible. Besides I take for granted that our formal 'meetings' will not be frequent.

Lastly I am convinced that it is most desirable that we should start by showing a united front to the public. Pray forgive this long letter.

[Postscript] — It is quite arranged between me and Harcourt that I am to be at liberty to call meetings if I think it desirable as well as he.

257. Caroline Currie[44]to Kimberley   1 Richmond Terrace,
     7 February 1897   Whitehall
     KP1 15/K2/21

I want to thank you for the kind letter you sent me after my dear Bertram's death.[45] You told me not to answer it but I always intended to do so when I had a little recovered from the strain of those months of anxiety and had got through the necessary business of the last few weeks.

As you are one of his oldest and best friends it will interest you I think to read the short paper which Bertram wrote giving the reasons for his conversion to Catholicism.[46] I have copied it for you as I do not like parting with the original.

He more than once referred to conversations he had had with you about

---

[43] Asserting that such meetings would be regarded as recognition of Harcourt as party leader. 24 January 1897, KP2 10245, ff. 105–07.

[44] Caroline Louisa Currie, wife of Bertram Wodehouse Currie; ardent Roman Catholic.

[45] Of throat cancer, 29 December 1896.

[46] The text of this "short paper" is included in John Powell, 'Testimony in High Places: The Conversion of Bertram Wodehouse Currie', *Recusant History*, 19 (October 1988), p. 207.

religion and was under the impression which I did not think was altogether a correct one, that your views were in accordance with those that were his during the greater part of his life[47] ....

258. Morley to Kimberley   Kincraig,
  18 September 1897   Inverness-Shire
  KP2 10245, ff. 142–43

Private

You are always so obliging to me in my hour of need that I venture to knock once again at your door. I have to make one or two speeches to my friends in Scotland in the course of a few days,[48] and I must say something about Ld. Salisbury's Eastern policy in its past and present aspect and result.

Of course one may say broadly that it has turned out as ill as possible, for it has ended in the exaltation of the Turk, and the smash of the Greek, and the failure to produce order in Crete. I find it less easy to *put my finger* accurately on this and that error — of omission or commission, in the last two years. He seems to have scored a point in the last phase of the matter? Or is this only superficial?

The Indian troubles seem to be an absolute vindication of our views about Chitral.[49] It is clear, is it not, that the reversal of our policy is a violation of Elgin's proclamation. Any points that occur to your expert mind will be very valuable.

Our highland weather has been fairly good in its own way. I hope all goes well in Norfolk.

259. Rosebery to Kimberley   Mentmore
  24 December 1897
  KP2 10247, ff. 41–42

I have been digging about those three infernal volumes of your correspondence with Sir W. H. for an unconscionable time.[50] But the truth is that I had a great aversion to look at them. But now I have begun to examine them and write to ask your permission to make some notes and copies[51]— of course in secret.

---

[47] That is, agnostic. She was correct. For a telling indication of Kimberley's Broad Church religious convictions about this time, see marginalia in Viscount Halifax and G. W. E. Russell, *The Present Position and the Common Creed of Catholics and Evangelicals*, 3rd ed. (London: England Church Union, 1898), KP6 MS.eng.d.2488, item four; Kimberley journal for 4 January 1897, KP6 MS.eng.e.2794, pp. 7-8.

[48] Delivered at Abroath on September 28 and at Bervie on the following day.

[49] See *Liberal Magazine*, 5 (September 1897), pp. 48, 370–72.

[50] Rosebery had had the Kimberley-Harcourt correspondence since mid-March, suggesting then that its perusal 'would be a wholesome exercise for Lent.' Rosebery to Kimberley, 13, 17 March 1897, KP2 10247, ff. 37–38.

[51] Typescripts now bound in RsP 10143.

They certainly present a livid picture of the difficulties under which foreign policy has sometimes to be carried on. One wonders how under such circumstances anything is done at all. When I have done with them I will bring them to you in person and talk them over with you — *non sine risu*.

I have not heard of you for an age. But happily the day enables me to send you and Armine my affectionate good wishes.

Kimberley annotation, n.d. — Answered (he may take copies)

---

260. Kimberley to Harcourt   Kimberley House
   31 December 1897
   HP53, f. 27

....I am entirely of opinion that we took the right course in not backing China. Japan may be an invaluable ally in case of need.[52]

---

261. Kimberley to Spencer   35 Lowndes Sq.
   9 April 1898
   SP K358

Private

I am much interested by your account of Italian affairs in your letter of April 3. I foresaw when the agreement with France[53] was published that we should offend Italy by drawing the line between us and France so as to leave the back-country of Tripoli within the French sphere of influence. Of course, strictly speaking, the effect of the agreement is merely to prevent us from exercising any influence beyond the line, and the claims of other powers are technically untouched: nevertheless the effect really is to hand it over to France. But it is not easy to see how we could avoid this result. Perhaps we might have inserted a General proviso, that the agreement was strictly limited in its effect to a renunciation by the two contracting parties of all claim to interfere beyond

---

[52] In response to Harcourt's certainty 'that we backed the right horse' in refusing to coerce Japan. KP2 10245, f. 65. Scholars have been reluctant to acknowledge the degree to which the Kimberley and Rosebery policy contributed to friendly relations with Japan. See Ernest Satow's record of conversations with Kimberley prior to taking up his post as minister plenipotentiary to Tokyo: 'The government saw no reason for interfering abt. Formosa, tho' of course wd. rather they had not taken it. As to Liaotung, that concerned Russia alone. Japan our natural ally, as agst. Russia....He thought the Engl. newspapers at Yokohama did a great deal of harm to our friendly relations with Japan. It was desirable to humour their vanity a little and cultivate their goodwill. It was no longer possible to treat them as semi-civilized and to bully them; they must be treated on a footing of equality.' 31 May, 28 June 1895, Satow Papers, PRO 30/33/15/17, ff. 95–101. Also, Nigel Brailey, "Sir Ernest Satow, Japan and Asia: The Trials of a Diplomat in the Age of High Imperialism", *Historical Journal*, 35 (1992): 127- 33.

[53] Convention of 18 September 1897, regarding the status of Tunis.

the lines fixed on either side. But this would have seriously weakened our title to hold the Soudan: and the French would have seen through any proviso of the kind. I think however if hereafter on the breaking up of the Ottoman Empire, Italy were to lay claims to Tripoli and the country immediately behind it we should not be precluded by our agreement with France from supporting Italy. It is an unlucky business, as I fear it will diminish the friendship of Italy for us. Sentiment, as you say, is very powerful. Your acct. of Harcourt's state of mind is very amusing. I think he will find C.B. much stronger than he expects, and the party in much better heart generally.

Meantime, what a sad loss T. Ellis is![54] We have no one I fear who can satisfactorily replace him. And the post of Head Whip is of immense importance now that the general Election is not far off.

The only event here just now is the local elections in Ireland, which as I fully expected, have gone everywhere except in Ulster in favour of Nationalists.

When will John Bull awake from his fond delusion that Home Rule is dead? It is as far as Ireland is concerned, as alive as ever, though for the moment weakened in Parliament by the dissension amongst the nationalist members and the want of a strong leader.

The 2nd reading of the Education Bill is fixed for Friday the 21st. If you do not mind cutting short your holiday, I need not say your presence will be welcome.

262. Kimberley to Spencer   35 Lowndes Sq.
      9 June 1898
      SP K358

I am sorry to hear that Lady Spencer is ill. As you surmise, it is not my intention to join the committee for cordial relations with the U.S.[55]

Like you I question whether such Committees do any good, and whilst I am profoundly convinced of the importance to us of a good understanding with the U.S., I doubt much whether a general treaty would be an advantage if obtainable, which seems to me very unlikely. If circms. should arise where the two countries were pressed to act together, a treaty or binding agreement

---

[54] Tom Ellis (1859–99), Liberal chief whip, whose untimely illness led to an early death. See Lucy, *Later Peeps at Parliament*, pp. 274–76.

[55] On 20 May 1898, J. Angus Hamilton of the *New York Journal* had written to Kimberley seeking support for an Anglo–American Alliance, freely dropping the names and titles of those who had already expressed sympathy or pledged support: the Dukes of Fife, Abercorn, Westminster, Portland, Argyll, Manchester and Marlborough, and the Marquess of Lorne, Baron Russell of Killowen and Lord Esher. Kimberley responded that he could 'only repeat what I said in my speech in the H. of Lords'. Spencer thought that Kimberley, 'as an ex-Foreign Secretary' would probably 'keep out of it'. KP1 15/K2/23; 4 *Hansard*, 57 (17 May 1898): 1512–14; Spencer to Kimberley, 8 June 1898, KP2 10247, f. 77.

of some kind *ad hoc* would naturally be concluded, but that is a very different thing from a *general* treaty for mutual defence.

If however you care to join the committee you can do no harm by following Asquith's and Bryce's example.

263. Hely-Hutchinson[56] to Kimberley Government House,
13 August 1898 Natal
KP1 15/K2/24

.... The Session here is just over, and I am glad to say the Customs Union Bill is through. We are now only waiting for the Cape Parliament to pass the Convention; and that, I am told, it is sure to do whichever party gets a majority at the general election now pending. The Convention tariff leaves much to be desired; but that is a minor matter. The great thing is, to get Customs Union established. As to the Cape Election, the wisest political prophets decline to forecast the issue; but in any case the majority, either way, will be small. And, if Schreiner[57] gets in, I do not think the results will be by any means so serious as some people out here seem to think. He and his will be on their best behaviour; and if a Bond majority means delay in 'progressive' legislation, any anti-Bond majority would be so small and uncertain that the 'progressives' would be scarcely less paralysed than under the Bond regime.

When I heard that Mr. G. Curzon[58] was going to India, I remembered what you said as to the mistake, for a man of ambition, of taking *any* post, however high, abroad.[59]

264. Carrington[60] to Kimberley 42 Parliament St.
23 November 1898[61]
KP2 10249, ff. 29–30

The Executive of the Home Counties Federation today passed a most important resolution, which I enclose. It is felt in the party that the present situation

---

[56] Sir Walter Francis Hely-Hutchinson, Governor of Natal, 1893–1901.

[57] William Philip Schreiner, Prime Minister of Cape Colony, 1898–1900, and brother of Olive Schreiner.

[58] George Nathaniel Curzon, Under-Secretary for Foreign Affairs, 1895–98, Viceroy of India, 1898–1905.

[59] While minister to St. Petersburg between 1856 and 1858, Kimberley chafed at being out of sight politically and later refused all posts abroad. See letters 23 and 28, herein; Wodehouse to Henry Wodehouse, 1 August 1861, KP1 15/K2/19; Kimberley journal, KP6 MS.eng.c.2790, p. 72a.

[60] Charles Wynn-Carrington, first Earl Carrington (1843–1928), Chairman of the Home Counties Liberal Federation.

[61] Cf. Stansky, *Ambitions and Strategies*, p. 253, which implies that the resolution was sent to Kimberley and Harcourt at the same time, almost two weeks later.

has become intolerable; and at the National Liberal Club and elsewhere, the younger members of the party are getting completely out of hand. Trusting in your sage counsel, and calm judgement, the executive are most anxious to see you on the subject, and as Chairman I am instructed to ask whether you would be good enough to grant some of us an interview on this most important subject. The feeling is as strong in the country as it is amongst London Liberals.

[*Enclosed*:]
Home Counties Liberal Federation,   42 Parliament St.
KP2 10249, f. 31

Resolution adopted at the Meeting of the Executive Committee, Novbr. 7th [1898]

'That this Meeting of the Executive Committee of the Home Counties Liberal Federation is of opinion that the early settlement of the question of the leadership of the Liberal Party is imperatively demanded, and that to allow a matter of such vital importance to drift on until a General Election is before the Country will seriously hamper the Liberal forces and will possibly destroy the fruits of a Liberal victory at the polls.'

Further Resolution adopted at the Meeting of the Executive Committee, November 23rd,

'That the Earl of Kimberley be asked to consider and advise the Executive as to the foregoing Resolution, in order that it may be ascertained whether an amicable outcome is possible and so that the publicity which the Committee considers would otherwise be unavoidable, may be obviated.'

265. Kimberley to Carrington   Kimberley House
     25 November 1898
     KP2 10249, f. 34.

Private and Confidential

As I have said in my other letter[62] I should be unable to move (even if I were so inclined) in the matter without consulting my former colleagues, and of course I should consult Harcourt. It would be rather awkward to show him a resolution of the Committee of the Federation of which he is President, which was not sent to him as well as to me.[63]

I of course note what you say as to the feelings of the younger members of the party of which I have heard from other quarters.

[62] In which Kimberley declined an interview, 25 November 1898, KP2 10249, ff. 32–33.

[63] Carrington responded that if the Committee was of the same mind at the next meeting, 'the first resolutions will be forwarded officially by the Secretary to yourself and to Sir William....' Carrington to Kimberley, 26 November 1898, KP2 10249, ff. 36–37.

266. Harcourt to Kimberley   Malwood
        7 December 1898
        KP2 10245, ff. 84–85

Secret

I have received a duplicate of the letter from the Home Counties Federation
which you enclose. It is not necessary that either you or I should make any
immediate answer to it. I am very well aware that a great deal is going on of
which it will be necessary — sooner or later, probably sooner than later — that
I should take some decided notice. As far as I know the action of the Home
Counties Federation is intended to be favourable — rather than the reverse —
to myself, but I am quite conscious that there is a great deal of underhand
machination at work elsewhere which is entirely in the opposite direction and
which is intended to make my position as Leader in the House of Commons
impossible. I have no intention of tolerating this state of things.[64]

I have a very strong and grateful sense of the cordial support I have always
received from you in the very difficult task that has been devolved upon us of
navigating the shattered barque of the Liberal Party. If there are others who are
desirous of taking that agreeable duty out of our hands the sooner, I think, they
make known their intentions and set about the work the better.

*I must beg that you will regard this letter and its contents as absolutely secret
and that nothing may be said upon the subject to which it relates to anyone
whatever.*

267. Lord Kimberley,   Wymondham, Norfolk
        Address to the Wymondham Liberal Association
        25 January 1899
        The Times, 26 January 1899, p. 5.

....It is rather singular that at this time last year when I addressed you
the attention of the nation was fixed upon the question of foreign policy, and
exactly the same state of feeling exists now. I do not suppose that any question
has deeply moved the feeling of the country for months which is not closely
connected with foreign policy. Now, a great deal has been said in many speeches
lately upon this subject, and one of the topics which it seems to many speakers
to be necessary to enlarge upon on such occasions is the difference between
what is called a "jingo" and a Little Englander. For my part I must say I think
it is a very barren and unprofitable discussion. (Hear, hear.) I do not think
that the mere nicknaming and the use of rather disagreeable expressions will
advance us the least in the world in the conviction of the political questions
which we have to face. However, I am not going to give any new definition of

---

[64] On circumstances, see Gardiner, *Life of Harcourt*, 2:466– 79.

a "jingo," but I should like to give the definition which we are provided with
by the maker of that celebrated song —
  "I don't want to fight,
  "But by jingo if we do."
(Laughter.) That is supposed to indicate a man of a most aggressive and
determined character as regards, I suppose, foreign nations. He begins by a
most peaceful declaration, "I am not going to fight" — I can conceive nothing
more peaceful than that. He does what is very proper; it is a very proper and
natural sentiment. "If I am forced to fight I am not afraid"; taken by itself
that is a very harmless expression. But it has now got to mean a man who
is pugnacious on all occasions. These things are not to be dealt with by such
sharply-defined lines. There are occasions when it is undoubtedly the duty, and
will always be the duty, of the nation not to be afraid to fight; but on the other
hand, I hold it to be the duty of the nation, and to the supreme interests of
the nation, to be in favour of peace. (Hear, hear.) It depends on the choice
of the nation; and no general proposition can be laid down. I suppose there is
no such person as a Little Englander who, under no conceivable circumstances,
would think it right to add to the dominions of the Empire; at all events, I never
have met with such a person, and I am quite sure that none of our distinguished
statesmen whom I have known ever held the doctrine in that bare form. I will
take only one most illustrious example, and that is Mr. Gladstone. (Cheers.)
I do not suppose that any one thinks that Mr. Gladstone was of an aggressive
temper or anxious to saddle this nation with heavier responsibilities than were
unavoidable. Yet Mr. Gladstone in the course of his career added not a few
territories to the dominions of the Empire. I remember that one of the first things
I was called upon to do, when I had the honour, many years ago, to be Secretary
of State for the Colonies under Mr. Gladstone's first Government, was to annex
that territory where a town was founded which they did me the honour to call
by my name — a territory where the diamond mines were in South Africa —
and very soundly I was abused by some people for doing it. However, I had
Mr. Gladstone's sanction for taking that step, and it is a remarkable fact, and
I do not pretend that we foresaw it at the time, that that annexation had far-
reaching consequences, as often happens, for unless you possessed that territory
you would have been absolutely cut off from all communication with the interior
of Africa from the Cape territory. That annexation has, as a matter of fact, been
followed by the annexation of Bechuanaland, which was also done during Mr.
Gladstone's Government. Further, you have that immense extension which we
now know by the name of Rhodesia. Then there was North Borneo, and very
recently indeed I had the duty of recommending the annexation of Somaliland
to the dominions of the Queen. I could go on with further instances, but I wish
you to observe that Mr. Gladstone was not one of those statesmen who, under
all circumstances, were adverse to the extension of the Empire. All these cases
must be judged by the particular circumstances, and no wise man would desire

unnecessary expansion, and no wise man would pledge himself absolutely that there should be no further expansion.

I wish to say one further word with respect to a peace policy. It is to my mind a grievous mistake to suppose that you always will preserve peace best by maintaining a very humble and a forbearing attitude. On the contrary, I am profoundly convinced that in the management of foreign affairs if you wish to preserve peace you must be firm upon occasions. If you are not you will not have that respect from other nations which is one of the greatest elements in the preservation of peace. I am old enough to remember the times of Lord Palmerston. He was certainly not a man who abstained from strong language nor even from what were strong acts, and probably he sometimes went too far, but, mark you, during his long career in the management of foreign affairs in times of the greatest difficulty he never involved you in war. He preserved the peace. But there was another distinguished Minister under whom I had the honour to serve on the first occasion I ever held office — I mean Lord Aberdeen. He was essentially a man of peace, but he involved this country in the Crimean war, and I have always believed, being then Under-Secretary for Foreign Affairs and knowing what took place, that that war might have been avoided if we had taken a firmer tone at the commencement of the dispute[65] ....

Last year during the Session of Parliament we were startled, almost electrified, by Mr. Chamberlain saying it was necessary for the country to seek for alliances. We thought that such an announcement as that could not be made without the authority of the Cabinet. We thought there was to be a change in the policy of the Government. We had heard it taught that blind, entangling alliances were not desirable, and I took occasion to mention the subject in the House of Lords. But Lord Salisbury was very wary indeed. He said he had not read Mr Chamberlain's speech (laughter) and would not give me any information except what I derived from his silence — namely, that he never authorized such a speech as that.[66] (Laughter.) Mr. Chamberlain has now quite changed his mind. I have ventured to point out that alliances of anything like a permanent nature are undesirable, but alliances for particular purposes are very desirable and are often made. But now Mr. Chamberlain gives us quite another account of the matter. He told us the other day at Wakefield that this country might be satisfied with what I think he termed its 'splendid isolation.'(laughter), and that alliances if they were to be concluded must be alliances for particular purposes, and not of any general character such as some persons had ascribed to him. I am much pleased to see that he has come back to that state of mind — namely, that it is not desirable to entangle ourselves with permanent alliances with foreign nations .... I may have said too much about Mr. Chamberlain, but he is a man

[65] See letter 17, herein.

[66] On this intra-party controversy, see Peter Marsh, *Joseph Chamberlain: Entrepreneur in Politics* (New Haven, CT: Yale University Press, 1994), pp. 430–441.

for whom I have great respect and admiration because of his ability. I always read his speeches with great attention, and one remark I always make to myself is this, ' I should certainly be sorry to be responsible for foreign affairs with Mr. Chamberlain as a colleague'(Laughter.) ....

Turning to Ireland you will see that the state of Ireland is just now in a very interesting phase, because we see what is happening under the very important Act passed under the auspices of the present Government during last Session— the Local Government Act. Thus far in the towns it has had exactly the result which I expected— namely, that it has greatly strengthened the Nationalist cause throughout the Irish towns, and I must add, though I may be a false prophet, that I fully expect precisely the same result will be found to prevail throughout the counties. We were in favour of the Local Government Act, because we thought it reasonable that the Irish people, as regards their local affairs, should have the same privileges that we have. I always believed it would strengthen the cause of Home Rule, and I am now more than ever convinced that it will do so. We know our opponents are not of that opinion.... It seems to me as clear as day that after they have used this gift of Home Rule as regards their local affairs they will be immediately strengthened in their demand for Home Rule in other affairs. Their argument will be a very strong one, and for the life of me I cannot see how Sir M. Hicks Beach can say that this grant of local government will do away with the demand for Home Rule I agree with what has been said by several of my former colleagues— that, whilst we made a strong, persevering, most vigorous effort to carry Home Rule, and having done that, we must hold ourselves entirely at liberty to choose our own time as regards the revival in Parliament of Home Rule, we will not, so far as I am concerned, be disposed to pledge ourselves with regard to it at all. We must look to all the circumstances and see when it may be possible to bring such a question forward. It is idle to bring forward a question of that magnitude unless there is some reasonable hope of advancing its future, and you will not do that by making efforts when there is no probability of being able to carry it. But that does not imply receding. For my own part I am as strongly convinced as ever of the policy of that measure. I know that it has been said that the Liberal party voted against their opinions for the most part, and I know that there are many Conservatives who believed that we turned round because Mr. Gladstone wished to do so. I certainly was influenced by the weight of Mr. Gladstone's policy, as I suppose any one would be, but this I know well— that as regards myself and my former colleagues, every one of us was firmly convinced that it was a measure of which we ought to recommend the adoption by Parliament. We must use our discretion as to when it is to be brought forward, though we do not for a moment recede from it. As for our relations with the Irish party, we look upon it as an independent party. We are glad when they act with us, but we regard them as entitled to take their own course as regards this national question.

And now as to the prospects of the Liberal Party. (Hear, hear.) the question suggests itself, Are we going to have any party at all? (Laughter) I read a most interesting letter from Mr. Goldwin Smith in *The Times*, in which he says that the day of parties in this country is gone by, and that nature has not drawn any political dividing line between people; that is to say, that people are not naturally divided into Liberals and Conservatives. Now I wholly differ from him. (Hear, hear). Men have a natural tendency one way or the other. One man will be, on the whole, averse to change, and another man will be naturally prone to change, and when questions present themselves they will judge the matter from different points of view. therefore, I believe there will always be a party which calls itself a party of progress and a party which calls itself a party of Conservatives. What are the prospects of the Liberal Party? We are told every day by gentlemen speaking from the Ministerial point of view that we are a disorganized, distracted, effete, and almost defunct party. We are divided, and, of course, there are differences amongst us. But would it be wholesome that there should be no differences, and that there should be a stagnant condition, in which people would not be allowed to have any independent opinion? But these differences have not prevented the party from working together in the past, nor will they in the future. Are the Conservatives always agreed amongst themselves? (Laughter.) Do you believe that Lord Salisbury and Mr. Chamberlain take the same view of foreign policy? You never know what passes in a Cabinet unless you are a member of it, and then you are bound by your oath not to give information. (Laughter.) I shall not be violating the oath if I say that 15 or 16 men round a table would find that there are many subjects on which they cannot altogether agree. They have to agree to differ, which often happens, and then they are a "united Cabinet." (Laughter.) When they come to act together they are obliged, if they mean to produce any definite result, to sink their differences. The same thing that happens in a Cabinet happens in a party. When men have to work together they are wise enough and patriotic enough to sink their differences, and it will be with the Liberal party as it has been in the past. Is this the first time that a party in this country has found itself in difficulties? We were defeated at the last election, and in the present Parliament we are not as effective in Opposition as we should wish to be; but these things right themselves. I can remember that, after the great secession, at the time of Free Trade, the Conservative party was in a melancholy plight for many years, and though they afterwards found a great leader in Mr. Disraeli, I can remember that in Palmerston's Government Disraeli was looked upon with the greatest distrust by a large number of members of the party, and it was notorious that Palmerston's Government, which came into power with something under 20 majority, was only kept in power by the fact that at least 40 members of the Conservative party were determined never to vote upon any question which could turn out the Government. (Laughter.) The Conservative party survived its troubles in those days, and we shall also survive. We are a powerful party in the country, although we are not a powerful party in Parliament. It may be that we shall have to wait for some time before we have the advantage of leaders of widespread influence and great genius; but I am sufficiently sanguine to believe that the time is not far distant when our fortunes will be very different from what they are now. The fortunes of a party do not depend only upon leaders. They depend also on the state of feeling of the whole bulk of the party, and I see no signs of decay or want of spirit in the party. There is a great deal of difficulty in finding candidates. But the Conservatives find a difficulty in that matter as well as we ourselves. Still, we do find candidates, and we have fought many elections this last year with success. Far from taking a desponding view, I believe that the time will come before long when we shall be able to satisfy even the aspirations of our friends on the other side, who not only commiserate our position, but express the most earnest desire for our health, and their earnest desire that the Opposition as a party should be strong enough to keep their own party in order. (Cheers.)....

268. Kimberley to Spencer   Kimberley House
    28 September 1899
    SP K360

I am sorry to say I agree with you that war appears to be imminent.[67] I also concur with you as to Harcourt and Morley's speeches.[68] You put the exact point as to the latter. I don't see how after making categorical demands we can sit still and do nothing. The effect throughout South Africa and indeed throughout the Empire would be most serious.

It is lamentable that we should be plunged into such a war, which I am convinced might have been avoided by more prudence in the earlier stages of the negotiations. If the F.O. were to conduct its business after Chamberlain's fashion we should be at war with half the world. He has managed by his language to aggravate to such a point the Boers suspicion of our designs (which after that abominable raid[69] are not unnatural) that now when the later despatches sanctioned by the cabinet are couched in moderate terms it is I fear too late.

I shall be very glad indeed to have a talk with you, but I am rather busy just now having done no shooting yet, waiting for Armine whom I expect tonight. I can manage to feed him and his wife, which is all I can do without a kitchen.[70]

---

[67] Spencer to Kimberley, 26 September 1899, KP2 10247, f. 94.

[68] Harcourt's at Tredegar on September 21, Morley's at Manchester on September 15. Morley, *Recollections*, 2: 86–87; F. W. Hirst, *In the Golden Days* (London: Frederick Muller, 1947), pp. 183–84.

[69] On the Jameson raid, see letter 248 and notes, herein.

[70] For accounts of the fire which destroyed the service wing of Kimberley Hall on August 26, see 'Kimberley Hall on Fire', *Eastern Daily Press*, 28 August 1899, p. 5; Kimberley to Ripon, 30 August 1899, RP 43527, ff. 148–51.

They and my daughter[71] are going to the Festival[72] next Wednesday, while I shall stay at home, (not being very musical). If you were able to come here on that day I shall be entirely at your disposal.

I wish I could pay you a visit but you will understand that I must just now be at home. What a nuisance a meeting of Parliament will be!

269. Kimberley to Campbell-Bannerman   Kimberley House
      5 October 1899
      CBP 41221, ff. 171–72

If the Boers have invaded our territory all talk about peace is at an end. Nothing is left but to wage war upon them and drive them out. We may criticise the Government as much as we like for bringing matters to such a pass, but it will be impossible not to support them in resisting the Boer attack. With war the Conventions of 1881 and 1884 cease to exist, and we shall have a clean sheet on which we may write what we please if we are successful in the war. Much as this Boer attack is to be lamented as putting an end to all hopes of peace, it will lighten our party difficulties, a poor consolation but still something to the good as far as we are personally concerned.

270. Kimberley to Spencer   Kimberley House
      18 November 1899
      SP K360

Private

Your kind letter gave me much pleasure.[73] It is a real satisfaction to me to know that you approved what I said at Newcastle.[74] You hit the point exactly in the distinction you draw between me and C.B., who in his very effective speech[75] rightly gave a more bellicose flavour in his utterances than I did. Were I to make fiery speeches, I should soon lose what little influence I have, and it can be but little in my case, in the House of Lords.

As to the criticism of such men as Ld. Grey and the D. of Northumberland,[76] I was not at all sorry that I did not please *them*. By the way, Spence Watson[77] told me that Grey is gaining much influence in Northumberland.

[71] Constance Wodehouse.

[72] Musical Festival, held triennially to benefit the Norfolk and Norwich Hospital.

[73] Of 17 November 1899, KP2 10247, f. 61.

[74] On 14 November 1899, where Kimberley made 'generous allusion' to Chamberlain, 'pinning him to the policy of 1881'. See *The Times*, 15 November 1899, p. 7.

[75] At the Free Trade Hall in Manchester, 15 November 1899. Wilson, *CB*, pp. 315–6.

[76] Albert Henry Grey, fourth Earl Grey; Henry George Percy, seventh Duke of Northumberland.

[77] Robert Spence Watson, President of the National Liberal Federation, 1890–1902.

The peace section of local Liberals had been howled down for three hours at a recent meeting held by them in the Town Hall, and never getting a hearing. Spence Watson was not without apprehension that I might experience some interruption. Happily, nothing could be more attentive and cordial than the audience which completely filled the hall. I spoke for 45 minutes, and did not find it so bad a place to speak in as I was led to expect. My speech at the luncheon which was well reported in the 'Leader' also went off very well.

It was a great help to have Edward Grey[78] in the chair at the Town Hall meeting. You say you wish I had expanded the 'fair grounds' for the annexation of the diamond fields. I purposely made only a slight allusion to them for altho' I was satisfied that our claim was sufficient to justify our action, I am not prepared to maintain that we had a perfect title; tho' it was, I believed, a better claim, to say the least, than that put forward by the Free State. It rested, if I remember rightly on a treaty which had been made by us with one Waterboer the native chief. It was still a question when I left office, whether we should not consent to refer the claim to arbitration, and Carnarvon[79] who succeeded me, very wisely offered the Free State £50,000 for any claims they might have. This the Free State accepted and so the matter ended. A very curious part of Carnarvon's arrangement which never became public was that, being I suppose unable to get the then Government, or being himself unwilling, to ask Parliament to vote this £50,000, he managed somehow to get the Bank of England to advance the money in the expectation that the Cape Govt. would undertake to pay it, and he himself went out of office without having been able to get the colony to do this, so that when I again became Col. Secy. I found the matter still unsettled and the Bank pressing for the money. Fortunately with some difficulty I succeeded in inducing the Cape Govt. to take over the territory and pay the money.

This is a long yarn but I thought you might like to know the whole history of the annexation. I do not recollect any speech of mine on the subject, but I think some papers must have been laid at the time.

I wonder whether you are going, as I am, (for my sins) to the Windsor banquet on Tuesday. If so I hope we may meet at Brooks' where I shall be at 4 o'clock on that day.

P. S. — I read your speech at Bath and need hardly say I entirely agree with your views on Educational Reform.[80]

---

[78] Liberal M.P. for Berwick-on-Tweed and formerly Under-Secretary to Kimberley at the Foreign Office, 1894–95.

[79] Henry Howard Herbert, fourth Earl of Carnarvon (1831–90), Conservative Secretary of State for the Colonies, 1874–78.

[80] Of November 15, opposing 'Government interference to fashion all schools in one mould', and hoping that religious teaching would not be 'dragged into secondary education.' *Bath Daily Chronicle*, 16 November 1899, p. 3.

271. Kimberley to Herbert Gladstone[81]   Kimberley House
    25 November 1899
    HGP 46057, ff. 218–20

Private

I have no difficulty in answering your letter.[82] My words as correctly reported
in the *Newcastle Leader*, were 'As far as I was concerned and to a great extent
Mr. Gladstone also, our reason was not, as some people seem to think, a mere
sentimental reason'; then I went on to say that President Brandt[83] who was very
friendly, at last told us that he could hold his Burghers no longer, and that
we had indications from the colony (i.e., the Cape) that there was a sympathy
which might give rise to serious difficulties, that in the event we came to the
conclusion 'that we were taking the right course to avert a calamity we saw
impending'. Observe I said not a *mere* sentimental reason.

I did not in the least exclude such reasons; and most certainly your father
and myself also (tho' in a less degree) were actuated by such reasons, I entirely
agreed with him that we had, as you say, been deceived in 1877 as to the
willingness of the Transvaal people to accept British sovereignty. My object
at Newcastle was to show that besides what are termed 'sentimental reasons',
there were powerful reasons of policy. There is really no inconsistency in this
as regards your father, tho' partisan critics try to extract this from my words.[84]

As to the 'fear' imparted to us, it was the fear of bringing on a terrible
disaster to South Africa. Events now taking place show that this 'fear' was well
founded.

I think after all it will be found that our divergence of opinion as to the
present state of things are not nearly so serious as they appeared to be at first.

272. Kimberley to Spencer   35 Lowndes Sq.
    19 February 1900
    SP K364

I agree with you that Rosebery's speech was too alarmist.[85] It 'savoured', as
you say, 'of panic'. I do not think it would have done for me to say nothing

[81] Herbert John Gladstone (1854–1930), Liberal M.P. for West Leeds, 1885–1910;
Chief Liberal Whip from 1899.
[82] Of November 24, seeking clarification of Kimberley's policy in the Transvaal,
1880–81. KP2 10249, ff. 87–88.
[83] Jan Hendrik Brand, President of the Orange Free State, 1864–88.
[84] See Spencer's keen assessment of Kimberley's position. *Red Earl*, 2:277–79. Also,
Acton's general remarks of 1881, noting the absence of a moral base in Kimberley's
politics. Herbert Paul, ed. *Letters of Lord Acton to Mary Gladstone* (London: George
Allen, 1904), p. 96.
[85] In the House of Lords, February 15. Spencer also found Kimberley's contribution
'alarmist'. *Red Earl*, 2:280–281.

and besides it was, it seemed to me, desirable to get up Salisbury. My opinion is strong that it would be most unwise to overlook the possibilities of a sudden demand for troops in India and the Soudan. Northbrook, who is not at all given to panic, told me that he entirely agreed in everything I said on these two points.

As to CB's speech there are some who blame it, as indicating that he is falling under the influence of the ultra peace party. This is not my own view. His position is an extremely difficult one, and I think he steered as successfully between Scylla and Charybdis as the situation admits.

With regard to conscription or ballot for the militia, I gather from your letter that we are agreed. We *may* have to come to ballot for the militia and we ought to have the machinery for it in good order but I am not disposed to commit myself to any thing beyond this.

As to immediate preparations for carrying on the war, I doubt their sufficiency. The statements of the Govt. on this point are not very clear, but the impression left on my mind is that they are not prepared with adequate reinforcement.

As to the fleet I am very glad to know that you are not in favour of immediate mobilization. I am not a competent judge on naval matters, but I was quite unable to see any sound reason for it.

273. Kimberley to Packe[86]　　　　　　　Kimberley House
　　　10 October 1900
　　　PkP DE 1749 19/11

As a member of the Opposition I ought to rejoice that you have not won a seat from us, but I can most sincerely assure you that it would have given me the greatest pleasure to see you in Parliament and that I am extremely sorry that you were beaten. It must be all the more disappointing as you ran so near.[87]

274. Kimberley to Ripon　　　　　　　Kimberley House
　　　15 November 1900
　　　RP 43527, ff. 169–74

Confidential

The prospects of our party look black.[88] C.B. wrote to me that he had to make a speech this week and that he proposed to say something friendly about Rosebery, holding out the 'olive branch' to him.[89] I think this may do some good. C.B. will at all accounts show that no personal antipathies or jealousies

---

[86] Hussey Packe, Kimberley's son-in-law since 1872; Liberal Unionist.

[87] Packe was defeated for Loughborough Division, Leicestershire in polling on October 9, the Liberal, Maurice Levy, receiving 4897 votes, Packe 4830.

[88] Responding to Ripon's inquiry regarding the 'pro-Rosebery intrigues.' Wolf, *Life of Ripon*, 2:262–63.

[89] At Dundee on November 15. See Spender, *Life of Campbell-Bannerman*, 1:301–07.

stand in the way of his return. The main cause of our dissension is not so much differences of opinion on public questions as these petty motives.

Of course if R. were to show a willingness to return, it would be indispensable, as you say, to have a clear explanation of his policy both as to the S. African settlement and domestic questions.

As long as R. stands aloof, keeping himself sedulously before the public eye but taking no open part in politics, he will act as a solvent on our party and render any united action impossible. Nor must we overlook Harcourt who hates R. as much as R. hates him.

For my own part the situation is so distasteful to me that I often wish I were out of politics altogether, but I feel that however dark the outlook may be, it is a public duty to strive to reorganise the opposition, the utter weakness of which is a national misfortune.

Unfortunately, we in the H. of Lords are able to do nothing but make a pretence of opposing the overwhelming majority against us. Meantime the war drags on and seems likely to drag on for some time, and we are a long way from making even a commencement of a peaceful settlement. I don't like the idea of a Crown Colony Govt., but I do not see how we can avoid what must be practically Crown Colony Govt., tho' it would be politic to call the interim Gt., which I fear must last a considerable time by some other name, which will not so directly remind the Boers of the Govt. against which they rebelled. If anything can be suggested which would enable us to draw a clear line between our policy and the Govt. policy as to the settlement, I should be in favour of it, but I am afraid we shall find that in the present stage of the business it will be extremely difficult to lay down in any definite shape the lines of settlement. 'Dolus' says the proverb, 'latet in generalibus,' but sometimes there is no alternative.

What a nuisance this autumn session is!

[*Postscript*] I quite agree with you that the complete abstention which you have heard that H. Gladstone proposes, is out of the question. If it were to be attempted, our hands would be forced by our 'followers' (if one can use that term).

An absurdity of the situation is that the quarrel between the two sections of the party is ostensibly about 'Imperialism' which has become a cant term capable of various interpretations. No one really wishes not to maintain the 'Empire'. The point is how best to do it, and that leaves ample scope for differences of opinion such as must always exist in a 'Liberal' party.[90]

---

[90] This evokes Morley's definition of Liberal Imperialism as 'Chamberlain wine with a Rosebery label'. Asquith, *Fifty Years of British Parliament*, 1:303; *Red Earl* 2: 285–87 and n. 3.

275. Kimberley to Campbell-Bannerman   Kimberley House
       1 January 1901
       CBP 41221, ff. 204–06

Private

I was very glad to receive your letter of yesterday, as altho' Spencer has kept me (generally) informed of what has been going on,[91] I did not before thoroughly understand the situation which is indeed as you say 'hideous'. I do not so much mind the real public differences which as you say are not incapable of adjustment, but the 'subterranean' personal intrigues are detestable.[92]

Your account of your interview with Rosebery is most interesting, and really as regards the war we are very nearly in agreement with him.

In my own mind I attribute his perverseness in an attitude of detachment to be in no small degree owing to his past most unpleasant relations with Harcourt.... I do not think anyone but myself knows what his relations with Harcourt were when we were last in office.[93] This however is mere conjecture, I mean the extent to which Rosebery may be affected by what is now of course ancient history. If R. really takes an active part in the Lords, this will be an important step on his part. Meanwhile how the war drags on! All my forebodings of the prolongation of the struggle have unhappily come too true.

I say nothing as to domestic questions, which are really swallowed up by the war. I do not suppose there would be any differences between you and me upon any of them.

As to myself, I am quite willing to remain nominal leader in the Lords for the present. My health tho' I am a complete invalid has improved lately. We have had on the whole pleasant weather here lately and I am very sorry to leave the country for London, which has always been to me in winter a detestable residence. I mean to move to town at the end of next week.

276. Kimberley to Morley
       n.d.
       KP2 10245, f. 154

I am vy. glad you have asked me whether the passage in my speech on the death of the Queen referred to the retrocession of the Transvaal in 1881 as I am able to assure you that it had nothing whatever to do with it.[94]

---

[91] See, for instance, *Red Earl*, 2:285–86.

[92] See Matthew, *Liberal Imperialists*, pp. 48–60.

[93] Kimberley was perhaps the most longsuffering of Gladstonian Liberals toward Rosebery. See *Red Earl*, 2:286.

[94] This letter written in answer to Morley's of 6 February 1901. KP2 10245, ff. 153–54. In a Lords speech on Queen Victoria's death on 24 January 1901, Kimberley mentioned that 'once' the Queen's opinion had been sounder than his own. For varying

277. Kimberley to Asquith					35 Lowndes Sq.
	29 June 1901
	AP 10, f. 13

I am much concerned to hear that you are to attend a dinner which I am told is to be the occasion of a further demonstration against the recent speeches of C.B. and others on the South African situation.[95]

To me, as a looker on, it seems that you have already so plainly defined your own position[96] that it cannot be essential to take part in a meeting to condemn the recent utterances of what I suppose I must term the other wing of the Liberal Party. Surely the accentuation of our differences cannot conduce to the public advantage.

We have before us immense difficulties after the war, and it is most important that there should be some check (it is only too weak already) on the extreme views of the ministerialists. If as I fear these repeated demonstrations should lead to a complete disruption of our party, I cannot see any light in a future already very dark.

I am, as you know, in no sense what is called a 'pro-Boer', but I have no confidence in the wisdom or energy of the Governt. and it will be disastrous if there is practically no opposition which can criticise their action, and expose their shortcomings.

278. Kimberley to Spencer					Kimberley House
	1 January 1902
	SP K372

Thanks for Rosebery's and CB's letters which I return.[97] I had a letter from CB this morning to the same effect as his letter to you.[98] I am quite ready for the present to remain nominal leader and *perhaps* if I continue to improve in

estimations of Kimberley's speech see Almeric Fitzroy, *Memoirs*, 2 vols. (London: Hutchinson, n.d.), 1:43; Viscount Mountmorres, 'Queen Victoria', *New Liberal Review*, 1 (March 1901), p. 198; Miss Dodson to Eleanor Wodehouse, 25 January 1901, KP1 15/K2/21; A. G. C. Liddell, *Notes from the Life of an Ordinary Mortal* (London: John Murray, 1911), p. 328; Henry Lucy, *The Balfourian Parliament, 1900–1905* (London: Hodder and Stoughton, 1906), pp. 24–25.

[95] On the politics of Liberal dining, see Spender, *Life of Campbell-Bannerman*, 1:338–50; Matthew, *Liberal Imperialists*, pp. 65–72.

[96] In a speech at Liverpool Street Station Hotel on June 20, dissociating himself from the 'pro- Boer' wing of the party. Asquith explained that Kimberley had been 'altogether misinformed'. He then sent a letter of clarification to the *Daily News* and suggested that Edward Grey speak with Kimberley about the matter. Asquith to Kimberley, 30 June 1901, KP6 MS.eng.c.4467, ff. 119–23; KP6 MS.eng.c.4470, f. 164.

[97] In Spencer to Kimberley, 31 December 1901, MS.eng.c.4474, ff. 88–89.

[98] See Campbell-Bannerman to Kimberley, 31 December 1901, KP6 MS.eng.c.4468, ff. 58–59; *Red Earl*, 2:295–96.

health as I have done during the last week or 10 days I may be able to appear again in the house.

I don't often see the 'Daily Mail' but nothing can be more miserable than that paper. I have long had a very poor opinion of the press generally. I am glad you are sending out your letters to the Peers and invitations to your dinner.

[*Postscript*] I shall go to town at the end of next week (either Friday or Saturday).

Appendix 1

Letters on the Death of Lord Kimberley

1. Ripon to 2nd Earl of Kimberley   9 Chelsea Embankment
9 April 1902
KP1 15/K2/21

I need not tell you how very truly Lady Ripon and I sympathise with you in your sad though long expected loss. In your dear father I have lost one of my oldest and best friends, with whom I have been closely associated for many years,[1] in whom I had the fullest trust, and for whom I cherished a warm affection. The public loss too is great indeed. There is no one exactly to take his place.

If it would be consistent with your arrangements I hope you will allow me to attend the funeral.

2. Arthur Godley to 2nd Earl of Kimberley   India Office
9 April 1902
KP1 15/K2/21

I must ask you to let me say how deeply grieved I was to hear of Lord Kimberley's death. I am sure that everyone in this office who came in contact with him felt it as a real personal loss. As you know, we were fortunate enough to have him three times for an official chief and if this was the general feeling, you may imagine that it was no small sorrow to me, who had been brought into the closest relations with him from 1883 onward, when he was in office. I owed my appointment to him and both in the office and out of it was treated by him with much kindness as I can never forget. I shall never forget the unmistakable signs of universal regret which were shown when he left us, for the last time, to go to the Foreign Office. It was a most genuine and unpremeditated display of feeling. I have never seen anything quite like it in a public office; and I could see that Lord Kimberley was much troubled by it, as indeed he could hardly fail to be.

[1] They began a regular and sustained correspondence in 1864.

Putting Mr. Gladstone aside, as in a class by himself, I say without hesitation that Lord Kimberley was the best *official* that I have ever served under, and I consider it a great privilege to have begun my work here under his auspices. I hope you will accept my most sincere sympathy.[2]

3. 2nd Earl of Kimberley to Campbell-Bannerman   35 Lowndes Sq.
13 April 1902
CBP 41237, ff. 28–29

Private

I cannot tell you how much I appreciate your excessively kind letter. My dear Father had the greatest regard for you, his mind was perfectly clear to practically the end, and he took a lively interest in everything that was going on. Your recent speeches that I read to him pleased him very much.[3]

His contempt of this Liberal League was absolute. Perhaps someday a little later if you wish I can come down and see you and tell you his views on the recent crisis in the Liberal camp.

4. 2nd Earl of Kimberley to Spencer   Witton Park, Norfolk
20 October 1902
SP K372

Private

I am sure you will not mind my troubling you for your advice upon the following matter. Lady Dufferin has written to me to let her have the letters written by Lord Dufferin to my Father and in return offers to let me have my Father's letters to Lord Dufferin. Her reason being that Sir Alfred Lyall[4] has undertaken to write her husband's life.[5]

My answer to her was that *all* my Father's papers are left to me unconditionally but that in a conversation I had with him he said he did not think anything ought to be published for 50 years, but his words were 'I leave it entirely to your discretion'. I said very well but I shall if anything arises consult Lord Spencer. My Father took hold of my hand and smiled so sweetly to me and said 'Quite

---

[2] Godley's appreciation must be reckoned sincere, and not merely perfunctory. He had attended the funerals of Lady Kimberley in 1895 and Armine Wodehouse in 1901, and published in his reminiscences an almost verbatim assessment of Kimberley's official abilities. Godley, *Reminiscences*, pp. 157–58.

[3] Wilson, *CB*, pp. 385–388.

[4] Alfred Comyn Lyall, Lieutenant Governor of North-West Provinces and Oudh, 1882–87; member of India Council, 1887–1902; Liberal Unionist.

[5] Subsequently published as *The Life of the Marquis of Dufferin and Ava*, 2 vols. (London: John Murray, 1905).

right, quite right, you cannot do better'. He never after that mentioned the subject of his papers again. This conversation took place at Kimberley in November last year....

Appendix 2

The Kimberley 'Biography'

Having had no biographer, Kimberley's historical reputation has been unusually dependent upon four standard sources. *The Times* obituary[1] has been a fundamental biographical source for information on Kimberley's life. It provides an admirably objective view of his departmental record, conceding that he failed in the Schleswig-Holstein negotiations of 1863–64 where 'probably no man could have succeeded'; that during his Irish viceroyalty 'his vigour and promptitude... were acknowledged by his political opponents as well as by his own party'; and that at the India Office he 'shared in the unpopularity of Lord Ripon's administration of native affairs' but was not 'so much afraid of Imperial responsibilities and Imperial expansion as a good Gladstonian is naturally expected to be.' *The Times* notice correctly associates Kimberley's lack of notoriety with a political philosophy of moderate reform, which during the late Victorian period most often required restraint of radicalism rather than 'original conceptions.' In a small way, too, Kimberley's personality is displayed — his 'reputation for common sense', his 'modesty and moderation', and, in a last wish, his characteristic avoidance of ostentation, desiring 'that no flowers be sent for the funeral'. Yet *The Times* obituary is virtually silent on cabinet politics. Had Kimberley been less reticent he might be better known today, but he kept cabinet secrets and seldom brandished his authority for outsiders. In Sir Garnet Wolseley's *surprise* at Kimberley 'abruptly and angrily' settling the question of 'war or no war' against the Ashanti 1873 over the objections of several ministers, one glimpses both the weight which enabled Kimberley to maintain his position in the front rank of Liberal ministers for thirty years, and the restraint which made him an agreeable colleague.[2] Because his style of politics, however, did not usually make good copy for contemporary reporters, it was little known and largely omitted from obituary accounts.[3]

---

[1] 9 April 1902, p. 3.

[2] Wolseley to Fleetwood Wilson, 22 September 1902, Wolseley Papers, Perkins Library, 18-H. Dilke and Rosebery each remarked upon their heightened estimation of Kimberley after sitting with him in cabinet. Dilke Diary, 30 August 1881, with later annotation, DkP 43924, f. 59; *EHJ1*, p. 830.

[3] For virtually a complete run of British and foreign obituary notices, which collec-

The *Dictionary of National Biography* has been more important as a biographical source because it has been widely accessible. Its avowed adherence to the word of 'authorities' has lulled generations of scholars into imagining that its errors are isolated to occasional factual slips and instances of temporal historiographical method which are easily detected.[4] But it is not quite uniformly true that early *DNB* entries were both 'artful' and 'accurate' condensations of lives, as has recently been suggested.[5] Criticisms of the accuracy and impartiality of the *DNB* have now gone well beyond the carping of the 'few experts' whom Augustine Birrell predicted would alone discover its faults.[6] No systematic study of the *DNB*'s 37,000 articles has been attempted, though mounting evidence suggests that faults are widespread. While others have praised it as 'the apex of the Victorian belief in, and commitment to, fact,' editor Leslie Stephen saw it as an albatross and not truly professional.[7] Great as the project was, and useful as were the results, Stephen was right. He simply did not have available to him either the pool of professional scholars who might have risen to a uniformly high standard of accuracy, or the technology which would have enabled him to correct the deficiencies which he did notice. And for the researcher at a given moment, no number of brilliant articles can compensate for the fundamentally flawed one lying open before one's eyes. The *DNB*'s entry on 'John Wodehouse', written by Lloyd Charles Sanders and published in 1912, is precisely such an article.

Sanders clearly was a writer of some ability, having won in 1880 the Stanhope prize for his essay on 'The Possibility of a Stewart Resoration on the Death of Anne'. Following his graduation from Christ Church, Oxford, he produced studies of Lord Palmerston (1888), Lord Melbourne (1889) and Richard Brinsley

tively draw a clearer picture, see KP6 MS.eng.c. 4478–4484.

[4] Though use of the *DNB* is usually too general to be noted, see an honest soul like G. H. Blore, who laments that if only boys would read the great dictionary his work would be superfluous. *Victorian Worthies* (London: Oxford University Press, 1920), p. vi; Jessop, 'The *Dictionary of National Biography*', *Nineteenth Century* 18, (1890), p. 1010.

[5] Ira Bruce Nadel, *Biography, Fiction, Fact, and Form* (New York: St. Martin's Press, 1984), p. 52.

[6] This jovial *bon vivant* went on to ask 'who would willingly associate' himself with such critics, who have 'few pleasures and of necessity lead dreary lives', certainly an important question in the evaluation of a standard book of reference. *Self-Selected Essays: A Second Series* (London: Thomas Nelson, 1916), pp. 182–83.

[7] Nadel, *Biography, Fiction, Fact, and Form*, pp. 52–54; Noel Annan, *Leslie Stephen: The Godless Victorian*, Univ. of Chicago ed. (Chicago: University of Chicago Press, 1986), p. 87. Among dozens of more recent accounts regarding the nature of the *DNB*'s deficiencies, Laurel Brake's 'Problems in Victorian Biography: The *DNB* and the *DNB* "Walter Pater"' may stand as a model. *Modern Language Review* (October 1975): 731–42. In 1992 funding was secured for a *New DNB*, in which longer articles are to be rewritten rather than revised. See project editor, Professor H.C.G. Matthew, 'The New DNB', *History Today* (September 1993), pp. 10–13.

Sheridan (1890), Palmerston's being part of the popular 'The Statesmen Series' which he edited for W.H. Allen & Co. (1888–95). His biographical dictionary, *Celebrities of the Century*, went through two editions (1887, 1890). He was at the same time writing 37 articles for volumes V-XIV of the *Dictionary of National Biography* (1888-1895), on individuals as diverse as James Donaldson, Georgian proprietor of the *Edinburgh Advertiser*; Adam Elliot, seventeenth-century traveller and priest; and Sir Stafford Northcote, contemporary Conservative Chancellor of the Exchequer and Foreign Secretary. Thereafter he produced a variety of historical works, including *Selections from the Anti-Jacobin* (1904), *Old Kew, Chiswick and Kensington* (1910), *The Holland House Circle* (1908), and *The History of England during the Reign of Victoria* (1907), the latter with Sidney Low. On the face of it, one must suspect Sanders' expertise on such a wide range of subjects. In Kimberley's case, however, nothing need be assumed, for the weaknesses can be specifically shown, and in almost every case can be traced to his reliance upon a half-dozen sources, including *The Times* obituary, which Sanders blatantly apes. Stephen's innovative listing of sources was a sound editorial idea, but could not guarantee that contributors would do more than attribute material, much of which had been misconstrued.

Three examples will suffice to show how Sanders' uncritical use of sources led him to draw an unreliable portrait of Kimberley. First, he asserts that 'the Palmerstonian tradition was strong' in Kimberley, leading him to dissent from Gladstone's anti-Turkish attitude of the 1870s.[8] In addressing the House of Lords on 20 February 1877, Kimberley did say that 'we have no need to turn our back upon our old policy in the East, of which the most typical representative was Lord Palmerston' — hence Sanders bald statement.[9] Yet it is clear that his speech had been prepared for political purposes. Refusing to turn one's back on the Ottoman Empire was not tantamount to active support. Five months prior to his speech, Kimberley had written to Lord Ripon that he believed it to be sufficiently obvious that 'the old Palmerston policy is played out', then went on to express his reasons for continuing to support the façade of a Palmerstonian policy —'the transition to a new policy is difficult, and should be cautiously managed, but I have no doubt what that policy should be — encouragement and support of the Christian population in the northern provinces of Turkey.'[10] Six weeks later he wrote to Lord Halifax expressing concern that Gladstone had unwisely antagonized the *Pall Mall Gazette*, yet rejoicing that the former prime minister had 'gained his point that a thorough pro-Turkish policy' was impossible.[11] Kimberley in fact supported Gladstone's policy, though not his method. But the diplomatic world of mixed principles was altogether foreign to

[8] *Dictionary of National Biography*, Supplement [1912] (London: Oxford University Press, 1921), p. 696.

[9] 3 *Hansard*, 232 (20 February 1877): 685.

[10] Kimberley to Ripon, 23 September 1876, RP 43522, f. 254.

[11] Kimberley to Halifax, 5 November 1876, HfP A4/151 (microfilm).

Sanders, who could only assume that Kimberley remained a firm Palmerstonian because he had once invoked his name.

By 1894 when Kimberley went to the Foreign Office, he had become so adamant in his opposition to Turkey that he refused Rosebery's request to do something 'to soothe the feelings of the sultan' in the wake of Gladstone's renewed agitation.[12] It would be harsh to judge the quality of Sanders' article on the basis of personal and official correspondence. After Kimberley's tenure at the foreign office, however, one need only have looked at the public record, or have gone to the press or to the columns of *Hansard* as *DNB* authors often did, to determine how Kimberley's views on the Ottoman Empire had evolved. In the House of Lords in 1897, for instance, in response to Salisbury's mock disappointment that a former and probably future foreign secretary would challenge the government's Ottoman policy on a party platform at Norwich by rejecting Palmerstonian support for the Turks, Kimberley defended his notorious and widely reported speech:

> I say there is nothing in the Treaty [of Paris] or in the present situation of the world which should preclude anyone in my position from announcing, as I did announce and as I wish to announce, and to repeat, that I believe it is in the interest of this country and it is for the interest of European peace that we should be disconnected for ever from regarding the integrity of the Empire of Turkey as a basis of British policy.[13]

It is common enough for statesmen change their views in the course of a half-century career, and any reliable biographical record must account for such changes. Sanders' Turkish statement was essentially false, but contained enough truth to seem plausible, and therefore to mislead when applied to the period of Kimberley's career when it really mattered to the nation, by which time he had explicitly rejected the 'Palmerstonian tradition'. However, as neither Kimberley nor relations with the Ottoman Empire were of paramount interest in 1912 when the first *DNB* supplement was produced, no one paid much attention to the error.

The case was very different with regard to South Africa, where Sanders' treatment has been widely followed by historians. Sanders asserts that in May 1881 Kimberley:

> directed Sir Robert Morier, British minister to Lisbon, to drop the treaty he was negotiating with the Portuguese government, by which a passage was to be granted both to the Boers and to the British troops through Lourenço Marques; such an arrangement might have prevented the South African war of 1899–1902 (*Letters of Sir Robert Morier*, i:400).[14]

---

[12] Letter 213, herein; Martel, *Imperial Diplomacy*, p. 232; Kimberley to Gladstone, 30 December 1894, 12 January 1895, GP 44229, ff. 228–30.

[13] 4 *Hansard*, 47 (19 March 1897): 1019. See generous allusions to his declaration in *Pamphlets and Leaflets of 1897* (London: Liberal Publication Department, 1898).

[14] *DNB*, Supp., p. 697.

It is difficult to imagine a more damning condemnation of a former Colonial Secretary written in the interval between the Boer War and the first campaigns of the Great War. Kimberley in fact had been an ardent supporter of the railway, and considered it a 'great misfortune' when popular opinion in Lisbon thwarted ratification of the treaty which would have made provision for it, a point absent from Morier's account and almost certainly unknown to Sanders.[15] The problem for posterity lies in the presumptive strength of the *DNB* — its reliance upon authoritative sources. Yet Morier was far from impartial, having believed since the 1860s that Kimberley and the Liberal government were conspiring against him. He wrote to Benjamin Jowett that Kimberley 'has twice done me deep wrong, and prevented my appointment to important posts', and to Dilke that he was 'systematically boycotted' by the Colonial Office.[16] When he complained to the Foreign Office that the Colonial Secretary was hindering his work out of personal animosity, Granville assured him that it was not true.[17] Morier's want of judgement and personal sensitivity was widely recognized at the Colonial Office and has since been noted by Agatha Ramm, who in her sympathetic biography wrote that he had 'gone forward without authorisation' in proposing an 'over-complicated (not to say fantastic) draft treaty' that forwarded 'a particular and personal policy.'[18] Morier's self-defence was taken by Sanders as authoritative, and thus reiterated.

The most serious objection to Sanders' portrait revolves around the highly-charged question of Irish Home Rule. Sanders suggests that Kimberley 'found

---

[15] Cf. Schreuder, *Gladstone and Kruger*, pp. 192–94; Extract, Kimberley memoir, RsP 10186, p. 266; Kimberley, minute of 14 June 1880, on CO 179/136; Granville to Morier, 23 June 1880, GrP 30/29/198; Kimberley to William Gurdon, 26 May 1881, CwP HA 54/970/2713.

[16] Wemyss, ed., *Letters of Morier*, 1:399–400; Morier to Dilke, 28 April 1881, DkP 43935.

[17] The disagreement stemmed from circulation of Morier's pamphlet, *The Dano-German Conflict and Lord Russell's Despatch of September 1862*, prior to Kimberley's plenary negotiations with the Germans and the Danes during December 1863 and January 1864, which had left him wondering 'what business an English Secretary of Legn. has to write anonymous partisan pamphlets.' Kimberley journal, 8 December 1863, KP6 MS.eng.e.2790, p. 250. Granville assured Morier that Kimberley was 'the least humbugging of men.... Since getting your private letter and interesting enclosures, I have communicated with him. He had entirely forgotten the episode of the pamphlet, but said that it now came back to his recollection, and he admits that at the time, he criticized very strongly its production. He considers your explanation to be a conclusive explanation and he affirms in the strongest manner that he has no feeling against you.' Granville to Morier, 23 June, 17 July 1880, GrP, 30/29/198.

[18] Hemming, minute, 5 May 1880; Kimberley, minutes 4, 8 May 1880, on FO to CO, 24 April 1880, CO 179/136; Grant Duff, minute, 11 June 1880, on FO to CO, 8 June 1880, CO 179/136; Tenterdon to Herbert, 5 November 1880, HbP 959/4; Ramm, *Sir Robert Morier*, pp. 105–07. On Morier's sensitivity, see *EHJ1*, p. 832; Horace Rumbold, *Recollections of a Diplomatist*, 2 vols. (London: Edward Arnold, 1902), 1:249–50.

no difficulty in supporting Gladstone's policy of home rule', a statement which 'authoritatively' substantiated his image as a loyal minion of Gladstone.[19] In fact, during the 1870s, he had been willing to treat Irish separation as 'the North did the question of breaking up the American union.'[20] As early as October 1885 he knew that Gladstone was leaning toward Home Rule, yet was among the last to declare his support. Torn between the necessity for providing a measure of autonomy for Ireland and the certainty that it would be unpopular in England, Kimberley preferred to force the Conservatives to declare their policy.[21] After the Hawarden Kite made public Gladstone's views, Kimberley still argued against committing 'ourselves either to Home Rule, or absolute refusal to consider the Irish grievance.'[22] Throughout January 1886 he remained adamant against specific declarations of policy while the Conservatives were in office. By January 28 he had accepted the need for some Home Rule measure, but thought that turning out the Irish members from the House of Commons essential for success, maintaining this position through frequent consultations with the Prime Minister.[23] On April 12, after Gladstone had secured Granville's written commitment to limited Irish representation at Westminster should it become necessary, Kimberley objected even to the small concession which Granville had made.[24] Five days later he finally agreed to retention of Irish members at Westminster, though he had consistently advised against it.[25] The patently false claim that Kimberley 'found no difficulty in supporting Gladstone's policy of home rule' suggests a well-defined policy which simply did not exist, important provisions of the complex Government of Ireland Bill, involving a wide range of practical as well as theoretical issues surrounding devolution, being decided after considerable consultation only days before the introduction of the measure.[26]

For political historians, these are only the most serious errors. Sanders follows the lead of *The Times* in omitting any reference to Kimberley's cabinet role. By saying nothing about an arena of public life in which Kimberley exercised substantial influence across thirty years, he unwittingly perpetuated the idea that his subject played no role in the development of Liberal policy, which was

---

[19] *DNB*, Supp., p. 697.

[20] Letter 74, herein.

[21] *DD3*, p. 46.

[22] Kimberley to Granville, 28 December 1885, GrP 30/29/22A/5.

[23] *DD3*, pp. 53, 55–56; Nancy E. Johnson, ed. *The Diary of Gathorne Hardy, Later Lord Cranbrook, 1866–1892, Political Selections* (Oxford: Clarendon Press, 1981), p. 592; Gladstone to Kimberley, 3 February 1886, GP 44228, f. 215; Kimberley to Gladstone, 15 March 1886, GP 44228, ff. 225–27.

[24] Kimberley to Gladstone, 12 April 1886, GP 44228, f. 243; Ramm, *Gladstone-Granville Coresp. 2*, 2:441n; Morley, *Life of Gladstone*, 2:410.

[25] See, Extracts, Kimberley memoir, RsP 10186, p. 273.

[26] On the variety of Kimberley's concerns, see his annotations on Sir Robert Hamilton's 'very secret' memorandum of 31 October 1885, KP6 MS.eng.c.4070, ff. 47–54; *Gladstone Diaries*, 10:clix–clx; letters 143–151, herein.

precisely the line taken by most historians for three-quarters-of-a-century after Kimberley's death. In the context of the enumerated errors of analysis and omission, mere inaccuracies such as the date and place of Kimberley's birth, and the nature of his family's politics, hardly bear mentioning. But these too suggest that Sanders was primarily an educated copyist.

Other standard sources have been equally misleading. George Edward Cokayne's *The Complete Peerage* is at once the most attractive and deceptive work on the peerage, eschewing the typically rigid factual approach for the more entertaining incorporation of anecdotal material. To the credit of Vicary Gibbs, a later editor, he freely admitted that he 'allowed himself a free hand' with the notes, acknowledging that such nearly contemporary comments must be largely 'coloured by political and personal prejudice, truth being often sacrificed to smartness.'[27] It should not be surprising, then, that Gibbs, Conservative M. P. for St. Albans, 1892–1904, would take a swipe at a recently departed Liberal 'greybeard' by annotating 'Envoy to St. Petersburg, 1856–58' with Lord Redesdale's opinion that Kimberley 'knew his trade', but 'had not the secret of treating business with charm.'[28] Quite apart from the merit of the assertion, one might ask why the assessment by Redesdale, an entry level clerk at the Foreign Office in 1858, writing forty years later, should be preferred to that of Lord Clarendon, Liberal Foreign Secretary, who found Kimberley's tone most appropriate and believed that his service in Russia pointed toward eventual succession to Clarendon's own office; or to that of Charles Greville, clerk to the Privy Council and noted diarist, who considered him a 'clever man' with 'plenty of courage and aplomb.'[29] Gibbs concludes his annotation with the reminder, clearly false and in any case irrelevant to the St. Petersburg mission, that Kimberley was 'one of the few peers who blindly followed Gladstone.' Considering the politics of the day, one should not wonder that *The Complete Peerage* represented Kimberley as it did, nor is it surprising that historians to whom Kimberley's role is incidental should have casually adopted its tone.[30]

---

[27] George Edward Cokayne and Vicary Gibbs, eds. *The Complete Peerage of England, Scotland, Ireland, Great Britain, and the United Kingdom*, new ed., 13 vols. (London: St. Catherine Press, 1910), 1:x. A volume of 'Addenda and Corrigenda' to deal with issues raised by such an approach and by new research over the long publishing period had early on been anticipated, but is only now being prepared for Alan Sutton Publishing.

[28] *The Complete Peerage*, 7:270.

[29] Clarendon to Wodehouse, 24 February 1858, KP2 46694, f. 127; Lytton Strachey and Roger Fulford, eds. *The Greville Memoirs, 1814–1860*, 8 vols. (London: Macmillan, 1938), 7:447. Upon Wodehouse's appointment, Clarendon advised that, though he and the Russian foreign minister had been 'rather intimate' in their youth, 'he must not expect us to join all Europe in flattering Russia. That is not our way and it is not necessary for the establishment or the maintenance of friendly relations.' Clarendon to Wodehouse, 22 July 1856, KP3 46692, ff. 39–40.

[30] See, for instance, Ethel Drus in *KJ*, pp. viii–x; Andrew Jones, *The Politics of Reform* (Cambridge: Cambridge University Press, 1972), p. 254.

The most recent biographical account of Kimberley is the fourteen-page introduction to the 'Journal of Events During the Gladstone Ministry, 1868–1874', written by Ethel Drus more than thirty-five years ago. Drus's edition is balanced, and based upon limited use of the Kimberley archives. Partisan judgements from 'authoritative' works such as the *DNB* and *The Complete Peerage* are countered, leaving the reader to weigh the relative merits of various points. However, because Drus is working primarily as editor rather than biographer, her introduction is meant to be little more than a sketch based upon familiar sources — the *DNB*, *Hansard*, *The Complete Peerage*, various published memoirs and biographies, and one or two small bundles of letters from among the vast Kimberley archive.[31] There is no discussion of his career after 1874 and the brief description which she thought necessary for the formative period before his admission to the cabinet is condensed to the point of obfuscation.[32] For example, Drus records that after Kimberley resigned as Under-Secretary of the Foreign Office upon Lord John Russell's elevation to the Lords in 1861, 'apparently he received no other offer and was out of office for the ensuing three years.'[33] In fact, Palmerston and Russell were both anxious to find a position for him, first as Under-Secretary at the India Office, then as Governor-General of Canada or as Governor of Bombay or Madras.[34] It was guessed in the highest political circles that he would 'have an embassy' and Constantinople was offered, though he declined.[35] The transfer to the India Office did not materialise because an anticipated vacancy could not be arranged, and Kimberley refused the other posts, having made it clear that he would accept none abroad.[36] Thus, although he had no permanent post until he became Under-Secretary at the India Office in April 1864, it quite misleads to say that 'apparently he received no other offer'.

[31] It is curious that although Drus apparently had access to all the Kimberley papers, she cites only sources which are now at the Norfolk Record Office.

[32] *KJ*, pp. viii–ix.

[33] *Ibid.*, p. xi.

[34] Palmerston to Russell, 19, 20 July 1861, RIP 30/22/21, ff. 508–09; Newcastle to Palmerston, 27 August 1861, in John Martineau, *Life of Henry Pelham, Fifth Duke of Newcastle, 1811–1864* (London: John Murray, 1908), p. 303; Kimberley journal, KP6 MS.eng.e.2790, p. 72a herein.

[35] Malmesbury, *Memoirs of an Ex-Minister*, 2 vols. (London: Longmans, Green, and Co., 1884), 2:257–58. Francis Cavendish, Foreign Office clerk from 1848–63, clearly states that 'the Embassy at Constantinople has been offered to, and refused, by Wodehouse.' *Society, Politics, and Diplomacy, 1820-1864*, p. 559. On Sir Henry Bulwer's possible removal see Walpole, *Life of Russell*, 2:423–24.

[36] Wodehouse to Henry Wodehouse, 1 August 1861, KP1 15/K2/19; Wodehouse to Russell, 12 September 1860, letter 28, herein.

Appendix 3

Kimberley's Residences

Country Houses

Letton Hall, Shipdham, Norfolk to 1846

Kimberley Hall, Kimberley, Norfolk, 1846 to 1902 – Kimberley referred to his home as Kimberley House, though most printed accounts style it Kimberley Hall

London Houses

20 Montagu Street, to 1850

37 Grosvenor Street, 1850

26 Lower Brook Street, 1850 to 1852

24 Upper Brook Street, 1852 – Purchased by Anne Wodehouse early in 1850; occasionally used by Kimberley while searching for other quarters

31 Lower Brook Street, 1852

48 Bryanston Square, 1852 to 1874

35 Lowndes Square, 1874 to 1902

Residencies Abroad

Place Michel, St. Petersburg, Russia, October 1856 to April 1958

Viceregal Lodge, Dublin, November 1864 to July 1866

Schools and Universities

Lyndon, Rutlandshire, 1835 to 1838

Eton, 1838 to 1843

1843 to 1847
Christ Church, Oxford

Appendix 4

Abbreviations of Principal Sources

I. Manuscript Sources

AP   Asquith Papers, Bodleian Library

BP   Bright Papers, British Library

BrP   Bruce Papers, Trinity College Library, Dublin

CBP   Campbell-Bannerman Papers, British Library

CdP   Cardwell Papers, Public Record Office

CfJ   Carlingford Journal, British Library

CfP   Carlingford Papers, Somerset Record Office

ChP   Chamberlain Papers, Birmingham University Library

ClP   Clarendon Papers, Bodleian Library

CO   Colonial Office Files, Public Record Office

CP   Currie Papers, Royal Bank of Scotland Archive

CrP   Cromer Papers, Public Record Office

CtP   Courtney Papers, British Library of Political and Economic Science

CvP   Carnarvon Papers, Public Record Office

CwP   Cranworth Papers, Suffolk Record Office

CzP   Curzon Papers, India Office Library

DfP   Dufferin Papers, India Office Library

DkP   Dilke Papers, British Library

DP   Derby Papers, Liverpool Record Office

DvP   Devonshire Papers, Chatsworth, Derbyshire

GBP   Great Britain Papers (Political), Perkins Library, Duke University

GDP   Grant Duff Papers, India Office Library

GP   Gladstone Papers, British Library

GrP   Granville Papers, Public Record Office

HBP   Hicks-Beach Papers, Gloucester Record Office

HfP   Halifax Papers, Borthwick Institute of Historical Research

HGP   Herbert Gladstone Papers, British Library

HmP   Hammond Papers, Public Record Office

HP   Harcourt Papers, Bodleian Library

HrP   Herbert Papers, Public Record Office

KP1   Kimberley Papers, Norfolk Record Office

KP2   Kimberley Papers, National Library of Scotland

KP3   Kimberley Papers, British Library

KP4   Kimberley Papers, Public Archives of Canada

KP5   Kimberley Papers, Cornwall Record Office

KP6   Kimberley Papers, Bodleian Library

KP7   Kimberley Papers, Mr. R.C. Fiske (privately held)

LP   Lansdowne Papers, India Office Library

LcP   Larcom Papers, National Library of Ireland

MBP   Monk Bretton Papers, Bodleian Library

MgP   Musgrave Papers, Perkins Library, Duke University

MlP   Malet Papers, Public Record Office

MP   Morley Papers, India Office Library

MtP   Minto Papers, India Office Library

NP   Northbrook Papers, India Office Library

OP   Overstone Papers, University of London Library

PkP   Packe Papers, Leicestershire Record Office

PP   Palmerston Papers, Southampton University Library

RlP   Russell Papers, Public Record Office

RP   Ripon Papers, British Library

RPD   Ripon Papers, Perkins Library, Duke University

RsP   Rosebery Papers, National Library of Scotland

SdP   Sanderson Papers, Public Record Office

SP   Spencer Papers, British Library

WO   War Office Files, Public Record Office

WP   Welby Papers, British Library of Economic and Political Science

II. Printed Primary Sources

CJ	A.B. Cooke and J.R. Vincent (eds.), *Lord Carlingford's Journal: Reflections of a Cabinet Minister 1885* (Oxford, 1971).
DD1	John Vincent, ed., *Disraeli, Derby and the Conservative Party, Journals and Memoirs of Edward Henry, Lord Stanley 1849–1869*, (New York, 1978).
DD3	John Vincent, ed., *The Later Derby Diaries. Home Rule, Liberal Unionism, and Aristocratic Life in Late Victorian England* (Bristol, 1981).
EHJ1	D.W.R. Bahlman, ed., *The Diary of Sir Edward Walter Hamilton 1880–1885*, 2 vols. (Oxford, 1972).
EHJ2	David Brooks, ed., *The Destruction of Lord Rosebery, From the Diary of Sir Edward Hamilton 1894-1895* (London, 1986).
EHJ3	D.W.R. Bahlman, ed., *The Diary of Sir Edward Walter Hamilton 1885–1906*, (Hull, 1993).
Gladstone Diaries	M.R.D. Foot & H.C.G. Matthew, eds., *The Gladstone Diaries*, 14 vols. (Oxford, 1968-1994).
Gladstone–Granville Corresp. 1	Agatha Ramm, ed., *The Political Correspondence of Mr. Gladstone and Lord Granville 1868-1876*, 2 vols. (London, 1952).

Gladstone–Granville Corresp. 2	Agatha Ramm, ed., *The Political Correspondence of Mr. Gladstone and Lord Granville 1876-1886*, 2 vols. (Oxford, 1962).
KJ	Ethel Drus, ed., *A Journal of Events during the Gladstone Ministry, 1868-74*, (London, 1958).
Notes from a Diary	Mountstuart Grant Duff, *Notes from a Diary*, 14 vols. (London, 1897–1905).
PMP: Gladstone	John Brooke and Mary Sorensen, eds., *The Prime Ministers' Papers: W. E. Gladstone*, 4 vols. (London, 1971-1981).
Red Earl	Peter Gordon, ed., *The Red Earl, The Papers of the Fifth Earl Spencer 1835-1910*, 2 vols. (Northampton, 1981, 1986).

Appendix 5

Document Summary

Letters from Kimberley	225
Letters to Kimberley	26
Memoranda	14
Notes on Reading	9
Speeches	3
Minutes	1
Total	278

Correspondent	*Letters to*	*Letters from*
Asquith	1	0
Birkbeck, H.	1	0
Boileau, J.	0	1
Campbell-Bannerman	4	0
Cardwell	1	0
Carrington	1	1
Chamberlain	1	0
Clarendon	1	1
Courtney	1	0
Currie, C.	0	1
Currie, R.	19	0
Derby, 15th	4	0
Dodson	9	0
Dufferin	1	0
Gladstone, H.	1	0
Gladstone, W.	36	4
Grant Duff	10	0
Granville	4	0
Grey, Earl	0	1
Grey, G.	2	0

Correspondent	Letters to	Letters from
Gurdon, B.	2	0
Halifax	8	0
Hammond, E.	1	0
Harcourt	9	3
Hartington	2	0
Hely-Hutchinson	0	1
Herschell	1	0
Hicks Beach	1	0
Lansdowne	3	0
Lorne	1	0
Malet, E.	1	0
Monkswell	1	0
Morley, J.	1	3
Morning Chronicle	2	0
Musgrave	1	0
Northbrook	3	0
Overstone	1	0
Packe, H.	1	0
Palmerston	1	0
Pratt, E.	1	0
Ripon	34	0
Rosebery	21	8
Russell	7	0
Somerset	1	0
Spencer	18	0
Windham, W.	1	0
Wodehouse, Anne	4	0
Wodehouse, H.	1	1
Wolseley	0	1
Totals	223	26

Index

Numbers shown in bold refer to the numbered letters in this volume